22.61

Trends Toward Corporatist Intermediation

Trends Toward Corporatist Intermediation

edited by

Philippe C. Schmitter
University of Chicago

and

Gerhard Lehmbruch
University of Konstanz

Contemporary Political Sociology Volume 1

SAGE Publications · Beverly Hills · London

For information address

**SAGE Publications Ltd
28 Banner Street
London EC1Y 8QE**

**SAGE Publications Inc
275 South Beverly Drive
Beverly Hills, California 90212**

British Library Cataloguing in Publication Data

Trends toward corporatist intermediation. —
(Contemporary political sociology; vol. 1).
1. Corporate state
I. Schmitter, Philippe C
II. Lehmbruch, Gerhard   III. Series
321.9   HD3611   79-63824

ISBN 0-8039-9836-8
ISBN 0-8039-9837-6 Pbk

First Printing

Contents

Introduction

This collection of essays represents an example — unfortunately a very rare one — of spontaneous, international and interdisciplinary collaborative research. The contributors formed and joined — completely without external inducements and occasionally without their initially being aware of it — an informal, nonspatial, unfunded working group on interest politics and policy-making in highly industrialized, advanced capitalist societies. This compilation constitutes the first in a series of volumes which the working group intends to publish. It explores broad issues of conceptualization and theory-building and focuses on the substantive question of recent trends in interest intermediation. It will be followed in the course of the coming year with a second volume containing empirical case studies "inspired and informed" by the perspectives discussed herein and emphasizing the public policy processes and consequences of corporatism.

Independent, simultaneous discovery, while apparently not uncommon in the physical sciences, is quite unusual in the social sciences. The essays in this book were touched off by one such rare occurrence — the independent and simultaneous revival of interest in corporatism. In 1974 there appeared three essays by scholars of different nationality, disciplinary training and research experience — all dealing with what the authors called "corporatism". Gerhard Lehmbruch prepared and presented a paper at an IPSA Round Table on Political Integration (9-13 September 1974) entitled:

"Consociational Democracy, Class Conflict, and the New Corporatism". It was never published and appears in this volume for the first time. Two British sociologists, Ray Pahl and Jack Winkler, predicted "The Coming Corporatism" in *New Society* (10 October 1974), while Philippe Schmitter speculated on "Still the Century of Corporatism?" in the *Review of Politics* (January 1974). For Schmitter's essay, the University of Notre Dame Press has kindly accorded its permission.

Perhaps even more surprising than the parallelism of the original discoveries is the fact that these scholars have joined together with others in a sporadic but intensive and repeated set of exchanges, some by correspondence and others by joint presentations at various scholarly meetings. The "follow-up" essays by Lehmbruch and Schmitter and those by Birgitta Nedelmann and Kurt Meier and by Charles Anderson were discussed at the working group's first formal session, a panel on "Modes and Models of Interest Representation" at the Congress of the International Political Science Association (Edinburgh, August 1976). One of the authors in this volume, Leo Panitch, was only later discovered to be a "member" by virtue of a paper he presented at the American Political Science Association meetings one month later (September 1976). He has since been enthusiastically coopted along with his essay on "The Development of Corporatism in Liberal Democracies". All of the foregoing are reprinted here from the special issue of *Comparative Political Studies* (April 1977) in which they first appeared.

At the annual meetings of the American Political Science Association the following year, Robert Salisbury brought the emerging perspectives of a corporatist approach to bear on interest politics in the United States and asked, "Why So Little Corporatism in the United States?" Published here for the first time, we welcome this "American connection" to what has been a largely Eurocentric enterprise.

The next major reunion of the working group came at the European Consortium for Political Research in Grenoble (6-12 April 1978). Over thirty papers were presented covering some aspect of corporatist theory or practice in almost as many countries. For this volume, we have selected the essay by Bob Jessop, "Corporatism, Parliamentarism and Social Democracy" because of the skillful and original manner in which it relates the themes of the corporatist discussion to those raised in the current debate on Marxist theories of the State. Many of the other ECPR contributions will be included in a second volume since they deal more specifically and empirically with single cases and delimited time periods.*

The last major gathering of what had by then become baptized as the "Corporatist Internationale" (or as most of its members would prefer, the "Anti-Corporatist 'Internationale'") came at the World Congress of the International Sociological Association in Uppsala (12-25 August 1978). From another set of innovative and provocative papers, we selected the one by T. J. Pempel and Keiichi Tsunekawa, "Corporatism Without Labor? The Japanese Anomaly", since it not only expanded our horizons far beyond the North Atlantic area but also raised new questions about the structure and process of interest intermediation in relation to the timing of capitalist industrialization and modern state-building.

The other essays from the Uppsala meeting have been "held over" for inclusion in our next collaborative publication. Gerhard Lehmbruch, who will be the principal editor of this second volume, has kindly consented to conclude this, our first effort, with a short summary of what he considers to be the present accomplishments and future problems of the *Korporatismusproblematik*.

The reader of these essays will discover that, despite this fortunate and extraordinary convergence of effort, the authors are by no means in complete agreement with respect to conceptual usage, substantive finding, causal inference, or normative preference. The recentness and tentativeness of their joint endeavor has by no means inhibited their capacity for criticizing each other, quite the contrary. This is no "mutual admiration society", and it does not offer the reader a self-satisfied, completely elaborated theory-cum-formula for the analysis of interest politics in the "First World".

What the volume does offer is a strong criticism — at times explicit and at times implicit — of the heretofore dominant way of conceptualizing the activities of interest groups, the pluralist model, and of the style of empirical research which has prevailed in this field, that of ahistorical, self-contained, configurative description. Beyond this negative contribution, the volume seeks to establish the positive foundation for an alternative *problématique*. Its authors agree that explanation of contemporary patterns of interest politics in Western Europe, North America and Japan demands a historical and comparative mode of inquiry which is

---

*G. Lehmbruch and P. Schmitter, *Consequences of Corporatist Policy Making,* to be published by SAGE Publications in the Modern Politics Series, volume 5.

sensitive to long-term developmental trends, the diffential impact of discrete events, the accumulated importance of past criticial decisions and the gradual accretion of normative standards, or what Charles Anderson has called "paradigms of public policy choice". Interest politics must be related to the generic context of social and economic transformation, as well as to the specific "national" experience of each polity. Whether that context is best conceptualized in terms of structural differentiation, capitalist development, postindustrial society, bureaucratic management, organized complexity and/or liberal-democratic values is an issue to which our authors give differential emphasis. Nor are they in agreement as to when this mode of historical, macrostructural explanation should begin. Anderson finds the problem already embodied in the legal traditions and political philosophy of the premodern or early-modern era. Schmitter emphasizes the associational configuration emerging from the period of accelerated capitalist development at the end of the nineteenth century and the crisis of the capitalist order ensuing from the aftermath of World War I. Panitch and Jessop stress the role of the changed patterns of class forces at the end of World War II.

"Corporatism" plays a central conceptual role in all the essays, hence its presence in the title of the volume. The authors agree that it offers an attractive alternative to the pluralist model, suggesting not only a different institutional configuration in the relationship between specialized interest associations and the political process, but also a different way of conceptualizing the role and importance of the state. To some extent they begin with the definition initially put forth in Schmitter's "Still the Century of Corporatism?" but they all, including Schmitter, impress reservations, criticisms, extensions and corrections upon its use. Lehmbruch prefers to speak of "liberal" rather than "societal" corporatism in advanced industrial societies, stressing its connection with liberal constitutional democracy and the degree to which such an arrangement is a matter of voluntary choice. For him, unlike Schmitter, corporatism is not "just" a mode of interest articulation, but a more encompassing pattern of policy formation, of concerted-cooperative action involving choice and implementation as well as intermediation or representation. For Winkler, such "politicological" approaches are too narrow. He and his co-author, Pahl, have argued that corporatism is a comprehensive economic system, a mode of allocating resources not of exercising influence or taking decisions.

Nedelmann and Meier criticize the static and descriptive aspects of Schmitter's initial formulation and stress the extent to which corporatist outcomes in Western Europe are less stable and enduring than has been commonly assumed. Panitch makes a similar point in this essay which emphasizes more strongly the dimension of asymmetric and contradictory class relations underlying contemporary corporatist formulae. Schmitter, to an extent anticipating these objections to his earlier work, attempts to trace the dynamic theoretical assumptions behind competing models of interest politics and ends on an inconclusive note, suggesting the greater than usually assumed importance of national differences in starting points and of internal factors emanating from within the processes of formalization, bureaucratization and centralization of intermediary associations. Jessop picks up (in part) from where Panitch left off and attempts to anchor the discussions of corporatism and parliamentarism in a specifically Marxist theory of the State. Anderson reminds us that these political and social processes are not merely limited to the satisfaction of material demands and/or to the objective reproductive imperatives of systems, industrial and/or capitalist, but require legitimation — at least eventually. In this area of private governance and social control which has been so stressed in the corporatist model, he finds an important, if not necessarily fatal, normative weakness. Contemporary corporatist practices, as well as pluralist ones, lack accepted criteria of public justification for the distributions and regulations they produce.

The study of "pressure groups", "lobbies", "interest associations" and the like has long been an area of conceptual torpor and theoretical orthodoxy in the discipline of political science. These essays hopefully will serve to awaken critical inquiry and even quicken the pace of discovery. They offer not only novel perceptions of the role of specialized interest intermediaries, but reach beyond them to raise important issues of comparative public policy, historical political development, the patterning of class relations, the nature of the modern state, the role of legal norms, and legitimating ideals. The authors offer them jointly to a wider public as part of their continuing, if episodic and inchoate, effort in comparative international collaboration.

To those of our readers who find these perspectives interesting and who share our commitment to critical inquiry, our penchant for historical and macrosocietal explanation, our willingness to engage in self- and collective-criticism, and our conviction that is this substantive area of interest intermediation-cooperative policy formation lies one of the major unexplored aspects of political life in Western Europe and North America, we extend an invitation to join our "informal, nonspatial and unfunded working group". The nature of membership is purely voluntary; the costs of joining are few; the barriers to the entry of new — even competing — participants are low; the access of persons of different academic status and national origin is rigorously equal; the amount of internal differentiation and authority is minimal; the degree of control over member attitudes and activities is nil; the correspondence between spontaneously expressed member interests and collectively implemented group functions is high; the freedom to leave is unrestricted. Indeed, if all this were characteristic of modern interest associations, there would be no need for our collaborative effort at conceptual redefinition and empirical reexamination. The pluralist paradigm would continue to do just fine.

Philippe C. Schmitter
University of Chicago
January 1979

1

Still the Century of Corporatism?

Philippe C. Schmitter
University of Chicago, USA

> The twentieth century will be the century of corporatism just as the nineteenth was the century of liberalism...
>
> Mihaïl Manoïlesco

Until recently, Manoïlesco's confident prediction could easily be dismissed as yet another example of the ideological bias, wishful thinking and overinflated rhetoric of the thirties, an *événementielle* response to a peculiar environment and period.[1] With the subsequent defeat of Fascism and National Socialism, the spectre of corporatism no longer seemed to haunt the European scene so fatalistically. For a while, the concept itself was virtually retired from the active lexicon of politics, although it was left on behavioral exhibit, so to speak, in such museums of atavistic political practice as Portugal and Spain.

Lately, however, the spectre is back amongst us — verbally at least — haunting the concerns of contemporary social scientists with increasing frequency and in multiple guises. Almost forty years to the day when Manoïlesco (1936:7) declared that "the ineluctable course of fate involves the transformation of all the social and political institutions of our times in a corporatist direction," perhaps we should again take his prediction seriously and inquire whether we might still be in the century of corporatism — but only just becoming aware of it.

The purposes of this essay are to explore various usages of the concept of corporatism, to suggest an operational definition of it as a distinctive, modern system of interest representation, to discuss the utility of distinguishing subtypes of corporatist development and practice and, finally, to set forth some general hypotheses "explaining" the probable context of its emergence and persistence.

I

The first step, I propose, is to rescue the concept of corporatism from various usages of it which have crept into the literature and which seem (to me) to do more to dissipate or to disguise than to enhance its utility. On the one hand, it has become such a vaguely bounded phenomenon that, like clientelism, it can be found everywhere and, hence, is nowhere very distinctive; on the other hand, it has been so narrowly attached to a single political culture, regime-type or macrosocietal configuration that it becomes, at best, uniquely descriptive rather than comparatively analytic.

Undoubtedly, the most difficult task is to strip the concept of its pejorative tone and implication. This is made all the more difficult by the fact that — unlike the thirties — there are very few regimes today who overtly and proudly advertise themselves as corporatist. It, therefore, becomes a tempting game to unveil and denounce as corporatist, practices which regimes are condoning or promoting under other labels, such as "participation," "collaborative planning," "mixed representation," and "permanent consultation." On the other hand, if corporatism is left to mean simply "interest-group behavior or systems I do not like" and/or used synonymously with such epithets as "fascist" and "repressive," then it can become of little or no utility for purposes of systematic comparison. This is not to say that those who use the concept must somehow be enjoined from uttering evaluative statements or even from expressing strong normative reactions to its role or consequences. I have now studied several corporatist systems and come openly to quite firm personal judgments about each of them. But, I hope that those who disagree on its desirability can at least arrive at some common prior agreement as to the empirical referents which identify its basic structure and behavior. They then can dispute the costs and benefits and the intrinsic "goods" and "bads" it produces.

In my work I have found it useful to consider corporatism as a system of interest and/or attitude representation, a particular modal or ideal-typical institutional arrangement for linking the associationally organized interests of civil society with the decisional structures of the state. As such it is one of several possible *modern* configurations of interest representation, of which pluralism is perhaps the best-known and most frequently acknowledged alternative — but more about that below.

Restricting the concept, so to speak, to refer only to a specific concrete set of institutional practices or structures involving the representation (or misrepresentation) of empirically observable group interests has a number of important implications. These sharply differentiate my preferred usage from those of several others who have recently employed the same conceptual label.

First, by defining corporatism in terms of its praxis, the concept is liberated from its employment in any particular ideology or system of ideas.[2] While as will become manifest in later sections of this essay, I am quite interested in the arguments put forth by particular proponents of modern or neocorporatism, my reading of its use in the recent history of ideas suggests that an extraordinary variety of theorists, ideologues and activists have advocated it for widely divergent motives, interests and reasons.

These range from such romantic, organic theorists of the state as Friedrich Schlegel, Adam von Müller, G. W. Friedrich Hegel and Rudolf Kjellen; to the pre-Marxist, protosocialists Sismondi, Saint-Simon and Proudhon; to the Social Christian, ethically traditionalist thought of Wilhelm von Ketteler, Karl von Vogelsang, the Marquis de la Tour de Pin, Albert de Mun and, of course, Popes Leo XIII and Pius XI; to the fascist authoritarianism of Giuseppe Bottai, Guido Bortolotto, Giuseppe Papi and Francesco Vito; to the secular modernizing nationalism of a Mihaïl Manoïlesco; to the radical (in the French sense) bourgeois solidarism of Léon Duguit, Joseph-Paul Boncour, Georges Renard and Emile Durkheim; to the mystical universalism of an Ottmar Spann; to the internationalist functionalism of Giuseppe de Michelis and David Mitrany; to the reactionary, pseudo-Catholic integralism of Charles Maurras, Oliveira Salazar, Marcello Caetano and Jean Brèthe de la Gressaye; to the technocratic, procapitalist reformism of Walter Rathenau, Lord Keynes and A. A. Berle, Jr.; to the anticapitalist syndicalism of Georges Sorel, Sergio Panunzio, Ugo Spirito, Edmondo Rossoni, Enrico Corradini and Gregor Strasser; to the guild socialism of G. D. H. Cole, the early

Harold Laski, S. G. Hobson and Ramiro de Maeztu; to the com-
munitarianism or bourgeois socialism of a François Perroux or an
Henri de Man — not to mention such contemporary advocates as
Bernard Crick, W. H. Ferry, Pierre Mendes-France and David
Apter.

All of these — and the list is by no means complete nor are the
above groupings by any means sharply distinctive[3] — have converg-
ed upon the advocacy of an institutional relationship between the
systems of authoritative decision-making and interest representation which can be considered as generically corporatist by my praxiological definition (and frequently defined as such by the authors
themselves), although they conceived of this arrangement as involving radically different structures of power and influence, as
benefiting quite distinct social classes, and as promoting
diametrically opposite public policies.

A French student of corporatism described the situation quite
well when he said:

> The army of corporatists is so disparate that one is led to think that the word,
> corporation, itself is like a label placed on a whole batch of bottles which are
> then distributed among diverse producers each of whom fills them with the drink
> of his choice. The consumer has to look carefully [Baudin, 1942: 4-5]

The situation is even further confused by the fact that many contemporary theorists, idealogues and activists are peddling the same
drink under yet other labels.

Not only is corporatism defined as an ideology (or worse as a
Weltanschauung) difficult to pin down to a central set of values or
beliefs and even more difficult to associate with the aspirations or
interests of a specific social group, but virtually all detailed empirical inquiries of corporatist praxis have shown its performance
and behavior to be at considerable variance — if not diametrically
opposed — to the beliefs manifestly advanced by its verbal
defenders. As another French scholar of the Forties (himself an advocate of corporatism *à sa manière*) observed, "The reality of existing corporatisms is, without a doubt, infinitely less seductive
than the doctrine." [Murat, 1944:206][4] Contemporary conceptualizations of corporatism based exclusively on the stated motives
and goals of actors or their apologists tend only to obfuscate this
"less than seductive" reality in praxis.

In short, I find there is simply too much normative variety and behavioral hypocrisy in the use of the corporatist *ideological* label to make it a useful operational instrument for comparative analysis.

Nor do I find it very productive to consider corporatism to be an exclusive part or a distinctive product of a particular political culture, especially one linked to some geographically circumscribed area such as the Iberian Peninsula[5] or the Mediterranean.[6] This approach to corporatism not only runs up against the usual (and in my view, well-founded) criticisms raised against most, if not all, political-cultural "explanations"[7] — especially against those based on impressionistic evidence and circular reasoning[8] — but also fails completely to explain why similar configurations and behavior in interest politics have emerged and persist in a great variety of cultural settings, stretching from Northern Europe, across the Mediterranean to such exotic places as Turkey, Iran, Thailand, Indonesia and Tawiwan, to name but a few. This form of pseudoexplanation also cannot contribute much to answering the question of why, even within the presumed homeland of such an ethos, that is, the Iberian Peninsula and its "fragments," corporatism has waxed and waned during different historical periods. Are we to believe that political culture is a sort of "spigot variable" which gets turned on every once in a while to produce a different system of functional representation? Also we might ask, why do societies supposedly sharing the same general ethos exhibit such wide diversity in interest-group values, practices and consequences? By all empirically available standards, Spain is more Catholic than Portugal, Colombia more so than Brazil, yet in each case it is the latter which has by far the more corporatist system. At best, then, culturalist arguments must be heavily supplemented to account for such embarrassing deviations in outcome.

Finally, since those who have advanced such an explanation also tend to place a great deal of emphasis on ideology (occasionally even accepting word for fact), we might wonder why the major ideologues of corporatism have *not* come from this part of the world. A quick glance at the admittedly incomplete bibliography attached to this essay will show that the intellectual origins of corporatism are predominately German, Belgian, French and Austrian and, secondarily and belatedly, English, Italian and Romanian. Those who advocated corporatism in the Iberian and Latin American areas unabashedly and unashamedly imported their ideas from abroad. Modern, nonmedieval, corporatism was diffused to the Iberian-Mediterranean area, not created within it.[9]

Another tendency which has cropped up in recent discussions of corporatism is to define or, better, submerge it into some wider political configuration such as "the organic state" or "the authoritarian regime."[10] The "organic state" concept runs up against many of the criticisms of definitional vagueness, lack of potential empirical specificity and circularity of argument leveled above at the political cultural approach. More importantly, it fails to take into account the historical fact that many "organically conceived" states were not composed of corporatist subunits, but built upon a great variety of "organs" ranging from the *curies* and *phratries* of Fustel de Coulange's ancient city,[11] to the "metallic" orders of moral excellence in Plato's ideal polity,[12] to the three to five estate systems of various anciens régimes,[13] to the phalanges of Fourier,[14] to the *régions* of Robert LaFont,[15] even to the autonomous, plural communities of Percival and Paul Goodman or Gar Alperovitz.[16] If one accepts that a special characteristic of modern corporatism (this in both ideology and practice) concerns the role of *functional* interest associations, then it is but one of many possible structural units, for example, familial, territorial-communitarian, moral, religious, "productionist," etc., which may go into the establishment of an "organic state." Emphasizing that macrocharacteristic does little to specify concrete relations of authority, influence and representation, except to differentiate them from equally vague notions of the "mechanical state."

The relation of corporatism in interest politics to a specific global type of political regime is a much more complicated (and, in my view, interesting) issue. For reasons which will, I hope, become apparent in the course of this essay I have found it more useful to define it as a concrete, observable general system of interest representation which is "compatible" with several different regime-types, i.e., with different party systems, varieties of ruling ideology, levels of political mobilization, varying scopes of public policy, etc. Then I will endeavour to specify distinct *subtypes* of corporatist representation which seem to have at least an elective affinity for, if not to be essential defining elements of, specific regime-types during specific periods of their development.[17]

Yet another tendency in the revived discussion of corporatism which differs from that proposed here is that which submerges the concept, not in some wider concept of regional political culture, state form or regime-type, but in some marcosocietal characteristic such as the presence of visual stigmata,[18] or the existence of religiously, ideologically or linguistically determined *zuilen, lager,* or *familles spirituelles*.[19] Here the problem is simply that stigmatized or pillared societies exhibit quite different degrees of corporatism in the sense used herein and that, vice versa, many heavily corporatized systems of interest representation exist in societies which have no marked visual stigmatization or pillared social and cultural structures. Sweden is no less corporatized because it lacks both dimensions;[20] Belgium no more so because it suffers from both.[21] These are interesting and salient dimensions of societies, in and by themselves, but they do not seem to bear any close association with the phenomenon upon which I recommend we focus our attention with the concept of corporatism.

In the present state of nominalistic anarchy prevailing in the discipline, it is absurd to pretend that scholars will somehow "rally" to a particular conceptualization, spurn alternative uses of the term, and, henceforth, agree to disagree on the basis of a common lexical definition. About all one can expect from an introductory discussion such as this may be to gain a few recruits for a more specific and bounded use of the concept of corporatism, and to warn the reader that a great deal of what has recently been written about corporatism and of what will subsequently be discussed in this essay may be of no mutual relevance at all.

II

Having rejected a series of alternative usages of the concept of corporatism and expressed a preference for a more empirically bounded specification which focuses on a set of relatively directly observable, institutionally distinctive traits involving the actual practice of interest representation, it is now incumbent upon me to produce such a conceptual specification:

> Corporatism can be defined as a system of interest representation in which the constituent units are organized into a limited number of singular, compulsory, noncompetitive, hierarchically ordered and functionally differentiated categories, recognized or licensed (if not created) by the state and granted a deliberate representational monopoly within their respective categories in exchange for observing certain controls on their selection of leaders and articulation of demands and supports.[22]

Obviously, such an elaborate definition is an ideal-type description,[23] a heuristic and logicoanalytical construct composed of a considerable variety of theoretically or hypothetically interrelated components. No empirically extant system of interest representation may perfectly reproduce all these dimensions, although two which I have studied in some detail (Brazil and Portugal) come rather close.[24] While the whole gestalt or syndrome is not directly accessible to measurement, its postulated components can be easily assessed, if not immediately quantified. Such detailed inquiry into the extent to which a given system of representation is limited in number of component units, compulsory in membership, noncompetitive between compartmentalized sectors, hierarchically ordered in internal structure, recognized or certified in some de jure or de facto way by the state, successful in exercising a representational monopoly within functionally determined categories and subject to formal or informal controls on leadership selection and interest articulation will not only enable us to distinguish what type of interest system it belongs to, but may help us gauge the extent to which these multiple dimensions are empirically as well as logically interrelated. It is, of course, quite conceivable at this early stage in research into these matters that what I have found to be a set of interrelated institutional practices coalescing into a distinctive, highly covariant and resistant modern system of interest representation may be quite limited in its scope of applicability, for example, only to Iberian authoritarian regimes, or restricted to only subtype of corporatism, such as ones "artificially" established from above by the state.

One purpose in developing this elaborate general model, beyond that of describing the behavior of a certain number of political systems which have interested me, is to offer to the political analyst an explicit alternative to the paradigm of interest politics which has heretofore completely dominated the discipline of the North American political science: *pluralism*. While a considerable number and wide variety of scholars have discovered that pluralism (and with it, the closely associated liberal democratic regime-type) may be of little utility in describing the likely structure and behavior of interest-group systems in contemporary developing polities, and while some have even gone so far as to suggest that it may no longer be of much utility when applied to the practices of advanced industrial polities, few if any of these scholars have proposed an alternative or contrasting model of modern representative association-state relations. Most of them merely mourn the passing or degeneration of pluralism and either advocate its return,[25] its replacement with some more formalistic, authoritative (if not authoritarian) "juridical democracy,"[26] or its periodic *bouleverse-ment* by spontaneous social movements.[27]

Pluralism and corporatism share a number of basic assumptions, as would almost any realistic model of modern interest politics: (1) the growing importance of formal associational units of representation; (2) the persistence and expansion of functionally differentiated and potentially conflicting interests; (3) the burgeoning role of permanent administrative staffs, of specialized information, of technical expertise and, consequently, of entrenched oligarchy; (4) the decline in the importance of territorial and partisan representation; and (5) the secular trend toward expansion in the scope of public policy and (6) interpenetration of private and public decision arenas. Nevertheless, despite this wide area of mutual agreement, pluralism differs markedly from corporatism as an ideal-typical response to these facts of modern political life.

> Pluralism can be defined as a system of interest representation in which the constituent units are organized into an unspecified number of multiple, voluntary, competitive, nonhierarchically ordered and self-determined (as to type or scope of interest) categories which are not specially licensed, recognized, subsidized, created or otherwise controlled in leadership selection or interest articulation by the state and which do not exercise a monopoly of representational activity within their respective categories.

Practitioners of corporatism and of pluralism would heartily agree with James Madison that "among the numerous advantages promised by a well-constructed union, none deserves to be more accurately developed than its tendency *to break and control* (my emphasis) the violence of faction." They would also agree that "giving to every citizen the same opinions, the same passions and the same interests...is as impracticable as [suppressing them altogether — PCS] would be unwise." Where the two practitioners would begin to diverge is with Madison's further assertion that "it is in vain to say that enlightened statesmen will be able to adjust these clashing interests and render them all subservient to the public good." Corporatists, basing their faith either on the superior wisdom of an authoritarian leader or the enlightened foresight of technocratic planners, believe that such a public unity can be found and kept. Their "scheme of representation," to use Madison's felicitous phrase, instead of extending the "number of citizens" and the "sphere of interests" would compress them into a fixed set of verticalized categories each representing the interdependent functions of an organic whole. Madison's metaphor was more mechanistic, and more dynamic. Hence, he was less sanguine about limiting and ordering the sources of faction — whether from above by imposition or from below by elimination. Corporatists of whatever stripe express confidence that an "enlightened statesman" (or an "enlightened state") can co-opt, control or coordinate not only those "most frivolous and fanciful distinctions [which] have been sufficient to kindle unfriendly passions and excite their most violent conflicts," but also that "most common and durable source of faction...the various and unequal distribution of property."[28]

In short, both pluralists and corporatists recognize, accept and attempt to cope with the growing structural differentiation and interest diversity of the modern polity, but they offer opposing political remedies and divergent images of the institutional form that such a modern system of interest representation will take. The former suggest spontaneous formation, numerical proliferation, horizontal extension and competitive interaction; the latter advocate controlled emergence, quantitative limitation, vertical stratification and complementary interdependence. Pluralists place their faith in the shifting balance of mechanically intersecting forces; corporatists appeal to the functional adjustment of an organically interdependent whole.

While time and space limitations prevent me from developing the idea further, I suspect that these two constrasting but not diametrically opposed syndromes do not by any means exhaust the possible alternative system-types of modern interest representation.

For example, the Soviet experience suggests the existence of a "monist" model which could be defined as

a system of interest representation in which the constitutent units are organized into a fixed number of singular, ideologically selective, noncompetitive, functionally differentiated and hierarchically ordered categories, created, subsidized and licensed by a single party and granted a representational role within that party and vis-à-vis the state in exchange for observing certain controls on their selection of leaders, articulation of demands and mobilization of support.

Much more difficult to specify in terms of the component dimensions we have been using for the other three because of its radical and utopian nature is the syndicalist alternative. Barely sketched in by a number of theorists (several of whom subsequently became corporatists), this projected model seems to reject or to seek to transform substantially many of the given characteristics of the modern political process — more or less accepted or even encouraged by the other three syndromes. Nevertheless, a brief description of its characteristics will be offered below, partly because it has emerged with increasing frequency (if not specificity) in recent discussions of participation and representation,[29] and partly because it seems to round out in logical terms the combinatorial possibilities of the variables used to define the other three types.

> Syndicalism could be defined as a system of interest aggregation (more than representation) in which the constituent units are an unlimited number of singular, voluntary, noncompetitive (or better hived-off) categories, not hierarchically ordered or functionally specialized, neither recognized, created nor licensed by state or party, not controlled in their leadership selection or interest articulation by state or party, not exercising a representational monopoly but resolving their conflicts and "authoritatively allocating their values" autonomously without the interference of the state.

With this last definition-model we have moved some distance from our stated limited concern with specifying the characteristics of corporatism as a distinctive and self-sustaining system of interest representation, and not confusing it with a whole system of political domination. Nevertheless, this excursion has served to remind us that the process of capturing organizing and articulating the demands of civil society as well as those of receiving, interpreting and even applying the "imperative coordinations" of the state is only part of the political process, and hence only intelligible in purpose and consequnce when considered in relation to other political subsystems and whole regime configurations. This wider set of concerns, ironically, leads us to a consideration of possible subtypes of corporatism.

III

To illustrate that the skeletonal connotation of corporatism offered above accurately describes the system of interest representation of a large number of countries, including many whose global political systems differ markedly, would not be difficult — even at the existing lamentable state of our empirical knowledge. Hence, it has been argued and rather convincingly shown that Sweden,[30] Switzerland,[31] the Netherlands,[32] Norway,[33] Denmark,[34] Austria,[35] Spain,[36] Portugal,[37] Brazil,[38] Chile,[39] Peru,[40] Greece,[41] Mexico[42] and Yugoslavia[43] have, by and large, singular, noncompetitive, hierarchically ordered, sectorally compartmentalized, interest associations exercising representational monopolies and accepting (de jure or de facto) governmentally imposed or negotiated limitations on the type of leaders they elect and on the scope and intensity of demands they routinely make upon the state.[44] As a result, such associations have attained "a quasi-legal status and a prescriptive right to speak for their segments of the population. They influence the process of government directly, bypassing the [parliament]. They are agents of authority. They deputize for the state in whole sectors of public life, and they have duties delegated to them that properly belong to the civil service." [Huntford, 1972:86] The summary above applies specifically to Sweden, but it is broadly descriptive of the countries cited above — and undoubtedly of many others yet to be investigated.

Such a demonstration of broad structural identity does have the virtue of debunking, if not divesting, some of these polities of the pluralist labels they have acquired — a prestigious title usually bestowed upon them for no better reason than the mere existence of a multitude of organized interests. It may also serve to call into question the relevance of many supposed properties associated with pluralism and assumed, therefore, to apply to these polities: competitiveness within sectors and, hence, accountability to members; cross-pressures and overlap and, hence, vacillation and moderation in demands; open competitiveness between interest sectors and, hence, incremental, split-the-difference solutions; penetration and subordination of political parties and, hence, broad aggregative party goals, low party discipline and absence of strong partisan ideologies; absence of stable hierarchies of organizational influence and, hence, irrelevance of class or ruling elite as political categories; low barriers of entry into the policy process and, hence, key roles assigned to "potential groups" and absence of systematic bias or exclusion; major importance attached to lobbying and, hence, concentration of attention upon parliament; assumption that policy initiatives are produced by group activity "from below" and, hence, passive roles assumed on the part of state executive and administrative bureaucracies; wide dispersion of political resources and, hence, neither omnipotent veto groups nor powerless marginal elements; and, finally, sheer multiplicity of interests and free associability ensuring spontaneous emergence of countervailing forces and, hence, a general tendency toward homeostasis or shifting equilibria.[45] Corporatist systems may manage to acquire and sustain similar outcomes of demand moderation, negotiated solutions, leader accountability, "deideologization," inclusive participation, countervalence of power and homeostatic balance, but they do *not* do so through the process which theorists and analysts of pluralism have emphasized. For example, in the studies I have conducted of one type of corporatism, I have found that such process features as preemption of issues; co-optation of leaders; vertical or sectoral policy compartmentalization; permanent institutionalization of access; "juridization" or legalization of group conflicts through labor and administrative courts; state technocratic planning and resource allocation; extensive development of functionally specialized, parastate agencies; political culture stressing formalism, consensus and continuous bargaining; symbiotic relation with clientelist and patrimonialist practices in certain issue areas and regime levels; deliberate narrowing and encapsulation of "relevant publics"; periodic but systematic use of physical repression and anticipatory intimidation and, finally, the establishment of what Dahrendorf called a "cartel of anxiety" among restricted elites representing the apexes of the differentiated hierarchic "orders" or "corporations" contributed to the persistence and viability of those systems — even over protracted periods of economic and social change and when faced with acute, externally induced political crises. While comparisons of institutional longevity are difficult to make, there is no evidence I can see that corporatist systems of whatever type are less stable or shorter lived than pluralist ones. There is, however, very strong evidence that they function quite differently — if often to produce generally similar outcomes.

This delineation of an equally elaborate, alternative model to pluralism may seem to some to be in and by itself sufficient justification for this exercise, but most readers must be feeling some vague sense of incompleteness if not of acute discomfort. After all, Sweden is not Portugal and Switzerland is not Greece; and yet, there they are — ignominiously grouped together under the same rubric.

The reason for this latent (or in some cases already manifest) sense of dissatisfaction lies, no doubt, in the stretch of the conceptual distinction I have made between corporatism and pluralism. While this may be an indispensable preliminary step in classifying interest systems, especially given the ubiquity and prestige of the pluralist label, it is still one which, to use Sartori's expression, "does not travel well," or better, "travels too far too easily." If our research objective is not to make universalizing suprahistorical comparisons, but to explore middle-range hypotheses which are explicitly qualified as to cultural, historical and even geographical space, then we must proceed further, *per genus et deifferentiam*, in our taxonomic trip. We must, in short, develop the notion of possible subtypes of corporatist interest politics (just as, of course, we should with pluralist ones, although that will not be attempted here).[46]

That most original and stimulating of corporatist theorists, Mihaïl Manoïlesco, provided the key distinction between two different subtypes. The one he called *corporatisme pur*, in which the legitimacy and functioning of the state were primarily or exclusively dependent on the activity of singular, noncompetitive, hierarchically ordered representative "corporations." The second in contrast he called *corporatisme subordonné*, in which similarly structured "corporations" were created by and kept as auxiliary and dependent organs of the state which founded its legitimacy and effective functioning on other bases. [1936:92][47] This radical distinction is one which, as we shall see, involves not only the nature of power and influence relations but also the developmental pattern by which corporatism emerges, has been reiterated, expanded upon and discussed at great length by Portuguese coporatist theorists where the two subtypes were labelled *corporativismo de associcao* and *corporativismo de Estado*.[48] For our purposes we could label the former, autonomous and penetrative, as *societal corporatism*; and the second, dependent and penetrated, as *state corporatism*.

Some clues to the structural and behavioral elements which differentiate these two subtypes of corporatism can be found in our initial global connotation, or more specifically in what was deliberately *not* included in that definition.

(1) *Limited number:* does not indicate whether established by processes of interassociational arrangement, by "political cartels" designed by existing participants to exclude newcomers, or by deliberate government restriction.

(2) *Singular:* does not indicate whether the outcome of spontaneous co-optation or competitive elimination by surviving associations, or by state-imposed eradication of multiple or parallel associations.

(3) *Compulsory:* does not specify whether de facto through social pressure, contractual dues checkoff, provision of essential services and/or acquisition of private licensing capacity, or de jure through labor code or other officially decreed, exclusively conceded authority.

(4) *Noncompetitive:* does not state whether the product of internal oligarchic tendencies or external, treaty-like, voluntary agreements among associations, or of the continuous interposition of state mediation, arbitration and repression.

(5) *Hierarchically ordered:* does not indicate whether the outcome of intrinsic processes of bureaucratic extension and/or consolidation, or of state-decreed centralization and administrative dependence.

(6) *Functionally differentiated:* does not specify whether arrived at through voluntaristic agreements on respective "turfs" and nonraiding provisions, or by state-established *enquadramento* (framing) of occupational-vocational categories.

(7) *Recognition by state:* does not differentiate between recognition granted as a matter of political necessity imposed from below upon public officials and that granted from above by the state as a condition for association formation and continuous operation.

(8) *Representational monopoly:* similar to above, does not distinguish between that which is independently conquered and that which is dependently conceded.

(9) *Controls on leadership selection and interest articulation:* does not suggest whether this is the product of a reciprocal consensus on procedure and/or goals, or of an asymmetric imposition by the "organized monopolists of legitimate violence."

Through this exercise in intention — the further elaboration of properties which combine to form a global concept — we have constructed two quite distinctive subtypes. The first, involving all or most of the initial elements in the either/or dichotomies made above, corresponds ideally to what we have called societal corporatism. Empirically, it is best exemplified by the cases of Sweden, Switzerland, the Netherlands, Norway and Denmark, as well as by emergent properties which have been observed by scholars in such other, supposedly pluralist, systems as Great Britain, Western Germany, France, Canada, and the United States. The second type, described by the latter elements in each either/or distinction, coalesces into a subtype we have labelled state corporatist and this conforms historically to the cases of Portugal, Spain, Brazil, Chile, Peru, Mexico, and Greece — as well of course to the defunct experiences of Fascist Italy, Petainist France, National Socialist Germany[49] and Austria under Dollfuss.

When viewed statically, descriptively, institutionally, these two subtypes exhibit a basic structural similarity, one which sets them apart from pluralist, monist or syndicalist systems of interest representation. When viewed in motion, however, they are revealed as the products of very different political, social and economic processes, as the vehicles for very different power and influence relations, and as the purveyors of very different policy consequences. Societal corporatism is found imbedded in political systems with relatively autonomous, multilayered territorial units; open, competitive electoral processes and party systems; ideologically varied, coalitionally based executive authorities — even with highly "layered" or "pillared" political subcultures. State corporatism tends to be associated with political systems in which territorial subunits are tightly subordinated to central bureaucratic power; elections are nonexistent or plebiscitary; party systems are dominated or monopolized by a weak single party; executive authorities are ideologically exclusive and more narrowly recruited and are such that political subcultures based on class, ethnicity, language, or regionalism are repressed. Societal corporatism appears to be the concomitant, if not ineluctable, component of the postliberal, advanced capitalist, organized democratic welfare state; state corporatism seems to be a defining element of, if not structural necessity for, the antiliberal, delayed capitalist, authoritarian, neomercantilist state.

IV

Corporatism appears under two very different guises: the revolutionary and the evolutionary. It is either the product of a "new order" following from a fundamental overthrow of the political and economic institutions of a given country and created by force or special "collective spirit"; or the outcome of a natural evolution in economic and social ideas and events. In the latter case, corporatism then emerges as an aspect of a certain *idée-force* progressing along with the amplification and specification of the process of associational development, generating what one calls today in several democratic countries, "the corporative mystique." [Malherbe, 1940: 13-14].

The Swiss author of these lines, himself rather caught up in "the corporative mystique" which swept his country in the 1930's, illustrates not only that theorists who contemplated the matter comparatively were well aware of the distinction between the two subtypes we have defined above, but were also quite conscious of the need for two essentially separate theories for explaining the emergence of modern corporatism. One of these would be more likely to emphasize long-term trends and slow, incremental change, cultural and institutional continuity, gradual intellectual awareness and passive political acceptance; the other more likely would be forged out of immediate *conjoncture* and impending collapse, strong leadership and repressive action, architectonic vision and inflated rhetoric. In a nutshell, the origins of societal corporatism lie in the slow, almost imperceptible decay of advanced pluralism; the origins of state corporatism lie in the rapid, highly visible demise of nascent pluralism.

The task of constructing this set of dual theories is enormous given the apparently bewildering variety of contexts in which one type or the other of corporatism has emerged, and the frustrating absence of empirical studies on the historical dynamics of whatever type of interest group system. Complicating the task even further is the natural tendency to confuse this problem with the more general and clearly interrelated one of the causes of the erosion/collapse of liberal democracy and the advent/consolidation of authoritarian rule. Even if we focus specifically and exclusively on those factors which hypothetically affect changes in the system of interest representation, we must admit from the start that the best we can do is to identify some probabilistically necessary but clearly insufficient conditions. We can only try post factum to strip historical cases of their idiosyncrasies of personality and culture, of their accidents of good and bad fortune, of their immediate but superficial catalysts and precipitants in order to reveal the underlying elements of structural conduciveness which led (and may lead in the future) to such similar and yet different outcomes as societal and state corporatism.[50] I hardly need to emphasize the preliminary and speculative nature of the following dual theories.

Nor should I have to stress that they may not contribute much to explaining specific occurrences or nonoccurrences. For example, why did the halting and tentative experiments in state corporatism by Sidónio Pais in Portugal (1917-18), Primo de Rivera in Spain (1923-30), Pangalos in Greece (1925) and José Uriburu in Argentina (1930-31) all fail to take hold when, ten to twelve years later, corporatism flourished in each case? Why did Sweden, Denmark, Switzerland and the Netherlands adopt internal "social peace" treaties between peak associations of employers and workers in the 1930s and then move rapidly and incrementally toward generalized societal corporatism in the 1940's and 1950's, while other countries such as Finland, Norway and Belgium moved more hesitantly and fitfully, and still others such as France, Great Britain, Ireland and the United States have proven consistently more resistant to the blandishments of corporatism? I doubt whether the following speculations can answer such specific questions very satisfactorily.

Whatever reservations one may have about the degree of determination exercised by the structure and mode of production upon such political variables as individual attitudes, voting choice, party systems and ideological doctrines, inquiry into the origins of corporatism of either type leads one very quickly to the constraints, opportunities and contradictions placed upon political actors by the operation of the economic system. More specifically for the cases which have interested me, it leads to a consideration of the basic institutions of capitalism and the class structure of property and power engendered by it.[51] Perhaps it is the directness of the linkage between the system of interest representation and these institutions of concentration of production and inequality of distribution, but the resultant situation is particularly "naked."

As a macrohypothesis, I suggest that *corporatization of interest representation is related to certain basic imperatives or needs of capitalism to reproduce the conditions for its existence and continually to accumulate further resources. Differences in the specific nature of these imperatives or needs at different stages in the institutional development and international context of capitalism, especially as they affect the pattern of conflicting class interests, account for the difference in origins between the societal and state forms of corporatism.*

Summarizing, again in a nutshell, the decay of pluralism and its gradual displacement by societal corporatism can be traced primarily to the imperative necessity for a stable, bourgeois-dominant regime, due to processes of concentration of ownership, competition between national economies, expansion of the role of public policy and rationalization of decision-making within the state to associate or incorporate subordinate classes and status groups more closely within the political process.

As for the abrupt demise of incipient pluralism and its dramatic and forceful replacement by state corporatism, this seems closely associated with the necessity to enforce "social peace," not by coopting and incorporating, but by repressing and excluding the autonomous articulation of subordinate class demands in a situation where the bourgeoisie is too weak, internally divided, externally dependent and/or short of resources to respond effectively and legitimately to these demands within the framework of the liberal democratic state.

Of course, to these general elements, one must add several other "overdeterminative" factors which combine with the former, making corporatism an increasingly likely outcome: (1) secular trends toward bureaucratization and oligarchy within interest associations; (2) prior rates of political mobilization and participation; (3) diffusion of foreign ideologies and institutional practices; (4) impact of international war and/or depression. Nevertheless, the core of my speculation about structural conduciveness rests on the problems generated by delayed, dependent capitalist development and nonhegemonic class relations in the case of state corporatism, and advanced, monopoly or concentrated capitalist development and collaborative class relations in the case of societal corporatism.

Turning to an explication of the advanced capitalism-societal corporatism relation, I shall be brief, partly because of my lesser familiarity with this side, partly because there exists a series of evocatively presented and excellently documented studies of the subject.

The first major theorist to perceive certain emergent imperatives of capitalism and to link them explicitly with corporatism was John Maynard (Lord) Keynes. In a startling essay published in 1926 entitled "The End of Laissez-Faire," Keynes first debunks the orthodox claims of liberalism:

It is *not* true that individuals possess a prescriptive "natural liberty" in their economic activities. There is *no* "compact" conferring perpetual rights on those who Have or those who Acquire. The world is *not* so governed from above that private and social interest always coincide. It is *not* a correct deduction from the Principles of Economics that enlightened self-interest always operates in the public interest. Nor is it true that self-interest *is* enlightened; more often individuals acting separately to promote their own ends are too weak to attain even these. Experience does *not* show that individuals, when they make up a social unit, are always less clear-sighted than when they act separately. [1952:312]

Given these negative results (and *sous-entendu* a growing awareness of them among wider and wider publics exercising the liberal voluntaristic rights accorded them by the open franchise and free associability), the *agenda* and *nonagenda* (as Keynes called it) of the state must be modified. Or, as he put it more bluntly in another essay, "In the future, the Government will have to take on many duties which it has avoided in the past." [1952:331] The objective of this imperative policy expansion is to exercise "directive intelligence through some appropriate organ of action over the many intricacies of private business, yet...leave private initiative and enterprise unhindered." More specifically, he noted the need for (1) "deliberate control of the currency and of credit by a central institution," (2) "dissemination on a great scale of data relating to the business situations," (3) "coordinated act(s) of intelligent judgement...as to the scale on which it is desirable that the community as a whole should save, the scale on which these savings should go abroad...and whether the present organization of the investment market distributes savings along the most rationally productive channels" and, finally, (4) "a considered national policy about what size of population...is most expedient." [1952:317-9] For 1926, that was a prescient statement about the future role of the state in capitalist societies — even down to the itemized content and sequential ordering of the new policy agenda.

Despite the unorthodoxy of these suggestions for "improvements in the technique of modern capitalism," Keynes wisely observed that "there is nothing in them which is seriously incompatible with what seems to me to be the essential characteristic of capitalism, namely the dependence upon an intense appeal to the money-making and money-loving instincts of individuals as the main motive force of the economic machine." [1952:319] The reason for his confidence in their compatibility stems from the political instrumentality he advocated to bring about this policy revolution, namely, societal corporatism.

I believe that in many cases the ideal size for the unit of control and organization lies somewhere between the individual and the modern state. I suggest, therefore, that progress lies in the growth and recognition of semi-autonomous bodies within the state — bodies whose criterion of action within their own field is solely

the public good as they understand it, and from whose deliberations motives of
private advantage are excluded, though some place it may still be necessary to
leave, until the ambit of men's altruism grows wider, to the separate advantage
of particular groups, classes, or faculties — bodies which in their ordinary course
of affairs are mainly autonomous within their prescribed limitations, but are
subject in the last resort to the sovereignty of democracy expressed through
parliament. I propose a return, it may be said, towards medieval conceptions of
separate autonomies [1952:313-4], my emphasis.

While there is no evidence (that I know of) that Keynes's slim
pamphlet exerted a direct, blueprint-like, influence or even provoked a general intellectual awareness of the issues he raised, in or outside of Great Britain,[52] the subsequent course of policy development in most developed Western nations confirmed his prognosis.
The fundamental paradox involved has been excellently put by a
Dutch scholar:

The more the private citizens succeed in organizing themselves into powerful
combines and associations for the promoting of their manifold and often conflicting interests, the more they undermine the conditions that are essential to the
actual functioning of the classical Liberalist concept of an automatically achieved equilibrium of freely competing societal forces. And the more this spontaneous harmonization proves to have little relation to reality, the more the
government is impelled to interfere in order to secure a deliberately regulated and
planned integration of interests. [Kramer, 1966:83]

To this I would simply add another: the more the modern state
comes to serve as the indispensable and authoritative guarantor of
capitalism by expanding its regulative and integrative tasks, the
more it finds that it needs the professional expertise, specialized information, prior aggregation of opinion, contractual capability
and deferred participatory legitimacy which only singular, hierarchically ordered, consensually led representative monopolies can
provide. To obtain these, the state will agree to devolve upon or
share with these associations much of its newly acquired decisional
authority, subject, as Keynes noted, "in the last resort to the
sovereignty of democracy expressed through Parliament."

This osmotic process whereby the modern state and modern interest associations seek each other out leads, on the one hand, to
even further extensions of public guarantees and equilibrations
and, on the other, to even further concentration and hierarchic
control within these private governments. The modalities are varied
and range from direct government subsidies for associations, to of-

ficial recognition of bona fide *interlocuteurs*, to devolved responsibilities for such public tasks as unemployment or accident insurance, to permanent membership in specialized advisory councils, to positions of control in joint public-private corporations, to
informal, quasi-cabinet status, and finally to direct participation in
authoritative decision-making through national economic and
social councils. The sequence by which societal corporatism has
crept into the polity probably varies considerably case by case,[53] but
to the extent that the Dutch pattern is representative, it shows a
peculiar circular trend. There it began with local and sectoral level,
jointly managed social insurance schemes (1913); then moved to
abortive attempts at establishing Conciliation Boards (1919, 1923);
to sectoral consultative bodies (1933); to public extensions of cartel
decisions (1935) and labor-management agreements (1937),
obligatorily covering nonmembers and nonparticipants; to sectoral
licensing boards on investment (1938); to the reestablishment of a
nationally coordinated wage determination board (1945); to indicative national planning (1945); then back to the establishment of
specialized Product and Industrial Boards, along with an overall
co-ordinating agency, the Social and Economic Council (1950);
then down to the establishment of consultative councils in each individual enterprise (1950) and, finally, to the creation of a national
level, joint coordination council for social insurance (1959) — right
back where they started in 1913.[54] The resultant pattern evolved
pragmatically and unevenly, not by the unfolding of some concerted, grand corporatist design. It moved *up and down* from
enterprise to local to national level; *back and forth* from a concern
with specific goods and services (insurance, health,
apprenticeship), to specialized vertical production areas
(metallurgy, electronics, chemicals, retail commerce) and to broad
horizontal sectors (industry, commerce, agriculture); and *sideways*
from one issue area to another (wages, prices, investment, indicative planning). While the Netherlands' osmotic adaptation may
be unique in many respects, I suspect that a sequential plotting of
measures of creeping corporatism in other advanced capitalist
societies would not be very different.[55]

Thanks to the effort of Andrew Shonfield, it hardly seems
necessary to pursue these speculations much further. In his
magisterial, *Modern Capitalism*, he has demonstrated in great
detail how, in order to correct inherent defects linked to processes
of internal concentration and external competition, the modern

"positive" state finds itself simultaneously attempting to foster full employment, promote economic growth, prevent inflation, smooth out business cycles, regulate working conditions, cover individual economic and social risks and resolve labour conflicts. This drastic modification of the governmental agenda/nonagenda has in turn led to (and is in part the product of) a major change in the relationship between interest associations and the public bureaucracy, as advocated and predicted by Lord Keynes. Shonfield unhesitatingly labels this formula as corporatist: "The major interest groups are brought together and encouraged to conclude a series of bargains about their future behaviour, which will have the effect of moving economic events along the desired path. The plan indicates the general direction in which the interest groups, including the state in its various economic guises, have agreed that they want to go." [1965: 231][56]

In postwar Western Europe, Shonfield finds this approach competing or combining with two others; (1) intellectualized, technocratic "indicative" planning, and (2) reinforced, direct economic control and ownership by the state. In a series of thoroughly researched and well-constructed case studies, he explores the extent to which this societally corporative approach has crept differentially into European policy process, alone or in combination with the other two. In specific instances, he emphasizes general historical-institutional-legal variables,[57] ideological residues,[58] prior levels of voluntary associational consolidation and decision-making style,[59] seriousness of demographic pressures and economic reconstruction,[60] well-entrenched conceptions of role on the part of organized interests,[61] as all providing a greater incentive for corporatization. Even more fascinating are his explanations of why certain European countries have resisted, or better, not so quickly or thoroughly succumbed to this approach. For France, he stresses the role of specialized training and corporate self-consciousness on the part of higher civil servants; [1965:122ff] for the United Kingdom, he finds the answer in "the traditional British view of the proper relationship between public and private power (in which) the two...are thought of as utterly distinct from one another," as well as resistance by industrialists to compulsory membership and jurisdiction. [1965: 99, 231-3] In a brilliant discussion of the American paradox — "the Americans who, in the 1930's, acted as the precursors of the new capitalism, seemed to stall in their course just when the system was coming to fruition in the Western world — showing its full powers to provide the great gifts of eocnomic growth, full employment, and social welfare" — Shonfield searches for the causes of this abortive attempt to encourage corporatist forms of policy-making during the early New Deal (1933-35). He finds them in the internally competitive, overlapping jurisdictions of the federal and state bureaucracies, the preferred leadership style of Roosevelt ("his penchant for the role of bargainer-in-chief, his evident delight in the exercise of a kind of administrative athleticism"), in the active, intrusive role of Congress in the administrative process, the juridical and legalistic imprint imposed on the American state by the special role which lawyers have played within it, and in the absence of a more professionalized, self-confident elite of civil servants. [1965:298-329] while Shonfield does carry his analysis into the mid-1960's, it is too bad that it stops before Lyndon Johnson and even more rapidly, Richard Nixon, managed to transform this "arm's-length relationship with private enterprise" (as Shonfield described it) into something more closely resembling the sort of "active huddle" which the NRA corporatists had advocated in the early thirties.[62]

Modern Capitalism provides us with a veritable gold mine of interesting general hypotheses concerning the emergence of societal corporatism and specific, if somewhat *ad hoc*, subhypotheses explaining its differential role in contemporary Western polities and its emergent relations with other policy-mechanisms of advanced capitalist management. From my admittedly less knowledgeable vantage point, I would tend to emphasize a longer period of historical regress, for example, to include planning, rationing, mobilization and reconstruction measures taken during and following World War I and their impact upon subsequent "public policy paradigms."[63] Add to these a more explicit discussion of certain political variables, such as degree of prior class consciousness and intensity of class antagonism, extent of prior party-interest association interpenetration (*lager*-type structures), ideological diffusion and international climate, plus prior rates of political mobilization and participation. Nevertheless, in our understanding of societal corporatism we are off to an impressive, if still speculative, start.

We are not so fortunately endowed at either the theoretico-deductive or the empirico-inductive level with respect to state corporatism. Of course, one reason is that there exists no companion volume to *Modern Capitalism* entitled *Dependent* or *Derived Capitalism* — not yet. But this lack of detailed comparative case studies or even good single country monographs is only part of the difficulty.

Theorists-apologists for state corporatism are usually not very helpful. This, not so much because they tended to be less perceptive and personally objective than, say, Lord Keynes, but because they were caught in a built-in contradiction between their subjective speculative task and the objective political function they were indirectly called upon to perform.

So, for example, there is scarcely a single state-corporatist theorist who does not proclaim his opposition to statism, his commitment to decisional decentralization and his desire for eventual associational autonomy.[64] Nevertheless, our theorist is aware that given the fragmented, ideologically charged and class-divided nature of the political system he is operating within, singular, non-conflictive, hierarchically ordered and functionally compartmentalized associations are not likely to be spontaneously forthcoming. He therefore advocates the temporary use of state authority to establish these compulsory structures — and to remove voluntaristic, competing ones — all, of course, in the name of national and/or public interest. Other than some vaguely specified reference to the eventual emergence of a "corporatist consciousness" (his equivalent to the New Soviet Man), our theorist conveniently forgets to specify the political mechanism by which the state's authoritarian presence can be made to "fade out," leaving those imagined self-governing agents of decentralized decision-making behind. Perhaps the most obvious case of this praxiological hypocrisy has been Portugal, if only because Oliveira Salazar so repeatedly and (apparently) sincerely expressed his fervent opposition to statism or even to any form of governmental economic intervention, while presiding over the creation of one of the most overbureaucratized, minutely regulated, centralized state apparatuses ever observed.

If such theorists can hardly be trusted with regard to the state, then neither can one expect them to be entirely candid about corporatism's relation to capitalism and specific class interests. One of their favorite themes — admittedly one which is today somewhat less loudly proclaimed — is that corporatism from above constitutes some sort of *tertium genus* between and distinct from either capitalism or socialism-communism. Hence, while they are often capable of decrying, in lurid and quite convincing terms, the inequitable and rachitic performance of existing capitalist institutions (and of conjuring up terrible visions of life under godless socialism), they are obviously not very concerned with revealing how the forceful implantation of corporatism acts as an instrument for rescuing and consolidating capitalism rather than replacing it. Given the unanimous emphasis they place on functional interdependence and group harmony, we should hardly expect them to delve too deeply into the elements of class conflict, status antagonism and centerperiphery tension that such an imposed system of interest representation is designed to suppress, if not overcome.

In short, as we attempt to put together speculatively some hypotheses as to the contexts in which this state corporatist response emerges and the possible range of variation and sequences of implantation it may encompass, we are not likely to get much help from its manifest theorists-apologists, as we did in the case of societal corporatism.

There is, fortunately one interesting exception: Mihaïl Manoïlesco. Manoïlesco was a sort of Salazar manqué. A professor of political economy (although an engineer by training) and minister of commerce and industry for a short period in his native Rumania,[65] he wrote *Le Siècle du Corporatisme* and its companion work, *Le Parti Unique*, after his political career had been cut short and published them in Paris. In the former he not only advanced his cosmic prediction about the ineluctable future of corporatism, but he supported his position with a complex, if schematic, argument — elements of which are strikingly modern.[66]

First Manoïlesco asserts (other corporatist theorists to the contrary notwithstanding) that his conception of this system of interest representation — actually he presents it as a complete system of political domination — has nothing to do, institutionally or ideationally, with an imagined revival of Catholic or medieval practices. Not only does he doubt the existence of natural harmony in such anciens régimes, but he accepts as definitive and desirable the rupture performed by nineteenth-century liberalism and capitalist development. His argument, then, is rigorously secular and, in his view, both progressive and realistic, looking forward prospectively rather than backward nostalgically.

Second, Manoïlesco makes his case on materialist grounds. While convinced, like Durkheim, that properly constructed corporations would provide the answer to overcoming modern man's moral and spiritual malaise, integrating him into society through new communal bonds, the imperative forces leading to corporatization were to be found in the political economy of his time, in the nature of ownership, production and distribution of capitalism itself. In fact, at several reprises, Manoïlesco approvingly cites Marx, although in general he regards him as theorist of the past rather than the present century.

Third, Manoïlesco denies that corporatism is merely a temporary defense mechanism for the mobilization and/or protection of class egoism which will somehow fade away when the conjunctural threat has passed. Rather, he presents it as a permanent institutional form, not intrinsically beholden to any social class or even to the maintenance of the status quo, capable of subduing particular interests to overriding national goals and eventually of transforming the capitalist basis of society itself.

In contemporary parlance, Manoïlesco was a theorist of "external dependence." While he occasionally hints at essentially internal political conditions, for example, "premature" radicalization of the working class through ideological diffusion, fragmentation and loss of nerve on the part of the bourgeoisie, urban-rural tensions, decline of local and regional loyalties, that might contribute to provoking a corporatist response, its essential "reason for becoming" lies in the system of unequal international exchange.

> Just as Marx's theory leads us to understand the social phenomena of the capitalist worlds and especially that of exploitation *by classes*, this theory of international exchange makes us understand the inequality *between peoples* and relations of exploiter and exploited that connect them. [1936:30]

Corporatism, as he understood and advocated it, is an institutional-political response to a particular process of transformation that the world political economy and its attendant system of international stratification is presently undergoing. Its "dominant cause" lies in the relations between *peoples*, rather than between *classes* within national units. In fact the latter are conditioned, if not determined, by the former. The entire spectrum of political forces has shifted: "The Nineteenth Century knew the economic solidarity of *class*. The Twentieth will know the economic solidarity of *nations*." [1936:35]

According to Manoïlesco, the dynamic element in this process of world economic transformation consists of a radical "national" demand for restructuring the international division of labor and its distribution of benefits. Peripheral capitalist nations are becoming

increasingly aware of the disparity in returns generated by their exchange of raw materials and foodstuffs for the manufactured
goods produced by the advanced, earlier developing economies and
are beginning to implement new national economic policies,
especially ones aiming at import-substituting industrialization and
control of foreign trade. This diffusion of industrialization and
policy techniques was greatly accelerated by World War I, but is an
autonomous secular trend which can be expected to continue on
throughout the century. In essence and embryo, Manoïlesco anticipated the general arguments and even many of the specific
points of what twenty years later came to be known as the ECLA
(Economic Commission for Latin America of the United Nations)
doctrine or, even later, the UNCTAD (United Nations Conference
on Trade and Development) position.

To this, he added a second, more static observation: the end of
territorial expansion. The twentieth century, he felt, would see the
exhaustion of both open internal frontiers and manifest external
imperialism. While he by no means could be credited with foresee-
ing the formal decolonialization of Africa and Asia (his perspective
was strictly Eurocentric), he did see that the international system
had in a physical sense filled out existing space. Borders and
loyalties were becoming fixed; territoriality from being a variable
had become a constant. Economic, social and political problems
would have to be tackled and especially organized with constant,
zero-sum parameters.

These compound changes in international relations — the collapse of the prewar liberal economic order, the rising demand for
equality of benefit and status between nation-states, the definitive
demarcation of territoriality — provided the materialistic (and
speculative) foundations for Manoïlesco's ideology of defensive,
nationalistic modernization from above. Each national unit, each
state, must henceforth act exclusively as its own agent in its own interests and with its own resources, bargaining continually for survival and self-advantage in a dangerous and unstably equilibrated
international system. Nineteenth-century assumptions about liberty
and initiative in the pursuit of individual self-interest and the
benevolent, self-corrective operation of free and competitive
markets and political processes were no longer valid. As a consequence of these new tensions between central and peripheral
capitalisms and between all autarkically minded nation-states, the
twentieth century would impose new conceptions of justice and

forms of political organization.

Corporatism, he argued, would be one of, if not *the* institutional response to these *impératifs de l'époque.* It alone would permit the state to fulfil the new functions which were being thrust upon public policy by external exigences. It would emerge first where those imperatives and tensions were the strongest, the southeastern and southern periphery of Europe, but once successful there, it would compel similar transformations in the organizational structure and policy practices of the earlier developing, liberal-pluralist systems.

But why corporatism? Why this particular set of *sous-instruments de l'Etat* as Manoïlesco unflinchingly called them? His arguments are multiple, if not equally convincing and consistent:

1) Such corporations would fill out a continuous hierarchy of authority, thereby providing the isolated and impotent individual with a set of well-defined intermediary ranks and loyalties "dragging him into society" à la Durkheim and offering the political system the means "to resolve from a unitary and logical point of view all the specialized problems posed by the complex relations between the individual and the state." [1936:74] To do this, Manoïlesco noted, these new units of representation would have to be *intégral*, not just cover economic interests as in Fascist Italy, but spiritual and moral ones as well.

2) The functional specialization of corporations would be "technologically self-determining" dividing the polity into vertical units of interest aggregation which in turn would enhance the role of technical expertise, depersonalize leadership and bring out naturally balanced interdependencies between issue areas. Most importantly and specifically, they would facilitate the expanding role of the state in national economic planning and international economic bargaining.

3) By devolving authority from the state to "neatly defined," "never contradictory" and "preestablished" interest hierarchies, the state would be relieved of decisional and implementational responsibility over "nonessential" matters (welfare, health, etc.) and could then devote more attention and effort to such "essential" tasks as internal security, external defense, foreign affairs, and national propaganda. In addition.

The multiplication of economic, cultural, intellectual and social functions of the state and the plurality of sources of public power creates a new function (or gives greater scope to a function already existing in embryonic form) which is the *function of arbitration and coordination of all national activities.* . . . The imperatives of our time oblige the state to recognize these [conflicts of collective interests]; they even oblige it to solve them. And they make the state the most active and solicited of arbitrators. . . [Even more] the state must have [its own power of initiative]. It must anticipate these conflicts of interest; it must have the initiative over all general decisions facilitating the coordination of national activities. Initiative becomes a new function unknown by the indvidualist state and embracing all manifestations of national life. [1936:131][67]

4) Corporatism through its compartmentalized vertical pillaring and internal hierarchy of authority would provide an antidote to the "spirit of class." This latter, outmoded form of "horizontal consciousness" would be replaced by the new spirit of national solidarity and functionally interdependent organization.

Despite the fact that corporative consciousness is presently weak, it will always triumph in the end. Because in the limited world we are entering today, where solidarity and organization are imperatives for survival, there will be no place for *artificial* social differences. Or, differences of class are mostly *artificial* and *temporary*, linked to the exceptional circumstances of the nineteenth century. [1936:107-8]

While Manoïlesco implies that this "benevolent" ninety-degree switch in the polarities of group consciousness would begin in the periphery and come as the result of, rather than the prerequisite for, the forceful implantation of state corporatism, he hints that it will be subsequently transmitted to the center where its adoption will be more spontaneous and voluntary:

In Western Europe, the owning class and the working class will draw together, impelled by the common danger they both face equally of witnessing the collapse of the industrial superiority from which they have both benefited. [1936:108]

Tactically speaking, Manoïlesco observes that in the short run "the best way to vanquish the actual antagonism of classes is to recognize it," that is, to incorporate "separate but equal" (*paritaire*) representations of owners and workers within the same corporation, but in the long run it will no longer be necessary to provide even such a simulated equilibrium, given the projected disappearance of class identification. [1936:108-9]

5) One reason Manoïlesco was able to soft-pedal the coercive, authoritarian aspects of the transition to state corporatism was his

belief that the twentieth century would see a major change in "the scales of moral and social values" held by citizens and subjects. The past century's ideals of individual equality and liberty would be replaced by new collective goals of *social justice*, based on differential rights and obligations according to the functional importance of one's role in society; and the goal of organization would place consensual restrictions on mutual activity in return for security and higher productivity. Both of these new *idoles de l'époque* would, of course, have to be made compatible with and subordinate to the highest ideal of all, that "indisputable criterion," which Manoïlesco exclaimed in a burst of totalitarian rhetoric to mean that: "All that conforms to the national interest is just; all that is contrary to that interest is unjust." [1936:110]

As complex and suggestive (if schematic and deformed by wishful thinking) as these hypotheses may be, Manoïlesco is much less explicit about the politics and the specific decisional sequence involved in the transition toward this new form of interest representation. Pure (read, societal) corporatism, he conceded three years later, can only be attained *after* the widespread development of "corporative consciousness" and such a high degree of national integration that "old" and "artificial" class and partisan loyalties had been eradicated or, at least, severely eroded. This, he admits, is a long way off and, in the meantime, those "imperatives of the epoch" demand action, especially in the periphery. There, subordinate corporatism is the only answer: "It is natural that the corporations must be held in tutelage. The indicated tutor...is the single party...for a transitory period. [1937:134]

In the present absence of comparative case studies, it is not easy to evaluate the merits of Manoïlesco's prototheory of the emergence of state corporatism, or to elaborate further upon it. In a very general way, there seems to be a correspondence between the context of peripheral, delayed-dependent capitalism; awareness of relative underdevelopment; resentment against inferior international status; desire for enhanced national economic and political autarky; extension of state control through regulatory policies, sectoral planning and public enterprise; emergence of a more professionalized and achievement-oriented *situs* of civil servants; and the forced corporatization of interest representation from above. Manoïlesco's belated remarks on the specific instrumentality responsible for this change have been less well confirmed. In no case was the single ruling party the primary or exclusive tutelary agent. Rather, state executive and administrative bodies tended to act directly in both establishing and subsequently controlling these new *sous-instruments*. The implantation of state corporatism, in fact, was compatible with a wide range of party contexts — from the no-party systems of Brazil, Greece and Austria, to the weak, reigning but not ruling, single-party systems of Spain and Portugal, to the strong monopolistic party systems of Fascist Italy and Nazi Germany.

On the surface, state corporatism was implanted much more dramatically, quickly, thoroughly and rationally than was the case with the hesitant, uneven, experimental, incremental, "creeping" pattern of its societal cousin. "Born at the stroke of the legislative baton," as one French critic put it, [Coornaert, 1941:293] overnight immense organizational hierarchics with sonorous names were created, covering all interest sectors and all levels of the polity with impressive symmetry of representative and equality of access. Subsequently, these monuments of political architecture persisted for years virtually without juridical or formal modification.

However, detailed analyses[68] have not only revealed the fictitious physical existence of many of these sonorous organizations and their marginal influence over public policy, but have also unmasked their pretence of class symmetry and equality of access. Moving ruthlessly to suppress all preexisting worker associations and to fill the resulting organizational vacuum as quickly as possible with the maximum number and most widely dispersed set of new compliant worker *sindicatos*, the state corporatists acted much more cautiously and "understandingly" with respect to producer and owner interests. Preexisting, voluntaristically supported associations were tolerated or incorporated with their leadership and functions intact; strategically placed elites were granted special organizational privileges and exemptions, for example, the right to form specialized national associations independent of the general sectoral hierarchies; rural landowners, except for those cultivating certain export crops, were left largely untouched, and associations for rural workers, where allowed to exist, were placed under their local control; no serious attempt was made to transform such preexistent, premodern corporations as the Church and the universities; corporatization of civil servants was expressly prohibited, as well as other forms of associability for this *situs*; finally, either no attempt was made to create "uniclass" peak associations of employers and workers (Brazil) or, where the attempt was belatedly made (Portugal), the resultant *corporacões* have been run by and for employers. In short, what appear at first sight to be architectonic monuments of great scope, foresight and symmetry turn out upon closer inspection to be just about as limited, improvised and lopsided as those of their societally corporatist relatives.

Some of Manoïlesco's prototheoretical assumptions about the political functions and policy consequences of state corporatism seem to have been confirmed by its subsequent praxis. It has been associated with the extension of state control over export commodities, sectoral policies of import substitution and attempts to exert greater influence in international economic negotiations. While by no means successful in eradicating horizontal (class) forms of consciousness, its imposition of verticalized decisional hierarchies and fragmented interest categories has definitely undermined the cohesion and capacity to act of the proletariat and even of the bourgeoisie with respect to general policy issues. It has advanced *pari passu* with an expansion in the role of technocratic expertise and impersonal (if not to say faceless) leadership styles. Most importantly, it has greatly advanced and facilitated the *verselbständigte Macht der Executivgewalt*, that "process whereby state executive power becomes progressively more independent" from accountability to organized social groups, that Marx so long ago suggested was the crucial element in modern authoritarian rule.[69]

Otherwise, Manoïlesco's specific functional hypotheses have not stood up so well. Horizontal consciousness shows no sign of disappearing no matter how suppressed. Class inequalities in access and benefit have not been erased; they have been institutionalized and augmented. The decision-making load on the state has not been lightened but burdened by the proliferation of dependent functional hierarchies; far from being freed to pursue bold and innovative national policies, the corporatist state has been trapped in a fantastically complex network of fiscal prebends, sectoral exemptions and entrenched privileges which ties it closely to a stalemated status quo. Popular demands for individual freedom and equality have yet to give way to respect for organizational hierarchy and acceptance of differential justice. Most striking, however, is the total lack of confirmation in praxis of Manoïlesco's assertion of pious hope that corporatism from above would result in a secular decline in the rate of profit, a devaluation of the role of entrepreneurial risk-taking, a diminution of the power of private property and the emergence of a new social or collective mode of production. So far, state corporatism has produced the contrary and one rather suspects it was always intended to do so.

V

> "*Kuppo!*" said the Shah, shaking his head.
> Khashdrahr blushed, and translated uneasily, apologetically.
> "Shah says, 'Communism'."
> "No, *Kuppo!*" said Halyard vehemently. "The government does not own the machines. They simply tax that part of industry's income that once went into labor, and redistribute it. Industry is privately owned and managed, and co-ordinated — to prevent the waste of competition — by a committee of leaders from private industry, not politicians. By eliminating human error through machinery, and needless competition through organization, we've raised the standard of living of the average man immensely."
>
> Kurt Vonnegut, Jr.,
Player Piano (p. 28)

If we accept Manoïlesco's belief in centennial longevity and my hunch that it all began during and immediately after World War I, then we are presently right smack in the middle of the century of corporatism and hence condemned to live with it for another fifty or so years. Kurt Vonnegut's poetic imagination offers us the "comforting" thought that full corporatization will only come in the aftermath of a third major world war. Nevertheless, barring his vision of a future global conflagration precipitating further change, and adopting a more suprise-free scenario, we may question whether corporatism, state or societal, will manage to fill out its century.

State coporatism is everywhere revealing itself more and more costly to maintain through repressive measures and less and less capable of providing the accurate information, semivoluntaristic compliance and contractual complicity needed for managing the modern capitalist state. The obvious answer, an institutional shift from the imposed, exclusionist to the invited, inclusionist type of corporatism, has yet to be made peacefully and incrementally. But the transition to societal corporatism seems to depend very much on a liberal-pluralist past, involving the following: a history of autonomous organizational development; authenticity of representation; protracted encounters between classes and sectors which acquired distinct self-images and loyalties and, eventually, a measure of mutual respect; the presence of competitive party and parliamentary arenas to which wider appeals could be addressed; and, perhaps most importantly, on a previous pattern of relative noninterference by the state which only gradually came to expand its role — and then usually at the request of organized private interests.

Countries locked into state corporatism at an earlier stage of development are likely to find it much more difficult to evolve toward such a consensual solution. There the established pattern is one of asymmetric dependence, unauthentic and fragmented representation, weak associational loyalties, suppressed or manipulated conflict, little mutual respect among groups, no effective means of appealing to wider publics and pervasive state bureaucratic control.[70] Under these conditions, it is difficult to imagine a politically continuous transformation toward societal corporatism; rather, one suspects that the state-corporatist system must first degenerate into openly conflictful, multifaceted, uncontrolled interest politics — pluralism in other words — as appears to be happening in contemporary Spain.

Established, societally corporatist systems are also facing new tensions which they, too, seem incapable of resolving.[71] They are being bombarded with demands for more direct and authentic forms of participation, undermining both the stability of their established internal hierarchies of authority and their claims to democratic legitimacy. More importantly, they are being bypassed with increasing frequency by broad social movements on the one side and specific spontaneous protest actions on the other. The very values and assumptions about society upon which corporatism ultimately rests, functional specialization and hierarchical organization, security and *prévision*, "productivism" and efficiency, economic growth and mass consumption as ends in themselves, are being called into question by these movements and actions. Here, the prospective associational answer is certainly *not* further societal corporatization, *nor* a reversion to past pluralism, *nor* even less a regression to state corporatism, but may be some experimentation with the sort of dispersed, nonspecialized, nonhierarchic, "hived-off", voluntaristic units, autonomously responsible for allocating their values and resolving their conflicts, an interest system which we earlier tentatively identified as syndicalist. Again, however, the peaceful and incremental route to such a systemic transformation has yet to be found.

Marx once suggested that societies only recognized the problems they stood some chance of resolving. From this optimistic perspective, renewed awareness that we may still be in the century of corporatism should contribute to making it the shortest century on historical record.

The next century, that of syndicalism, already awaits its Lord Keynes or its Mihaïl Manoïlesco!

NOTES

1. Mihaïl Manoïlesco, *Le Siècle du Corporatisme*, rev. ed. (Paris, 1936). The original edition was published in 1934.

2. For an example of such a definition by ideology, see James Malloy, "Authoritarianism, Corporatism and Mobilization in Peru," in F. B. Pike and T. Stritch (eds.), *The New Corporatism* (Notre Dame: Notre Dame University Press, 1974), pp. 52-84.

3. To this essay I have appendixed a reference bibliography of some 100 titles which seem important to an understanding of the ideological and praxiological bases of corporatism up to and including the interwar period.

4. For excellent critical treatments of corporatist practice in the 1930's, see Roland Pré, Louis Rosenstock-Franck, 1934; and François Perroux, 1937, 27-178.

5. For a subtle, institutionally sensitive presentation of this argument, see Ronald Newton, "On 'Functional Society,' 'Fragmentation' and 'Pluralism' in Spanish American Political Society," *Hispanic American Historical Review* L, no. 1 (February, 1970), 1-29. For an approach which relies essentially on an ill-defined, Catholic weltanschauunglich argument, see Howard Wiarda, "Toward a Framework for the Study of Political Change in the Iberic-Latin Tradition," *World Politics* XXV, no. 2 (January, 1973), 206-235.

6. See especially the argument by Kalman Silvert, "The Costs of Anti-Nationalism: Argentina," in K. Silvert, ed., *Expectant Peoples* (New York, 1967), pp. 358-61. Also his *Man's Power* (New York, 1970), pp. 59-64, 136-8; "National Values, Development, and Leaders and Followers," *International Social Science Journal* XV (1964), 560-70; "The Politics of Economic and Social Change in Latin America," *The Sociological Review* Monograph XI (1967), 47-58.

7. As Max Weber scornfully put it to earlier advocates of political cultural explanations, "the appeal to national character is generally a mere confession of ignorance." *The Protestant Ethic and the Spirit of Capitalism*, p. 88, as cited in Reinhard Bendix, *Max Weber: An Intellectual Portrait* [New York, 1962] p. 63, fn. 29.

8. Such reasoning has been particularly prevalent among Anglo-Saxon students of Latin America where, from the start, these area specialists seem to have drawn the following syllogism: "Latin Americans behave differently from North Americans; Latin America was colonized by Spain and Portugal; North America by Great Britain; Latin Americans are Catholics, North Americans are predominantly Protestant; *ergo*, Latin Americans behave differently from North Americans because of their Catholic-Iberian heritage!"

The few systematically comparative studies of attitudes which have included both Latin and North American samples have generally concluded that once one controls for education, class, center-periphery residence, age, etc., residual differences that could be assigned specifically to culture are statistically insignificant. See especially Joseph Kahl, *The Measurement of Modernity* (Austin, Texas, 1968).

9. It is also worth mentioning that many, if not most, of the theorists of modern corporatism have not been Catholics. Many were in fact militantly secular. Even those who most publicly claimed to be inspired by "Social Christian" ideals, such as Salazar and Dollfuss, followed a much more bureaucratic, statist and authoritarian praxis. Also worth stressing is that among "Social Christians" or more broadly, progressive Catholics, not all by any means advocated corporatism. Such prominent figures as Jacques Maritain and Emmanuel Mounier opposed it. See Henry Guitton, *Le Catholicisme Social* (Paris, 1945).

Also worth mentioning is that corporatism has been considered quite compatible with many non-Catholic, non-Iberian cultures. See, for example, Samuel H. Beer, *British Politics in the Collectivist Age* (New York, 1969) and Thomas Anton, "Policy-Making and Political Culture in Sweden," *Scandinavian Political Studies* IV (Oslo, 1969), 88-102.

10. See the concept of "limited pluralism" in Juan Linz, "An Authoritarian Regime: Spain," in E. Allardt and S. Rokkan, eds, *Mass Politics* (New York, 1970), pp. 251-83, 374-81.

In subsequent conversations with this author, Linz has advanced and defended the idea of an "organic state model" as the appropriate framework for the discussion of coporatism. See also the essay cited above (fn. 2) by James Malloy.

11. Fustel de Coulange, *La Cité Antique*, 4th ed. (Paris, 1872).

12. Plato, *Laws*, 5-6.

13. Emile Louss,e *Organizacão e representacão corporativas* (Lisbon, 1952), a translation of his *La Société d'Ancien Régime* (Bruxelles, 1943).

14. F. Charles Fourier, *Théories de l'Unité Universelle* (1822) and *Le Nouveau Monde industriel et sociétaire* (1829).

15. Robert LaFont, *La Révolution Régionaliste* (Paris, 1967).

16. Percival and Paul Goodman, *Communitas* (Chicago, 1947) and Gar Alperovitz, "Notes toward a Pluralist Commonwealth," *Warner Modular Publications*, Reprint No. 52 (1973).

17. In earlier works, I tended to define corporatism exclusively in relation to authoritarian rule. See the concluding chapter of my *Interest Conflict and Political Change in Brazil* (Stanford, 1971); also, "Paths to Political Development in Latin America," *Proceedings of the American Academy* XXX, no. 4 (1972), 83-108 and "The Portugalization of Brazil?" in A. Stepan III, ed., *Authoritarian Brazil* (New Haven, 1973).

18. Ronald Rogowski and Lois Wasserspring, *Does Political Development Exist? Corporatism in Old and New Societies* (Beverly Hills, Sage Professional Papers, II, no. 01-024, 1971).

19. For example, Arend Lijphart, *The Politics of Accommodation* (Berkeley, 1968) — where in all fairness the concept of corporatism itself does not appear. In an essay by Martin Heisler, however, these "pillared" notions are expressly linked to a corporatist model of European politics: "Patterns of European Politics: The 'European Polity' Model," in M. Q. Heisler et al., *Politics in Europe: Structures and processes* (New York, 1974).

Also relevant are Arend Lijphart "Consociational Democracy," *World Politics* XXI, no. 2 (January 1969), pp. 207-25; Val R. Lorwin, "Segmented Pluralism: Ideological Cleavages and Political Cohesion in the Smaller European Democracies," *Comparative Politics III*, no. 2 (January, 1971), 14-75; Gerhard Lembruch, *Proporzdemokratie: Politisches System and politische Kultur in der Schweiz und in Österreich* (Tübingen, 1967).

20. Roland Huntford, for example, argues that it is precisely social and economic homogenization which contributes to the thoroughness of Swedish corporation; see *The New Totalitarians* (New York, 1972), pp. 86-87ff. Also Olaf Ruin, "Participation, Corporativization and Politicization Trends in Present-day Sweden" (Paper presented at Sixty-second Annual Meeting of the Society for the Advancement of Scandinavian Study, New York, May 5-6, 1972).

21. On the contrary, a recent analysis of Belgium's associational structure argues persuasively that multipillared conflicts in that polity serve to sustain a more pluralist (i.e., nonmonopolistic, competitive, overlapping) system of interest representation; see A. Van Den Brande, "Voluntary Associations in the Belgian Political System 1954-1968," *Res Publica*, no. 2 (1973), pp. 329-356.

22. At this point it is perhaps worth repeating that this constructed definition does not correspond to any of the ones advanced by specifically corporatist theorists. Moreover, it ignores a number of institutional and behavioral dimensions they tended to stress. For example, it does not specify the existence of singular associations (corporations) grouping both employers and workers. (These rarely exist and where they have been formally established — Portugal, Spain and Italy — they do not function as units.) Nor does it say anything about the presence of a higher council or parliament composed of functional or professional representatives. (Many polities which are not otherwise very corporatist, France or Weimar Germany, have such a *Conseil Economique et Social or Wirtschaftsrat*; many heavily corporatist countries which do have them, e.g. Portugal, do not grant them decisional authority.) Nor does the definition suggest that corporatist associations will be the only constituent units of the polity — completely displacing territorial entities, parties and movements. (In all existing corporatist systems, parties and territorial subdivisions continue to exist and various youth and religious movements may not only be tolerated but encouraged.) These institutional aspects as well as the more important behavioral issues of how and who would form the unique and hierarchical associations, what would be their degree of autonomy from state control and whether whole scheme really could bring about class harmony and constitute a *tertium genus* between communism and capitalism were the subject of extensive debate and considerable fragmentation among corporatist ideologues.

The ideological definition closest to my analytical one is Mihaïl Manoïlesco's: "The corporation is a collective and public organization composed of the totality of persons (physical or juridical) fulfilling together the same national function and having as its goal that of assuring the exercise of that function by rules of law imposed at least upon its members [1936: 176]

23. Actually, the concept is more "a constructed type" than an ideal type. The former has been defined as: "a purposive, combination, and (sometimes) accentuation of a set of criteria with empirical referents that serves as a basis for comparison of empirical cases" (John C. McKinnes, *Constructive Typology and Social Theory* [New York, 1966], p. 3).

24. See my *Interest Conflict and Political Change in Brazil* (1971) and "Corporatist Interest Representation and Public Policy-Making in Portugal" (Paper presented at the Conference Group on Modern Portugal, Durham, N.H., October 10-14, 1973). Also "The Portugalization of Brazil?" (1973).

25. For example, Henry Kariel (ed.), *Frontiers of Democratic Theory* (New York, 1970), and his, *The Decline of American Pluralism* (Stanford, 1961); also Grant Mc-Connell, *Private Power and American Democracy* (New York, 1966).

26. Theodore Lowi, *The End of Liberalism: Ideology, Policy and the Crisis of Public Authority* (New York, 1969).

27. Theodore Lowi, *The Politics of Disorder* (New York, 1971).

28. The quotations are all from *The Federalist Papers*, no. 10.

29. See especially the article by Gar Alperovitz and works cited therein (1973) even though the author associates his proposals with the tradition of pluralism, rather than that of syndicalism. Also Jaroslav Vanek, *The Participatory Economy* (Ithaca, 1971).

30. Nils Elvander, *Interesse-organisationer i Dagens Sverige* (Lund, 1966); Thomas J. Anton (1969), Olaf Ruin (1972) and Roland Huntford (1972). Also Hans Meijer "Bureaucracy and Policy Formulation in Sweden," *Scandinavian Political Studies*, no. 4 (Oslo, 1969), pp. 103-16.

31. Hans Huber, "Swiss Democracy" in H. W. Ehrmann, ed., *Democracy in a Changing Society* (New York, 1964), esp. p. 106.

32. P. E. Kraemer, *The Societal State* (Meppel, 1966). Also John P. Windmuller, *Labour Relations in the Netherlands* (Ithaca, 1969).

33. Stein Rokkan, "Norway. Numerical Democracy and Corporate Pluralism" in R. Dahl, ed., *Political Opposition in Western Democracies* (New Haven, 1966), pp. 105-106ff.

34. Kenneth E. Keller, *Government and Politics in Denmark* (Boston, 1968), esp. pp. 169-70ff.

35. Alfred Diamant, *Austrian Catholics and the First Republic. Democracy, Capitalism and the Social Order 1918-1934* (Princeton, 1960). Also, Gehard Lembruch (fn. 21) and Frederick C. Engelmann, "Haggling for the Equilibrium: the Renegotiation of the Austrian Coalition, 1959," *American Political Science Review* LVI, 3 (September, 1962), 651-620.

36. In addition to Juan Linz, "An Authoritarian Regime: Spain", see Juan Linz and Armando de Miguel, *Los Empresarios ante el Poder Público* (Madrid, 1966); Juan Linz, "From Falange to Movimiento-Organiacion: The Spanish Single Party and the Franco Regime, 1936-1968" in S. P. Huntington and C. H. Moore, eds., *Authoritarian Politics in Modern Society* (New York, 1970), esp. pp. 146-183. Also Fred Witney, *Labor Policy and Practices in Spain* (New York, 1964).

37. Schmitter, "Corporatist Interest Representation and Public Policy-Making in Portugal".

38. Schmitter, *Interest Conflict and Political Change in Brazil* and "The Portugalization of Brazil?"

39. Constantine Menges, "Public Policy and Organized Business in Chile," *Journal of International Affairs* XX (1966), 343-65. Also James Petras, *Politics and Social Forces in Chilean Development* (Berkeley, 1969), pp. 199-203, 209-19.

40. Julio Cotler, "Bases del corporativismo en el Peru," *Sociedad y Política*, I, no. 2 (October, 1972), 3-12.

41. Keith Legg, *Politics in Modern Greece* (Stanford, 1969).

42. Robert E. Scott, *Mexican Government in Transition* (Urbana, Illinois, 1959), esp. chapters 5 and 6.

43. International Labour Offices *Workers' Management in Yugoslavia, Geneva, 1962).* Also Dusan Sidjanski, *"La Représentation des intérêts et al décision politique" in* L. Moulin (ed.), *L'Europe de Demain et ses Responsables* (Bruges, 1967). Something approaching the corporatist model has been implicitly but not explicitly advanced in describing certain "degenerate" varieties of totalitarian ("partialitarian") rule in other Eastern European polities: Poland, Czechoslovakia, Hungary and Rumania, even the U.S.S.R. itself. For an intelligent survey and critique of this literature's misuse of the pluralist paradigm, see Andrew Janos, "Group Politics in Communist Society: A Second Look at the Pluralistic Model" in S. P. Huntington and C. H. Moore, eds. (1970), pp. 537-50.

44. In an even wider range of polities, authors have suggested that parts, if not substantial portions, of the interest group universe can be described as "corporatized"; e.g., the United States: Grant McConnell (1966); Theodore Lowi (1969); Great Britain: Samuel Beer (1968); Western Germany: Ralf Dahrendorf, *Society and Democracy in Germany* (London, 1968); Canada: Robert Presthus, *Elite Accommodation in Canadian Politics* (New York, 1973); France: Suzanne Berger, "Corporative Organization: The Case of a French Rural Association" in J. Pennock and J. Chapman (eds.), *Voluntary Association* (New York, 1969), pp. 263-84.

45. These hypotheses about the functioning of pluralist systems are develped further and contrasted with corporatist ones in my "Inventory of Analytical Pluralist Propositions," unpublished MS of Chicago, 1971.

46. I am following here the advice (and occasionally the vocabulary) of Giovanni Sartori, "Concept Misformation in Comparative Politics," *American Political Science Review* LXIV, 4 (December, 1970), esp. pp. 1034-5.

47. Manoïlesco also noted the existence of "mixed corporatism" combining the two ideal-types.

48. João Manuel Cortez Pinto, *A Corporacão,* vol. I (Coimbra, 1955); also José Pires Cardoso, *Questões Corporativas* (Lisbon, 1958). A somewhat similar distinction, but one which placed primary emphasis on its role in furthering class collaboration by different means, is François Peroux's between *corporatisme lato sensu* and *corporatisme stricto sensu* [1937:7-19].

49. Actually, Nazi Germany is an ambiguous case. For an excellent analysis of the struggles involving competing conceptions of interest politics and the eventual demise of corporatist tendencies after 1936 in that polity, see Arthur Schweitzer, *Big Business in the Third Reich* (Bloomington, Indiana, 1964).

50. For the theoretical model underlying these distinctions between "structural conduciveness" and "precipitating factors," see Neil Smelser, *Theory of Collective Behavior* (New York, 1963).

51. Incompetence prevents me from even speculating about the tendencies toward corporatization which appear to exist among societies with a quite different system of economic exploitation, namely, bureaucratic-centralized socialism. For an initial

treatment of these issues, see the excellent article by Janos (1970) and the works discussed therein.

52. The much later discussion of these issues in the United States was, as might be expected, even more privatistic and antistatist than that of Keynes. For a critical evaluation of this literature, see Hal Draper "Neo-corporatists and neo-reformers," *New Politics* (Fall, 1961), pp. 87-106.

53. A study which illustrates this particularly well in a nicely controlled cultural and developmental setting is Nils Evander, "Collective Bargaining and Incomes Policy in the Nordic Countries: A Comparative Analysis" (Paper prepared for delivery at the APSA Annual Meeting, New Orleans, Sept. 4-8, 1973).

54. The work from which this primitive sequential account is drawn [Kraemer, 1964, 54-65] leaves off in 1958. No doubt further private-public interpenetration has occurred since then.

55. Not all treatments of the emergence of societal corporatism place as much emphasis as I do on the role of advanced capitalism and the imperative transformations it forces on the modern state. Huntford [1972:87] for example, places most of his explanatory emphasis on the traditional agricultural system of Sweden, the role of temperance societies and a particular type of industrial settlement (*bruk*). Thomas J. Anton bases his argument on a distinctive "Swedish policy-making style and elite culture" [1969:92-99]

56. Shonfield goes on to remark: "It is curious how close this kind of thinking was to the corporatist theories of the earlier writers of Italian Fascism, who flourished in the 1920's. Corporatism got its bad name, which has stuck to it, essentially because of its association with the one-party state" (p. 233).

57. "The corporatist form of organization seems to be almost second nature to the Austrians. It is not that they are undemocratic; they nearly all belong to their business and professional associations, their trade unions, their religious and other groups, indeed membership in some of them is compulsory. And the Government is in turn under legal compulsion to consult these organizations before it takes legislative or administrative action of certain specified kinds" [1965:193-94]

58. "It is interesting to find the old corporatist ideal which was deeply embedded in Italian pre-war thinking — the ideal of a balanced and responsible economic group with quasi-sovereign powers administering itself — cropping up again in this new guise" [1965:192]

59. "In Sweden there is a society in which interest groups are so strongly organized, their democratic basis so firm and their habit of bargaining with each one another independently of the government so well established...(yet) the Swedish Government still manages to act in a decisive fashion when circumstances require... It just happens that it is the Swedish way to treat the process of government as being in large part an extended dialogue between experts drawn from a variety of bodies, official and unofficial, whose views are expected to be merely tinged rather than finally shaped by those who pay their salaries" [1965: 199-200]

60. "The remarkable willingness of the trade unions to collaborate actively in this policy of wage restraint is to be explained by their anxiety about the future supply of jobs for Dutchmen" [1965:212]

61. "The general point is that German *Verbände* have traditionally seen themselves as performing an important public role, as guardians of the long-term interests of the nation's industries, and they continue to do so. The development one observes since the war is that the approach to problems of policy has become more

consultative, with the emphasis on technical advice. Power and influence are still present; but the manner is different" [1965:245]

62. Mark Green and Peter Petkas, "Nixon's Industrial State," *The New Republic*, September 16, 1972, p. 18.

63. Shonfield concentrates almost exclusively on the post-World War II period. Only in the case of the United States does he systematically probe further back. Is it just a coincidence that those European countries which were neutral in World War I moved more rapidly and thoroughly towards corporatization (except Austria), than the belligerents? Also worth exploring in greater detail are the diverse policy responses to the Great Depression — as our rapid sketch of the Netherlands illustrated.

64. A partial exception would have to be entered for the Fascists: Bottai, Bortoloto, Papi and Vito but not, for example, for Ugo Spirito who even went so far as to suggest that *corporazione* should replace both private individuals and the state as the basis for property and decision-making, thereby causing a minor scandal at the 1932 Ferrara Congress on Corporatism, *Capitalismo e Corporatismo*, 3rd ed. (Florence, 1934). Interestingly, Spirito's works have been recently reedited.

65. For a brief description of his role in relation to Rumanian politics, see Andrew Janos, "The One-Party State and Social Mobilization: East Europe between the Wars" in S. Huntington and C. H. Moore, eds. (fn. 38), pp. 213-14.

66. In the following summary of his argument I will not cite specific page references, except in the case of direct quotes, since the elements of his position are frequently scattered rather widely and I have synthesized them freely. All quotes are from the 1936 edition.

67. This is the same author who thirty pages before had claimed: "Between the corporatist conception of the state and the pure individualistic one, there is a certain coincidence in outcomes. Both systems result (*aboutissent*) in a minimal state"!!

68. This and the following generalizations about the praxis of state corporatism draw on my case studies of Brazil and Portugal. The Italian Fascist case, however, does not appear to differ markedly. See Roland Sarti, *Fascism and Industrial Leadership In Italy, 1919-1940* (Berkeley, 1971).

69. The expression is from Marx's *The Eighteenth Brumaire*. For a further development of these ideas, see August Thalheimer "Über den Faschismus" in O. Bauer *et al., Faschismus und Kapitalismus* (Frankfurt, 1967), pp. 19-38; H. C. F. Mansilla, *Faschismus und eindimensionale Gesellschaft* (Neuwied u. Berlin, 1971); and Nicos Poulantzas, *Fascisme et dictature* (Paris, 1970); also my "The Portugalization of Brazil?"

70. These conclusions about the difficulties inherent in the transformation from one type of corporatism to the other are based on the study I have conducted on Portuguese corporatism and are discussed more fully therein; see "Corporatist Interest Representation and Public Policy-Making in Portugal."

71. These and other tensions and contradictions of advanced societal corporatism are explored in Christopher Wheeler, "The Decline of Deference: the Tension between Participation and Effectiveness in Organized Group Life in Sweden," unpublished MS, Beloit College, 1972. Also Ruin (1972.

A REFERENCE BIBLIOGRAPHY ON CORPORATISM:
ca. 1800-1950

The following is a list of approximately 100 works dealing with the doctrine and/or practice of modern, i.e., nonmedieval, corporatism up to and including the 1930's and 1940's.

I — *Original works dealing primarily with the theory or doctrine of corporatism*

Charles Anciaux, *L'Etat Corporatif* (Bruxelles, 1935).

Joaquín Aspiazu, *El Estado Corporativo*, 5th ed. (Madrid, 1952).

Raoul Andouin and P. Lhoste-Lachaume, *Le Corporatisme pseudoremède contre l'étatisme* (Paris, 1962).

Eduardo Anuós Pérez, *El Estado Corporativo* (Madrid, 1928).

Guido Bortolotto, *Diritto Corporativo* (Milan, 1934).

Giuseppe Bottai, *Esperienza Corporativa (1929-1934)* (Florence, 1934).

M. Bouvier-Ajam, *La doctrine corporative*, 3d. ed. (Paris, 1941).

Jean Brèthe de la Gressaye, *Le syndicalisme, L'organisation professionnelle et l'Etat* (Paris, 1931).

Jean Brèthe de la Gressaye, "La corporation et l'Etat," *Archives de Philosophie du Droit et de Sociologie Juridique* (1938), pp. 78-118.

Martin Brugarola, *Régimen Sindical Cristiano* (Madrid, 1948).

Marcello Caetano, *Lições de direito corporativo* (Lisbon, 1936).

Marcello Caetano, *O sistema corporativo* (Lisbon, 1938).

António de Castro Fernandes, *Princípios Fundamentais da Organizacão Corporativa Portugesa* (Lisbon, 1944).

G. D. H. Cole, *Self-Government in Industry* (London, 1920).

J. Manuel Cortez Pinto, *A Corporação*, 2 vols. (Coimbra, 1955-6).

J. Pinto da Costa Leite (Lumbrales) *A doutrina corporativa em Portugal* (Lisbon, 1936).

Raymond Devrient, *La corporation en Suisse, ses principes et ses méthodes* (Neuchâtel, 1935).

Léon Duguit, *Traité de Droit constitutionnel*, 5 vols (Paris, 1924-27); vol. II.

Émile Durkheim, "Préface," *De la division du travail social*, 2nd ed., (Paris, 1902).

Anne Fremantle, ed., *The Papal Encyclicals* (New York, 1956).

Otto Von Gierke, *Deutsches Genossenschaftsrecht*, 4 vols. (Berrlin, 1868).

Georges Guy-Grand, "Vue sur le corporatisme," *Archives de Philosophie du Droit et de Sociologie Juridique* (1938), pp. 7-26.

Maurice Hanriou, *La Théorie de l'Institution et de la Fondation* (Paris, 1925).

S. G. Hobson, *National Guilds* (London, 1919).

Pierre Jolly, *La mystique du corporatisme* (Paris, 1935).

W. E. von Ketteler, *Ausgewählte Schriften*, ed. J. Humbauer, 3 vols. (Kempten-Munchen, 1911).

John Maynard Keynes, *The End of Laissez-Faire* (London, 1926).

Rudolf Kjellén, *Der Staat als Lebensform*, 4th ed. (Berlin, 1924). Original Swedish edition in 1916.

Harold Laski, *Studies in the Problem of Sovereignty* (New Haven, 1917).

Harold Laski, *Authority in the Modern State* (New Haven, 1927).

Bernard Lavergne, *Le gouvernement des démocraties modernes*, 2 vols. (Paris, 1933); especially vol. I, pp. 176 *et seq.*

Ramiro de Maeztu, *La Crisis del Humanismo*, 2nd ed. (Buenos Aires, 1951). Originally published as *Authority, Liberty and Function* in 1916.'

Ramiro de Maeztu, *Un Ideal Sindicalista* (Madrid, 1953).

Henri de Man, *Corporatisme et Socialisme* (Bruxelles, 1935).

Mihaïl Manoïlesco, *Le parti unique* (Paris, 1937).

Mihaïl Manoïlesco, *Le siècle du corporatisme*, "Nouvelle édition," (Paris, 1936). Original edition in 1934.

Eugène Mathon, *La corporation, base de l'organisation économique* (Paris, 1935).

Charles Maurras, *Oeuvres Capitales. Essais Politiques* (Paris, 1973).

Giuseppe di Michelis, *World Reorganisation on Corporative Lines* (London, 1935).

David Mitrany, *A Working Peace System* (Chicago, 1966). Originally published in 1943.

Robert von Mohl, *Politische Schriften*, ed. by Klaus von Beyme (Köln u. Opladen, 1966).

Adam Müller, *Die Elemente der Staatskunst*, 2 vols. (Wien/Leipzig, 1922). Originally published in 1809.

Albert de Mun, *Discours*, 7 vols. (Paris, 1895-1904).

Albert de Mun, *Ma vocation sociale* (Paris, 1909).

Auguste Murat, *Le Corporatisme* (Paris, 1944).

——, *L'organisation corporative* (Angers, 1935).

Sergio Panunzio, *Stato nazionale e sindicati* (Milan, 1924).

Giuseppe Ugo Papi, *Lezioni di economia politica corporativa*, 5th ed. (Padua, 1939).

Joseph-Paul Boncour, *Le Fédéralisme économique*, 2d. ed. (Paris, 1901)

Pedro Teotónio Pereira, *A Batalha do Futuro*, 2nd. ed. (Lisbon, 1937).

François Perroux, *Capitalisme et Communauté de Travail* (Paris, 1937).

José Pires Cardoso, *Questões Corporativas. Doutrina e factos* (Lisbon, 1958).

Gaétan Pirou, *Essais sur le corporatisme* (Paris, 1938).

Gaétan Pirou, *Néo-Libéralisme, Néo-Corporatisme, Néo-Socialisme* (Paris, 1939).

A. Prins, *La démocratie et le régime parlementaire, étude sur le régime corporatif et la représentation des intérêts*, 2nd ed. (1887).

Pierre-Joseph Proudhon, *De la capacité politique des classes ouvrières* (Paris, 1873).

Walter Rathenau, *La triple révolution* (Paris, 1921).

Georges Renard, *L'Institution* (Paris, 1933).

Henri de Saint-Simon, *Oeuvres*, esp. Vol. XIX (Paris, 1865-73).

Henri de Saint-Simon, *L'Organisateur* (Paris, 1966).

A. de Oliveira Salazar, *Discursos*, 4th ed. (Coimbra, 1948), esp. Vol. I.

A. de Oliveira Salazar, *Une révolution dans la paix* (Paris, 1937).

Louis Salleron, *Naissance de l'Etat corporatif* (Paris, 1942).

Louis Salleron, *Un régime corporatif pour l'agriculture* (Paris, 1937).

Friedrich Schlegel, *Schriften und Fragmente*, ed. by E. Behler (Stuttgart, 1856).

Adérito Sedas Nunes, *Situacão e problemas de corporativismo* (Lisbon, 1954).

J. C. L. Simonde de Sismondi, *Etudes sur les constitutions des peuples libres* (Paris, 1836).

Georges Sorel, *Matériaux d'une théorie du prolétariat* (Paris, 1919).

Othmar Spann, *Der Wahre Staat*, 3rd ed. (Jena, 1931).

Ugo Spirito, *Capitalismo e corporativismo*, 3rd ed. (Florence, 1934).

Ugo Spirito, *I fondamenti della economia corporativa* (Milano-Roma, 1932).

Marcel Tardy and Edouard Bonnefous, *Le corporatisme* (Paris, 1935).

J. J. Teixeira Ribeiro, *Lições de Direito Corporativo* (Coimbra, 1938).

M. de la Tour de Pin, *Vers un odre social chrétien: jalons de route (1882-1907)*, 6th ed. (Paris, 1942). Originally published in 1907.

M. de la Tour de Pin, *Aphorismes de politique sociale* (Paris, 1909).

Union de Fribourg, *Réimpression des thèses de l'Union de Fribourg* (Paris, 1903).

P. Verschave, "L'organisation corporative aux Pays-Bas" in Semaine Sociale d'Anger, *L'organisation corporative* (Angers, 1935), pp. 465-482.

F. Vito, *Economia política corporativa* (Milan, 1939).

Karl von Vogelsang, *Gesammelte Aufsältze über sozialpolitische und verwandte Themata* (Augsburg, 1886).

Max Weber, *Economy and Society*, ed. by G. Roth and C. Wittich, 3 vols. (New York, 1968); especially vol. I, pp. 40-56, 292-299, 339-354 and vol. III, pp. 995-1001, 1375-1380, 1395-1399.

II — *Works discussing Corporatist theorists*

Ralph H. Bowen, *German Theories of the Corporate State* (New York, 1947).

Richard L. Camp, *The Papal Ideology of Social Reform* (Leiden, 1969).

Edouard Dolléans *et al.*, "Syndicalisme et corporations," Ed. spéciale de *L'Homme Réel* (Paris, 1935).

Hal Draper, "Neo-corporatists and Neo-formers," *New Politics* (Fall, 1961), pp. 87-106.

Matthew H. Elbow, *French Corporative Theory, 1789-1948* (New York, 1966).

G. Jarlot, *Le régime corporatif et les catholiques sociaux. Histoire d'une doctrine* (Paris, 1938).

Walter Adolf Jöhr, *Die ständische Ordnung; Geschichte, Idee und Neubau* (Leipzig-Bern, 1937).

P. Keller, *Die Korporative Idee in der Schweiz* (St. Gallen, 1934).

Peter Cornelius May-Tasch, *Korporativismus und Autoritarismus* (Frankfurt, 1971).

III — *Works dealing primarily with the practice of corporatist institutions (often however heavily ideological):*

Max d'Arcis, *Les réalisations corporatives en Suisse* Neuchâtel, 1935).

Firmin Bacconnier, *Le Salut par la corporation* (Paris, 1936).

Louis Baudin, *Le Corporatisme: Italie, Portugal, Allemagne, Espagne, France* (Paris, 1942).

Georges Bourgin, *L'Etat corporatif en Italie* (Paris, 1935).

Simone Comes, *L'organisation corporative de l'industrie en Espagne* (Paris, 1937).

Emile Coornaert, *Les Corporations en France avant 1789*, 4th ed. (Paris, 1941).

Freppel Cotta, *Economic Planning in Corporative Portugal* (London, 1937).

Fritz Ermath, *Theorie v. Praxis des fascistisch-Korporativen Staates* (Heidelberg, 1932).

J. Félix-Faure, *L'Organisation professionnelle aux Pays-Bas* (Paris, 1938).

Antonio Ferro, *Salazar: Le Portugal et Son Chef* (Paris, 1934).

José Figuerola, *La colaboración social en Hispanoamérica* (Buenos Aires, 1943).

Herman Finer, *Representative Government and a Parliament of Industry* (Westminster, 1923); especially pp. 3-34, 210-230.

Daniel Guerin, *Fascisme et grand capital*, 2nd ed. (Paris, 1945).

Carmen Haider, *Capital and Labor under Fascism* (New York, 1930).

J. E. S. Hayward, *Private Interest and Public Policy: The Experience of the French Economic and Social Council* (London, 1966).

Camille Lautaud and André Poudeux, *La représentation professionnelle. Les conseils économiques en Europe et en France* (Paris, 1927).

Jean Lescure, *Etude sociale comparée des régimes de liberté et des régimes autoritaires* (Paris, 1940).

Emile Lousse, *La société d'ancien régime* (Bruxelles, 1943).

Jean Malherbe, *Le corporatisme d'association en Suisse* (Lausanne, 1940).

Jacques Marchand, *La renaissance du merchantilisme à l'époque contemporaine* (Paris, 1937).

Fr. Oliver-Martin, *L'organisation corporative de la France d'ancien régime* (Paris, 1938).

F. Pereira dos Santos, *Un Etat corporatif: La Constitution sociale et politique portugaise* (Paris, 1935).

Roland Pré, *L'organisation des rapports économiques et sociaux dans les pays à régime corporatif* (Paris, 1936).

L. Rosenstock-Franck, *L'économie corporative fasciste en doctrine et en fait* (Paris, 1934).

L. Rosenstock-Franck, *L'Expérience Roosevelt et le milieu social américain* (Paris, 1937).

Martin Saint-Léon, *Histoire des Corporations de métier depuis leurs origines jusqu'à leur suppression en 1791*, 4th ed. (Paris, 1941).

Carl T. Schmidt, *The Corporate State in Action* (London, 1939).

William G. Welk, *Fascist Economic Policy* (Cambridge, 1938).

2

Consociational Democracy, Class Conflict, and the New Corporatism

Gerhard Lehmbruch
University of Konstanz, Germany

"**Consociational democracy**" or "Konkordanzdemokratie" has been described as the response of political elites in certain countries to the challenge of strong subcultural segmentation. [Lehmbruch, 1972; also Lijphart, 1968 and the articles compiled in McRae (ed.), 1974] Conflict within "fragmented political cultures" is settled by bargaining among the top leadership of rival groups. "Consociational" strategies, however, may not only serve to manage conflict of highly integrated and mutually incompatible value systems. The proposition of this paper is that they have also been employed for stabilizing and steering highly developed capitalist economies by promoting a new type of social integration. In this patterned arrangement, the relations between government and organized interest groups take the form of a new coporatism which we shall call "liberal corporatism". While consociational democracies have moved strongly towards the corporatist model of policy-making, the question arises whether both — consociationalism as well as corporatism — will not disintegrate as a consequence of an increase in social mobilization by the rank and file and a revival of class conflict in advanced capitalism.

By the term "liberal corporatism" we mean a special type of participation by large organized social groups in public, especially economic, policy-making. Consultation and cooperation among administrations and organized interests is, of course, common in all constitutional democracies with a highly developed capitalist economy. But the distinguishing trait of "liberal corporatism" is the high degree of cooperation among these groups themselves in the shaping of public policy.

The decision-making process in some liberal corporatist systems is characterized by the existence of two levels of bargaining (more or less distinct from each other). First, bargaining occurs among the "autonomous groups" (this is the significant expression used by the West German Council of Economic Advisers). Then, bargaining shifts to exchanges between the government and the "cartel" of organized groups. An influential defender of liberal corporatism in Austria recently stressed the difference between this "bilateral bargaining", and "multilateral" or separate consultation between the government and different interest groups. In the multilateral model the government perceives its role as that of a "turnplate" in economic policy-making, while in the bilateral model its impact on economic policy is said to be much less. [Kienzl, 1974:287]

Liberal corporatism should be distinguished from the traditional corporatism of pre-industrial Europe, on the one hand, and from authoritarian corporatism of the fascist type, on the other. Its essential feature is the large measure of constitutional autonomy of the groups involved, hence the voluntary nature of the institutionalized integration of conflicting social groups. Among the developmental conditions for liberal corporatism are: (1) the replacement of classical liberal-competitive capitalism with "organized capitalism" (Hilferding) and a growing "politicization" of the market, by the transformation of competitive economies through the social power of oligopolistic firms and organized interest representatives; (2) the traumatic experience of the economic crisis of 1929 with its subsequent disastrous consequences for political stability in the liberal democracies. Due to this experience, economic policy became subject to the political imperative that full employment, monetary stability, balance of payments, and, increasingly, economic growth (which is perceived as a precondition for social pacification through the distribution of increments in national product) should be guaranteed and maintained in a balanced condition. Such management of the business cycle and of economic growth is a high priority policy objective of liberal corporatism, but its scope may also involve decisions about the institutions of the economic system and related social policies, as we shall see below in the case of Austria.

Liberal corporatism rests on the theoretical premise that there exists strong interdependence between the interests of conflicting social groups in a capitalist economy. This "interdependence of interests" image of society is clearly opposed to a "conflict of interests" image which (as in the Marxist concept of class conflict) stresses the ultimate incompatibility of antagonistic demands. One of the most elaborate versions of the "interdependence of interests" model can be found in modern versions of macroeconomic equilibrium analysis in the Keynesian tradition (known in German economics as *Kreislauftheorie*). The strong influence which economists of the Keynesian and post-Keynesian persuasion have gained in the formation of economic policy in a number of West European countries has doubtlessly contributed to the advance of liberal corporatism. This can be demonstrated, for example, by the importance which economic expertise has gained for the policies of trade unions in West Germany and Austria.[1] Macroeconomic analysis in these associations has become an important frame of reference for the strategy of elaborating and promoting wage demands.

AUSTRIA AS AN ADVANCED CASE OF LIBERAL CORPORATISM

"Social partnership" (*Sozialpartnerschaft*) in Austria can serve as a particularly conspicuous example of the above phenomenon. Its main elements are the following:[2]

(1) The large interest groups are organized into "Chambers" which are statutory public corporations with compulsory membership. [Pütz, 1966; Secher, 1960]. The most important are the Chambers of Business (*gewerbliche Wirtschaft*), of Agriculture, and of Labor; the latter is strongly tied to the Austrian Confederation of Trade Unions (ÖGB) which, though of a different legal status, is an equivalent partner in the bargaining processes. The Chambers and the ÖGB are strongly centralized bodies, both *de jure* (e.g. sectoral industrial unions, need the consent of the ÖGB for wage demands and strikes), and *de facto* (e.g. the Chambers of Agriculture of the provinces [*Länder*] enjoy a considerable theoretical autonomy, but are in fact governed by the "Conference of the Presidents of the Chambers of Agriculture" and its rather in-

fluential bureaucracy). Centralized leadership is strengthened by the considerable influence which experts trained in economy or law enjoy within all these associations. It appears that a majority of university economists have strong ties to one or other of the organized interest groups. In Austria, it would be difficult to find economic expertise independent of the interest group system.

(2) Cooperation among interest groups has been institutionalized since the 1950s by agreements between business and labor leaders. The most important body is called the *Paritätische Kommission für Preis- und Lohnfragen* (Paritary Commission for Questions of Price and Wage Regulation). The "Paritätische" consists of representatives of the four above mentioned associations plus two members of the government who, however, have only deliberative voice in the commission.[3] The sessions are preceded by the *Präsidentenbesprechung* in which the presidents and staff of the four associations clarify their positions before meeting in the presence of government representatives. Decisions are prepared by subcommissions consisting of experts from the associations' headquarters. There is one subcommission on wages and another one on prices. Collective bargaining on wages is under the complete control of the "Paritätische". In addition, it controls about one quarter to one third of the consumer prices — another quarter is governed by administrative controls. In practice, the price decisions of the Commission (which are based on calculation of costs and can serve only to slow down inflationary tendencies to some degree) have the same effect as price recommendations by a cartel. The result, therefore, is to restrain competition.

A third subcommission is the *Beirat für Wirtschafts- und Sozialfragen* (Advisory Council for Economic and Social Problems). This may be considered an Austrian counterpart of the American Council of Economic Advisors but it is, of course, exclusively composed of experts from the different groups on a "paritary" basis. The government is not represented in the *Beirat* although its function is precisely to advise the government on economic and social policy. Furthermore, the *Beirat* has no formal legal basis and the government is not entitled to demand its advice. This is a good illustration of the "bilateral" model through which "cartelized" interest groups may assume an initiative role in economic policy-making. Budgetary forecasts, for example, have been established by the government at the demand of the *Beirat*.

The influence of the *Beirat* has somewhat declined since the formation of a Socialist government in 1970. The Socialist ministers of finance and economy (who had been before leading labor spokesmen in the "Paritätische") prefer "multilateral" bargaining with different interest groups simultaneously present. Yet the influence of organized interests continues to be very strong. Economic forecasts are discussed every quarter of the year in the *Verbändebesprechung* (consultation of associations) with the minister of finance and the president of the *Nationalbank*. In this context we should also mention that the major organized groups are strongly represented in the governing council of the *Nationalbank*. Its actual Generaldirektor served before as head of the economic division of ÖGB headquarters, while his predecessors had been former officials of the Chamber of Business.

(3) The Chambers and interest groups are entitled to give their opinion on all government bills *before* they are submitted to parliament (*Begutachtungsrecht*). In practice, of course, this amounts to a great deal of negotiation among government and interest groups. Changes in the income tax, for example, have been discussed and sometimes have been agreed upon after much log-rolling among government and the trade unions. While this corresponds more to the "multilateral" model, the "bilateral" model too is of considerable importance in law making. Legislation on restrictions to competition has been prepared by prior agreements between business and labor. The conservative government of Josef Klaus (1966 to 1970) tried to depart from this routine when submitting a bill changing the cartel law by having it drafted by the legal division of the Chancellor's Office with the aid of some experts of the Chamber of Business. This bill, however, met such vehement opposition by Socialist union representatives in parliament that the government preferred to withdraw it. A new bill was then negotiated, on the demand of the Chancellor, between the Chambers of Business and of Labor, and afterwards ratified without any change by the government and parliament. Another important example of such bargaining has been the *Mitbestimmungsgesetz* (Bill on Workers' Participation in the Management of Industrial Firms) which, too, was drafted in negotiations between the Chambers of Business and Labor.

(4) The *Sozialpartnerschaft* rests upon the voluntary cooperation of interest groups. Each of them could denounce the agreement without risking sanctions other than the disapprobation of a large part of public opinion. Demands for statutory institutionalization (on the pattern of the Dutch or French Social-

Economic Councils) have been raised by a number of constitutional lawyers, but they have been rejected by the majority of interest group leaders as well as by party leaders. Support for social partnership has been strong in public opinion and within the organized groups themselves, in spite of criticism by *étatiste* or legalistically minded academics and civil servants.

The predominance of certain economic doctrines and the strong influence of economic experts has contributed to this consensus to a degree which should not be underestimated. The experts in the staffs of business, agricultural and labor organizations often have been trained within the same academic institutions (e.g. the *Hochschule für Welthandel*) and tend to share a common approach to the analysis of economic and social problems. Informal communication between business and labor headquarters is frequent and intense. On the basis of reciprocity, information is exchanged even if it may serve the other side and prejudice some members of one's own clientele.

OTHER EXAMPLES
OF LIBERAL CORPORATISM

The Austrian system is one of the most elaborate examples of liberal corporatism; the most elaborate except perhaps for the case of the Netherlands from 1945 to 1963. [Busch-Lüty, 1964] In Switzerland, classical liberal and anti-etatiste traditions have hindered formal institutionalization of corporatism, but in fact here too the "bilateral" model seems to play an important role in legislation and policy-making. There are comparable phenomena in other West European countries as well: "Harpsund democracy" in Sweden and what Rokkan has described as the "two-tier system" of decision-making in Norway for example [1966], the "Konzertierte Aktion" in West Germany [Hoppman, 1971; Adam, 1972] and the National Economic Development Council in the UK. However, the extreme examples of liberal corporatism are to be found in those countries which belong (or have belonged) to the type of *Konkordanzdemokratie* or "consociational democracy" which has been earlier analyzed by this author and by Arend Lijphart. There are obvious genetic relations between the one and the other: The *Paritätische* in Austria was established during the era of the coalition of conservatives and socialists, just as the West German *Konzertierte Aktion* has been instituted by the government of the "Great Coalition". [Lehmbruch, 1971] Austrian *Sozialpartnerschaft* has survived the end of the coalition in 1966 but has since, significantly, been described as a sort of *Bereichskoalition* (sectoral coalition). It is true, on the other hand, that the Dutch system of income policies by agreement among the groups was discontinued not very long after the departure of the Labor Party from government in 1959. But it is, nevertheless, possible to insert these heterogeneous developments into a single explanatory context. On the one hand, as we have argued in earlier publications, bargaining strategies of the "consociational" and of the "liberal corporatist" type presuppose some learning from successful experience by the elites of the rival groups, so that the newly acquired strategic approaches may be transferred to other spheres of conflict management. [Lehmbruch, 1967] On the other hand, trade union leaders will be more inclined to participate in bargaining on income policies if they feel that their interests are adequately represented in government, that is, if the socialist party is governing or is a partner in the governing coalition.

More important, however, is the structural isomorphy of the "consociational" and the "liberal corporatist" pattern. In both, bargaining and log-rolling serve to reconcile the conflicting interests of highly cohesive groups which can not be adjusted by electoral competition and/or by majoritarian devices. Bargaining power is concentrated in the hands of top level leadership, a sort of interlocking directorate of the competing groups. While pragmatic consensus among elites is rather highly developed, there is little communication among lower levels of the groups. An essential condition is strong vertical integration of each group. The resulting latitude of action by its top leadership is necessary for a smooth functioning of the bargaining process. This means, in the case of liberal corporatism, that trade unions as well as employer organizations must be strongly centralized. The anarchic mood of a large part of the French *patronat*, for example, would be almost as embarrassing for such a system as the autonomy of British shop stewards. On the other hand, if the top leadership has established a monopoly of bargaining power on the basis of reciprocity — as in the Austrian case — this may contribute further to strengthen the dependence of the membership.

FUTURE TRENDS

It has been pointed out that, since the last decade, "consociationalism" is declining due to the attenuation of certain subcultural (especially religious) conflicts and the corresponding decrease in vertical integration within the segmented subcultures and due furthermore to the growing mobilization and politicization of grassroot members which has taken place since the mid-60s. "Ontzuiling" in the Netherlands [Lijphart, 1975] is, of course, not typical of all consociational democracies as can be seen in the case of linguistic conflicts in neighboring Belgium. However, Austria, Switzerland and West Germany are equally characterized by the decline of subcultural conflicts and of vertical integration within the groups. This raises the question of eventual consequences for the system of liberal corporatism.

"Ontzuiling", the decrease of vertical integration, seems to result in a diminution of conflict. Yet, reality is more complex than that. The incompatibility of cultural value patterns may decrease but that does not mean that class conflict caused by inequality in the distribution of income and by alienation in work will decline equally. On the contrary, the decomposition of traditional (and rival) value systems may weaken vertical integration within the groups to such a degree that acquiescence of the rank and file and, consequently, the bargaining power of elites may be greatly diminished. This may lead to strains within the liberal corporatist system, especially if within organized labor members begin to perceive the results of the bargaining process as biased in favor of business. Available empirical evidence on the West German wildcat strikes of 1969, which dealt a decisive blow to the *Konzertierte Aktion*, indicates that among the motives of the strikers one of the foremost was that the expectation of a "fair share" in the distribution of income had been disappointed by the lag of wages behind rising profits. [Schumann, 1971] Similar stresses led to the end of the Dutch system of wage controls in 1963.

Growing mobilization of the grass roots union membership contributes further to the crisis of liberal corporatism. In order not to lose control over the rank and file, the union leadership of metal workers in West Germany, for example, had begun to establish a shop steward system which, of course, strengthens the power of the lower levels of the organization. Top leaders were forced, consequently, to take a more militant stand in wage conflicts and, thus, have had growing difficulty in accepting wage restraints. A conceivable alternative to save the liberal corporatist system might be to extend its reach beyond collective bargaining on wages, for example by negotiating structural changes in the economy which might serve as a compensation for wage restraints and thus might contribute to perceptions of greater "symmetry" in class relations.

This, however, is a largely speculative alternative. It is quite probable that the "interdependence of interests" image of society may increasingly lose its persuasive power in favor of the "conflict of interests" image. The revival of radical and Marxist economics might play an important role in this respect, if, as we have argued, the rather broad consensus upon Keynesian policies among interest group experts has contributed to the establishment of liberal corporatism, this consensus may vanish when young Socialist and Marxist intellectuals are increasingly recruited into trade union staffs. In the Austrian as well as in the German case this hypothesis seems to be quite realistic.

NOTES

1. On the growing role of experts in West German trade unions see the unpublished research report of the Institut für Sozialforschung: Zwischenbericht über den Stand der Arbeiten am Forschungsprojekt, "Die Funktion der Gewerkschaften im Prozess der gesellschaftlichen Enwicklung Westdeutschlands," Frankfurt am Main, Marx 1969 (mimeographed), p. 204 ff.

2. On "social partnership" in Austria, see Pütz (1966), Klose (1970) and Klose et al. (1974). (Note that some details of the Austrian situation have of course changed since 1974 when this paper was written.)

3. Representatives of the government had the right to vote until the breakup of coalition government in 1966. Since then it has been abandoned in order not to endanger the political equilibrium within the commission.

3

Modes of Interest Intermediation and Models of Societal Change in Western Europe

Philippe C. Schmitter
University of Chicago, USA

Comparative analysis of the similarities and differences in the historical patterns of emergence of "systems of interest intermediation"[1] in modern Europe is a relatively unexploited topic. Without this basic knowledge, needless to say, there has not been much systematic exploration of the consequences these systems have had, now have, and will continue to have for public policy and the role of the state in that part of the world. For example, this area of inquiry has attracted much less concerted attention than the study of party systems and such related issues as electoral mobilization, voting preference, and coalition formation.

Hence, in the currently fashionable discussion of the declining "governability" of Western polities, attention among academics tends to focus on narrowing margins of electoral victory, shifts in partisan allegiance, minority governments, unstable "reigning" coalitions, the possibility of communist participation in cabinets, and so forth. This, despite a descriptive awareness that many of the contemporary crises are rooted in the network of highly organized and specialized representatives of class, sectoral, regional, sexual, and generational interests. The collapse of new "social contracts," the burgeoning demand for guaranteed and privileged access; the clash of representational jurisdictions, the frustrated negotiation of incomes policies, the explosion of subnational ethnicity, the quest for authenticity and participation at all levels of authority, private as well as public, the mobilization and militancy of such previously quiescent groups as public employees, the insistence upon and the revolt against rising state expenditure and regulations, the growing ineffectiveness of public policy implementation, the increasingly acute sensitivity to relative deprivation within as well as between social classes, the sudden emergence of single issue movements, the tendency to resort to unprecedented, extralegal means of political expression — many, if not most of these "ills" of advanced industrial-capitalist societies can be traced to their systems of interest intermediation — their complexes of specialized associations often bypassing, if not boycotting, more traditional and more general partisan and legislative structures of articulation and aggregation. In short, formally organized interest associations in these societies have tended to acquire an indispensability and ubiquity in civil society, a penetration and influence within the apparatus of the state, and a presence in the formation and promotion of ideology and collective consciousness that radically alter the liberal-bourgeois-parliamentary-democratic mode of political domination. With the partial exception of North American critics of "interest group liberalism" and European theorists of corporatism in the interwar period, this "sea change" within the structure of the political process has gone relatively unexplored. Its consequences are being experienced; many of its surface manifestations have been described; but its past roots, present nature, and future implications are hardly understood.

GENERIC MODES
OF INTEREST INTERMEDIATION

Any tentative charting of these murky waters must begin with some sensitivity to the diversity of historical patterns and contemporary configurations that have emerged in Western Europe. Despite such general communalities as more extensive coverage, higher membership density, increased bureaucratization, more formalized participation in decision-making, greater multiplicity of organizational tasks, and an expanded role in ideational manipulation, the polities of this region demonstrate a rather wide range of modes of interest intermediation. They differ considerably in number and scope of component units, degree of voluntarism and overlap in membership, extent of centralized hierarchic coordination within interest domains and of noncompetitive compartmentalization across them, success in exercising a representational monopoly within categories, importance of de jure or de facto recognition by state authorities, degree to which they are subject to formal or informal controls on leadership selection or agree to respect regime-defined limits on their means of interest articulation, and, finally, extent to which they demand or accept the performance of quasi-public governmental tasks.

Elsewhere (Schmitter, 1974) I have suggested that these multiple dimensions are not randomly distributed, but cluster into a finite number of ideal-typic configurations of state-interest association relations. In each of these "modes," a set of relatively directly observable, institutionally descriptive traits would tend to cohere in an interdependent, mutually supportive manner, making it possible to categorize historically specific systems (or, at least, parts of them) by generic type. While no empirically extant system of interest intermediation may perfectly reproduce or replicate any of the following types, many come rather close. In any case, it would seem possible *both* to group together for closer comparative scrutiny structurally similar modes at a given point in time *and* to use them as a means of capturing fundamental changes in the nature of civil society-association-state linkages within the same polity over longer periods of time.

The three modes most appropriate for describing and analyzing interest politics in Western Europe are pluralism, corporatism, and syndicalism (Schmitter, 1974:93-98).[2]

(1) Pluralism can be defined as a system of interest intermediation in which the constituent units are organized into an unspecified number of multiple, voluntary, competitive, nonhierarchically ordered, and self-determined (as to type or scope of interest) categories that are not specifically licensed, recognized, subsidized, created, or otherwise controlled in leadership election or interest articulation by the state and that do not exercise a monopoly of representational activity within their respective categories.

(2) Corporatism can be defined as a system of interest intermediation in which the constitutent units are organized into a limited number of singular, compulsory, noncompetitive, hierarchically ordered, and functionally differentiated categories, recognized or licensed (if not created) by the state and granted a deliberate representational monopoly within their respective categories in exchange for observing certain controls on their selection of leaders and articulation of demands and supports.

(3) Syndicalism can be defined as a system of interest intermediation in which the constituent units are an unlimited number of singular, voluntary, noncompetitive (or better hived-off) categories, not hierarchically ordered or functionally specialized, neither recognized, created, nor licensed by state

or party, nor controlled in their leadership selection or interest articulation by state or party, not exercising a representional monopoly but resolving their conflicts and "authoritatively allocating their values" autonomously, without the interference of the state.

These *gestälter* are static and descriptive — deliberately so. They are intended to indicate acquired, not emergent, properties, mutually coherent rather than contradictory dimensions, and "disembodied" characteristics, not ones contingent upon a particular culture, productive structure, distribution of property, system of stratification, or type of regime. While all "require" a certain degree of societal complexity, organizational skill, material resources, and normative secularization — i.e., all are descriptions of *modern* modes of interest intermediation — sociologically or politico-logically speaking, all are compatible with a wide range of contingent contexts. It is precisely the effort to chart some of these contingencies with respect to competing paradigms-cum-theories of the development of contemporary industrial, advanced capitalist societies that provides the principle focus for this paper.

As statically specified above, the three generic modes of interest intermediation could have come into being by two radically different processes and, hence, may embody diametrically opposite relations of power and influence They could have emerged "from below" in more-or-less spontaneous response to prior changes within civil society and the associational sphere itself; or they could have been imposed "from above" as a matter of deliberate public policy contrived and controlled by preexisting authority groups. In the previously cited article (Schmitter, 1974, 103-104), I proceeded *per genus et differentiam* in a taxonomic exploration of the corporatist syndrome, distinguishing a societal and a state version. There, I argued that precisely what was *not* included in the definition of the genus could be used to differentiate two historically distinct subtypes.

(1) *Limited number:* does not indicate whether established by processes of interassociational arrangement, by "political cartels" designed by existing participants to exclude newcomers, or by deliberate government restriction.

(2) *Singular:* does not indicate whether the outcome of spontaneous cooptation or competitive elimination is by surviving associations or by state-imposed eradication of multiple or parallel associations.

(3) *Compulsory:* does not specify whether de facto through social pressure, contractual dues checkoff, provision of essential services, and/or acquisition of private licensing capacity, or de jure through labor code or other officially decreed, exclusively conceded authority.

(4) *Noncompetitive:* does not state whether the product of internal oligarchic tendencies or external, treaty-like, voluntary agreements among associations, or of the continuous interposition of state mediation, arbitration, and repression.

(5) *Hierarchically ordered:* does not indicate whether the outcome of intrinsic processes of bureaucratic extension and/or consolidation, or of state-decreed centralization and administrative dependence.

(6) *Functionally differentiated:* does not indicate whether arrived at through voluntaristic agreements on respective "turfs" and non-raiding provisions, or by state-established *enquadramento* (framing) of occupational-vocational categories.

(7) *Recognition by state:* does not differentiate between recognition granted as a matter of political necessity imposed from below upon public officials and that granted from above by the state as a condition for association formation and continuous operation.

(8) *Representational monopoly:* similar to above, does not distinguish between that which is independently conquered and that which is dependently conceded.

When viewed statically, descriptively, and/or institutionally, these two subtypes exhibit a basic structural similarity, one that sets them apart from pluralist, monist, or syndicalist systems of interest intermediation. When viewed in motion, however, they are revealed as the products of very different political, social, and economic processes, as the vehicles for very different power and influence relations, and as the purveyors of very different policy consequences. Societal corporatism is found embedded in political systems with relatively autonomous, multilayered territorial units; open, competitive electoral processes and party systems; ideologically varied, coalitionally based executive authorities — even with highly "layered" or "pillared" political subcultures. State corporatism tends to be associated with political systems in which territorial subunits are tightly subordinated to central bureaucratic power; elections are nonexistent or plebiscitary; party systems are dominated or monopolized by a weak single party; executive authorities are ideologically exclusive and more narrowly recruited; and, finally, political subcultures based on class, ethnicity, language, or regionalism are rigorously repressed.

I have become increasingly convinced that the other two syndromes, pluralism and syndicalism, also have distinct "societal" and "state" subtypes. For example, pluralism, with all its multiple associations, overlapping structures, autonomous organizations, and nonmonopolistic representation may be the unintended product of long-term social and economic trends, slow incremental changes, cultrural continuity, and the gradual emergence of distinctive consciousness in a setting of passive indifference and/or respect for constitutional freedoms on the part of authorities. More rarely, those same properties may be the deliberate outcome of rather short-term calculations, rapid policy changes, and externally stimulated group consciousness on the part of authorities who, following James Madison's advice (if not instrumentality), deliberately seek to extend "the number of citizens [and] the sphere of interests" by following a classic *divide et impera* strategy in the official encouragement and promotion of multiple, overlapping, and competing associations.[3] Even syndicalism, for all its triumphant antistatist ideology, might be thought to have a "state" version which, rather than have all political authority devolve to self-governing associational monads, would use the resources of an existing central state to create encapsulated islands of privileged class or sectoral autonomy without destroying, or even by extending, a wider system of exploitation and domination. Alongside "socialism for the rich, capitalism for the poor," one might find "syndicalism for the powerful, pluralism for the weak."[4]

CAVEATS ON THE NOTION OF A "MODE" OF INTEREST INTEREMEDIATION

We have, then, identified tenatively three generic modes of intermediation and placed them in motion, so to speak, to create six distinct types of structural interest linkage between civil society and the state: pluralism, corporatism and syndicalism, each with a state and a societal variant. Needless to say, these are by no means equally frequent in empirical occurrence, nor equally subject to normative praise and/or scholarly scrutiny. Before attempting to situate them with respect to several competing models of societal transformation, we must take note of some serious "operational" problems which impede the development of a systematic theory of specialized interest intermediation comparable in parsimony, elegance, generalizability, and predictability to that which exists (however precariously) — for party systems, electoral competition, and coalition formation. To the extent that progress to these ends depends on a typology of modes, we are faced not only with the peculiarities and vicissitudes of historically specific cases incompletely resembling idealtypic configurations, but also with manifest gross inconsistencies in structure and behavior. Not only may a given country's interest system appear quite differently configured when viewed from the municipal, provincial, regional, or national levels (that often holds for party systems and coalition strategies), but, within the same level, different interest sectors also may be organized and relate to the state in quite different ways. The most obvious reason for this persistent structural heterogeneity is that, unlike party systems or coalition-formation situations, usually all interest associations in a given polity do *not* interact with each other. There often is no central, simplifying, zero-sum competitive logic of political choice forced on all participants. In some cases they may quite literally go their own way or, more often, form competitive subsystems seeking to influence and/or control only segmented policy arenas, each with a distinctive pluralist, corporatist, or syndicalist mode. Even the extent of their information about how other interest actors operate in the polity may be low, weakening the diffusion of organizational and strategic techniques. In the contemporary world, specific interest intermediaries may be better informed about the activities, successes, and failures of their analogs in adjacent or competing polities, adding yet another element of structural heterogeneity.

Another peculiarity of "interest systems" is their legal heterogeneity. Regimes quite regularly enforce discriminatory norms with respect to freedom of association upon different interest sectors, tolerating, or even encouraging, spontaneous and autonomous collective action for some groups, while repressing, coopting, or channeling it for others. The two state corporatist systems I have studied in some detail, Brazil and Portugal, despite their impressive architechtonic symmetry and ideological pretense of "unitary, compulsory, monopolistic, balanced mode of interest representation," quietly tolerated the practice of pluralism among certain propertied groups. Irrespective of sonorous constitutional provisions guaranteeing freedom of speech and assembly to all, in the accumulated minutiae of administrative practice and judicial precedence are lodged incentives and disincentives differentially affecting the capacity to organize of social classes, productive sectors, ethnic groups, and the like — when such discrimination is not openly proclaimed against "workingmen's combinations," "secret societies," "alien and seditious" groups, and so forth.

Finally, "interest systems" are peculiarly historical constructions. They are laid down, frequently in waves of accelerated organization and counterorganization, in distinct time periods, for divergent purposes, and under different legal and political circumstances. Successive layers with their peculiar compositions often remain in a sedimentary state, relatively unaffected by subsequent or antecedent developments. Even the potentially metamorphic impact of revolution, civil war, rebellion, defeat in war, and/or foreign occupation may fail to rearrange or displace them. For example, such thoroughly discredited regimes as Vichy France and Fascist Italy have left a considerable residue in the contemporary interest systems of those two countries. The recent rapid and spontaneous collapse of the state corporatist scheme in Portugal was hardly complete, as new "management" moved quickly into the same singular compulsory structures, and the revolutionary regime dutifully certified their "unicity." Party systems, electoral support, and coalitional propensities do occasionally survive such political cataclysms, but interest associations, their membership patterns, and their influence practices seem to have an even greater, if less visible, resiliency.

Hence, while for analytical purposes it may be desirable to use generic modes and for descriptive purposes it may be useful to label whole national units as state corporatist, societal pluralist, state syndicalist, and so on, in point of fact, all the interest intermediation systems of Western Europe are "mixed." They may be predominantly of one type, but different sectors and subsectors, classes and class factions, regions and subregions are likely to be operating simultaneously according to different principles and procedures.

A BRIEF COMPARATIVE
HISTORICAL OVERVIEW OF THE PROBLEM

Keeping these caveats in mind, let us turn briefly to the remarkable differences that exist and persist in the nature and role of interest associations in contemporary Western European polities, despite the otherwise impressive similarities in levels of living, development of productive resources, systems of class and status stratification, degree of urbanization, and so forth. In a few, according to national surveys, more than 75% of the adult population reports membership in at least one association, while elsewhere the proportion hardly exceeds 35%. Aggregate data inform us that in Sweden almost 90% of the economically active population is at least formally inscribed in a trade union or professional association, while in Switzerland the figure hardly reaches 30%. Moreover, the differences are just as striking if one looks at the financial bases, organizational resources, decisional centralization, characteristic style of influence, frequency and intimacy of interaction with the state, performance of quasi-governmental functions, and so forth. A longitudinal-historical comparative survey would no doubt reveal even more striking disparities in the timing of associational spurts, rates of change in membership, unevenness in interest coverage, level at which interests were aggregated, degree of resistance by previous social formations to new entrants, extent of militancy and violence in the promotion of new demands, and/or explicitness of group consciousness and ideological project.

And, yet, all Western European societies passed, unevenly and asynchronically, through some of the same structural transformations in their organized-mediated relation between civil society and the state. From a set of "ancient associations" — involuntary, exclusive, monopolistic, quasi-public, semireligious guilds — most moved (with varying degrees of partiality and brevity) toward a situation of "freedom of contract" or "freedom of labor" as a result of the abolition of guild privileges and monopolies and the more gradual assertion of liberal notions of individual citizenship and territorial-parliamentary representation — those reforms in turn impelled by the spread of capitalist relations of production and distribution. In extreme instances, e.g., France under the Loi Le Chapelier, all forms of effective intermediation between citizen and state were formally abolished. Elsewhere, legal codes and judicial practice were differentially destructive of class-based organizations, e.g., the Combination Acts and Taff Vale Judgment in Great Britain. Finally, in a few Western European cases, the intervening period of individualistic liberalism was quite short and incomplete as monarchic autocracies and conservative oligarchies attempted to make over from above medieval corporations into modern interest associations (e.g., Germany and, especially, Austria).

By the last quarter of the nineteenth century, the "art of association" could no longer be formally denied — even to potentially subversive working-class majorities and ethnic minorities. With varying degrees of delay, reluctance and reservation, European

governments began to recognize "freedom of association and petition" as one of the fundamental rights of citizenship. In at least
one case — Switzerland — the constitution also recognizes one's
"freedom not to be forced to associate," prohibiting all forms of
Zwangsverbände. This change in legal norms and ideology, combined with a protracted economic depression, a wider agenda of
policy choices (e.g., tariff debates and the institutionalization of
social insurance), changes in the nature and structure of productive
units, and the full extension of capitalist relations to all sectors of
the economy seems to have produced an outburst of formal interest
associability in the 1870-1890s. During this period something like a
modern system of representation based on extensive functional
coverage and intensive interest specialization began to emerge at
the national, as well as in the municipal and provincial subunits. At
first, most of this associability took a pluralist form. The units of
representation were spontaneous in formation, multiple, dispersed,
overlapping in their claims to jurisdiction, competing for members,
ideologically divergent in their goals, and praxiologically distinct in
their techniques of intervention. Nevertheless, differences in modes
of representation emerged quite early. The degree of hierarchy and
vertical structure and, with it, the relative importance of peak
associations (*Spitzenverbände*) varied considerably, as did political
and organizational independence from the state and political parties, and influence in setting the agenda and determining the outcomes of public policy.

Some of this initial diversity in structure and behavior was reduced by the impact of World War I. Everywhere, even in
nonbelligerent powers, the tasks of wartime mobilization, rationing, planned resource allocation, price control, and so forth encouraged the consolidation of previously competitive associations,
the formal delimitation of jurisdictions, the nationalization and
centralization of organizational structures, the monopolization of
representation, the acquisition of quasi-public functions, and the
interpenetration of public and private realms of decision-making,
as well as enhanced the legitimacy and influence of interest associations in their direct interaction with the state bureaucracy. When,
as Maier (1975) has argued, bourgeois Europe was "recast" in the
tense aftermath of the war, a reinforcement of neomercantilist
policies and neocorporatist organization was part of the mold. In
the 1920s and 1930s, the primary issue in many European countries
was whether these trends would develop autonomously and selec-

tively within the sinews of civil society, often culminating in privatistic "social peace treaties," or whether they would be forced to develop under the watchful eye and compulsory muscle of the state, eventuating in the impressive corporatist façades of Fascism and other forms of authoritarian rule.

Meanwhile, North American political and social scientists — in a polity exceptional for its nonfeudal and noncorporative origins, for its spontaneous and relatively free associability, and for the brevity of its abortive neocorporative experience (the early New Deal) — had discovered the "pressure group." They proceeded to create an elaborate and impressive theory-cum-ideology of pluralism, which justified the existence and celebrated the presence of these collective intermediaries. By making their emergence "respectable," by stressing their autonomy, competitiveness, multiplicity of origins, criss-cross of allegiance and effort, ease of entry, and equality of resources, and by postulating an inherent tendency toward equilibrium in their activity, monitored by the influence of consensually motivated "potential groups" that could be counted upon to act as "trimmers" in the event of asymmetric access or exploitation by privileged organizations, the pluralists provided a model for explaining the relative stability and moderation of the U.S. polity — despite its evident heterogeneity and centrifugal impulses. They also provided a normative framework for making these corporate actors appear perfectly compatible with individualistic bourgeois norms and classical democratic theory.

When, after World War II, "pressure group politics" was uncovered in the entrails of Western European polities — and discovered to be often of earlier vintage and even greater virulence than their U.S. counterparts — political observers either confined themselves to descriptive inventories (almost every Western European country has at least one by now) or uncritically accepted the pluralist paradigm and its assumptions for analytical purposes. They failed to notice that the existing structure and behavior of interest associations in most Western Eurpean systems hardly exhibited the spontaneous, overlapping, chaotic, and competitive properties said to characterize their U.S. analogs, or, where there was evidence of such pluralism, that it was rooted in polarized ideological conflicts and/or ethnic-religious-linguistic diversity and hardly so conducive to the same consensual, moderate, equilibrated outcomes.

One task, therefore, facing Western European social scientists is to capture and render intelligible this diversity in the interest politics of their countries and to use the historical understanding so acquired as a basis for interpreting the likely future course of policy and political change. The task has been made all the more difficult by an emergent context in which previously "sovereign" subunits of a wider world system find themselves in ever more interdependent exchanges, entangling alliances, and binding policy negotiations that have added yet another layer — a supranational regional one — to their patterns of interest intermediation. Part of the answer, I have suggested, lies in a more variegated notion of differing modes. The rest lies in relating these modes to major interpretive paradigms — models, if you will — of societal change in advanced industrial-capitalist societies.

MODELS OF SOCIETAL CHANGE

In my first attempt at relating the two corporatist modes to their societal contexts, I suggest,

> as a macrohypothesis...that the corporatization of interest intermediation is related to certain basic imperatives or needs of capitalism to reproduce the conditions for its existence and continually to accumulate further resources. Differences in the specific nature of these imperatives or needs at different stages in the institutional development and international context of capitalism, especially as they affect the pattern of conflicting class interests, account for the difference in origins between the societal and state forms of corporatism.
>
> Summarizing, again in a nutshell, the decay of pluralism and its gradual displacement by societal corporatism can be traced primarily to the imperative necessity for a stable, bourgeois-dominant regime, due to processes of concentration of ownership, competition between national economies, expansion of the role of public policy and rationalization of decision-making within the state to associate or incorporate subordinate classes and status groups more closely within the political process.
>
> As for the abrupt demise of incipient pluralism and its dramatic and forceful replacement by state corporatism, this seems closely associated with the necessity to enforce "social peace," not by coopting and incorporating, but by repressing and excluding the autonomous articulation of subordinate class demands in a situation where the bourgeoisie is too weak, internally divided, externally dependent and/or short of resources to respond effectively and legitimately to these demands within the framework of the liberal democratic state. [Schmitter, 1974: 107-108]

Since this hypothesis was clearly "overpredictive," i.e., it implied that all Western European (and extra-European for that matter) societies that fall into the two domestic institutional and international contexts of capitalist development should exhibit equally the properties of the respectively appropriate corporatist mode of intermediation — and this was descriptively not the case — my response was to add some "overdeterminative" elements that might combine with broader structural affinities to account for specific national differences. When faced with a similar dilemma in his *Modern Capitalism*. Shonfield (1965) tended to resort to arguments based on national character and historical precedent. I suggested that such generic factors as (1) variation in secular trends toward bureaucratization, centralized control, and oligarchization within interest associations, (2) differences in prior rates of political mobilization and degrees of ideological polarization and, hence, the resilience and vitality of competing pluralist organizations, (3) disparities in the diffusion of foreign ideologies and institutional practices, and (4) differences in the impact of international war and variations in the magnitude and effect of business cycles could be used to predict differences in the modal outcome.

In retrospect, this first approach to the problem seems to me less wrong than limited and premature. On the one hand, it will hardly serve to explain those countries or cases of predominantly pluralist or syndicalist representation, whether societal or state, except to explain them away as deviant exceptions. On the other hand, it probably is not "fine-grained" enough to account for class, sectoral, or regional differences within the same polity. These and other deficiencies may be due in part to the fact that this first guess was exclusively rooted in only one of the competing "models" for explaining the structural transformation of European capitalist societies and the evolving role of their capitalist states. Examining what these alternative models have to contribute to theoretical speculation about changing modes of interest intermediation may considerably improve our capacity for understanding those changes that have occurred, and even help us to predict those which are likely to happen in the future.

Grosso modo, three such models (or paradigms if you prefer) of societal change compete for our attention. Each has its own demiurgic process impelling structural transformation, its own laws of motion, its own "axial structures and axial principles," its own cast of characters and leading role,[5] its own contradictions generating crises, its own "prototypic" cases, its own teleological outcome, and, not surprisingly, its own distinctive origin in sociological and political theory. The first could be called the *structural differentiation* model, and its modern genealogy begins with Durkheim and runs through Parsons to contemporary theorists of postindustrial society. The second model, *historical materialism*, can be initially discerned in Marx's historical and journalistic writings, then follows an agenda set primarily by Weber and Marxist revisionists. Hilferding in his analysis of "organized capitalism" offers what may be the most explicitly relevant effort in this perspective. The third, *political economy*, begins, of course, with Marx's more abstractly theoretical writings, especially Volume II of *Das Kapital* and, more recently, the *Grundrisse*. These pioneering thoughts have been expounded and developed in various directions by Lenin, Trotsky, Mandel, Althusser, Balibar, Baran, Sweezy, Kidron, Hirsch, Altvater, Yaffe, Poulantzas, Boccard, and (rather ambiguously) O'Connor, not to mention the "official Marxism" of scholars and ideologues in the Soviet Union and Eastern Europe. The trichotomy of models is admittedly crude.[5] Some authors conceptualizing the role of the state in responding to and stimulating the transformation of civil society do not fall exclusively or neatly into one of the three.[6] Some falling under the same rubric disagree stridently with each other. Irrespective of the problem of classifying any one work, however, these three general models do have the specific virtue of offering divergent interpretations of why, when, in what manner, and with what effect specialized interest associations would emerge to influence and be influenced by the course of the modern state and its policies.

STRUCTURAL DIFFERENTIATION
AND POSTINDUSTRIAL SOCIETY

Explicitly or implicitly, this manner of conceptualizing the nature of "modern" societal transformation lies at the root of all pluralist notions about the resultant mode of interest intermediation. Linear, crescive, irreversible increases in the division of labor produce greater and greater occupational specialization, organizational differentiation, and institutional interdependence. These, in turn, interact with prior differences in geographic location, religiosity, language, culture, local norms, and, as Madison put it so expansively, "those most frivolous and fanciful distinctions [which] have been sufficient to kindle unfriendly passions and excite their most violent conflicts'' to create spontaneously a pattern of interests which is multiple, voluntary, competitive, dispersed, overlapping, and independent of external — i.e., state — control. The invention and assimilation of new technology is the underlying propellant force, if not the singular determinant, of these changes. Its differentiating impact on the physical and mental tasks of production promotes the splitting up and hiving off of occupations, which in turn lead to processes of professionalization, bureaucratization, rationalization, secularization, status and interest specification, and multiple-role identification. Since these infusions of endogenously produced or exogenously diffused technological change are random and/or episodic in nature, the resultant pattern of associational response tends to consist of irregular and disruptive ''waves'' of organization and counterorganization interspersed with periods of relative equilibrium and stability. Synchronic intersocietal differences in existent and future systems of interest representation, while roughly explicable in terms of ''levels of economic development,'' are fundamentally unpredictable (or, better, only comprehensible *post festum*). Their total number, degree of specialization, level of aggregation, extent of coverage, density of membership, manner of overlap, variety of organizational forms, and diversity of practical action will be determined in each specific historical case by that unit's previous cleavage structure, prior level of organizational complexity, peculiarities in timing and sequence, and, catchall-to-end-all-catchalls, ''political culture.''

This way of conceptualizing societal change and interest intermediation is ''economistic'' (admittedly with varying degrees of reductionism) in that the occupational structure engendered by the production-distribution of goods and services is the system's fundamental determinant and motive force. Theorizing cast in this mold by no means ignores associability based on noneconomic criteria (indeed, it often exalts and celebrates the existence of other factors of differentiation). It does, however, tend to treat the multitude of civic groups, choir societies, *schutzenvereine*, ethnic associations, sports clubs, voluntary organizations, and so forth as ''side products'' affected by externalities deriving from the more basic structure of production and consumption (and, hence, of leisure). Important as these other organizations may be as elements of civil society or as influences upon the state, their emergence and role is contingent upon the interests, resources, and loyalties established by the structural differentiation of an industrial or, more lately, postindustrial economy.

This anticipated pattern of wavelike crescive development of a theoretically unlimited number and variety of interest associations is hardly conflict free, despite the repeated emphasis in pluralist writings on political continuity, procedural consensus, negotiated substantive agreement, homeostatic equilibration, and even intrinsic "harmonic" interdependence. To an important extent, conflict generated by structural differentiation and interdependence serves as the midwife to pluralistic association formation through jurisdictional disputes over newly differentiated occupations, intersectoral clashes over proportional benefits from economic growth, intrasectoral competition among alternative producers and consumers, struggles between upwardly and downwardly mobile groups differentially affected by changing technology, and, perhaps, most saliently, countervailing mobilizations against initial organizational successes and emergent disequilibria in influence relations. What is intrinsic to this conceptualization of change is the assumption that conflict can be contained within a continuous, preexistent set of norms and practices, and that its outcome reinforces, rather than diminishes, associational tendencies toward multiplicity, dispersion, competitiveness, relative equality, ease of access, fluidity of combinations, and so forth. Pluralism as a mode of interest intermediation, in other words, tends to be self-perpetuating, even self-extending, in nature, not self-limiting and certainly not self-canceling, at least in the minds of its proponents-cum-exponents.

Until relatively recently, this way of explaining the emergence and role of interest associations led to conclusions that were both praxiologically optimistic and normatively benign. Additional interests were constantly being created (or, better, differentiated); the barriers to their finding formal organizational expression and to obtaining access to the polity were regarded as low, if not nil; associational newcomers would be reliably socialized to the appropriate rules of the game and would not make demands of such a magnitude or such intensity that they could not be somehow materially accommodated or symbolically manipulated; the payoff from continuous further development would ensure both sufficient resources to meet demands and an ample pad of private economic satisfaction and collective political apathy; the whole bargaining process would not, indeed could not, be dominated by some hegemonic actor or set of actors, and, even if such a danger were to appear, "potential groups" of previously quiescent conformists would mobilize to meet the threat. Interest representation and societal transformation — at least in those developed countries in which such process had been properly institutionalized — combined dynamically to produce both political stability and democratic accountability.[7]

Critics of the pluralist paradigm have, needless to say, been attacking virtually all of these assumptions for at least a decade or two, but only recently have theorists working from within this paradigm begun to express doubts about the benignity of its outcome. The displacement of the previous model of industrial society by a new one of postindustrial society, they suggest, has served to raise a number of new questions and serious doubts.[8] What if the spread of education and diffusion of associational techniques began to produce a fully organized, aware and mobilized polity, with less and less "slack resources" and satisfactional apathy? What if this new "tautness" resulted in an enormous increase in demands for imperative coordinations and public allocations, and a concomitant stalemate in the parallelogram of group influences? What if the expansion of public policy resulted not in the removal of items from the agenda, but greater and more transparent impingement on citizen concerns and a consequent reinforcement of mutually exclusive associational demands? What if the growing complexity of social organization led to problems of restricted span-of-control and coordination of tasks within the state? What if increased international interdependencies narrowed rather than expanded the range and flexibility of possible national policy responses? What if the bureaucratic-technical personnel necessary to run the proliferating interest associations and specialized agencies of the state began increasingly to act on professional norms of their own and/or to follow self-serving interests of their own? What if the shift in "axial principles" from property to knowledge, from energy to information, from market to plan should be resisted and "irrational" nonexpert citizens continue atavistically to demand participation, accountability, and communal satisfaction? Under any or all of these eventualities, what might happen or already have happened to the pluralist mode of interest intermediation?

While the speculative answers have hardly been unanimous, they have all been pessimistic in tone — ranging from expectations of an authoritarian, technocratic reaction in a corporatist mode to bureaucratic assertions of "juridical democracy" designed to regulate against associational excesses, to disruptive plebiscitary populist movements appearing to eliminate all forms of interest intermediation, to "socialist" revolutions with their *gleichgeschaltet*, party-directed monist systems of representation. In short, whatever its pretense to having successfully described-analyzed the relations between societal change and interest representation in the past, the structural differentiation-pluralist paradigm seems at best stymied and at most incapable of understanding the contemporary emergent properties of civil society and interest intermediation, even within its own, rather limited perspective of "postindustrial society."

HISTORICAL MATERIALISM
AND ORGANIZED CAPITALISM

From this perspective-cum-paradigm, the pattern of emergence and the political role of formal interest associations are seen as affected primarily, not by the linear, crescive structural differentiation of industrial and, later, postindustrial society, but by the peculiar discontinuous, cyclical process of capitalist development. The emphasis is not upon universal trends in professionalization, rationalization, secularization, and so forth interacting with relatively fixed national bases of preindustrial social-cultural stratification, but upon the way in which historically specific social classes are able to use and enforce their property rights to organize production and control the distribution of its surplus. While the first perspective leads one to expect a pluralist associational outcome (at least, until recent theorists of postindustrialism interjected a new note of puzzlement and pessimism), the second suggests, at least for the modern period, that corporatism is (or already has been) the most likely development outcome.

Rather than the potentially limitless and presumably inexorable advance of an ever more complex division of labor leading to more and more interest specialization and competitive associational activity in a world of expanded resources and consensual values, the historical determinist sees the development of productive forces as necessarily constrained by the social relations they assume under capitalism and limited by the capacity of such a system to extract surplus value from its own wage earners and/or from its own colonies or peripheral dependencies. The result of this shift from the relatively benign concern with consumption and distribution to the more malignant problem of production and accumulation brings out the compulsory and coercive aspects of the linkage between civil society and the state and the possible role that "less than voluntary" monopolisitic interest associations may come to play in controlling that relationship, whether from above as a matter of deliberate public policy or from below as the product of class, sectoral, and/or institutional efforts.

The major analytical device of this historical (if not historicist) approach is a "staircase" conceptualization of capitalism. Pirenne (1914) seems to have pioneered the notion when he suggested that economic development in the West had not been the result of the efforts of a continuous capitalist class "changing itself to suit changing circumstances," but of a multiplicity of succeeding "distinct and separate" capitalist classes. "In other words, the group of capitalist of a given epoch does not spring from the capitalist group of the preceding epoch. ...That history [of capitalism] does not present itself to the eye of the observer under the guise of an inclined plane; it resembles rather a staircase, each step of which rises abruptly above that which precedes it" (Pirenne, 1914: 515).

Having suggested such a stepwise notion of capitalism was, of course, only a start — and not one the non-Marxist Pirenne or others took very far. Leaving aside the ticklish issue of whether or not this particular generic mode of production is best described as on its last or its next-to-last step and whether "stepping up" requires revolution, we still must identify what specific institutions, behaviors, motives, urges, and so on serve to identify successive "epochs," as Pirenne called them, and from there attempt to trace why such emergent properties might result in quantitative and qualitative changes in the systems of interest representation. There has been no shortage of scattered suggestions with respect to the nature of these "epoch-making" changes: (1) shift in the source of recruitment to the capitalist class, (2) change in the organizational form and degree of concentration of ownership, (3) movement of the basis of power from property to management, (4) shift in the sectoral locus of power within the productive system, (5) transformation in the type of wage-earning proletariat, (6) alteration in the mix of private and public ownership, (7) modification in the objectives pursued by ownership-cum-management. Combinations and permutations of these (and no doubt other) structural assumptions about change have produced a bewildering variety of "prefix-capitalisms" (to use the expression of Hernes): "modern-," "advanced-," "state-," "bureaucratic-," and, of course, "post-." Most, if not all, of these have been invented in an ad hoc fashion to "explain" particular periods (usually the one just past) or specific cases (usually a rather extreme one). None (that I know of) is sufficiently systematic and generic in its delimitation of constitutive properties to serve as the basis for valid cross-sectional comparisons; least of all, for longitudinal inferences about emergent "futurist" properties. Rarely, if ever, do they come accompanied by more than a hint about the politicological implications of the changes they describe for interest consciousness, associational activity, or institutionalized patterns of intermediation. While the cumulative effect of reading about "prefix-capitalisms" does point in the direction of an increasing likelihood of corporatist-type outcomes for the contemporary period, the logic of inference for arriving at such a hypothesis is hardly consistent; the structural and behavioral properties such an interest system might be expected to exhibit are hardly uniform; the temporal and spatial validity of such a prediction is hardly clear.

Further exploration of Pirenne's pioneering thoughts, for example, suggests a possible cyclical theory of interest intermediation. Each initially progressive capitalist class, as it loses its innovative spirit, reorganizes itself representationally to appeal to the state for protection through regulation against rising foreign and domestic competitors. Its initially dynamic, competitive associations are replaced by hierarchically ordered, monopolistic ones, through the imposition of the state where the crisis in class hegemony is particularly acute or through relatively autonomous class efforts where the challenge to established wealth and privilege is less threatening. In either case, "the descendants of the new rich wish to preserve the situation which they have acquired, provided public authority [or delegated private associations] will guarantee it to them, even at the price of a troublesome surveillance" (Pirenne, 1914: 515). Such a corporatist outcome prevails until the next "distinct and separate" class of capitalists (perhaps state capitalists) either infiltrate the interest system with their parallel, competitive, pluralist associations or replace it dramatically with their own singular, "fused" monist organizations in the service of a revolutionary movement. The endless repetition of this pattern suggests trendless cycles of privatistic competition and state regulation, associational proliferation and consolidation, interest pluralism and corporatism. However, to the extent that each declining set of capitalist "epoch makers" was not violently and definitively displaced and, therefore, managed to encapsulate itself corporatistically in the policy structure of the state, the historical pattern of interest representation would increase both the quantity and variety of associational forms. If the rise and decline of successive capitalist classes were technologically determined (something not suggested by Pirenne), it would in superficial empirical terms be difficult to distinguish this outcome from the sort of waves of organization and counterorganization set off by technological disturbances predicted by the pluralists — except that the latter might find it puzzling to explain the simultaneous presence of qualitatively distinct modes of representation, and would be at a loss to understand the interim periods of regulation, retrenchment, and monopolization in associational activity.

Another effort at "prefixing" capitalism has been a good deal more specific in its treatment of associational consequences. Some revisionist Marxists in the early twentieth century and, more particularly, Hilferding, arrived at the conclusion that there had occurred a bundle of concomitant changes in the structure of productive property, the role of the state and the nature of class intermediation such that the old model of individualistic-disorganized-spontaneous capitalism leading inevitably to economic collapse, class polarization, and violent social revolution was no longer applicable.[9] A new *organisierter Kapitalismus* had emerged, he argued, in which the concentration of ownership and vertical integration (especially in the form of finance capital) and the establishment of specialized cartels and employers' peak associations, on the one hand, and the creation of a well-organized, permanent union movement and the spread of electoral suffrage to the working class, on the other, had combined to expand the policy role of the state, to dominate the anarchy of the market through planning, to infuse the domain of collective choice with a new technocratic ethos, to mediate the contradictory clash of labor and capital through joint collective negotiation, and, hence, to stabilize and extend the viability of capitalism. Furthermore, continuation of this process of organization would lead pacifically and inevitably to an "economic democracy" in which production would become fully socialized and the working class by virtue of superior numbers would become the hegemonic element. The naive (in retrospect) optimism of Hilferding's scenario and the quietistic praxis it entailed for the socialists in Germany and Austria when confronted by subsequent economic crisis (Gates, 1972), coupled with its complete failure to foresee a bourgeois and petit-bourgeois reaction to these trends in the form of a radical authoritarian political movement, no doubt served to discredit the notion of "organized capitalism" as a descriptive-cum-predictive model.[10] For a while the apparent neoliberalism and neopluralism of Western German politics seemed to make it even less relevant, until German scholars, faced with the paradigmatic competition of a more orthodox, state monopoly capitalism (*Stamokap*) model, revived it as a tool for analyzing the complex institutional interpenetration and policy concentration of twentieth-century Western Europe and in the process began to test its comparative validity in other polities.[11]

Tempting as the "organized" prefix may be for our purposes, given the explicitness with which it links changes in the social relations of production and the authority role of the state to both quantitative and qualitative aspects of interest intermediation, a number of deficiencies must be overcome before it furnishes anything like a valid, testable model.

1. The Hilferding specification is clearly too "Germanic" in its emphasis on high concentration of ownership, large-scale of enterprise, hierarchic authority patterns, the role played by banks, the timing of enfranchisement, the nature of party-trade union linkages, and so forth (Kocka, 1974). What are the quintessential elements and what are the circumstantial, unit-specific ones of an organized capitalism?

2. The model is ambiguous and hesitant on the causal relations that produce this "bundle" of reciprocal traits. To what extent is this an unplanned, spontaneous, even accidental outcome of independent conflicts and/or disaggregated copings with multiple crises and unselfconscious efforts of various elites, or is it a calculated project of domination by a new propertied class which seizes upon events and manipulates their issue to ensure the survival of a capitalist mode of production, albeit under different rules and personnel (Rokkan, 1970:40-43)? Must the role of the state (i.e., public policy) be treated as purely reflexive in the emergence of such a new configuration, or might not those acting in its name have resources, goals, and interests which they can autonomously bring to bear to mold the associational outcome they prefer?

3. The model is incapable of differentiating adequately between national situations in which the corporatist outcomes it predicts emerged in a continuous, accommodative, consensual manner and those in which it was a "solution" imposed by coercion after a breakdown in influence relations and a change in regime configuration. What is it about the contending societal and state actors that allows, in some cases, such a smooth transformation from a polity based on individuals acting on their beliefs to one based on groups reacting in their occupational or sectoral roles? How can some polities change from a plebiscitary to a functional conception of democracy, in which elites (or the general pubic) are almost unaware of the magnitude and import of what has occurred, e.g., Sweden, Norway, and The Netherlands (Ruin, 1974; Kramer, 1966), while, in others, the switch is a much-celebrated and much-contested event in which everyone acknowledges its magnitude and import, e.g., Fascist Italy, Salazarist Portugal, and Vichy France?

4. The model is conspicuously silent on the effect of extrasocietal and international processes. Are we to believe that such a set of changes is the isolated product of purely endogenous changes in the structure of production, development of class consciousness, extension of political rights, and formation of the national administrative state? Or should the paradigm be extended to include the world-systemic properties of exchange and exploitation within capitalism and/or the regional-system effects of diffusion and emulation within a geographically contiguous interpenetrative cultural area?

5. Finally the model of "organized capitalism" is suspiciously static (once shorn of Hilferding's optimism about a peaceful, continuous transition to socialism). What comes next? A reaction in the form of disorganized, unregulated competitiveness in production and interest relations? An extension in the form of supranational cartels, trade unions, and political processes? Or merely more of the same? Is it possible to specify the generic processes-trends that initially contributed to its gestalt-like emergence and presumably will contribute to its eventual dialectical transformation? Would such a theoretical speculation be adequate, or must one introduce into a more dynamic analysis new processes-trends which only begin to emerge once the interdependent practices in production, intermediation, and domination have been consolidated and institutonalized?

My own perception, inchoately expressed in the "Still the Century" piece, is that both societal and state corporatisms at their respectively different developmental levels of organized capitalism have already revealed contradictory tendencies, and that this was being manifested contemporarily in a double crisis of legitimacy and performance. The decline of faith in the public interest produced by minoritarian *consortio* policy segmentation, and the absence of public deliberative forms; the reduction in legitimacy of leaders of oligarchic, highly bureaucratized interest associations and owner-managers of large, monopolistic firms; the demand for individual authenticity and participation instead of mere role-satisfaction and vicariously obtained advantagement; the persistent emergence of new "style and quality" issues cutting across established functional hierarchies resulting in single-issue movements and spontaneous protest actions; the growing awareness of inflation as the real hiding hand equilibrating outcomes and invisibly redistributing benefits; the reassessment of the burgeoning role of the state and of the formulas used for distributing its benefits and "socializing" its costs — all these suggest the existence of serious dilemmas in the syndrome of organized capitalism which focus specifically on the corporatist intermediation so central to its past success.

Again, our heuristic explorations have led us to the same conclusion. However superior the historical materialism-corporatism paradigm (especially if extended and explicated in the directions discussed above) may be over the much more common structural differentiation-pluralism one, it is resolutely oriented toward a retrodictive-reconstructive form of understanding. It may help us to analyze better the past nature and role of interest politics in Western Europe, but it fails to provide us with a set of categories and expectations capable of capturing emergent properties and consequences. Faced with ubiquitous evidence of change, we lack criteria for judging their significance, much less for assessing whether or not the capitalist staircase is being ascended, descended or transcended, and, if so, whether this movement will produce a revival of pluralism, a refinement of corporatism, or, as I have suggested in the "Still the Century" piece, a renaissance of syndicalism.

POLITICAL ECONOMY AND
THE "CAPITALIST STATE"

This approach to the politics of interest intermediation shares, of course, a great deal of assumptions with historical materialism. The broad referential context is again capitalism or, more specifically, the way in which the reproductive and expansive imperatives of this mode of production define the nature of interests, establish the distribution of power resources, determine the level of consciousness, and delimit the role of the state. However, unlike the previous approach that treats the mode and outcome of interest intermediation, along with other political outcomes, as historically contingent, the more abstract, deductive political economy approach regards them as necessary products of the operation of scientific laws. These universal tendencies or "laws of motion" of capitalism toward comodification, falling rate of profit, underconsumption, emiseration, underemployment, concentration, surplus profits, uneven development, underemployment, socialization of the forces of production, bipolarization of class relations, emergence of proletarian consciousness and organization, delegitimation, imperialist expansion, and so on result not in mere conflicts to be resolved by amelioration and redistribution or occasional dilemmas to be overcome by institutional reform and ideological manipulation, but in unavoidable contradictions which destroy the society's capacity to reproduce itself and, hence, can only be solved by structural revolution in the mode of economic production itself, and, with it, in the mode of political domination, including that of interest intermediation.[12] In its Leninist version, at least to the extent that Soviet practice provides a prototype, the resulting configuration of associations linking the new "socialist" society to the proletarian-dictatorial state would be "monist" in nature:

in which the constituent units are organized into a fixed number of singular, ideologically selective noncompetitive, functionally differentiated and hierarchically ordered categories, created, subsidized and licensed by a single party and granted a representation role within that party and vis-à-vis the state in exchange for observing certain controls on their selection of leaders, articulation of demands and mobilization of support.[Schmitter, 1974:97]

In its utopian version, partially exemplifed by the *Rätebewegung* and Consigli at the end of World War I and by the recent movement for *poder popular* in revolutionary Portugal, the collapse of bourgeois political order could result in what we described supra as a syndicalist intermediate system of dispersed, voluntary, self-managing, producer-controlled units. In either case, the pluralist and corporatist outcomes would prove incapable of coping with or containing the contradictory forces of capitalist development, or of guiding the emergent forces of socialist transformation.

The usual *problématique* of "interest politics" renders it largely, if not completely, inaccessible to analysis from this perspective. For one thing, its conception of "interest" is quite different. The political economist infers it as an objective property deriving from his or her lawlike understanding, whereas the pluralist or historical materialist either establishes it from subjective preferences of actors or "projects" it on the basis of some contextual assessment of actual behavior or likely effect (Balbus, 1971; Connolly, 1972; Greenstone, 1975). The former, when not content with demonstrating the plausible existence of such objective interests with selected illustrations from class actions and postulating their eventual triumph, tends to dismiss nonconcordant or aberrant expressions of collective interest as mere "false consciousness." Since much of the content of contemporary associational intermediation often seems to contravert, if not the laws, at least the interest articulation and class structuration based on them, the political economy paradigm is not of much positive help to those analysts that take such empirical data seriously.

Nor are certain contemporary efforts to extend the paradigm into a theory of the state of much more help. In its orthodox "state monopoly capitalist" version, on the one hand, the degree of concentration of ownership and vertical integration of production is postulated as so advanced that collective representation would seem superfluous and, on the other, the extent of interpenetration between such monopoly producers and the state as the supreme monopolist is seen as so great, that interest intermediation would appear unnecessary (cf. Wirth, 1972; Valier, 1976; Vincent et al., 1975). Precisely what is recognized as an arena of constant change, contentious friction, uncertain linkage, indeterminant choice and intersocietal differentiation by the other two macroapproaches is virtually defined out of existence by the symbiotic coupling of private and public producers and allocators presumed by this approach.

Contemporary "structuralist" versions of the political economy model also tend to dismiss observed expressions of interest politics as irrelevant. By defining the state as a unitary actor and endowing it with both a responsibility and a capacity for guaranteeing the long-run reproductive imperatives of capitalism, the demands and protestations of existing social classes and their "factions," even those of bourgeois beneficiaries from state largesse and protection, can be dismissed. These specific, short-term, partial, fragmented, atavistic, or even irrational perceptions of interest are — cannot be — the real mainsprings for public policy and state action. If they were, the capitalist state might well prove incapable of accomplishing the higher functional mission with which it is endowed according to this paradigm. This, however, is assured either by selected "hegemonic" fractions of the dominant class (which may or may not be distinctively localizable in the formal associational structure) and/or by the superior capacities of certain technological and intellectual cadres who can best discern and implement the common interests of the capitalist class — which may or may not exhibit empirically and collectively an appropriate gratitude (Poulantzas, 1974; Hirsh, 1974). In any case, a political economy perspective which accords such primacy (even exclusivity) to structural essence at the expense of empirical substance is not likely to offer many clues about the behavior of observable collective agents, even such a historically destined one as the proletariat, or to attribute much significance to their expressions of interest, except perhaps as evidence of miscalculation and/or a source of minor contradiction. The Marxism of the historical materialist, while it also conceptualizes politics in terms of efforts to overcome the intrinsic dilemmas of capitalism, accords to the processes of intermediation through specialized collective representation a major and autonomous role both in the articulation of conflicting goals of social classes, sectoral capitals, central and peripheral subjects, and national and international interests *and* in the emergence of new organizational properties which distort and amplify these cleavages: displacement of bureaucratic goals, assertion of professional norms, rationalization of procedures, standardization of outputs, education and manipulation of clienteles, and so forth. The structuralist political economist may recognize these very same dilemmas and even describe them as contradictions, but uncouples their expression from the relatively autonomous realm of civil society and incorporates them within a greatly extended notion of the unitary state with its component distributional, repressive, and ideological apparatuses.

The primary utility of this third generic model of societal change to the study of interest politics, in my view, is as a source of negative warning rather than positive inspiration. It signals out empirical instances in which interest politics may be superfluous, if not misleading — i.e., states (or, more likely, agencies of the state) where concentration of ownership and interpenetration of allocation are so fused that the processes of intermediation and exchange, of representration and control are mere formalistic façades. It also points to substantive areas in which the content of demands and range of policy alternatives may be predetermined, if not rigged — i.e., situations in which interest representatives, even of exploited and oppressed classes, act within a restricted realm of imagined feasibility and felt constraints imposed by the structure of the capitalist mode of production, be it global, regional, or national. In this latter sense, the student of interest politics, no matter how imaginatively and concertedly he or she attempts to incorporate "real" interests and not just "subjective" preferences into his or her analysis of political action, will always be dealing with an incomplete and, hence, distorted portion of the totality of the means of domination in a given society. Furthermore, to the extent that these structural parameters may be overthrown, surpassed, or just made more transparent and obvious in the future, the mode of interest intermediation is likely to differ radically from those presently exhibited in Western Europe.

CONCLUSION

Our effort in this essay to link modes of interest intermediation and models of societal change has been only a partial success. The first two paradigms, structural differentiation and historical materialism, did provide us with some positive if different expectations about why, when, and who would exercise "the art of association" and what would be the resultant institutional-behavioral configuration of their efforts. The third approach, political economy, has served to warn us what not to expect from a theory of "interest politics" by alerting us to specific situations and total contexts in which this range of activity might be misleading or irrelevant.

One direction that future conceptual effort might take is to relate the three macroapproaches to each other. This could be done either by *juxtaposition*, i.e., by specifying their independent relevance for explaining the emergence of different types of associability,[13] or by *synthesis*, i.e., by combining them into a single theory with appropriate temporal lags, issue shifts, interactive properties, dependency relationships, parametric changes, and crisis effects. My suspicion is that, even if we could sociologically and politicologically combine all the different assumptions about invariant structures, linear trends, cyclical processes, and discrete events, there would still be a whopping "error variable" in our formula, and that we would find ourselves relying heavily upon it to "explain away" cross-sectional and longitudinal differences in outcome.

The reason for this, I submit, lies in a basic assumption shared by all three approaches, namely, that changes in the mode of interest representation are primarily the product or reflection of prior and independent changes in economic and social structure. Beyond the fact that this discounts for the continued impact of possibly relevant "differences in historical intercept and starting point," e.g., differences in the nature of premodern associability, geographic location, intersocietal diffusion patterns, "paradigms of policy choice," national character, and/or political culture,[14] it also ignores the importance of emergent organizational and political processes. For the purposes of understanding initial associational responses, this economism-societalism may be appropriate, but once the new collective actors begin to acquire resources and organizational properties of their own and once the state has expanded the scope and volume of its policy interventions, the mode of interest intermediation may be molded "from within" and "from above," so to speak, in relative independence from the conditions of civil society and even in disregard for the preferences and interests of the individuals, firms, sectors, classes, and so on whose interests are supposedly being represented.

Michels was perhaps the first to stress these emergent properties of modern bureaucratic organizations, but his comments on the Iron Law of Oligarchy have now been extensively supplemented by a vast literature on the importance of organizational routines, standard operating procedures, goal displacement, incrementalist strategies, cooptation, professional norms, administrative leadership, diffusion of innovations, incentive structures, manipulation of client preferences, selective benefits, and so forth. Interest associations, even in the rare instances in which they are non-monopolistic in their coverage and voluntaristic in their member support, are no less (and possibly more) susceptible to acquiring these properties than business or governmental organizations. For example, many new associations are created by preexisting ones whose leaders are able to use their installed capital to invest in new ventures, even in the absence of member demands (Salisbury, 1970: 61-63). Also, the consolidation and centralization of previously overlapping and competing associations often obey the motives of administrative convenience or connivance, and not the imperatives of prior social or economic change.[15]

Nor should the state and public policy be conceptually confined to a merely reflexive or responsive role. By introducing a distinction between voluntaristic societally induced and compulsory state-produced configurations into the typology of modes of intermediation, we have already hinted at a possibly "perverse" causality in which interest associations are the product of, rather than the producers of, public policy. Leaving aside those obvious cases of direct and deliberate "recasting," even where public authorities do not seek to create from above a complete configuration of interest politics compatible with their mode of political domination or regime type, the indirect and often unintended impact of public policy may well determine the timing, form, internal structure, area of representation, mode of action, and type of leadership of associations. The mere announcement of a policy intention, the categorical definition given a policy problem, the request expressed for policy relevant information, the choice of a specific modality of implementation, and so forth may create interests and associational responses where none were evident or likely before. Beyond these catalytic effects, the preference of discrete and/or semi-autonomous agencies of the state for correspondingly organized functional "partners" in the issue arenas they are mandated to regulate legally, subsidize materially, or placate symbolically is a powerful force contributing to the formation of *clientelas* (Lapalombara, 1964: 262-271) and symbiotic productive-allocative *complexes* (Alford, 1975). These unintended policy consequences and interorganizational affinities, plus the deliberate attempt to create encapsulated segments of associational privilege and policy protection especially for groups, sectors, and classes threatened by the secular trends of industrialization and capitalist development, go a long way to explaining the persistent differences in mode of intermediation across Western European societies of otherwise rather similar economic and social structures, but different administrative payouts, political institutions, and patterns of public policy. If the nature and role of interest associations were exclusively determined by prior changes in the occupational structure, historic social relations, the laws of capitalist reproduction, and/or generic organizational processes, Western Europe would hardly exhibit the variation in outcomes it historically has had and currently does have.

NOTES

1. In an earlier draft of this essay I used the concept, "interest representation." Subsequent criticism has convinced me that such a label can be doubly distortive: (1) it conveys the impression that formal interest associations accurately and faithfully transmit the demands and preferences of their members, or, worse, are "representative" in some statistical sense of the term: (2) it implies that representation is the exclusive or even predominant task of such specialized organizations.

By switching to the more awkward and less frequently used expression, "interest intermediation," I mean to emphasize that the associations not only may express interests of their own, fail to articulate or even to know the preferences of their members, and/or play an important role in teaching their members what their interests "should be," but also often assume or are forced to acquire private governmental functions of resource allocation and social control. Representation (or misrepresentation), hence, may be only one of the activities of these associations, occasionally not even the most important one.

2. This article also delineates a fourth mode of interest intermediation, monism, characteristic of the Soviet Union and the People's Republics of Eastern Europe at a certain moment in their political development.

3. For this theme of "state pluralism" I am indebted to the doctoral dissertation of Chattopadhyay (1975).

4. Recent developments in Australia during the Labour Government of Whitlam (1972-1975) would seem to have illustrated such tendencies.

5. A subsequent reading of a recent article by Alford (1975: 145-160) which also makes use of a trichotomy of paradigms reminded me how easy and insightful it can be to classify according to different distinctions. Alford is more impressed by the pluralist-elitist difference than I am, whereas I tend to find the singular "class" paradigm he proposed differentiated into two separate analytical approaches.

6. In his criticism of this article, Panitch has reminded me how difficult it is to classify contemporary British Marxists by its criteria. Hobsbawn, E. P. Thompson, P. Anderson, Nairn, Gough, and Miliband are all "historical materialists" in some sense (and definitely not "political economists" as the term is used here), but would presumably scornfully reject the Weberian-revisionist descent. Nor do they engage in the sort of periodization and conceptual exploration of "stages" of capitalist development which is so marked among continental historical materialists.

7. Perhaps the *locus classicus* of this line of thought with respect to Western Europe is to be found in Graubard (1963), especially the essays by Haas, Lipset, and Dahrendorf.

8. While the two best known presentations of the postindustrial syndrome — Brzezinski (1970) and Bell (1973) — are studiedly vague but generally optimistic about the political implications of this new era/age, subsequent essays have had a more pessimistic tone: Huntington (1974), Ionescu (1975), Lindberg (1976). Ironically, the first person to use the concept "postindustrial" was an advocate not of pluralism, but of corporatism (Penty, 1922).

9. Hilferding's original writings on this subject appeared in a variety of socialist journals and party congress documents from 1915 to 1931. For my understanding I had relied heavily on Winkler (1974), especially the essays by Winkler, Kocka and Wehler. For an interesting critique, see Bade (1975:293-307).

10. The scenario, however, is not so far-fetched when applied to the evolution of capitalism, interest associations, and the state in Sweden. For the concept of "functional socialism" see Adler-Karlsson (1970).

11. Kocka (1974:19-33) contains a discussion of the basis of this revival of interest in the "organized capitalism" concept. The Winkler (1974) volume incorporates case studies on Great Britain, Italy, France, and the United States, as well as Germany.

12. The distinction between dilemmas and contradictions within capitalism is explored in Offe (1975:245-246).

13. For example, it is tempting to suggest that the historical materialism paradigm applies best to the emergence and institutionalization of associations representing property and labor, while the structural differentiation paradigm applies more appropriately to the associational expression of middle-class, white-collar, and liberal professional interests.

14. For an approach which relies (excessively, in my judgment) on political culture to explain differences in Canadian and US interest politics see Presthus (1974), also Beer (1969) and Anton (1969).

15. For example, the impending fusion of the National Association of Manufacturers and the Chamber of Commerce in the United States does not seem to have come from either explicit demands from the base or from prior implicit imperatives within the production process. For a scathing critique of the distortions in "group politics" stemming from organizational processes, see Lowi (1974).

4

Theories of Contemporary Corporatism Static or Dynamic?

Birgitta Nedelmann
Kurt G. Meier
University of Mannheim, Germany

The following comments are concerned with certain problems associated with the use of the concept of corporatism as an analytical tool to describe macroscopic political configurations in contemporary Western Europe. As will be argued here, however, some of these problems are not just specific to the concept of corporatism, or better, societal corporatism, but reflect general theoretical and conceptual difficulties in the discipline of the social sciences.

We begin by asserting that the general approach reflected in the construction of a model of corporatist interest representation can only be approved. Its intentions appear to be twofold. First, the concept of corporatism rejects explicitly the concept or model of pluralism as empirically inadequate. Seen from this point of view, the concept has somewhat polemical connotations and is directed against those students which continue to describe the political sphere in metaphors derived from the liberal image of a perfect market system. In the idea of corporatism some of the basic criticisms which can be directed against this pluralist image are summarized and an attempt is made to construct a more empirically adequate model of interest representation in advanced industrial societies. Second, as becomes quite clear in Schmitter's (1974) explication of the concept of corporatism, it is a model constructed on the same level of analysis as that of pluralism: i.e., both constitute macroscopic models of political institutional and behavioral configurations focusing on the aspect of interest representation. This seems to us an advantage: in this way the equally dangerous alternatives of either reducing the analysis of political systems to an examination of individual actions and orientations or of replacing concepts potentially rich in substantive content by technically impressive, but politically empty, labels of "input," "output," and the like are avoided.

One last point should be mentioned. In contrast to pluralists, students of corporatism place special emphasis on the importance of the state as an actor and do not reduce it to an arena in which competing interests operate in order to determine policy. Instead, the state is credited with initiatives, interests, and politics of its own, in at least relative autonomy from associational activity. While these features of the concept of corporatism can only be but welcomed, one should not ignore that the very fixation of the concept of corporatism with the previously dominant model of pluralism contains a number of pitfalls. By taking over the dimensions of the latter — such as "number of organizations," "intrasectoral monopoly of interest representation," "degree of competition between the organizations," and so on — and just changing or inverting the empirical values of these dimensions or variables, one risks importing the same conceptual and theoretical difficulties already connected with their previous utilization. It is to some of these risks and pitfalls that the following remarks are devoted.

One of the basic ambiguities of the pluralist model concerns its epistemological status. It is not clear whether the pluralist conception should be regarded as a descriptive account of certain empirical phenomena, or whether it represents an attempt at an explanatory model. Equally ambiguous is the corporatist model. Our impression is that the corporatist model should be regarded principally as a descriptive model, that is, as a set of assumptions concerning selected features of reality which does not relate these features explicitly to each other. From its descriptive character, however, follows one problem typical of descriptive models in general: it seems rather arbitrary in its selection of the types and range of structural elements included. It is not clear whether it should contain only two basic dimensions, namely, the associational organizations and the state, or whether it should also include a third one, namely, the socioeconomic structure or, more specifically, the nature and extent of the unorganized population.

Although the corporatist conception should be regarded principally as a descriptive effort, it is nevertheless quite obvious that it has, at least implicitly, explanatory ambitions as well. Here, we again can see the pitfall in paralleling the pluralist model which has as a consequence that the conceptual possibilities of the model of corporatism are not fully utilized. Although the idea of the state as a relatively autonomous actor is stressed on a general level, it is only used in the classificatory level in order to distinguish between different types of corporatism. This is most obvious in Schmitter's (1974) description of societal corporatism. The most general hypothesis implied by both the model of pluralism and the societal version of corporatism can be formulated in this way: the decisions of the state reflect or are the product of the constellation of interests articulated by associational organizations. In other words, the concept of corporatism, as well as that of pluralism, implies the same old-fashioned theory of power in which state behavior is accounted for by reference to interest group pressure. This hypothesis, of course, immediately raises questions. What is it that makes these organizations able to determine the action of the state? In other words, what is the power base and the mechanisms of influence of these organizatons? Instead of attempting an answer to these fundamental questions, the corporatist model moves on to make another claim. In strong opposition to the pluralist model, it asserts that the organizations which determine the action of the state are always the same, not changing, shifting in importance, partially disappearing, being complemented by new ones, and finding themselves in constant mutual competition. This proposition does not answer the above question about the power base and influence mechanisms of interest associations. Neither fluidity nor stability in the structure of associational representation and pressure has an immediate and predictable implication for the power base necessary to determine the actions of the state. Nevertheless, the proposition that the structure of associations in advanced industrial societies tends to be fixed and collusive, instead of fluid and competitive, is interesting in itself, and one wonders how to account for such a change in organizational character.

However, instead of answering this question, the model of corporatism refers to yet another range of empirical phenomena — namely, the increasing level of functional and structural differentiation of the social structure. Again, this may be a valuable empirical observation in its own right, but there is no obvious connection between structural and functional differentiation in society and fluidity or nonfluidity of the structure of interest associations. Since in the corporatist model the state and the social structure are mediated via formal representative organizations,[1] this lack of a theoretically grounded argument explaining the connection between social and organizational structure merely reveals that there is also no explicit statement about the connection between societal differentiation and state behavior (which can be regarded as a or the classical problem of political science and political sociology).

Summarizing these remarks, we find that first, the model of corporatism contains three elements: the state, the structure of interest associations, and the social structure; second, one of the main issues the model addresses is the problem of the determination of state actions by pressure groups;[2] third, neither is the assumed stability of the organizational structure related in a theoretical way to state behavior, nor is a theoretical connection made between the differentiated social structure and the stable structure of interest representing organizations; fourth, although the model itself, being descriptive, does not give an answer to these questions, it nevertheless has the virtue of posing them and, hence, of pointing to the theoretical necessity for answering them. However, because of its vaguely formulated epistemological base, key elements of the model are left rather ambiguous and underdefined.

In the following, some examples will be drawn upon to illustrate these difficulties. It should be clear, however, that they are, for the most part, not specific to the corporatist model of interest representation, but equally relevant for many other approaches in political science and political sociology. Nevertheless, they should be taken into account more explicitly by students of corporatism if this approach is to prove useful.

Crudely stated, corporatism conceives of societies as a dualism between the state on the one side and civil society (organizations and social structure) on the other side. With reference to the former "pole," it remains unclear what its theorists understand by the concept of the state. As the concept of corporatism is concerned with a description of the link between the decisional structure and interest organizations, it would seem necessary to define which action units constitute the state: is it, for example, the government, or the administration, or the parliament, or is the state composed of all three of these units?[3] As associations have to use different strategies when trying to influence state decisions depending on whether they are made by the government or by the parliament or by the administration, it seems to be necessary to differentiate between the different possible counterparts which interest organizations must meet within the decisional structure.

Another question left unanswered by students of corporatism is whether or not parties are to be included into the concept of the state. One reason why parties are not mentioned in the definition and theorizing about corporatism could be the tacit assumption that they are "bypassed" by interest associations and, therefore, are negligible in importance. But it would be worthwhile to make such an implicit assumption explicit and to include in the definition of the problem which action units within the state complex are allegedly bypassed by corporations. By stating this as an explicit problem it would become possible to ask under what conditions, concerning which problems, to which extent, and by which means parties are left out from the decision-making process.

There are some other open questions, too, when looking at the second "pole," that of the associations. First, the fact that only occupational and economic organizations are considered should be openly acknowledged. Perhaps one can try to justify this exclusion and, hence, the exclusion of so many other formal interest associations. One such justification could be simply pragmatic, but there are other and perhaps more interesting justifications possible. For example, one could argue that it is in the economic sphere that the macroscopic functional differentiation of society is especially pronounced and effective with respect to interests. Since the corporatist model, especially the societal corporatist one, refers to advanced industrial societies, it seems appropriate to concentrate on the economic sphere. Now, obviously, this argument is at least problematic, if not clearly wrong empirically. One has, for example, to think only of the cultural sphere with its increasing differentiation or of the legal sphere with its increasing multiplicity of types of laws and legal institutions to see that the economic sphere cannot claim a monopoly or even an exceptional position with respect to differentiation.

Another justification for the restriction to economic organizations could be strategic. It could be argued that it is the economic sphere which seems most relevant for societal development, and for this reason one should concentrate on economic issues, interests, and interest groups. Whether such a claim of prominence is valid or not, the decision to concentrate only on economic problems and associational organizations does not justify the exclusion of "noneconomic" interest groups ex ante. Organizations which represent moral or ideological interests could have an important moral or ideological influence not only on those issues for which they claim to be primarily competent, but also on economic issues. In fact, one of the most interesting problems concerning interest groups consists exactly in the examination of the capacity of these groups to define given issues as belonging (and in other cases not belonging) to their area of representation. To imply in one's approach a total correspondence between issue areas and interest groups is to exclude the possibility of analyzing the dynamics of absorption and repulsion of issues by organizations.

This argument also implies a certain scepticism on our part concerning the definition of interest groups as "functionally specific." For example, in the Swedish case (which is often taken as the example par excellence for societal corporatism), the temperance association would have to be excluded from the analysis according to the definition of intermediary organizations, which prevails in the corporatist model since it represents principally moral interests, in spite of the fact that it has a major influence on economic questions, as could be demonstrated by the decision of the Riksdag to abolish "mellanöl" (beer with a certain percentage of alcohol) from free sale in the shops. Other examples of such functional contamination would be the church concerning itself with the issue of workers' participation in firms or the unions trying to influence issues within the educational sector. To restrict the analysis to only occupational and economic organizations is, of course, legitimate as far as this restriction is kept in mind when making final classifications of total societies as belonging to the corporatist or some other type of representational system. In the mentioned Swedish case, for example, the picture would change substantially if other important organizations were to be included into the analysis (Lindroth, 1975; Lundkvist, 1973).

Concerning the different characteristics given by Schmitter (1974) to describe the mode of associational representation, it remains in some cases unclear what is meant by them. He seems to argue that interest associations are characterized by (1) functional specifity with respect to the economic sector they represent; (2) monopolistic position within the respective economic sector — that is to say, absence of competition concerning sectoral representation; (3) compulsory membership for those represented by the organization in the sense of severe negative consequences for those units which do not join; (4) hierarchical structure, which means that within a given economic sector only the monopolistic association structures the relationship to the state (no direct participation by the members or subunits). All these features refer primarily to the structure of interest groups characteristic of corporatism itself. However, Schmitter (1974) also makes some references to the socioeconomic structure (that is, to the third, largely implicit, element of the model), and here there seem to be some difficulties. Consider characteristic 1: functional specificity. To characterize organizations as being "functionally specific" or representing functionally specific interests or sectors is in some cases problematic because of the definitional stretching or compressing of domains within which competences are claimed. But there are two other more general problems involved. First, in most concepts of societal differentiation its unidimensional character is implied. So, for example, one could use as a criterion for societal differentiation in the economic sphere the kind of technology of production or the type of product. Accordingly, one could distinguish between different branches within the agrarian, industrial, and service sectors. One could talk of "functionally specific" interest organizations if there would exist interest organizations for each of these different branches.[4] Obviously, there are other criteria as well which could be used for societal differentiation. To take another example, if "type of control over the means of production," "private" and "public ownership," is used as a criterion for societal differentiation, there ought to be at least two types of interest organizations if one could talk about their functional specificity. If these different criteria (technology of production, type of product, and type of control) are combined, then, a "functionally specific" interest organization would, for example, be the "association of the privately owned wheat producers"; the "association of wheat producers," however, including both privately and publicly owned farms, would have to be regarded as "functionally diffuse." These simple examples show that the concept of functionally specific interest organizations is meaningful only in relation to an explicit definition of the criteria of societal differentiation.

Second, not only does there exist a variety of criteria for societal differentiation which constitutes the base for interest organizations, but it should not be overlooked that the interest organizations themselves influence the social definition and evolution of these criteria of societal differentiation. As has been shown, for example, in the sociology of professions, when social differentiation is looked upon historically and in dynamic terms one finds that many of its aspects can be regarded as the result of the strategies of interest organizations trying to find, to create, to strengthen a specific clientèle by inventing new or exploiting old (but until then not relevant) social differences. Seen from this angle, it does not seem justified to think of interest organizations as only representing interests in a functional specific way; instead, it would be more appropriate to investigate also the degree to which and the mechanisms by which such organizations produce subjective notions of relevance concerning differences, objective societal differentiation, and corresponding differences of interests.

Obviously, there is no one-to-one relationship between a given social structure and the structure of interest organizations. There is a certain indifference or indeterminism between the organizational and the social structural levels which goes further than the three structural versions of pluralism, societal, and state corporatism suggest. The construction of these different models can be credited for paying attention to this indifference, but the explication of these models has not yet gone far enough to also realize that the relationship betwen social differentiation and the differentiation on the level of the structure of interest organizations (their "functional specifity") itself has to be treated as being theoretically problematic. Especially important, then, seems to be the explanation of different degrees of interest aggregation and the analysis of the consequences of these different degrees in relation to both the constituent members of interest organizations and the decision-making structure.

If this line of argumentation is plausible, it follows, of course, that some of the other characteristics of corporatism have to be modified accordingly. What might appear as competition in the social structural level does not have to be competition on the organizational level; and competition or noncompetition for members of interest organizations has to be sharply distinguished from competition or noncompetition concerning the influence on the behavior of the state.

There are some other definitional characteristics of corporatism which do not refer to the organizational level per se or to the relation between the organizations and the social structure, but to the link between state and civil society. Here, mainly three such characteristics are distinguishable: (1) recognition by the state, (2) controls on leadership selection, (3) controls on interest articulation. With reference to the first characteristic, it should be asked if a state confronted with monopolistic associations representing the central economic interests has any other alternative but "recognizing" them in one way or the other (it is left open to the definition of the subtypes of corporatism how the state recognizes the organizations). Which state could afford to overlook and ignore such central associations? This characteristic seems to be a consequence of prior monopolisic sectoral dominance. Of course, one has to distinguish sharply between recognition in the sense of the state regularly taking into consideration the existence of organizations and the state conforming to the demands of such organizations. The state might be able to form coalitions with either other interest groups or the unorganized population (for example, in elections with the voters) and, thereby, effectively refuse to meet the demands of a given monopolistic interest organization. What seems to be important, then, is the theoretically guided development of types of alternative reactions of the state in relation to the pressure of interest organizations including as an extreme version attempts of the state to suppress interest organizations.

In exchange for the recognition of the associations' status, the state — it is said — gets "certain controls on their selection of leaders and articulation of demands and support" (Schmitter, 1974: 94). Here it would be interesting to specify whether the state has control over the content of the interests expressed, over how violently they are pressed, over the point of time when they are articulated, to which stage of the decision-making process they are addressed (i.e., the initiating stage, the consultative stage, or the final decisive stage). Here one should at least differentiate between different action areas in which organizations' influence, on the one hand, and the state's influence, on the other hand, is made effective. As Elvander (1966:272ff.) has shown, for example, interest organizations in Sweden have influence not so much on the final decision-making process, but more in the preliminary consultative phase of decision-making in their capacity as advisors and experts. Whether the advice and suggestion given by the interest organizations are taken into consideration in the final decision-making process is still very much an open question. In other words, to be able to specify the type of influence and the area of influence of both the interest organizations and the state, it is necessary to differentiate in more detail what is meant by control over "interest articulation" and influence upon the decision-making process. Influence mechanisms by associations and means of control by the state respectively will vary widely according to the area in which the state tries to control interest articulation and the area in which the interest organizations try to affect public policy.

We would suggest the need to differentiate among at least the following three action areas which both interest organizations and the state could try to dominate. First, there is the area of *initiating* certain issues. Here, one could think of the state as having control over what kind of issues are initiated by interest associations and having the capacity to recognize problems and to confront organizations with them. This type of control over the area of interest initiation has been especially prominent in the 1950s and 1960s, when the Swedish Social Democratic government took over the initiative in the central reform questions, leaving the interest organizations in a position of reacting to its proposals. In other questions, however, the contrary could be observed. There associations, mainly the Workers' Central Union (LO), took the initiative in central reform questions, such as in the recently promoted question of "wage earners' funds" (löntagarfonder), and the government was pushed into a defensive position.

A second, already mentioned, action area in which the influence of the state over associational activity could be realized is the *consultative* stage of decision-making. Theorists labeling Sweden as corporatist usually refer to the fact that interest organizations in Sweden are integrated into the Royal Commissions and into the process of *"remiss-yttranden"* (Heckscher, 1958; Ruin, 1974; Heclo, 1974: 41, 184). Once an issue has been initiated — regardless by whom — the main associations are invited to give their opinion and advice. However, influence in this area does not necessarily mean that these organizations also have an influence on final decision-making, which is probably what theorists labeling Sweden as corporatist primarily have in mind. Therefore, it seems desirable to differentiate yet a third action area, namely, the decision-making area or, as it will be called here, the area of issue *resolution*.

In relation to these three action areas one could imagine one form of "state corporatism" in which the state dominates all three: initiating all issues, preparing them within its own administrative bureaucracies, and selecting the solutions without advice or interference. The opposite extreme form of "societal corporatism" would involve interest organizations not only initiating issues, but also dominating both the preparatory consultative phase of the decision-making and the final phase of issue resolution. In the last case, the state would only play the role of an executor of the solutions made by the associational organizations.

Without going into the way different subtypes might be constructed (which probably have more empirical relevance than these extreme types), it should be emphasized that such a differentiation could be of more than mere classificatory interest. It would permit one to ask more precisely on what issues which actors have which type of influence, in which area of the policy process. The problem, then, would be to ask whether there are specific problems or conflicts which facilitate "state corporatism" and others which facilitate "societal corporatism." The focus of interest would then be upon the way certain types of conflict areas structure modes of influence in special action areas.

SUGGESTIONS FOR A DYNAMIC APPROACH TO CORPORATISM

So far we have only tried to point to some weaknesses connected with the model of corporatist interest representation. There is, however, a more general point to be made which is connected with the way in which society is conceptualized in this approach. It is presented as consisting of certain elements or "levels," of which two are emphasized particulary — namely, the level of decision-making and the level of interest representation. One consequence of such a "level" image of society is that it encourages approaching macropolitical problems in a static manner. The focus of interest is directed to the question of institutional arrangements between associations and the state. If "processes" come into the picture at all, they refer only to macrohistorical changes (such as the transformation of capitalism) to which the origin of the structural configuration called corporatism is attributed. What is less often done, however, is to deal with two other types of processes: first, those processes by which the "changed nature of capitalism" is mediated into the structure of both interest groups and the state, with the joint result of bringing about corporatism; and second, the internal processes which constitute a structural configuration such as corporatism.

The following arguments are directed to the latter type of processes. This emphasis is based on two assumptions, one theoretical and one empirical. First, it is assumed that in general one can regard "structures" and "structural arrangements" such as corporatism as the result of or as consisting of continuing processes repeating themselves. If this assumption is plausible, it follows that one can and perhaps should analyze structural arrangements like corporatism in a dynamic way — that is, as the result of the continuous reproduction of certain processes. Second, it is assumed empirically that corporatism as a structural configuration is rarely an adequate characteristic of total societies. Instead, it seems more likely that corporatist representation can be used to characterize specific aspects or sectors of society. Rokkan (1975:219), for example, makes a similar point when arguing that in modern European countries it is especially in the primary economic sector where corporatist constellations are to be found, whereas in the secondary and the tertiary sectors pluralist constellations are predominant. If, however, the degree of "corporatization" of a society changes according to economic sector or if, as it is argued below, corporatist features are likely to disappear and reappear quite quickly, it would appear more realistic to regard corporatism just as a type of interaction constellation and not as a stable, fixed, or "basic" structural characteristic.

Based on these two assumptions, there seem to exist both theoretical and empirical reasons to treat corporatism as an interaction configuration based on or consisting of processes. Changes in this interaction constellation would then have to be explained by changes in underlying processes. In order to advance this dynamic process-oriented approach to the problem of corporatism, however, speculative revisions of some concepts are necessary. The first task of such a reformulation would be to replace the existing "level" approach, substituting for it a distinction between different action units which promote demands and interests. For this purpose the concept of state has to be redefined, and this raises the question of whether the differentiation between three institutional components as suggested above — government, administration, and parliament — is sufficient. On the other hand, the concept of representative associations must be differentiated according to the type of interests they represent and the degree of aggregation of interests. These two criteria seem to be important for assessing the chance that certain actual interests will be expressed politically and effectively. In other words, as a first step in the reformulation of the corporatist model in dynamic terms it seems necessary to focus more on differences in relevant actors instead of differences in social and political levels.[5] As a second step, one would have to combine this redefinition in terms of action units or actors with the different action areas, in which the interests and demands of the actors have an influence upon the others' interests and demands. Of course, it is an open question whether the specific differentiation suggested above between initiation, consultation, and resolution will prove sufficient.[6]

Two further tasks have to be accomplished in order to be able to analyze corporatist constellations in a dynamic way. First, it is necessary to define more strictly that aspect of corporatism which can be taken as the theoretical focus. Ruin (1974), for example, has concentrated on the repercussions which corporatism has on the rank-and-file membership of interest organizations. Alternatively, one could also try to analyze the conditions that make for more or less competition among interest organizations. But we have decided to focus on changes in the actors participating in decisional processes concerning economic policy. Second, what are the processes which constitute and change corporatist constellations? In this regard only two types of processes which seem to be especially relevant will be considered: (1) processes relating to the "definition of the issues or conflict objects," and (2) processes involving the "definition of the situation" in which such issues are raised, or "transformed."

In the context of this essay, we cannot enter into a detailed discussion of how to conceptualize these two aspects or dimensions in a more refined way. We have discussed the concept "definition of conflict objects" elsewhere (Nedelmann, 1975). There, two main dimensions were distinguished along which the definition of conflict objects may vary — namely, their "value-load" (*Wertladung*) and their "divisibility (*Teilbarkeit*). As regards the dimension "definition of the situation," corresponding theoretical and conceptual refinements eventually will have to be made. What we will attempt in this paper, however, is to demonstrate, by sketching some recent developments in Swedish politics, that interaction constellations of interest representation and state decision are far from being "fixed" or "frozen," and that the type of dynamic approach suggested above is useful for analyzing both stability and change in such relationships. The general hypotheses guiding the following analysis may be stated succinctly in the following way. Interaction constellations change according to (1) the dominant way in which the actors *define an issue* (or conflict object) on which their interaction is concentrated, and (2) the dominant way in which the actors *define the situation* in which the interaction takes place.

THE CASES OF "HAGA"

In the years 1974 through 1976, three different major policy decisions were made in Sweden. According to the place where the bargaining occurred, they were called "Haga" decisions. In all three situations the following actors participated at least in the consultative stage: the Social Democratic government, the Conservative Party, the Center Party, the Liberal Party, the Communist Party, the main trade unions (LO, TCO, and SACO/SR), the Swedish Employers' Federation (SAF), and the central bank (Riksbanken). In essence, two issues were debated: (1) the general outline of economic politics, especially anti-inflationist measures, and (2) tax politics. The first two bargaining situations resulted in a constellation which comes close to what Schmitter defines as "societal corporatism," whereas the third Haga situation in 1976 resulted in a quite different constellation, which, according to the hypothesis suggested here, is related to both changes in the definition of the issues and the situation in which the issues were debated upon.

HAGA I AND HAGA II

The background of the three bargaining situations was constituted by the outcome of the general elections of 1973, which had produced a deadlock in the Swedish parliament. The Social Democrats and the Communists had the same amount of seats as the bourgeois opposition (the Conservatives, the Center Party, and the Liberals), or 175 mandates apiece (Petersson, 1974). In spite of their weakened position, the Social Democrats constituted the government. According to the Swedish constitution, in such a situation choice by lot is used to decide upon questions for which no majority could be found in the Riksdag. And, in fact, a couple of questions have been decided by lot in the last three years. This type of decision-making threatened not only the government, but the whole parliamentary system, and that is why the government tried hard to avoid this procedure, at least for questions which were considered to be too important to be decided by pure chance. Therefore, the parties and the government had to evaluate every issue according to its importance and, therefore, to decide whether they could risk the choice by lot. For those issues which were defined as too important, the actors had to find alternative forms of decision-making.

Definition of the Issues

Two issues according to the definition of the actors were highly important and, therefore, could not enter the decision process in the Riksdag without being assured of a majority in advance — namely, the politics of inflation and the issue of taxes. Since the Social Democratic government had not succeeded in presenting to the parliament a far-reaching proposal for tax reform, tax politics had to be formulated year by year. Another factor which made the tax question a yearly item on the agenda was the collective agreements between LO and SAF which take place in every autumn. Under inflationary conditions tax reductions were interpreted as income for wage earners which should be taken into consideration by the labor market "partners" in their collective negotiations. Hence, the issue of inflation policies was by definition combined with and conditioned by the question of fiscal politics.

By defining the issues in such an interconnected way, three effects were produced: first, the representative organizations in the labor market were defined as important interaction partners without whom the solution of both issues would be impossible; second, by thus including the interest associations of the labor market as important actors, the Riksdag was no longer the appropriate place for bargaining. Instead, a place outside the parliament had to be found where the labor market partners could participate officially. Third, since the decision would be taken into consideration by employers' and workers' associations in their wage agreements in autumn, the question demanded an urgent solution. Furthermore, anti-inflationary measures had to be decided upon immediately in order not to prolong or exacerbate the economic crisis.

Definition of the Situation

This context of urgency and crisis was not only evident in relation to the interpretation of Sweden's own economic and political situation, but also in relation to the general situation in the neighboring countries. It was — according to the point of view of the Swedish actors — not only the capacity to act of the Swedish parliamentary system that was challenged, but that of other countries as well. Other Nordic countries were also characterized by either minority or weak coalition governments in the end of 1974. This general definition of the situation suggested that parliamentary democracies were in principal difficult to govern and powerless when confronted with crisis situations such as inflation or the oil crisis. As an expression of this crisis atmosphere, people recalled the years during World War II (*beredskapsåren*). This was expressed not only in a diffuse wave of nostalgia, but in several books and films about the war experience. In particular, the all-party government under the leadership of Hansson from 1939 to 1945 was brought back to mind.

This way of defining the two issues and the situation constituted the political context within which the negotiations of Haga I and Haga II were undertaken. Both resulted in a more or less corporatist constellation. Briefly, the government and the Liberals (along with the Center Party in the second Haga constellation) on one side and the trade union centrals and the employers' organization on the other decided how to finance tax reductions and to take these tax reductions into consideration in the collective bargainings. Only the Conservatives and the Communists did not take part in this final decision. In other words, the state — although not backed up by all parties — and interest associations decided upon a question in which usually the national government had not intervened. Thus, the autonomy of both sides was curtailed and mutually conditioned.

As Elvander (1966: 184ff.) has shown, such decisions are not unusual in Sweden. So, for example, during and for some years after World War II inflation was fought by committing the unions to hold back their demands voluntarily. However, the more the situation was defined as "normal," the more difficult it was to bind the organizations to such "*stabiliseringsöverenskommelser*," because under normal conditions the partners sought to demonstrate their organizational independence and autonomy. As soon as the situation is defined as "abnormal" (either due to war or some other type of crisis), they tend to act more in response to the whole country than to the narrow interests of their own organization. In order to protect "national" interests, the associations and the state stress the norm of cooperation on the base of mutual dependence — a feature which, according to Schmitter, is typical of corporatism.

In summary, the main features of the first two Haga situations which resulted in a corporatist decision-making constellation were the following: (1) because of the deadlock situation, the parliament was weakened in its decisions-making capacity; (2) the central issues of economic and tax policies were defined as being too important to risk choice by lot in the Riksdag, and another forum for decision-making had to be chosen; (3) since the wage and price issue was defined as conditional upon the resolution of the tax issue, the principal organizations of the labor market had by definition to be incorporated into the negotiations; (4) since the general situation was defined in crisis terms, the norm of cooperation was predominant over that of competition in organizational interactions.

HAGA III: IDEOLOGICAL COMPETITION

In the spring of 1976 the same actors which had participated in the negotiations of Haga I and II were invited by the government to a third round of negotiations on economic policy and tax issues. This time the Riksdag formally decided to initiate such a "forum för samräd," so another decision outside the parliament was legitimized in advance. By this time, however, the constellation had shifted considerably.

The main factor which from the beginning reshuffled the old constellations of Haga I and Haga II was connected with a significant change in the definition of the situation. The focus of attention shifted from collective bargaining to the coming general elections in September. Due to the impending elections, the actors followed competitive norms instead of cooperative ones. It was no longer the nation as a unit which had to be supported, it was the different ideological and interest positions which had to be defended. The clear ideological differentiation thus contradicted the cooperative norms to which they were presumably committed by the Riksdag decision. In order to escape this dilemma they redefined the central issues which were to be subject to negotiation. Although the economic and fiscal policies still were considered to be too important to risk a random choice, and although the issues still demanded an urgent decision, they were no longer defined as issues which could be only solved by the coordinated efforts of all the principal associations. Instead, the voters now were considered to be the actors having the final decison-making power, and it was to them that the issues were ultimately to be addressed. To put it in other terms, the issues were now defined as central issues in the struggle for votes.

The resultant final constellation of actors could be described as follows. The main unions (LO and TCO) that had participated in the first two Haga decisions now refused to take part in any further negotiations. They legitimized their withdrawal by arguing that in situations which could be called "normal" (in contrast to crisis situations) it was their task as organizations representing labor to maintain their autonomy and not to let the state interfere in their collective bargainings with the employers' organization. The withdrawal of the two unions from further Haga negotiations had as a consequence that the bourgeois parties refused to include the tax issue in another Haga bargaining situation. Instead, they wanted the voters to decide on the issue. The bourgeois parties wanted to discuss only the general economic policies in the third Haga round. Having thus separated the fiscal issue from the general anti-inflationary problem, the Social Democratic government had a free hand to take the initiative in tax matters. And, in fact, only one day after the first Haga III meeting had taken place, the Social Democrats presented a common solution with the LO and TCO in which they promised voters to reduce the taxes considerably if the Social Democratic government were reelected. The unions promised to take these reductions into consideration in the forthcoming collective negotiations on wages. The Social Democrats, the labor union central (LO), and — to a minor degree — the TCO presented themselves as a coalition of the working-class movement and addressed their position on the tax decision very clearly and directly to the voters. Thus, the government in its role as Social Democrats created an alliance with both unions and thereby definitely broke up the cooperative constellation with the bourgois parties which had been typical of the preceding two years.

But there still remained the second issue, the outlines of the general economic policies, to be negotiated upon in the Haga III round. However, the Conservatives refused to participate any longer, accusing the government of double-dealing on the tax issue. The other actors (the Center Party, the Liberals, SACO/SR, the central bank, and SAF) oriented themselves mainly toward one goal — to finish the cooperative Haga constellation to enable them to differentiate themselves as competing parties to the voters. Therefore, they decided upon a vaguely formulated declaration, in which they roughly expressed their will to fight inflation, to control prices and expenses, and to stimulate employment. The Communist Party also joined in this declaration; only the Conservatives refused to participate. Thus, one could define this situation as one in which the partners demonstrated their consensus with the most fundamental outlines of economic policies, but having thus demonstrated their willingness to cooperate and their loyalty to the most fundamental values of economic management, the parties now had a good starting position to compete according to ideological lines.

In summary, this third Haga situation could be described as having the following characteristics. (1) Similar to the first two negotiations, there was still a deadlock situation in the Riksdag, but now, in 1976, the government had demonstrated its action capacity and its ability to cooperate across party lines. The government was, hence, stronger than in 1974 and 1975. (2) The central issues of fiscal and economic policies were still considered to be important and urgent issues demanding a quick decision. It was still held necessary to "predecide" them outside the Riksdag. This opinion was expressed in a formal parliamentary decision and, hence, further decisions outside the parliament were from the beginning formally legitimated. (3) In contrast to the first two situations, however, the focus of attention according to which the actors defined the situation had changed. The "crisis" definition had been replaced by the definition of "election-year," in which it was considered "normal" to fight for specific organization interests. Thus, the role of the actors changed, and they now appeared as spokesmen of different ideological convictions rather than as bearers of national responsibility. (4) The issues were no longer defined as being conditionally dependent on each other. Instead they were separated, and different constellations were constructed in which each issue would be decided upon separately. Concerning the first issue, the working-class coalition of Social Democrats, Labour Union, and TCO presented a proposal on tax reduction which it addressed to the voters for final decision. On the second issue, general economic policies, the other parties (with the exception of the Conservatives), the government, and the SACO/SR unions presented a general document in which they declared their consensus on the fundamental economic values.

However, there is a last important point to be made which is related to some of the cirticisms advanced above. From the point of view of corporatism, the main emphasis is placed on the associations and the state as the most important elements in the decision-making constellations. However, as has already been pointed out, this restriction to organized interests can be problematic, because in certain cases "unorganized interests" may play an important role in the decision-making process. To take those actors explicitly into account appears all the more necessary, since these unorganized interests can be the outcome of the way in which associations and the state have treated certain problems. In other words, the state or representative organizations may produce interests for which there is no organizational representation as yet. The description of the Haga cases would have been incomplete if the emergence and role of such unorganized interests had not been taken into consideration. Without being able to go into detail, it can only be said that the first two Haga decisions concerning the tax issue resulted unintentionally and unexpectedly in severe injustices for small businessmen who had to pay higher taxes than other professional groups. In March 1976, the famous author Astrid Lindgren published an article in the newspaper *Expressen* in which she accused not only the Minister of Finances, Sträng, but the whole state apparatus for exploiting taxpayers, especially small entrepreneurs. This unconventional tax protest and system critique (Lindgren expressed it in the form of a fairy-tale on "Promperipossa i Monismanien") had for a short period the dimension of a wider tax movement directed against the Social Democratic government. As a result, the tax issue could no longer be treated more or less secretly in separate negotiative rounds, but had from that point on to be treated in public. The decision of the Social Democrats, the LO, and the TCO to reduce taxes if the Social Democrats were reelected was, in part, a reaction to this sudden and violent tax protest.

This event demonstrates that decisions made in collusion by interest associations and the state can produce new problems for which no organization is responsible and which therefore stimulates the rise of new movement or, eventually, even new interest organizations. These new movements in turn could disrupt the corporatist interaction pattern and produce a change in the traditional mode of decision-making.

CONCLUSION

The purposes of this paper have been threefold. After having advanced some general critical remarks concerning the concept of corporatism and advocated the desirability of reformulating this model in more dynamic terms, some specific suggestions as to how this could be done were offered. Finally, some recent decision-making processes in Swedish economic politics have been used to illustrate the approach suggested.

The first conceptual step should be a specification of different actors and of different action areas in which there might be a competition for influence between associations and the state. It is necessary to differentiate at least among the areas of issues initiation, consultation, and final resolution. As has been demonstrated, there were different constellations in the area of consultation than in the final decision area, in which not all actors participated. If one speaks of societal or liberal corporatism, one has to specify in which action area the interest organizations are expected to dominate state policies, whether it is in only one area, or in two of them, or in all three. At the very least, one cannot simply presuppose that a corporatist constellation, let us say in the consultative area, automatically leads to a corporatist constellation in the area of final resolution. This argument applies specifically to the Swedish system, often held to be a case of "societal corporatism." The fact that the interest organizations in Sweden regularly participate in the Royal Commissions and in the "remiss" procedure cannot be taken as an indicator for corporatism everywhere, particularly if corporatism involves the question of the final outcome of public decisions.

Second, after having redefined corporatism in terms of interaction constellations, a very general conceptual frame of reference and specific hypotheses have to be constructed in order to account

for changes in these constallations. Specifically, it appears promising to conceptualize the processes underlying these interaction constellations as involving both definitions of issues and definitions of
situations. An attempt has been made to illustrate how redefini-
tions of issues and situations resulted in a change of interaction
constellations.

The constellations of Haga I and Haga II, which could be defined as "societal corporatist," were constructed under specific conditions: a weak government, a crisis situation, a disturbance of the
normal decison-making process due to the deadlock-situation in the
Riksdag, and a definition of issues supported not only by the parties, but also by the main partners of the labor market, which
recognized the need for an urgent solution. According to the actors' definition, the situation demanded the coordinated decisions
of all actors in order to save the whole country from severe
economic difficulties. Influence in such a situation, then, rests
mainly on the capability of defining the situation in a manner convincing to those actors whose support was needed. In these cases
(Haga I and Haga II) it was the Social Democratic government
which was able to convince the bourgeois parties, employers' and
workers' organizations to cooperate in rather unconventional
ways. For this purpose the government not only had to define the
situation but also to initiate new forms of interaction and decision-
making. The other actors had to overcome traditional commitments and positions in order to be able to participate effectively. For this purpose the new place of interaction, Haga, was appropriate, since no commitments concerning the number of participants, the manner of negotiation, and the mode of resolution
were yet connected with it.

This change in the corporatist constellation was brought about
by a change in the definition of the issues and by a change in the
definition of the situation. Here, too, the type of effective influence
involved a redefinition of the situation as being no longer "abnormal," but "normal" and, more particularly, "preelectoral." This
redefinition was promoted by a coalition between the government
and the principal unions. The foundation of this coalition was
made possible by still another type of redefinition — namely by a
change in the definition of the role of these action units. Instead of
claiming to continue to act as "government" and as "interest
groups," these actions units now claimed to act as elements of the
working-class movement. That is to say, the change of the previous

corporatist constellation was brought about by redefining the role in which the actors interacted with each other. Usually such changes in the definition of the roles of the actors are not taken into consideration by theorists of corporatism or pluralism. They assume fixed definitions of the role of the state and associational organizations and, thereby, predefine the mode of interaction between them. As the Swedish example illustrates, the meaning of the coalition between the government and the trade unions shifts according to the definition of the role which is inherent in a changing interaction situation.

Unfortunately, another hypothesis will be stated, but cannot be fully elaborated. The Swedish case suggests that in relation to other kinds of issues the constellation of state and representative associations may shift and even acquire a more pluralistic configuration. This could be demonstrated by analyzing, for example, the issue of the politics of alcohol (e.g., the "mellanöl" decision), which has major consequences for the state revenue, or it coud be shown with the issue of family policies. In both cases no such corporatist constellations can be found. Another interesting example would be the conflict object initiated by the labor union central, which concerns wage earners' funds (*löntagarfonder*). In this case, the central initiated the issue and pressed the Social Democrats to take it up; the Social Democrats, however, tried hard to avoid the issue in the election campaigns. Palme defended the Social Democrat's autonomy vis-à-vis the labor union: "We are glad that Social Democracy has been able to realize important demands by the wage earners. . . . Of course, this does not mean that the Social Democratic government would be obliged to realize everything what has been decided by the labour union."[7]

NOTES

1. However, the associational organizations' functions of mediating between the social structure and the decisional structure is not worked out by corporatist theorists as clearly as has been done in the classic work of Durkheim (1964) or by Kornhauser (1959).

2. There are, of course, other problems, too, for which the model seems interesting. For example, it provides a frame of reference for the analysis of the attitudes and actions of the members of the interest organizations. However, these problems cannot be dealt with in this essay.

3. This distinction is made by Elvander (1966). But one could, of course, think of the state as consisting of even more relevant subunits.

4. In the context of this essay, the problem of whether criteria like the two mentioned (technology of production and type of product) are in fact very meaningful for the specification of the notion of social differentiation cannot be discussed. However, the question has to be raised whether more reasonable criteria for social differentiation should refer to action units, such as firms, instead of to the products of these enterprises. It is, for example, only from such a perspective that the developments in late capitalism can be conceptualized, namely, the decrease of social differentiation via the fusion of structural and functional elements. Furthermore, this line of argument implies that the degree of differentiation could be greater on the level of interest organizations than on the social level.

5. Almond, Flanagan, and Mundt (1973) in their interesting process model of crisis and choice still have a "level" approach which gives the model a static bias.

6. There is, of course, another important action area, the area of "implementation" or "realization" of decisions already taken; here the influence of the different actors could be of vital importance for the issue under question.

7. Palme as cited in *Dagens Nyheter* (July 25, 1976).

5

The Development of Corporatism in Liberal Democracies

Leo Panitch

Carleton University, Canada

I

Corporatism as an ideology has a long history. It finds its modern roots in those versions of nineteenth-century social and political thought which reacted against the individualism and competition which characterized the emerging dominance of the capitalist mode of production, and against the industrial and political conflict between classes which was the ineluctable product of this development. Although the varieties of corporatist theory are many, the common premise was that class harmony and organic unity were essential to society and could be secured if the various functional groups, and especially the organizations of capital and labour, were imbued with a conception of mutual rights and obligations somewhat similar to that presumed to have united the medieval estates in a stable society. Accordingly, corporatist programmes advocated a universal scheme of vocational, industrial or sectoral organization, whereby the constituent units would have the right of representation in national decision-making, and a high degree of functional autonomy, but would have the duty of maintaining the functional hierarchy and social discipline consistent with the needs of the nation-state as a whole. A limited organizational pluralism, generally operating under the aegis of the state as the supreme collective community, would guarantee the major value of corporatism — social harmony.[1]

When we turn to actual corporatist structures, the most famous — or rather infamous — instances of corporatism in practice, that of the fascist states, gave a rude answer to the question of how the social harmony trumpeted in theory would in fact come to replace the competition and class conflict of capitalist society. Corporatism was introduced concomitantly with the abrogation of liberal democracy and the smashing of the indigenous organizations of the working class to the end of repressing both political and industrial class conflict. Harris (1972:72) has observed of this experience:

> The relationship between forces and the appearance of unanimity is not settled in the modern, anymore than in the earlier corporatist writings: it is assumed. Yet, as Pirou notes in relationship to Italian Fascism and Neumann with reference to the Nazis, corporatism in these countries was not, and could not be, much more than a decorative façade for force. For the harmony which it is assumed is intrinsic to society — if the squabbling cabals can be swept away — can in practice only be reproduced by the use of force. And the use of force directly contradicts the assumption of intrinsic harmony. In Vichy France and in Salazar's Portugal, overtly corporatist societies, the same comment is appropriate. Corporatism assumes what it is designed to create, and destroys what it seeks to create by pursuing the only practicable means available: coercion.

But the historical experience with corporatism in this century has not been confined to fascist states. In liberal democracies implicit tendencies toward corporatist structures developed both before and concurrently with the emergence of fascism.[2] One British Cabinet member contended in the 1930s: "it seems to me to be courting failure to tell people that they have first to dress themselves in black shirts and throw their opponents downstairs in order to get the corporative state. . . . This new economic order has already developed further in England than is generally recognised" (quoted in Harris, 1972: 55). Bowen (1947: 3-4) observed more generally of the pre-World War II period:

> In countries where liberal-democratic political institutions continued to function, these authoritarian versions of "corporatism" were generally repudiated with some vehemence. At the same time, however, there appeared signs of a growing awareness that in modern industrial society certain fundamental tendencies which might be described as "corporative" had for some time been at work. Economists and historians found one such tendency to be the decline of atomistic competition in economic life, a sphere in the "free play of individual forces" was increasingly being superseded by the operation of collective agreements concluded among solidly organized "communities of interest." Jurists and political scientists observed a parallel decline of atomistic in-

dividualism in politics, noting that private bodies claiming to represent the group interests of labour, of employers, of farmers, of consumers, of particular branches of industry and of other economic and social groups tended to become more inclusive and more highly integrated with a view to increasing their direct influence upon governmental policies. In some democratic countries notably in pre-Nazi Germany, in France and in Czechoslovakia, groups of this kind were given a degree of official recognition when they were allowed representation in National Economic Councils created to serve as advisory "parliaments of industry."

In the late thirties, during World War II, and especially in the postwar period, these tendencies toward corporatist structures have accelerated and been more systematically developed in liberal democratic societies. They have been particularly associated with the increased state involvement in managing the advanced capitalist economy, and have centered on the integration of central trade union and business organizations in national economic planning and incomes policy programmes and bodies. This development has taken place within the framework of the maintenance of liberal political freedoms, has entailed the integration of indigenous class organizations for the most part, and state coercion has played a secondary, or at least sporadic and indirect, role in the process. For the most part, however, this development has rarely, or at least only in very specific contexts, been announced or even acknowledged as corporatist by politicians, group leaders, or bureaucrats, or described as such in even the "serious" press. Corporatism, not surprisingly, had become a term of denigration in the course of the antifascist war throughout liberal capitalist societies, and especially among western labour movements whose participation in the new structures was the "sine qua non" of their development. Indeed, insofar as the term was used — outside of intellectual or academic circles — it was used by labour leaders or left-wing social democrats and Marxists, as a means of opposing trade union integration in these structures.[3]

Among scholars, however, and especially among social scientists interested in questions of interest group representation and economic planning in liberal capitalist societies, the term corporatism, usually prefixed by "neo" or "quasi" or qualified by the adjective "liberal," has become increasingly common. Well over a decade ago, Beer (1969:419) identified a "new group politics" in Britain, a "system of quasi-corporatism bringing government and producers' groups into intimate and continuous relationship" in framing, applying, and legitimating state policies. "The welfare state and especially the managed economy of recent decades," Beer (1969:395) contended, "simply could not operate without the advice and cooperation of the great organized producers groups of business, labour and agriculture. And the history of these groups displays the powerful influence of government in calling them into existence, shaping their goals and endowing them with effective power." More generally, Shonfield's influential *Modern Capitalism* (1965:161) explicitly argued: "The term 'corporatist' is not to be understood in a pejorative sense. All planning of the modern capitalist type implies the acceptance of some measure of corporatism in political organization: that follows from basing the conduct of economic affairs on the deliberate decisions of organized groups of producers, instead of leaving the outcome to the clash between individual competitors in the market." More recently, Lehmbruch has defined "liberal corporatism" as "a special type of participation of large economic social groups in public especially economic policy-making. Consultation and cooperation among administrations and organized interests is of course common in all constitutional democracies with a highly developed capitalist economy. But the distinguishing trait of 'liberal corporatism' is a high degree of cooperation among those groups themselves in the shaping of public policy." Significantly, Lehmbruch (1974:1-2) carefully warns that: "Liberal corporatism must be distinguished from the traditional corporatism of pre-industrial Europe on the one hand, from authoritarian corporatism of the fascist type on the other. Its essential feature is the large measure of constitutional autonomy of the groups involved, hence the voluntary character of institutionalized integration of conflicting social groups."

The most rigorous contemporary specification of the corporatist concept in ideal-typical, but nevertheless in empirically bounded structural and behavioural terms, has recently been provided in an outstanding article by Schmitter (1974:93-94). His definition is purposefully constructed to cover both authoritarian and liberal democratic corporatism, but Schmitter (1974:105) goes on immediately to distinguish between "societal" and "state" subtypes. The distinguishing structural and behavioural differences between the two are seen to depend on whether the nature of the constitutent units, in terms of their limited numbers, singularity, compulsory character, and monopolistic representation of functional groups is a product more of general socioeconomic developments and voluntarist arrangements than of state imposition, and whether the state's controls on their leadership selection and interest articulation is a product of "reciprocal consensus on procedure and/or goals, or of an asymmetric imposition by the 'organized monopolists of legitimate violence' " (Schmitter, 1974: 103-104).

The foregoing examples of the employment of the concept of corporatism in the liberal democratic context are presented not merely as indicators of its growing acceptance in social science, but because, more as a corpus than individually, they capture the essence of the "neo-," "quasi-," "liberal-," "societal-" corporatist paradigm. Whereas many mainstream social scientists have joined the company of corporatist apologists and have seen the above developments as constituting "a distinct form of economic structure,"[4] an alternative or sequel to capitalism, even of the mixed economy variety, corporatism as used herein is a *political structure* that attends if is not actually produced by, the emergence of the *advanced capitalist economy*. Whereas some scholars have carelessly characterized virtually any and all intimate interest group-state relations which have become accepted as legitimate in the political culture as corporatist (e.g., Lowi, 1969; Presthus, 1973), corporatism as used herein carefully stresses the centrality of the large socioeconomic groups' relationship to the state and the cooperative interaction among them as essential to the paradigm. Whereas some scholars have attempted to conflate consociationalism and corporatism, so that religious and ideological pillarization and elite accommodation are characterized as corporatism,[5] the concept as used herein maintains a careful distinction between the two, stressing the centrality of *functional representation* in socioeconomic policy-making. Finally, whereas many scholars have used the term one-dimensionally to apply only to interest group *representation*, corporatism as used herein focuses as well on the state's *reciprocal* influence on interest groups, and their consequent employment as agencies of mobilization and social control for the state vis-à-vis their members.

The corporatist paradigm as understood to connote *a political structure within advanced capitalism which integrates organized socioeconomic producer groups through a system of representation and cooperative mutual interaction at the leadership level and of mobilization and social control at the mass level* can be a heuristic tool for appropriating the social reality of many western liberal democracies. As a working model in political analysis, it has manifest advantages over pluralist theory unencumbered as it is by the latter's unwieldy assumptions of extensive group multiplicity, passive state behavior, and stability as a product of overlapping membership and the unseen hand of group competition.[6]

Nevertheless, even considering the more careful and rigorous practitioners of the corporatist paradigm, one cannot but come away from a reading of the literature with a profound sense of unease. Schmitter, in assessing the use to be made of "state corporatist" theorists in constructing an operational paradigm of the beast, decries their lack of candour, indeed their apologetics, about "corporatism's relation to capitalism and specific class interests," as well as the role of state coercion in the implementation of corporatism "as an instrument for rescuing and consolidating capitalism rather than replacing it." The unanimous emphasis they place on functional interdependence, he suggests, leads them to ignore factors of class conflict, status antagonism, and centre-periphery tension that state corporatism is designed to suppress. Schmitter (1974: 115-116) finds the record of societal corporatist theorists, especially Shonfield, better, suggesting they have set us off to an "impressive, if still speculative, start" in our understanding of this animal. But if the theory of corporatism within liberal democracies is better, that does not make it good. For there is herein also a pronounced — indeed, unmistakable — tendency in most instances to ignore the question of which class interests liberal corporatism serves. This tendency is the product of the widespread assumption that liberal capitalist societies, while subject to tension and strain, are no longer subject to contradiction with the coming of the welfare state and state economic planning. It is assumed, rather than demonstrated, in other words, that there is in fact an underlying social harmony in modern capitalist societies and that in the circumstances the concept of national or public interest is an unproblematic one. Characteristic in this regard is Shonfield's (1965:128) assertion that French planning is a "conspiracy in the public interest between big business and big officialdom." As Watson (1975:461) has recently pointed out, "whether and why it is in the public interest, he seems to take for granted."

There are three specific, although highly interrelated, areas in which the liberal corporatist paradigm may be judged deficient. There is, first of all, a critical lack of a rigorous theory of the state in advanced capitalist society, despite the large, important, even determining role that is assigned to the state in the corporatist framework. There appears to be a theoretical closure to the question of whether the increased role and changing functions of the state is not a product of the changing needs of the capitalist class in terms of maintaining its political, economic, and ideological dominance. That is not to say that instances of bias are not discerned (although it is usually assumed that the state's role has been to reduce power differentials between the classes), but that the question of a *systematic* bias toward capitalist class dominance on the part of the state is not addressed.

Second, there is an assumption that the functional representation in economic decision-making of trade unions and business organizations takes place within the framework of an equivalence of power and influence between the two. This assumption is one that derives from traditional liberal theory. It is based on the view that if producers' organizations voluntarily enter into a "social contract," they must do so on the basis of equality, just as liberal economic theory assumes with regard to individuals in the market. As Macpherson has pointed out, liberal freedoms allowed capitalism to appear "as the system in which production is carried on without authoritarian allocation of work on rewards, but by contractual relations between free individuals (each possessing some resources be it only his labour-power) who calculate their most profitable course of action and employ their resources as that calculation dictates." But at the same time, "the market economy, with its concentration of capital ownership and its distribution of rewards in accordance with the marginal productivity of each of the contributors to the product, maintained a massive inequality between owners and workers" (Macpherson, 1973:180-181). The importance of liberal democracy for capitalism lies in the guarantee of individual legal and political equality which makes the wage contract *appear* as an exchange between equals in a massively unequal society. The importance of liberal democracy for corporatism in such a society is that the guarantee of legal and political equality for functional groups makes the "social contract" appear as an exchange between equals, despite vast inequalities between the groups in power and distributional terms. The assumption of equivalence within the liberal corporatist paradigm has led to the valid concern that "it may be that corporatism obscures as much about different configurations of power as the notion of pluralism has" (Martin,

1975a: 56 n.19).

Finally, there has been a tendency to ignore the high degree of instability that marks corporatist structures within liberal democracy. This has been particularly evident in the crucial area of incomes policy, where tripartite structures have proved difficult to establish in the first place, and much more difficult to protect from breakdown once established. But it extends to economic planning structures as well, or at least to the instability of cooperative group behaviour within them. The tendency to ignore, or at least the inability to explain, this instability is largely a product of the above-mentioned defects — the assumptions of underlying social harmony, state neutrality vis-à-vis the groups, and power equivalence between them. In the absence of underlying social harmony between classes, and in the face of policy outputs which reflect capitalist class dominance vis-á-vis the state and trade unions, the latter have often had to opt out of corporatist structures, or at least abstain from accommodative behavior if they were not to be repudiated by their rank-and-file membership. This very instability brings us directly back to the question raised at the beginning, i.e., whether state coercion, at least in the form of repressing rank-and-file actions and insulating union leadership from its effects, is not a "sine qua non" of establishing stable corporatist structures. And this raises in turn the fundamental question of the contradiction between corporatism and political freedom.

It has not been our intention to suggest that these concerns have been entirely overlooked among students of corporatism within liberal democracy. Lehmbruch (1974) addresses the question of instability in the face of class conflict; Schmitter (1974) explicitly raises the element of class dominance; and all the above concerns are central to Harris's (1972) study of modern British Conservatism and my own study of modern British Labour (Panitch, 1976a). But these contributions have been made by a minority of students of liberal corporatism, and have yet to be systematically developed. In the pages that follow we shall attempt to make a further contribution toward that development.

II

In his seminal essay, Schmitter suggests that students of corporatism avoid the tempting game of finding fascism under the bed of every tripartite structure in liberal democracies, and, more generally that we avoid tying it to any particular ideology or political movement. The advice is well taken. But it does not mean that we should ignore the question of the similarities between fascist and liberal corporatism in terms of origin, structure, behavior, or internal contradiction. And Schmitter himself places fascist and liberal corporatism under the same definitional and historical rubric, while discerning the important differences between them. Bowen (1947:5-6), writing shortly after the end of World War II, insightfully noted:

> Italian Fascism and German Nazism lie in ruins, but many of the economic and cultural forces that brought them into existence have not ceased to operate. ...Unless Germany's social structure should be completely revolutionized in the near future, important sections of the community may well continue to see in some kind of non-Marxian, non-liberal social ideal the promise of class harmony, national solidarity and economic stability.

Before turning to an examination of the structural factors which may be seen to account for the development of corporatism within liberal democracies, therefore, a short discussion on the admittedly less crucial ideological influences is necessary. What is most important to note, at the ideological level, is the common affinity of the three major governing ideologies in European liberal democracies — Catholicism, liberal-conservatism, and social democracy — to corporatist thought. Indeed, the common affinity is striking enough upon examination to have led one student of The Netherlands (Scholten, 1976:2) to suggest that consociationalism is less a product of ideological cleavage than of ideological congruence between "pillars" influenced by the common corporatist goal and that this congruence has been mobilized to "moderate, retard or even prevent the development in salience of other identification criteria which have greater potential for leading to social instability" (i.e., revolutionary socialism).

The corporatism of modern Catholic thought has been stressed enough to need no repetition here. What has been less noticed is the affinity between fascist corporatism and modern conservatism, at least in terms of their analysis of society's ills (but see Harris, 1972; Carpenter, 1976). This may be illustrated by comparing the following two quotations. The Italian Fascist Confederation of Industrialists, in a 1939 publication, stressed the necessity of correcting and neutralizing a condition brought about by the industrial revolution of the nineteenth century which associated capital and labor in industry, giving rise on the one hand to a capitalist class of employers of labour and on the other to a great propertyless class, the industrial proletariat. The juxtaposition of these classes inevitably led to the clash of their opposing interests. [quoted in Arendt, 1967:258 n.94]

The British Conservative industrialist, politician, and theorist, Aubrey Jones, a prime mover of corporatist structures under both Conservative and Labour governments, similarly contended in 1950:

> The greatest evil of all wrought by individualist capitalism was the division it drove between the two classes...status had been replaced by contract, and the labourer, preoccupied with the day, was left bargaining helplessly against an employer secure in the present and uncertain only about the future. ...The classic remedy for labour's plight, trade unionism, in fact solves only part of his troubles. ...[It] was never calculated to bridge the gap that had grown between employers and employed; it served rather to widen it and to exacerbate the strife between the two sides. For trade unionism itself became infested with the doctrine that the struggle of the classes was something inevitable; this struggle was looked upon as scrawling itself across the whole of history; and the more inevitable it is accepted to be, the more implacable and the more permanent does it become. [Jones, 1950: 24-27]

But if the analysis of the problem was common, the proposed remedy differed in important respects (although both, of course, addressed themselves to the need to eliminate conflict within capitalism, rather than capitalism itself).

> The Fascist answer is by organizing the people in groups according to their respective activities, groups which through their leaders...rise by stages as in a pyramid, at the base of which are the masses and at the apex the state. No group outside the state, no group against the state, all groups within the state...which...is the nation itself rendered articulate. [quoted in Arendt, 1967:258 n.95]

Jones, while a major Conservative spokesman for state intervention in the economy and a subsequent architect of a tripartite incomes policy enforced with the state's coercive powers, looked, on the other hand, to a more reformist, integrative solution:

> Conflict follows only because labour is an outsider in industry...the bigness or smallness of the common pool of profits means nothing to it; it is intent only on the size of its own share; and so it is tempted to act irresponsibly. It is so acting

today. This irresponsibility can be overcome only if labour is made to feel that it has the same purpose as capital, and that while they remain rivals, their rivalry is subordinate to a unity. That, after all, is the first condition of a healthy society. [Jones, 1950:28-29]

To this end, Jones recommended that the consultative system of voluntary joint union-employer production committees, which had evolved during World War II, be promoted: *"Authority remains with the employer, it is he who still controls. But those who are controlled are taken into his confidence; their views are solicited; and so the control, by becoming less of an imposition, is made to operate more effectively"* (Jones, 1950: 31; emphasis added). A more candid view of the liberal-conservative corporatist position is hard to come by.

The ideological affinities of social democracy and corporatism are less readily apparent. Certainly the movements that have evolved under their respective banners differ enough in social base as well as philosophy and practice to render ludicrous any attempt to revive the ill-conceived and tragic (in its consequences) strategy of the Communists in the late 1920s of attacking social democracy as social fasicsm. To be sure, the more stable tripartite arrangements in Europe have been established or at least sustained by social democratic parties, and it is a telling sign that social democracy has been reduced in some eyes to tripartism itself (see note 5). But social democracy, for all its gradualism and promotion of class cooperation, has always entailed more than a call for tripartism within capitalism. This is because its strategy did involve at least reducing the capitalist class's power through some public ownership and because it was a political movement with a predominantly working class base.

How, then, is the social democratic proclivity toward corporatist structures to be explained? Although the major factors are structural, set in the historical context of the timing of the ascension to office of social democratic parties, an important facilitating factor has been that dominant ideological strain within social democracy which rejects the notion of the class struggle as the dynamic of social change (see Panitch, 1971). Those who would search for the corporatist roots of social democracy will find them less in its explicit programmatic links with guild socialism as a left-wing variant of corporatism or even with the Fabian or Bernsteinian dislike for the "class war" methods of industrial bargaining, and more in the fundamental differences between social democracy and Marxism. A succint expression of the difference is to be found in Durbin's *The Politics of Democratic Socialism* (1940):

> if there is a principle of living more fundamental than another, of the human species — and therefore of history — it is the principle and practice of coopera-tion. [p. 186]
> It is radically false, therefore, to suppose that the dynamic element in social life is solely that of warfare and struggle — especially that of class struggle and class warfare. [p. 189]
> There is no end to the sectional disputes of free people. . .how are these disputes to be resolved?. . .the only solution that is compatible with the maintenance of social peace and the growth of mutual respect between contending groups is that of open and honest compromise. [p. 264]
> When individuals or groups disagree — including nations and classes and Parties within the state — the most important question is not what they disagree about, but the method by which their disputes are to be resolved. [p. 271]

This ideological linchpin of social democracy fits well with liberal corporatism, which, as Lehmbrunch (1974:3) points out, also "rests on the theoretical premise that there exists strong in-terdependence among the interests of conflicting social groups in a capitalist economy. This 'interdependence of interests' image of society is clearly opposed to the 'conflict of interests' image which (as in the Marxist concept of class conflict) stresses the ultimate in-compatibility of antagonistic group interests."

The importance of this ideological factor is to be seen in terms of the fact that corporatist structures and practices have developed more fully in the postwar period in those countries where confes-sional and social democratic unions have dominated the labour movement, including in the three countries which we examine in some detail in the following sections: The Netherlands, Sweden and Britain. Where a large communist movement has existed, on the other hand, the establishment of corporatist structures and prac-tices has been much less marked. Postwar Italy, and even postwar France, despite the major role played by the state in their post-war economies, have furnished far fewer examples of tripartism. Heisler's (1974:57) contention that societies that approximate his corporative "European polity model" exhibit a high level of development to coopt groups "virtually without regard to their supportive or opposing orientations to the regime and its norms" cannot be supported. If the communist movements of Italy and France are being "coopted" at present, it is far more due to their participation in the parliamentary institutions of liberal democracy than in the corporatist ones.[7]

But if ideology is an important factor, it is primarily a facilitating one rather than a creative one. To understand how and why ideology becomes operative, we have to understand the deeper structural factors that have impelled corporatist developments in liberal democracies. The example of Canada is instructive in this regard. Despite a strong Catholic corporatist tradition in Quebec (including the establishment of a Catholic trade union confederation), an English-speaking trade union leadership which was predominantly social democratic, and a powerful Liberal prime minister for almost a quarter of a century who explicitly ascribed to corporatist principles as early as 1918[8] and consistently held to them throughout his career, Canada has seen very little of liberal corporatist developments. Why? Because the petite-bourgeoisie remained the largest subordinate class in Canada until World War II; because, even subsequently, labour has rarely posed a *centralized* threat politically or industrially with which the state has been forced to deal; and because the Canadian economy has had so little autonomy from the American (the problem of incorporating multinational corporations in national economic planning is particularly marked in Canada's "branch-plant" industry). Ideas, if they are socially disembodied in the sense of not correlating with the major socioeconomic forces in a society, can themselves have little impact.

III

As we suggested earlier, although corportist tendencies in liberal democracies may be traced as far back as World War I, the introduction of corporatism as a widespread systematic process, with corporatist structures playing a significant political and economic role, is more properly traced (as it is by most scholars) to the World War II period. The crucial factor, and the fact that allows us to locate its development in a country like Sweden, or Norway, *before* the war, is the state's commitment to full employment. This provided the material basis for industrial militancy in the postwar period and for the reactive (in some cases preventative) introduction of incomes policies and social welfare measures designed to coerce or induce wage restraint on the part of trade unions. From its very inception, state social expenditure in the postwar period was introduced with the threat of wage pressure a key element in the policy equation.[9] More important, from our immediate perspective, is the fact that in virtually every liberal democratic country in which corporatist structures become at all important an incomes policy designed to abate the wage pressure of trade unions was the frontispiece of corporatist development.

The full employment commitment, and the consequences it had for greater state involvement in the economy and corporatism, was a product of *political* forces. It is often presented as a technical achievement, based on the Keynesian discovery of the budgetary deficit as a solution to the disease of underconsumption and the attendant depressionary symptoms of the capitalist economy, and on the administrative planning experience and political confidence acquired by the state in the war economy. Yet not only had the experience of the war economy existed before (and in any case the kind of planning adopted during World War II was largely abandoned afterwards), but the Keynesian "discovery" (as advocated by Keynes as well as other economists) had been available for well over a decade before its widespread acceptance. Governments in capitalist democracies, with the main exceptions of Sweden and Norway, had explicitly rejected a policy of increasing employment through budgetary deficits during the depression. As the economist Kalecki pointed out in a brilliant article in 1943, the reason for this rejection largely lay in the negative attitude of big business. This attitude was based on a number of concerns. First, the desire to maintain the powerful controlling device over governments which the need to sustain "business confidence" entailed in a "laissez faire" economy governed by the principles of "sound finance"; second, the suspicion of government spending, particularly of the kind of spending necessary to maintain effective demand in the Keynesian context, i.e., public investment and the subsidising of mass consumption (the former constituting a potential competition to private investment, the latter undermining the fundamentals of cpaitalist ethics — as Kalecki puts it: "You shall earn your bread in sweat — unless you happen to have private means"). Their main concern, however, was that

> under a regime of full employment, "the sack" would cease to play its role as a disciplinary measure. The social position of the boss would be undermined and the self assurance and class consciousness of the working class would grow,

> strikes for wage increases and improvements in conditions of work would create political tension. It is true that profits would be higher under a regime of full employment than they are on the average under "laissez-faire," and even the rise in wage rates resulting from the stronger bargaining power of the workers is less likely to reduce profits than to increase prices, and to affect adversely only the rentier interests. But "discipline in the factories" and "political stability" are more appreciated by the business leaders than profits. Their class instinct tells them that lasting full employment is unsound from their point of view and that unemployment is an integral part of the normal capitalist system. [Kalecki 1971:140-141]

As Kalecki pointed out, business leaders in the Allied countries had come during World War II to agree that "something must be done during a slump," but the conflict continued as to the direction of government intervention and as to whether it should be used merely to alleviate slumps or to secure sustained full employment. But, although the outcome was still indeterminate at the time Kalecki wrote, he recognized the possibility that continuing opposition to full employment might at least temporarily be overcome "under the pressure of the masses." It was precisely this pressure that did turn the tide, as the political dangers of not introducing full employment loomed far larger and far more immediate than the political danger of introducing it. The necessity of sustaining trade union cooperation during the course of the war with the promise of continued prominence in decision-making after the war and a commitment not to return to prewar conditions; the recognition that the experience of full employment and comprehensive planning had led to rising expectations of a postwar rise in living standards and security on the part of the working class; the example of the Soviet economy (much played up during the wartime alliance) and the concern regarding its effect on the working class in the postwar period; and, finally, the mass radicalism that exhibited itself in the electoral success of working class parties in the immediate postwar years — these were elements in the final decision.

It was the changing balance of class forces which attended the commitment to full employment and the consequent development of economic planning to deal with its consequences that lay at the heart of corporatist developments. The point has been made by Warren (1972:3-4): "Full employment policy...was a product of the fear of the *political* repercussions of a repetition of the mass unemployment of the 1930s. Capitalist planning was, on the contrary, designed to deal with the economic, as much as the political, consequences of full employment policies." The consequence of full employment was that trade unions were in a much stronger position than heretofore to raise money wages. If these increases were passed on in price increases, however, this had the effect, given the growth rate of productivity, of affecting a country's foreign competitiveness. If the increases were not passed on in an inflationary spiral, on the other hand, the motor force of the capitalist economy — profits — tended to be squeezed. It was this problem that provided the spur to state economic planning in the postwar era, directed both at raising productivity (and hence economic growth) and inducing trade unions to cooperate in an incomes policy which would restrain money wage demands.

Although specific factors have affected the character and timing of developments in each country, corporatist structures have been most pronounced precisely in those countries where incomes policy has been at the heart of economic planning. Although the operative details of the various systems cannot be adumbrated here, Sweden (see Shonfield, 196: 189-211; Martin, 1975b; Van Otter, 1975; Sunesson, 1966) and The Netherlands (see Shonfield, 1965: 211-220; Peper, 1975; Edelman and Fleming, 1965) may be taken as two major examples of postwar economic planning being secondary or at least facilitative to the early establishment of incomes policy as the central focus of economic policy, although direct state intervention in the wage bargaining process differs markedly in the two systems. Britain, on the other hand, provides a prime example of tripartite economic planning structures being developed in the first place with the primary aim of inducing the trade unions to cooperate in the incomes policy (see Panitch, 1976a; Corina, 1975; Dorfman, 1973). However, where a tripartite incomes policy has not been central to economic planning, as in France, planning has been a much more closed exercise, largely confined to senior civil servants and big business, with "functional representation," including that of organized labour, largely passed by. When emphasis has been given to achieving tripartite consensus in the context of French planning, wage restraint via an incomes policy has provided the motivation for, and the central content of, discussions (Shonfield, 1965: 130-131, 143; Hayward, 1966, 1972).

It would be wrong, of course, to tie corporatist developments solely to incomes policy. For instance, the specific geopolitical location of Austria and West Germany in the postwar balance of international forces may be seen as a particularly powerful factor in cementing an institutionalized alliance between capital and social democratic-led labour. Moreover, even within the economic policy framework, the transition to advanced capitalism required much more state involvement in the economy than was directly necessitated by the full employment commitment or the formalized process of indicative planning. To facilitate capital accumulation under monopoly capitalism (as well as to the end of securing the economic growth and higher productivity to accommodate consumer demand and increased wage costs), the state promoted the tendency toward even greater industrial concentration, undertook to socialize the risks of private production through subsidies, tax write-offs, building infrastructure, manpower training, and so on, and sought to integrate private and public investment and planning decisions. To the end of legitimating this increased state-business interface, as well as to facilitate labour cooperation at the level of individual industries, joint consultative structures, works councils, and the like were often promoted. Moreover, access to the state was made relatively easy for groups other than business. But insofar as this entailed the *offer* of an effective say for labour in national economic policy (rather than a formalized, legitimating process such as the annual presentation of views to the Cabinet), the topic of the unions administering a wage restraint policy to their members or at least moving toward centralized wage bargaining (to contain as much as possible wage drift) never lagged far behind.

The reason that incomes policy generally lies at the heart of corporatist developments is that, far more than is the case in other fields of state intervention in the economy, it requires the direct cooperation of the trade unions. Unions might be induced to legitimate other policies, such as taxation policy, automation, manpower policy, asnd so on, but the administrative arm remains the state or the corporation. The union is the direct object of an incomes policy, however, for it is its behaviour the policy is designed to affect, and it must be the vehicle for administering the policy to the rank and file. And because business groups must in turn agree to at least nominal state supervision of prices, profits, and dividends, the stage is set for that cooperative behavior between the groups themselves in the framing and administering of public policy that is the "distinguishing trait" of liberal corporatism. Moreover, the establishment of a wage norm inevitably involves the unions in discussions of what fiscal, monetary, and even private and public investment policies are consistent with the norm. With a social democratic party in office, the prospect of union influence on decision-making and of state control over profits and prices and thus the distribution of incomes becomes a tempting inducement to union cooperation in wage restraint.

The process we have been describing can be theoretically explicated by employing a theory of the state along the lines suggested recently by Miliband (1969) and Poulantzas (1973). If we employ a theory of the state which permits it to respond *only* to the needs and demands of the capitalist class, our location of the origin of corporatist planning and incomes policy developments in the victory of the working class on the full employment issue makes little sense. If we employ a theory of the state, on the other hand, which sees the state as relatively autonomous from this class, acting on its behalf but not necessarily at its behest, we can discern how the state responds directly to various class pressures. As Miliband has pointed out with regard to Marx's famous formulation that "the executive of the modern state is but a committee for managing the common affairs of the whole bourgeoisie": "The notion of common affairs assumes the existence of particular ones; and the notion of the whole bourgeoisie implies the existence of separate elements which make up that whole. This being the case, there is an obvious need for an institution of the kind [Marx and Engels] refer to, namely the state, and the state *cannot* meet this end without enjoying a certain degree of autonomy. In other words, that nature of autonomy is embedded in the definition itself, is an intrinsic part of it" (Miliband, 1973: 85 n.4). Precisely because of this relative autonomy, the actions of the state have to be "situated within the field of the class struggle" (Gough, 1975:64). At times, the state will intervene against the short-term interest of the capitalist class as a whole, or even against the long-term interests of a fraction of that class to the end of engaging in compromises and sacrifices which will maintain the long-term interests of the whole class. This was precisely the basis for the introduction of successful reforms in the postwar era; they were reforms in the true sense — i.e., they left untouched the fundamental structure of capitalist society, but nevertheless constituted material economic and social gains for the working class.

The shift in the balance of class forces after World War II (and before it in Sweden and Norway) has been widely recognized by most students of advanced capitalism. Unfortunately, however, it has been usually correspondingly assumed that at this time the state shed its systematic relationship with the class structure and emerged as Brenner (1969:119) puts it, as "the political arm of the community." But the autonomy evidenced in the state's interventionism and the access given to noncapitalist groups do not entail state independence from the system of class domination. Indeed, the fact that the state operates within the confines of capitalism usually ensures that the functions of state activity often diverge from their historical origins. As Gough (1975:76) puts it: "Social policies originally the product of class struggle will, in the absence of further struggle, be absorbed and adapted to the benefit of the dominant class."

This can be seen from the conclusions to the major recent survey of planning in the liberal democratic state since Shonfield's study.

> The nature of planning is to be judged in the first place by its works. Such a balance sheet shows that the social reforming potential, which has not lacked government sponsors, has proved largely illusory, dominated by the preoccupation with management of the economic system of modern capitalism. This establishes the real sense in which planning is compatible with the mixed economy, insofar as it works for the maintenance of the social and political structure associated with it rather than for its change. [Watson, 1975:447]

The outcome in terms of the distribution of resources may be seen by taking what is generally judged to be the strongest case of corporatist planning with a social purpose — that of Sweden. Despite the widespread myth with regard to the income redistribution effects of Swedish policy, a report submitted to the Landsorganisation (LO; the Swedish confederation of trade unions) shortly before the strike explosion of the late sixties which shook the corporatist system found that not only had there been no marked change in income distribution since 1948, but that the fraction of persons with 40% or less of mean income had considerably increased, while the group with "normal" income decreased and the proportion with high incomes increased. This was matched by a growing concentration of wealth in Sweden (Anderman, 1967:111).[10]

This kind of outcome may be attributed partly to the imbalance between the groups in corporatist arrangements. In characterizing the postwar British system as "quasi-corporatist," Beer identified the source for the power of functional organizations in the state's need for the expert advice in the formation of policy, for their acquiescence or voluntary agreement to administer state policies, and for their approval and legitimation of state policy in the eyes of their members. It was particularly the state's need of these things from the unions, according to Beer (1969:211), which accounted for their "unrecognizably transformed power position." My own study of economic policy-making in Britain in the postwar period (Panitch, 1976a) has shown, however, that government policies were repeatedly formed either without first securing the advice of the unions, or after having explicitly rejected their advice. It was not their advice, but their acquiescence and approval which were studiously courted, usually *after* policy decisions were reached. The advice on which the 1966 Labour Government acted in introducing massive deflation and a statutory wage freeze and abandoning the economic plan was that of the Confederation of British Industry, the City of London, and Britain's foreign creditors, in light of the latter's immediate concern to protect the pound against devaluation. Indeed, even when this advice proved faulty in the extreme, as devaluation was eventually forced on the Government, Labour had to continue to promote private business incentive to foster economic growth. For insofar as the logic of class cooperation ruled out command reformist planning, it also ruled out a redistributive fiscal policy.

Watson (1975:468) has put the point more generally, summing up the planning experience of France, Italy, and Britain:

> Notwithstanding the participation of a variety of interests, an established hierarchy has exerted on the effectiveness of their contributions. A *de facto* convergence between planners, officials and industrial management has dominated the process. . . . Undoubtedly some planners and officials have regretted the extent of this alignment, but seen it as virtually inevitable, given the lack of trade union expertise. Notwithstanding the great improvement that has occurred in national accounts and statistics, information from industry remains crucial for the planners designs, especially when they are seeking to deal directly with specific problems, which the strategic, operational orientation of planning involves. Yet the reluctance of industrialists to disclose information, particularly to the unions, has not diminished. Here planning has singularly failed to bring about explicitness in decision-making.

That a similar situation existed in Sweden, despite the vaunted "partnership" between the LO and the central employers federation, can be seen in the LO's demand in the early seventies, after the system was shaken by rank-and-file unrest, that the unions be provided information by employers on their recruitment policy and labour force planning. Without direct access to managerial information, and with a staff of 90 at the LO headquarters, for the requisite "expertise" the LO had to develop for corporatist policy-making it was obviously highly dependent on its "partner."

What this suggests is that the bias of the system is less attributable to direct pressure from business than to the logic entailed in state planning in a capitalist economy. To quote Watson (1975:458) again:

> The expertise on which planning has been based requires that there be definite constants in the economic process, above all in its authority structure. Social science solutions rely on people behaving as their assigned role requires. Insofar as planning has been the medium for propagating the reasoning underpinning such solutions, the circle involved has remained the very restricted one of those having a direct relationship to the management function, whether at the micro or macro level, since they are the ones on which successful steering is taken essentially to depend. The system is viewed as structured to permit management a discrete, specialized, and hierarchical function.

The consequence of this is that planning's success rests on the participants' speaking the same language as management, given the state's prior acceptance of the prevailing authority structures in industry. Indeed, one of corporatism's main functions appears to be a matter of diffusing this language among the union leadership, who have often been willing apprentices since without it their concerns appear to be irrelevant, if not hostile, to the planning exercise. It is in this manner, as much as through the overt pressure of particular capitalist interests, that corporatism within liberal democracies has become a powerful vehicle for reinforcing class dominance.

But it is also in this light that the instability of corporatism within liberal democracies must be understood. For in accepting the one-dimensional rationality entailed in its decision-making, trade union leaders become unable to promote the interests of their membership. Moreover, since their primary involvement in the system relates to the economy's problem with wage pressure, rather to a mere legitimizing role they might play, they are forced to carry this rationality back to their members in the concrete, if unpalatable, form of wage restraint. Not surprisingly, in the absence of effective union input in economic decision-making and in the absence of extensive price and profit controls and a redistributive fiscal policy, union leaders eventually come under heavy pressure from their membership to withdraw from the incomes policy structures and abstain from cooperative behaviour in broader economic planning structures. The legitimation and union action which the state needs, in other words, delegitimizes the union leadership in the eyes of their base.

IV

The foremost example of corporatism's instability is that of Britain. The Trades Union Congress (TUC) was first forced to withdraw from the tripartite wages policy in which it had cooperated for two years when the General Council suffered a rare defeat at the 1950 congress on the issue. Having been once burned, and without the pull of loyalty to the Labour Party, the TUC refused participation when the question was broached by the Conservatives in the 1950s, and although they joined the tripartite National Economic Development Council when it was established to induce them to cooperate in an incomes policy in the early sixties, they refused to cooperate with the Conservative Government's pay pause or National Incomes Commission. When the latter was swept away after Labour's 1964 victory, the unions joined in a voluntary tripartite policy on the promise of full employment, a national economic plan, and extensive trade union input in decision-making. But under the impact of the introduction of statutory backing (only three months after the policy was inaugurated, at the insistence of Britain's foreign creditors and the domestic financial community), the abandonment of planning and full employment, and price control of a mainly symbolic nature, the unions, after three years of extensive cooperation, were forced by the defeat of right-wing union leaders, and rank-and-file dissent which culminated in the wage and strike explosion of 1969, to withdraw their cooperation. Since then we have seen the Heath government's unsuccessful attempt to reestablish corporatist arrangements through its incomes policy of 1972-1974, and the eventual breakdown of the more successful Social Contract at the end of the 1974-79 Labour Government's term of office.

It is mainly those union leaderships which are highly insulated from membership pressures at the plant level which can sustain participation in corporatist arrangements for any considerable period of time. It is no coincidence that those societies most commonly listed as corporatist — Austria, Norway, Sweden and The

Netherlands — contain the most highly centralized union confederations in the western world.[11] This insulation may be provided
by central bargaining and control over strike funds, the purposive
atrophy of union locals, and the underrepresentation of opposi-
tional elements at the central level, as well as by the state's use of its
coercive powers to prohibit unofficial strikes and provide a
statutory framework for collective bargaining and incomes policy
with severe penalties against their breach.

Under many of these conditions, the corporatist arrangements of
Sweden and The Netherlands have proved more stable than the
British. But what is striking as one examines these systems more
closely is that this stability was highly precarious while it lasted.
The voluntaristic incomes policy contained in the Swedish annual
central negotiations was effectively established during the 1950s only after the unions had opted out of a state-imposed wages policy
similar to the British in the late 1940s (Martin, 1975b:429-432).
And even this system, sustained as it was by an active manpower
policy pursued by the government, was far more subject to disruptive influences than is generally recognized or admitted by the central actors. As has been recently demonstrated, unofficial strikes
have been fairly common in Swedish industry at the plant level
throughout the postwar period, although "the myth of labour
peace and the focus of interest on the institutional structure have
long obscured this fact" (Fulcher, 1973:52). It is this shop-floor
power which has provided the basis for the extensive wage drift
which occurs outside the central wage agreement. This suggests that

> in the Swedish case more and more open conflict appears as one descends from
> the central level of organizational interaction to the shop-floor. The pattern of
> this conflict and its similarity with that of other industrial societies suggest that
> whatever the institutional superstructure, the economic and technological
> substructure tends to impose their own pattern. [Fulcher, 1973:54]

To those less subject to accept the LO's explanation of employer-
union peace in terms of "we has a meeting" (Shonfield, 1965:199),
then, the explosion of industrial strife in the late 1960s and early
1970s was likely to come as less of a surprise. The industrial unrest
of this period weakened the power of the central union organization, and, following the 1974 settlement, a new wave of unofficial
strikes hit the economy.

In the Dutch case, the debacle came earlier, as should perhaps be expected from a policy that was much more obviously one of wage restraint, and one in which the state was much more directly involved. The policy for years held back The Netherland's real wages to a level below that of other European countries, and it would have been impossible to sustain but for the coercive powers that backed it up and the extremely high degree of central union bureaucratic independence from rank and file. By the late 1950s, rank-and-file pressure (including the formation of independent unions outside the recognized structure) led to a reorientation of the policy (significantly, after the socialists left the governing coalition, thus weakening the pull of loyalty on the socialist union leadership). The unofficial strikes and wage explosion of 1963 finally convinced the union leadership that they could not hold the line and led to their subsequent rejection of central wage controls. The strikes of the last decade, and the union decentralization that has accompanied them, have indicated that the system cannot easily be put together again (see Peper, 1975; Marx and Kendell, 1971; von Tijn, 1964; Turner and Jackson, 1969).

The manifest instability of corporatist arrangements in liberal democracies by the late sixties and early 1970s has led in most cases to a state response of a coercive kind. In Sweden this was seen in the government taking the unprecedented step of suspending the right to strike for public employees in 1971. In The Netherlands, it was seen in the Law of Wage Formation (submitted to Parliament in 1968 and passed in 1970) which permitted the government to invalidate wage contracts which were considered detrimental to the national economy. It must be noted again that in neither of these countries was this coercive intrusion entirely new. Since 1928, unofficial strikes in Sweden (more particularly strikes and related actions during the period of an agreement) have been prohibited by law. The famous 1938 Basic Agreement between the LO and the employers federation, the linchpin of the postwar incomes policy, was itself struck under an immediate government threat of legislation. In the "guided wage policy" of The Netherlands, statutory powers played a major role. These older coercive elements already tainted the much-vaunted voluntarist nature of liberal corporatism. The new controls did even more so.

The shift toward coercion was more striking in Britain because of the previous absence of statutory interference in collective bargaining. It began with the statutory incomes policy of 1965 (which required unions to refrain from pursuing any agreement referred to the Prices and Incomes Board for a four-month period) and was maintained in the face of union opposition throughout the life of the Labour Govenrment. It took on new dimensions in 1968-1969 when the Government attempted to impose a compulsory cooling-off period on unofficial strikes. This development had indeed been foreseen as necessary inside the Government as early as 1965, when the incomes policy was inaugurated. The Ministry of Labour had seen "one obvious general problem" with the new tripartite arrangements:

> If trade union leaders accept these wide responsibilities there is a risk they will cease to be regarded as representative of their members' interests and their influence and authority may be transferred to unofficial leaders. [U.K. Ministry of Labour, 1965:3]

The proposed legislation was withdrawn when the furor it produced in the labour movement led to the revolt of the party caucus, but not before the Government attempted to get the TUC to rewrite its constitution to expel unions which failed to apply sanctions against unofficial strikers. The effort failed in the face of pressure on the union leadership from the rank and file. This was followed, after the Labour Government's defeat in 1970, by the Conservative's Industrial Relations Act, which reserved the very term "trade union" only for those organizations that registered under the act and which undertook to discipline unofficial strikers, whose actions were in any case now made illegal by the act.

The primary aim of these coercive measures was not to destroy trade unions, as was often alleged in the course of the labour movement's struggle against them, but rather to define, codify, and back by state sanctions the obligations of unions to employers and the state in a way consistent with securing a stable corporatism. The philosophy behind them was perhaps best expresed, in explicitly corporatist terms, by none other than Shonfield (1968:284) as a member of the Royal Commission on Trade Unions and Employers Associations:

> The distinction between labour organizations which explicitly accept certain responsibilities towards society as a whole, as well as toward their members, and those which refuse to do so needs to be pressed further. This should be done by demanding of trade unions the fulfilment of certain minimum standards of behaviour...notably those which express the duty of trade unions to conduct their industrial relations in such a way as not to hold back improvements in the standard of living of the community as a whole.

If trade unions as voluntary democratic organizations were not going to adopt a corporatist conception of the national interest, then state coercive force was necessary to make them do so.

But the line between authoritarian and liberal corporatism is not as thin as this would suggest. For what has been remarkable about the recent development of the state's coercive force over labour is its ineffectiveness. The inability of the Swedish labour courts to stop the dockers' strike of May 1970, despite its application of maximum fines on 78 workers, was symptomatic of the problem, and in most cases the unofficial strikes did not lead to prosecution (Fulcher, 1973:54-55). The Law of Wage Formation in The Netherlands was met with implacable union opposition and led to the withdrawal of the two largest of the three labour centres from the preparation of the semiannual economic reports in the Social and Economic Council, "an act of key significance, an open show of noncooperation, which ruptured the established system of industrial relations" (Peper, 1975:132-133). This action, together with the mobilization surrounding the one-hour general strike of December 1970 and the setbacks suffered by the Christian parties in the 1971 elections, led to the emasculation of the law by the new government. In Britain, the Industrial Relations Act was rendered inoperative within three months of its implementation by the refusal of most trade unions to register under it, and more significantly by the real threat of a general strike in the face of the imprisonment of five unofficial docks leaders.

The reason behind the ineffectiveness of the new state coercive measures in this area is to be found in the contradiction they pose to liberal democracy itself. To meet the challenge of a working class united against the operation of laws that contradict the freedoms of their indigenous class organizations, coercive measures have to go far beyond the immediate field of industrial relations. To have made these laws operable, the extensive use of police powers would likely have been necessary, and probably would have involved limiting the rights to mobilize opposition through free speech and assembly. It woud have entailed, in other words, the abrogation of liberal democracy itself. It should be pointed out that, even under fascism, industrial class struggle continued to take place in the form of indiscipline, abstentions from work, and even sectional wage demands (Mason, 1966). What kept the conflict closed (it was never healed) was the iron fist of the state preventing the working class from mobilizing and unifying itself industrially or politically.

That the advanced capitalist state has backed off from such a venture may be attributed partly to the self-identification of political leaders and the capitalist class itself with the principles of liberal democracy. More important still, however, must be the risks it would entail for a capitalist society with a large working class prepared to defend its indigenous organizations and itself highly conscious of the value of political freedom.

The foregoing does not suggest by any means that we have seen the end of corporatist developments in advanced capitalist liberal democracies. On the contrary, in the absence of much evidence of the immediate emergence of a political movement (with the possible exception of Italy and France) which would merge with and go beyond the massive industrial militancy of the last decade, and particularly in countries with social democratic governments, we are likely to see a further cycle of the establishment, breakdown, and reestablishment of corporatist structures. To be sure, it is unlikely that these cycles can be continued indefinitely, and, in the face of the inability of the working class to effect its own resolution to capitalism's contradictions, the dynamics of these repeated cycles will eventually lead to a fully authoritarian response by the state. In any event, it is certainly clear that the much-vaunted view of corporatism as representing a new avenue of democratic stability for advanced capitalism contains no fewer contradictions than the traditional corporatist theory itself.

NOTES

1. For useful discussions, in English, of European corporatist theory, see especially Bowen (1947), Elbow (1966) and Harris (1972). Schmitter's "Still the Century of Corporatism?" (1974) provides an outstanding bibliography and introduction to the range of corporatist thinkers.

2. The early American experience is covered in Draper (1961) and in Weinstein (1968), although both are too ready to identify as corporatism any form of class collaboration.

3. For examples of this form of use of the term see my *Social Democracy and Industrial Militancy* (Panitch, 1976a: 4, 124, 131). In the mid-1970's it became more commonly employed, at least in the Canadian and British press, as a descriptive term (with only continuing nuances of opprobrium) for Trudeau's "New Society" and Wilson's "Social Contract" programmes of wage restraint. And the Executive Council of the Canadian Labour Congress went so far in the "Manifesto" presented to the May 1976 convention as to condemn Trudeau's "New Society" proposals as

"liberal corporatism" (where "tripartism would mean that the institutions of organized labour would function to ensure the acquiescence of workers to decisions in which their representatives have no real power"), but to advocate a system of "social corporatism" where labour would be an "equal partner" in economic decision-making with business and government. The use of the term in a positive sense produced widespread outrage at the convention, however, and the leadership amended the document, perhaps tellingly, to read "social democracy" rather than "social corportism." See Canadian Labour Congress (1976).

4. The phrase is from Paul and Winkler (1975:31). This widely read article, by two British sociologists, is not without its insights, but stands as a prime contemporary example of the lack of definitional rigour and loose thinking in much theorizing about corporatism.

5. Apart from Presthus's (1973) utter confusion between the two, Heisler (1974: 42ff., 88) also tends towards a conflation of corporatism and consociationalism.

6. Both Brenner (1969) and Schmitter (1974) provide useful contrasts between the pluralist and corportist paradigms.

7. Heisler (1974:87) does not explicitly consider Italy as approximating his model, but he does France.

8. See King (1973). The consistency with which the views expressed in this book were held over time may be seen from an entry to the *King Diaries* on June 29, 1937. On a visit to Germany at the time, King had been impressed above all with the corporative element in German fascism, almost to the total neglect of its effects on working class institutions and the freedom of working people. "They are truly establishing an industrial commonwealth, and other nations would be wise to evolve rapidly on similar lines of giving to labour its place in the control of industry." For a fuller discussion of this see Panitch (1976b).

9. The widely influential Beveridge report (1945), which laid the programmatic foundations for the British welfare state and, it might be argued, for the postwar capitalist state generally, explicitly placed the responsibility for the avoidance of inflation on the unions, demanding a unified wage restaint policy as a "quid pro quo" for full employment and social services.

10. Anderman's (1967) conclusions are drawn from the findings of the 1964 Swedish Royal Commission on Taxation. On the regressivity of the Swedish tax system see Van Otter (1975: 222-223). For similar findings in Britain see Nicholson (1967) and Blackburn (1967).

11. For an index of union centralization see Headey (1970: Table 5, 434-433). On the index, the confederations of the countries mentioned score from 25 to 35 in centralization — as compared with those of France, Britain, the United States, and Italy, which score from 0 to 5.

6

Liberal Corporatism and Party Government

Gerhard Lehmbruch
University of Konstanz, Germany

The progress of corporatist ideas since the late nineteenth century
and the advent of authoritarian "corporatist" regimes in the twentieth century have been strongly fostered by critiques of parliamentary and party government. To be sure, corporatist doctrines have
not been unanimous in their assessment of universal suffrage,
parliament, and competitive party systems. While on the one hand
authors such as Spann (1934) proposed to abolish parliament, that
"*Schwatzbude*," and to replace it by a representation of "estates,"
others merely proposed to redress the alleged shortcomings of
parliamentary democracy by adding a system of corporate
representation. For example, Catholic "Solidarists" (a school
which has been important in the German-speaking countries), proposed a Chamber of Corporations which should supplement, but
not substitute for, a parliament based on political parties (Mayer-
Tasch, 1971:60). On the other hand, a socialist party leader, the
"Austro-Marxist" theorist Bauer, under the influence of early
Soviet experience as well as English "guild socialism," pleaded for
the improvement of merely "formal" or "political" democracy
(i.e., bourgeois-dominated parliamentary government based on
universal suffrage) by "functional democracy," which demands
that "the government in each single branch of its activity rests in
continual understanding with the organized whole of the citizens,
who, according to their profession or their plant, according to their
social and economic function are immediately concerned by that

particular branch of government activity" (Bauer, 1923: 187). But
for all variations in corporatist doctrine, in their majority they did
have an antiparliamentary flavor. This is still more true of the
praxis of authoritarian regimes who have adopted corporatist
devices. Having abolished free universal suffrage, the competitive
party system, and parliamentary government, modern dictator-
ships use alternative techniques of consensus mobilization: either
the disciplined mass "movement" or a system of "state corporatism" (Schmitter, 1974).

It has been asserted that in a number of Western European countries patterns of associational interest representation have been
emerging that might be covered by the label of "neocorporatism."
Schmitter (1974) has described them as "societal corporatism." I
have stressed other aspects of the phenomenon by distinguishing
"liberal" from "authoritarian" corporatism (Lehmbruch, 1974a).
For, in contrast to the latter, the "new corporatism" of Western
and Northern Europe has remained embedded in a system of liberal
constitutional democracy, comprising institutional rules such as
freedom of association. It is true that with "neocorporatism" the
classical liberal distinction between the "state" and "society" is
being blurred. And the voluntary character of membership in large
interest associations due to strong social pressures may often
become rather a fiction. Instead, the relationship of the individual
and the organization may in practice come close to compulsory
membership (Schmitter, 1974).[1] However, the large organizations
themselves enter voluntarily into such "corporatist" relationships.
In principle they even remain free to terminate them. This may
eventually involve considerable costs, such as disapprobation by
"established public opinion." But the Dutch experience in particular (where the once extremely cooperative labor unions later
went into strong opposition) demonstrates that withdrawal of
organizations from corporatist "partnership" is by no means impossible. A central problem of a genetic theory of neocorporatism,
thus, is how — in the absence of coercion from the state — the decision of large organizations to enter (or to continue) a "liberal corporatist" cooperation may be explained.

I will argue in this article that the conditions of such choices are
at the same time relevant for understanding the relationship of
liberal corporatism with party government and its cross-national
variations. The problem here is whether in liberal democracies, too,
corporatism tends to replace parliamentary government and the

party system in their functions for policy-formation. It might be that under this functional aspect "authoritarian" and "liberal" corporatism bear a fundamental resemblance. Perhaps this resemblance is only somewhat concealed, due to the fact that liberal corporatism is a much less doctrinaire phenomenon than the classical variety. Of course, supporters of liberal corporatism in general have not proposed to substitute an alternative institutional arrangement for parliamentary and party government.[2] But since "liberal-corporatist" patterns have evolved in a rather pragmatic manner, they may quite imperceptibly be on the point of superseding representative government. Apprehensions of this sort are obviously entertained by supporters of the classical liberal tradition.

To speculations of this sort I propose to oppose a somewhat more refined hypothesis: the relationships of corporatism and party government, in highly developed capitalist countries with liberal constitutional governments, tend to develop toward a structural differentiation into subsystems which permits them to absorb higher problem loads. Instead of being rivals, both subsystems are interconnected by a sort of symbiosis which may take varying forms. This relationship, however, may not be a stable one. In some cases there seems to exist a trend toward a corporatist "spillover." Thus, it is an open question whether the subsystem of party government will (and should) retain the character of a "functionally primary subsystem" (in the sense of Parsons, 1959: 118) under certain specifiable aspects.[3]

THE CONCEPT OF CORPORATISM

Before continuing the discussion, some conceptual clarifications are appropriate. "Corporatism" has only recently made its reappearance on the terminological stage of political science, and it would be somewhat premature to take its meaning for granted. So far, Schmitter (1974: 93-94) has given the most elaborate definition.

The object of his definition is to distinguish "corporatism" from other types of "interest intermediation," such as "pluralism" and "syndicalism." However, in my opinion, this has some disadvantages. Being cast into the conceptual framework of Easton and Almond's input-output model, the definition covers only the "input" functions ("interest articulation"). But the input-output model quite obviously has a strong affinity to the pluralist paradigm of "pressure politics," which Schmitter otherwise seeks to amend. Thus, important aspects of "corporatism" are not really covered by the definition. The state, in corporatist systems, not only confines itself to "recognizing or licensing" or "granting a monopoly" on the one hand, exerting "controls" on leadership selection and demand (or support) articulation on the other (besides, the latter may be doubtful for most cases of "societal corporatism").[4]

Corporatism is more than a peculiar pattern of articulation of interests. Rather, it is an institutionalized pattern of policy-formation in which large interest organizations cooperate with each other and with public authorities not only in the articulation (or even "intermediation") of interests, but — in its developed forms — in the "authoritative allocation of values" and in the implementation of such policies. It is precisely because of the intimate mutual penetration of state bureaucracies and large interest organizations that the traditional concept of "interest representation" becomes quite inappropriate for a theoretical understanding of corporatism. Rather, we are dealing with an integrated system of "societal guidance" (Etzioni) which — particularly in the variety of Western European "neocorporatism" — seems to constitute that serious challenge to the traditional institutional and organizational framework of liberal democracy which we are discussing here.

From what has been said, it follows that liberal corporatism should not be confounded with simply more consultation and cooperation of government with organized interest groups which is, of course, common in all constitutional democracies with a highly developed capitalist economy. The distinguishing trait of liberal corporatism is a high degree of collaboration among these groups themselves in the shaping of economic policy. For analytic reasons we may distinguish two levels of bargaining in liberal corporate systems: first, bargaining among the "autonomous groups" (as they are called in the annual opinions of the West German Council of Economic Experts); second, bargaining between government and the "cartel" of organized groups. These two levels may often merge into a "one-step" bargaining process in which the government engages in "multilateral" talks with a plurality of associations and thus serves at the same time as an active "mediator" between them. But, instead, we may encounter a "two-step" bargaining process — whether because associations engage in autonomous clearing processes on the first level before seeking coordination with the authorities, or because they negotiate autonomously on the basis of recommendations or a mandate from the government. We shall see that this is a conspicuous pattern in Austrian "social partnership."[5] From these varieties of "multilateral" corporatist policy-formation, we shall distinguish "bilateral," separate bargaining between the government and individual groups as, for example, in the "social contract" between the British government and the Trades Union Congress (TUC). The latter may at best be considered an embryonic variety of liberal corporatism.

Bargaining procedures in liberal corporatism often retain a quite informal character, even if the participants are formal organizations. Strong institutionalization through the parliamentary representation of groups in a chamber (e.g., "Economic and Social Council"), which had been advanced by the theorists of the more democratic versions of classical corporatism, is viewed with skepticism by the practitioners of corporatist policy-making in countries such as Austria. Elaborate institutional arrangements as in The Netherlands remain an exception. In general, because of the pragmatic manner in which liberal corporatism has evolved, it has by no means reached a degree of explicit institutionalization similar to that of parliamentary government.

THE POLITICAL ECONOMY
OF LIBERAL CORPORATISM

How can one explain the apparently growing importance of liberal corporatism in a number of Western European countries? To arrive at a probabilistic theory (predicting under what conditions this pattern of policy-formation is likely to appear), we obviously have to consider certain functional exigencies of the economic system. Corporatism (in its liberal as well as its authoritarian varieties) seems to be "related to certain basic imperatives or needs of capitalism to reproduce the conditions for its existence and continually to accumulate further resources" (Schmitter, 1974: 107). More specifically, corporatism appears to serve such imperatives by regulating the conflict of social classes in the distribution of national income and in the structure of industrial relations. As for the liberal variety of corporatism, it obviously is specifically related to problems of economic policy-making which arise in in a rather advanced stage of capitalist development. Here the regulation of class conflict is an important element of macroeconomic "system politics' which are expected to replace pluralistic "process politics" (Lehmbruch, 1974a).[6]

A rather cursory comparative inspection of issue areas characterized by a frequent occurrence of the liberal corporatist pattern of policy-formation yields some important observations.

1. The corporatist pattern is most conspicuous in economic policy-formation, above all in the domain of policies affecting the business cycle, employment, monetary stability, and the balance of trade. In particular, income policies appear to constitute a core domain of liberal corporatism. A "cooperative" variety of income policies[7] is common to virtually all systems to which this label (or that of "societal corporatism") may be applied. In contrast to this, policies affecting the organizational and institutional framework of the economy (*Ordnungspolitik* in the terminology of German neoliberal economics), for example, the regulation of competition or industrial codetermination, are less frequently included in corporatist policy-making.

2. The most important interest groups included in the corporatist pattern are organized labor and business. This may comprise a plurality of associations on the side of labor as well as of business. The central feature is, however, the collaboration of "capital" and "labor" in a corporatist scheme. Other associations — organized agriculture, for example — seem to be less frequently included and, when participating, apparently have no decisive voice. Hence, they remain largely confined to the classical pluralist "pressure politics" and may try to influence government within the limits set by the "cartel" of organized business, labor, and the administration (cf. Böckenförde, 1976).

CONSENSUS-BUILDING IN ECONOMIC POLICY

These observations point to important developments in the pattern of economic policy-formation in highly developed capitalist economies. While Ordnungspolitik, the regulation of economic institutions, has always been among the prerogatives of parliament — at least to the degree that law has remained an effective instrument of policy-making — business-cycle policy has largely remain-

ed the domain of central bank and governmental authorities. From
this rule there is one possible exception, namely — in those countries where parliament has an effective influence on taxation —
"Keynesian" fiscal policy. In West Germany, for example, since
1967 the government may, as an anticyclical measure, increase or
reduce the income tax by an ordinance which is subject to the consent of parliament. Interestingly, however, this provision has
never worked. When in 1970 the federal government considered
such an anticyclical increase in taxation, it met with strong opposition from the social democratic caucus, which accepted only a sur-
tax reimbursable at a later date. Apparently it proves difficult to
reconcile effective political management of the business-cycle with
the parliamentary process of consensus-building.

Now it appears to be a characteristic feature of advanced
capitalist societies that economic policy-making — which in earlier
periods, to adopt the conceptual framework of Etzioni (1968), was
largely based on "control" (supplementing self-regulation of the
market economy) — is more and more dependent upon processes
of "consensus-building" within the political system. This is the
burden which interventionism places on policy makers. Classical
laissez-faire economics could afford to neglect the problem of consensus. Market processes were supposed to proceed from a
"natural" and, hence, just order (cf. Habermas, 1973). And, in the
eyes of liberal economists, one of the advantages of policy-making
by *marktkonforme*, or automatic devices, especially of monetary
steering by the central bank, is precisely that it may relieve policy
makers from the constraints which the requirement of explicit consensus places on them and may thus protect the political system
from "overload." But it appears that, to the degree that such
methods are workable, they may serve to elude the consensus problem only within certain limits.

Of course, bankers may not be so preoccupied with being
reelected. And it is likely that they are less eager about facilitating
reelection of the government than top-level administrators (at least
in those countries where political nominations are current in the
civil service). However, even the policies of central banks are more
or less constrained by the requirement of public consent. Take, for
example, the West German case. Here the central bank is under the
legal obligation to give priority to the maintenance of price stability
which implies, of course, that this objective may have precedence
over eventually conflicting goals such as full employment. This

legal requirement on the one hand is intended to protect the political system from an erosion of consensus. Even though the high priority given to anti-inflationary policies may be justified by purely economic reasoning, it cannot be fully understood without taking into consideration the historical trauma of two strong inflationary crises and the resulting apprehension that — as presumably was the case in the 1920s — inflation may bring on a massive crisis of political confidence. On the other hand, such a policy may nonetheless endanger the very same objective. When, for example, in 1966 the central bank stuck to a rigid deflationary line, the unanticipated consequence was to upset the latent consent of the electorate.

In a more general manner it appears that decades of economic interventionism have conditioned the expectations of the public in a particular manner. Policy makers now are increasingly held responsible for all essential economic parameters that are within the reach of the nation-state, monetary stability as well as full employment.[8] Hence, neither inflation nor unemployment are accepted any longer as "natural occurrences," except if they are engendered by processes on the world market apparently beyond the reach of national decision makers.[9]

Apart from the fact that market processes and market mechanisms have largely lost their quasi-natural justification, the deficiencies of "control" are responsible for increasing requirements of consensus-building in economic policy. It has become obvious that in a national economy subject to strong interpenetration within international markets, monetary policies often are of rather limited effectiveness. The same is more and more true of "Keynesian" techniques of macroeconomic budgetary and fiscal demand management, especially since the progress made by "stagflation" in the 1970s. Faced with "control deficits" of this sort, governments increasingly turn to more direct attempts at influencing the economic behavior of business and/or labor, be it by "moral suasion" or by more or less "dirigiste" measures, especially "income policies." Such direct steering, however, poses acute problems of consensus. It is a common experience that, for example, wage and price freezes fail because compliance cannot be obtained. Direct controls, therefore, tend to be supplemented or replaced by political bargaining of governments with the large interest associations, that is to say, by corporatist consensus-building.

Trends toward policy-making by "corporatist" bargaining sometimes are perceived as constituting a serious challenge to the established pattern of parliamentary government, where parliament and the party system are supposed to be the privileged agencies of consensus-building. Indeed, they might be a more serious challenge than the specter of "administrative government" (Rose, 1968). For an "ideal-type" administrative government would presuppose that no consensus-building is required, and this is rather unlikely as soon as conflicting interests (or values) are concerned by a decision. Hence, "corporatist" collusion of administrative authorities with the large interest associations seems to be the more realistic perspective, precisely because this apparently permits the "short-circuiting" of the party system and parliament by the establishment of a direct "bridge" for consensus-building.

It would, however, be premature to speculate that corporatist policy-making signifies the displacement of parliamentary and party government by a new pattern of consensus-building. As will be shown later, in liberal corporatist systems there exist strong links between interest associations and the party systems which do not fit with this hypothesis. Therefore, it seems more plausible to interpret the trends in the relationship of "liberal corporatist" patterns and the party system as an instance of increasing *structural differentiation and functional specialization* of the political system brought about by certain requirements of consensus-building specific to economic policy-making.

To explore this further, let us assume that the party system plays the dominant role in consensus-building. This would mean that the actors are organizational units and subunits or individuals acting within these units, from the local association to the central executive of the party and to the party caucus in parliament. Consensus-building takes place within the party system if, for example, the caucus of the majority party or the leaders of a party coalition decide to introduce a bill in parliament, or if some local party meeting votes to back (or to oppose) certain policies. And the party system would play the dominant role in consensus-building in those instances where policy-formation presupposes obtaining the assent of a majority within the party membership or (in a more "oligarchical" variant) its leadership. This would, of course, include electoral processes if they worked according to that model where "political parties...mold their policies to suit voters so as to gain as many votes as possible" (Downs, 1957: 88).

The consensus-building capacity of the party system is, of course, subject to certain characteristic restrictions. Some of these seem to be particularly relevant in economic policy-formation and may explain the partial substitution of alternative patterns of consensus-building.

1. The first aspect is the contradictory temporal constraints placed upon consensus-building within the party system. On the one hand, political parties often are 'stratarchies'' rather than ''hierarchies'' (Eldersveld, 1964) and, as such, have high requirements of time needed for consensus-building.[10] On the other hand, elections induce a certain (though not absolute) preference for shorter time perspectives rather than longer ones. This may lead certain party leaders to choose conflict-minimizing strategies which reduce the requirements for consensus-building, but may impair the rationality of decisions made within this restricted perspective. It seems reasonable to hypothesize that one of the consequences of these contradictory restrictions is that consensus-building within the party system tends to produce more rational output for long-term policy decisions (e.g., reforms of criminal law or of constitutional provisions) than for short-term ones. Economic policy decisions often have a strong short-run component, and the pressure of time may be high. Political parties, then, either are incapable of building sufficient consensus within a short time span or they produce irrational decisions.[11] This may induce the decision makers to shift responsibility for consensus-building toward the subsystem of interest associations.

2. The capacity of competitive party systems to structure conflicts and thus to produce consensus seems to vary with the nature of the specific choice. Competitive strategies may be appropriate for structuring a qualitative choice, where possible outcomes could be arranged upon a nominal scale — e.g., the choice among different superannuation schemes. If, however, possible outcomes differ only according to their level (and hence may be arranged upon an ordinal scale), as in the case of a higher or lower increase in pensions, then the tendency to outbid each other would strongly risk blurring programmatic differences. It is particularly difficult to imagine how a consensus on the eventual distribution of the GNP for, say, the next twelve months could be worked out by a strategy of party competition and the building of electoral majorities. A viable consensus rather presupposes bargaining processes, and if the government wishes to influence the outcomes it has to

engage in bargaining itself. On the other hand, decisions on the structural bases of economic policy (e.g., control of private investments) may eventually be made by a parliamentary majority and implemented by an administration controlled by that majority.

This has important consequences for a majority party. If it wished to play a leading role in consensus-building in business-cycle policies, the necessity to engage in bargaining might restrict its freedom to choose competitive electoral strategies. Therefore, it may be in the interest of political parties to shift responsibility for matters such as business-cycle policies to a "corporatist" subsystem formed by organized interests and the administration.

A COMPARATIVE OVERVIEW
OF CORPORATIST INCOME POLICIES

Accordingly, it is not surprising that income policies is the field in which the role of liberal corporatism is most conspicuous. Generally speaking, the "cooperative" variety of income policy (Rall, 1975) has for some time been practiced in practically all countries which we may classify as "liberal corporatist": Austria, The Netherlands, the Scandinavian countries, Switzerland, and West Germany. In some, but not all of these, "corporatist" forms of policy formation also extend to economic Ordnungspolitik, and this in turn signifies a further restriction of the "reach" or "scope" of the party system as an agency of policy formation. We shall discuss this in some detail using two examples: Austria and West Germany. These cases present the advantage of resembling each other in various aspects relevant to our problem: in particular, in the configuration of their party systems — which in both cases is characterized by competition between a large conservative and a large socialist party, while a relatively small liberal party retains some importance. In addition, the structure and role of interest associations exhibit marked similarities: for example, in the importance of interest representation by statutory public corporations in which membership is compulsory (the "chambers," whose importance dates from the "neomercantilist" stage of economic policy which characterized these countries after the end of the short liberal era in the nineteenth century). Both countries have a rather strong trade union movement based on the principle of industrywide organization, predominantly tied to the respective socialist parties, but with a minority of Christian Social unionists represented among the leadership and remaining loyal to the conservative parties. On the other hand, in both countries employers' organizations are strong and rather disciplined and, in general, support the conservative parties, although they have come to terms rather easily with governments led by socialists. This in turn has much to do with the fact that socialist party leadership in both countries has pursued a very cautious "reformist" line. In both countries, moreover, the ideology of "social partnership" has long played an important role in industrial relations, supported by the legal institution of shop representation of labor (*Betriebsräte*) with some influence on working conditions and personnel management. Finally, due to language and historical factors, communication across the border is quite intense, especially North to South. West German newspapers are widely read by the Austrian elite, and Austrian political leaders are remarkably well informed on West German political and social problems. This should — and indeed does — facilitate diffusion processes which might reinforce existing affinities. All the more striking, however, are continuing dissimilarities in political strategies, including "cooperative" income policies in both countries.

THE AUSTRIAN CASE

Austria probably is one of the clearest examples of income policies by accommodation on the liberal corporatist pattern. An elaborate system has been established which has been working smoothly and without any interruption for two decades. In general this is referred to as *Sozialpartnerschaft* (social partnership), a term which strongly underlines the consensual and cooperative aspects. Since 1948, unions and business had collaborated intermittently to restrain wages and prices. This collaboration was turned into a more formal and permanent one in 1957: on the basis of an agreement of Chancellor Raab (Conservative) with the trade union president Böhm,[12] the government established a formal (but extralegal) institution, the *Paritätische Kommission für Preis- und Lohnfragen* (Joint Commission on Prices and Wages). *Parität* (equal representation) here consists in giving organized labor the same number of seats as business and agriculture taken together. Labor is represented by the *Österreichische Gewerkschaftsbund* (ÖGB,

Austrian Federation of Trade Unions) and by the Chambers of Labor (these statutory public organizations are strongly dominated by the OGB, which is a voluntary organization). The other side is represented by the Federal Chamber of Business (*Bundeskammer der gewerblichen Wirtschaft*) and by the Conference of Presidents of (*Länder*) Chambers of Agriculture. It should be noted that on the side of labor the chambers are restricted to rather technical functions while the political functions of interest representation are in the hands of the ÖGB, whereas in the cases of business and agriculture organizational preponderance rests with the chambers. (The "Union of Austrian Industrialists" is of rather limited importance since it represents private and, hence, small and medium industries only; almost all important industrial firms belong to the public sector.) This difference in organizational structure seems to reflect the historical fact that the trade unions still respond to the tradition of a workers' movement which stressed the voluntary aspects of membership, while on the side of business and agriculture there is a stronger corporatist tradition. That "parity" is obtained by practically doubling the representation of labor derives primarily from political motives. Organized business and agriculture are strongly tied to the conservative *Österreichische Volkspartei* (ÖVP), while the socialists have a majority within the ÖGB and the Chambers of Labour.[13]

Formal reunions of the Joint Commission are presided over by the Federal Chancellor or the Minister of Interior and minutes are kept by the Chancellor's Office. In addition, the government is represented by the Minister of Commerce and Industry and by the Minister of Social Affairs. But characteristically since the end of coalition government in 1966, the representatives of government sit in advisory capacity only, in order not to upset numerical "parity." Still more important, since that time formal reunions are preceded by an informal meeting of the presidents of the four organizations (together with their secretaries general and some staff) in which the most important decisions are anticipated without participation of cabinet members. This most clearly marks the shift toward autonomous clearing between interest groups and the diminution of the role of the government. There exist two subcommissions to the Paritätische, on wages and on prices, which normally make concrete routine decisions and are manned by "experts" — in general, trained economists from the staff of the chambers and the

ÖGB. Only if these do not reach unanimity, or when important questions arise, is the matter submitted to the Joint Commission itself, which comprises leaders and top managers of the associations. Collective bargaining is tightly controlled. An industrial union which wants to open negotiations first has to obtain the approval of the federation (ÖGB) headquarters; after this internal screening the matter is submitted to the Joint Commission, which must give the green light and has to approve the eventual final agreement. In the case of serious disputes — for example, strikes (which have been quite rare) — the matter is again taken from the hands of the industrial (labor and employers) associations and settled at the "summit" in direct negotiations between the presidents of the ÖGB and the Federal Chamber of Business. Price controls are much less effective, and today cover no more than one-fifth of consumer prices (another quarter is subject to administrative regulations). Producers have to show that their costs (wages and supply costs) have risen if they want to raise prices; other elements (such as the degree of competition) are not taken into consideration. Producers in general comply with the procedure, largely as a consequence of informal pressures from the Federal Chamber of Business. But, as the Federal Chamber represents a large number of small and medium enterprises, it is not surprising that the whole system has a strong protectionist bias. Employers agree with unions (who want to protect existing jobs) to conduct wage policies in such a manner as not to endanger the profitability of marginal enterprises.

THE WEST GERMAN CASE

We now turn to cooperative income politics in West Germany.[14] During the period of neoliberal economic policy, there was, of course, no ostensible incomes policy, in accordance with the official ban on economic "planning." When in 1963-1964 some officials of the Federal Ministry of Economy discussed principles of an eventual incomes policy together with union spokesmen, they were disavowed by the government of Chancellor Erhard. A first turning point was marked in 1964 by the creation of a Council of Economic Experts (*Sachverständigenrat zur Begutachtung der gesamtwirtschaftlichen Entwicklung*), which was to present to the government opinions on the macroeconomic situation, including forecasts based upon alternative projections. Although the law demands that the experts abstain from formulating policy recommendations, the council soon began to plead for an incomes policy oriented in accordance with increases in productivity and for a *Konzertierte Aktion* (a term reminiscent of *économie concertée*) or a "new *contrat social*" in order to establish a "relationship of trust" between "autonomous groups." This prepared the ground for the law "on the advancement of economic stability and growth," adopted in 1967 during the Grand Coalition period and strongly influenced by the Social Democratic Minister of Economy Schiller. According to its third paragraph, in the case of a danger to one of its macroeconomic goals (price stability, full employment, balance of foreign trade, continuous and "appropriate" growth), *Orientierungsdaten* for the "coordinated behaviour [*abgestimmtes Verhalten*] of territorial authorities, trade unions and business associations" shall be made available by the federal government. The practice has developed in a different and somewhat more complicated manner. On the one hand, the policies of the federal and Länder governments and of the associations of local authorities are coordinated by two separate bodies, the *Konjunkturrat der Öffentlichen Hand* (Council of Public Authorities on Business-Cycle Policies) and the *Finanzplanungsrat* (Council on Budgetary Planning).[15] The Konzertierte Aktion, on the other hand, has developed into a regular meeting with economic interest associations convened by the Federal Minister of Economy several times a year.

Some interesting contrasts appear if we compare the Konzertierte Aktion with the Austrian Paritätische Kommission. In West Germany, the government apparently plays a more active leading role, at any rate a role much more visible to the public. On the other hand — and this facilitates governmental leadership — the organizational representation of interests is much more broadly dispersed. The number of participants is rather high (more than 50, plus the respective staffs), since a large number of associations is invited. On the side of business, these are the federal associations of employers, of industry, of commerce, trades, and banking, as well as the central organization of the chambers of industry and commerce, besides the farmers' association (*Deutscher Bauernverband*). Labor is represented by the *Deutsche Gewerkschaftsbund* (German Federation of Trade Unions, DGB), together with its most important industrial unions, as well as the (autonomous) union of white collar workers (*Deutsche Angestelltengewerkschaft*) and the association of civil servants (*Deutscher Beamtenbund*). On the side of government, the Federal Minister of Economy presides over the meetings and has the main responsibility. In addition, there are officials from the Ministries of Finance, Interior, Social Affairs, and Agriculture and of the Chancellor's Office, and representatives of the Federal Bank, of the Council of Economic Experts, and of the federal authority on cartels (*Bundeskartellamt*). The most important political figures, besides the Ministers of Economy and Finance and the president of the Federal Bank, are the presidents of the Employers' Association and of the German Federation of Industries (both held for some time in personal union), the president of the DGB and the presidents of the two most important industrial unions within the DGB (namely, the metal workers union and the union of public employees and transport workers). But the power structure within the Konzertierte Aktion is clearly more diffuse than within its Austrian counterpart. This is primarily due to the fact that, although German interest associations, too, are rather highly centralized from the bottom to the top, the degree of interorganizational concentration is clearly lower. This is true in particular of the DGB, which has no formal authority (and little real influence) over the wage policies of its constituent industrial unions. Since the power structure within the interest group system is much more diffuse than in Austria, coordination is of course much more difficult to obtain. This is, however, not the only (and probably not even the major) explanation of the lower degree of effectiveness of the Konzertierte Aktion (KA).

Above all, the KA has never had the powers of its Austrian counterpart; its functions have been described as confined largely to communication among the groups. On the one hand, this has to do with a continuing disinclination for open intervention of the government in the economy — and, as we have seen, the KA is perceived as an instrument of the government, not (as in Austria) of the autonomous *Sozialpartner. Tarifautonomie* (the autonomy of collective bargaining) is not to be impaired by the state. On the other hand, the emphasis placed upon the communication functions of the KA derives from the theoretical considerations that have been put forward by the Council of Economic Experts and by Minister Schiller. The council has held that — because of the interdependency of macroeconomic aggregates, in particular because of the probability that business will pass increased wage costs on to prices and that labor will react by obtaining higher wages and thus squeezing profits — conflicts about the distribution of income were unproductive (*funktionslos*) and unsuited to obtaining long-term changes in the ratio of wages to profits. The continuing existence of such conflicts was explained by Schiller as being due to a lack of information, and, quite logically, the function of the KA was to inform the "social partners" about their real (and interdependent) interests. The government took a leading role by publishing the Orientierungsdaten derived from a macroeconomic "goal-oriented projection" (*Zielprojektion*), in particular on the expected growth of the GNP and on employment, prices, and incomes (wages and profits). The expected consequences on the part of the interest associations were a reduction of uncertainty, on the one hand, and a modification of behavior in the direction of strong consideration of *gesamtwirtschaftliche* (overall economic) objectives (cf. Rall, 1975: 217), on the other hand. The Orientierungsdaten, by the way, are not supposed to constitute formal "guidelines." (Interestingly, the government has become increasingly reticent in publishing such data since union membership might consider them as minimum objectives which have to be attained. However, it is obvious that bargaining in the KA and contacts of the government with unions largely center around certain percentages put forward by the government in an informal manner as the desirable limit of wage increases and which take on a symbolic value).

The record of the KA is controversial. Wage restraint, which was its principal objective, has been obtained mainly in periods of slump when unions felt able to obtain the agreement of their rank and file with a policy of wage restraint under the pressure of threatening unemployment. This has especially been the case in 1967-1969 and in 1975-1976. But in 1969 it became clear that the system did not work in periods of economic recovery and continuing boom. The wildcat strikes which in 1969 broke out in the steel industry and repeated themselves on a still larger scale in 1973 demonstrated a growing lack of compliance of the rank and file and an increasing degree of militancy. Therefore, in 1970 the trade unions turned to rather aggressive policies and obtained the highest increases in the real wages since the end of the war. A second critical point was marked by the highly controversial wage conflict in the public services in 1974 which demonstrated that militancy had begun to spread to this sector too, forcing the government to yield after several days of large-scale strikes. During all this time, however, the regular meetings of the KA were carried on and the unions continued to participate in spite of strong criticism from parts of their rank and file. Apparently they were anxious not to embarrass the socialist-led government and, in addition, not to incur the disapproval of the mass media. The slump of 1975-1976 induced the unions to return to a policy of wage restraint, with the notable exception of the printers' union that fought a bitter conflict to break the informal guideline that had been respected by the other unions.

In practice, hence, the KA has mainly served as an instrument of crisis management, not of continuous economic guidance. In general, this is explained by its bias toward wage restraint (e.g., Hardes, 1974; Pfromm, 1975). It has never advanced a full-fledged incomes policy, including both prices and profits, and has largely disregarded the issue of income distribution, although this has remained central among the goals of organized labor. However, it is significant that, in spite of its major deficiencies, the Konzertierte Aktion has never been openly challenged as an instrument of consensus-building. (On later developments, cf. infra, p. 305).

CORPORATIST INCOME POLICIES
IN OTHER EUROPEAN COUNTRIES

The cases of Austria and West Germany may be placed into a broader comparative perspective since, in a number of other European countries, cooperative incomes policies have been developing as a core element of corporatist management of the economy. There are significant differences as to the degree of institutionalization, to the autonomy of the "cartel" of organizations in relation to the government (one-step or two-step bargaining), and to the degree of concentration within the associational subsystems. Here we shall not discuss these variations in a systematic manner, but simply point to two rather extreme examples which may illustrate them.[16]

In Sweden the autonomy of the associational subsystem appears to be still more pronounced than in Austria. Swedish wage policies in particular have been described as a "borderline case" (Rall, 1975: 142). Strictly speaking, there exists no official incomes policy, but only a highly centralized system of collective bargaining without even that minimum of formal interference of the state which we encountered in the Austrian case. Of course, cooperation between unions and employers has been highly developed since the Saltsjöbaden agreement of 1938, but to label such cooperation as "corporatism" would imply that functions of public policy have been taken over by interest organizations. Except for a short period of cooperative wage and price controls in 1949-1950, there have been no such formal examples in this domain up to 1970. In an informal manner, however, information from the government on the economic situation and on desirable outcomes is obviously taken into account in collective bargaining between the central organizations. If we place this in the larger context of what has been called "Harpsund democracy," it seems justified to place Sweden in the "liberal corporatist" category.[17] The degree of institutionalization is very low in Sweden, and it seems plausible to relate this to the high degree of centralization and concentration of the associational subsystem which permits it to renounce more formal institutional arrangements. It is true that the Trade Union Federation (*Landsorganisationen*, LO) and the Employers Association (*Svenska Arbetsgivarföreningen*, SAF), which for a long time had succeeded in enforcing a strongly egalitarian wage policy, have recently met strong opposition from the autonomous white collar unions (especially from SACO, the Union of University Graduates). However, corporatist policies in Sweden apparently have been much more successful than, e.g., in neighboring Denmark (cf. Ulman and Flanagan, 1971).

The most elaborate institutionalization of liberal corporatism is to be found in The Netherlands. This example makes clear that the degree of formalization of corporatist policy-making does not necessarily correspond directly to what we might call the steadiness of cooperative income policies. We have here a quite complex network. First, the "Foundation of Labour" (*Stichting van den Arbeid*) was created in 1945 by an agreement of unions and employers organizations as a private institution recognized by the government. The task of this institution, in which the organizations are represented in equal strength, is to give expert opinions on all problems of industrial relations, including wage policies. The "Social-Economic Council" (*Sociaal-Economische Raad*), established by law in 1950, is a tripartite board consisting of 15 representatives of labor, 15 representatives of the employers' organizations, and another 15 members nominated by the crown (among which are economic experts, the director of the central bank, and the director of the *Central Planbureau*). It serves as an adivsory body to the government in matters of economic policy (especially on macroeconomic decisions) and has at the same time the function of adjusting diverging interests. The law on the Social-Economic Council provided, in addition, for an organization of the different branches of industry and trade in corporate *bedrijfsraden*. These provisions, however, have only been partially implemented. Nevertheless, an institutional framework for cooperative income policies similar to the Austrian case exists. Indeed, after the war, unions and employers cooperated in a system of strict wage controls through a process of bargaining which included the Foundation of Labour, the Social-Economic Council, and the Board of Government Conciliators (*College van Rijksbemiddelaars*). The cooperative attitude of trade unions at that time is indicated by the fact that the socialist union (NVV), in order to combat wage drift, opposed proposals to allow prosperous employers to pay higher wages. Cooperation, however, has declined since 1959, and, although the government for some time continued trying to enforce guidelines in the sixties, wage restraint largely broke down. Opposition of trade union rank and file which had developed since the late 1950s contributed strongly to this decline. When, in 1970, the government put forward a law on wages permitting an "imperative" incomes policy by intervention into collective bargaining, the unions registered their strong opposition. A new central agreement on wage controls was concluded in 1973, but did not work very well, and in 1974 the government returned to "imperative" incomes policy.

THE INTEGRATION OF ORGANIZED LABOR

Interestingly, in West Germany as well as in Austria, the trade unions have played an active role in the establishment of cooperative income policies, whereas employers and conservative political leaders in the beginnning were much more reluctant. Union leadership expected that institutions such as the Paritätische Kommission and the Konzertierte Aktion might serve as a strategic point of departure for arriving at a larger participation of organized labor in the formulation of overall economic policy. Such hopes have not materialized in an appreciable manner, at least in the West Germany and Austrian cases. Enlarging the field of corporatist economic decision-making beyond income policies (or, more exactly, control of wage policies) would have meant, among others, control of profits and of investments and, hence, a considerable structural transformation. This would have necessitated a shift in power relations which certainly could not be obtained within a corporatist system. Liberal corporatism operates by processes of accommodation of interests and consequently is characterized by high thresholds of consensus.

On the contrary, incomes policies — as the core domain of corporatist policy-making — have largely served the function of integrating organized labor into the economic status quo. For corporatist incomes policies have largely been confined to wages, and union demands for a redistribution of national income had to be put aside. It is true that it is precisely this neglect of the problems of distribution which in the long run tends to jeopardize cooperative incomes policies since, in situations where profits rise much faster than wages, unions may be tempted to free themselves of corporatist chains. (At least this has been a central impediment for the steady working of the Konzertierte Aktion.) On the other hand, however, wage restraint appears to be a preferred instrument of economic policy, since wages set by collective bargaining are more easy to control (the problem of wage drift notwithstanding) than other parameters. Moreover, anticipation of profits and willingness to invest are the crucial variables of capitalist economy oriented toward the goal of economic growth, and they have to be respected by a cooperative incomes policy.

Consensus-building in liberal corporatism is therefore largely contingent on the degree to which the labor union movement is integrated into the process of policy-formation. For, obviously, union leadership, more than other elite groups in the corporatist subsystem, risks facing serious problems of rank-and-file compliance — especially if it continues to proclaim objectives such as a redistribution of income relations and of national wealth, as West German unions do in principle. Outbursts of a renewed militancy such as have been observed in West Germany, The Netherlands, or Sweden, especially since the end of the sixties, have demonstrated the fragility of the social bases of liberal corporatism. For example, an important element among the causes of the West German wildcat strikes in 1969 was that expectations of "social symmetry" had been deceived when profits rose much faster than wages, which had been fixed by long-term agreements (Schumann et al., 1971).

This explains why corporatist steering of *Konjunkturpolitik* seems to presuppose some particular structural characteristics of the trade union organization. Above all, a high degree of centralization and concentration, as in Austria or Sweden, seems to be required. Of course, this condition holds equally for employer organizations, but is probably of more vital importance in the case of organized labor. Cooperative incomes policies become more difficult, but still remain possible, if the union movement is centralized but not concentrated, as in the case of West Germany. Here the power of leaders within the large industrial unions (centralization) is considerable; the influence of the federation over industrial unions (concentration), however, is weak. Therefore, the strong industrial unions have to be included into the central consensus-building process. Lack of both conditions and a large measure of rank-and-file autonomy, especially if combined with shop-level bargaining as in Great Britain, tend to impair severely the capacity of union leaders to cooperatie in liberal corporatist system.

Correspondingly, in countries where the labor movement either has a strong "class conflict" orientation or a high degree of rank-and-file autonomy, liberal corporatism is not strongly developed. In France, for example, the institutional framework exists. We only need to mention the *Conseil Economique et Social* or, within the planning system, the *commissions de modernisation* in which business and labor are represented. But unions have always been reluctant to cooperate, so that business and the state bureaucracy largely work in a tête à tête within the modernization commissions. When, in 1963, it became clear that the *cohérence* of planning could not be obtained without an incomes policy, the planning authorities turned to organized labor for cooperation. But the CGT maintained its strictly negative attitude, while the CFDT made its cooperation contingent on the establishment of certain elements of labor influence in entrepreneurial policies which employers would not accept. Governments did not fare much better in further attempts to obtain union cooperation, such as de Gaulle's scheme of participation (Cohen, 1969; Ulman and Flanagan, 1971).

But the greater or lesser willingness of organized labor to cooperate within a liberal corporatist framework apparently is not to be explained only by structural properties of union organization. Another important independent variable seems to be the position of the "labor movement" (a term which in German usage comprises socialist parties) within the party system. Generally speaking, liberal corporatism is most important in those countries where the working class movement had obtained participation in political power by the channel of the party system and where, in consequence, the trade unions had gained privileged access to governmental and administrative centers of decision. We may conjecture that this is an essential compensation for the peculiar strains to which trade unions expose themselves by cooperating in income policies. Essentially two groups of countries seem to fall into this category: (1) those where the socialists have been the leading party in government, in particular the Scandinavian countries; (2) those where the socialist party is integrated into an elite cartel of the "consociational" type. The latter is well illustrated by the case of Austria. Here the rise of the Sozialpartnerschaft and the establishment of the Paritätische Kommission quite clearly have been concomitant with the cooperation of the conservative and socialist parties in the "black-red" coalition which lasted from 1946 to 1966. In West Germany, the Konzertierte Aktion likewise was established after the Social Democrats had entered the government in 1966. On the other hand, the decline of cooperative incomes policy in The Netherlands was obviously influenced by the withdrawal of the Labour Party from the coalition in 1959. The example of Great Britain, too, seems to demonstrate that unions are more likely to support an incomes policy if the socialist party is in government.

That is not to say that the continued working of liberal corporatism is under all circumstances dependent upon continued socialist participation in government. In Austria, the end of the coalition and the formation of a conservative government in 1966 (which remained in power until 1970) had practically no influence on the smooth working of the Sozialpartnerschaft. But this does not really disconfirm our hypothesis, for in that country — as I shall demonstrate later — the importance of the corporatist subsystem has become such that it now can be regarded as "self-sustaining." However, the hypothesis seems to permit some cautious predictions regarding France and Italy. An electoral victory of the Left in France, or a realization of the *compromesso storico* in Italy (that is to say, the coalition with the *Democrazia Cristiana* for which the PCI is striving), might result in the establishment of liberal corporatist schemes in these countries, too, beginning with cooperative incomes policies. In France, the institutional framework (including the Conseil Economique et Social, which might gain in importance) is ready, as I have mentioned earlier. In Italy, with the advent of the Andreotti government in

1976, Communist Party as well as union leaders already have made clear their sympathies for corporatist solutions to the economic crisis of the country. However, since rank-and-file autonomy is extremely well developed within the Italian labor unions, it may seem doubtful whether communist leadership really will be able to obtain their compliance.

LIBERAL CORPORATISM
AS ELITE CONSENSUS-BUILDING

This points to an important aspect of the liberal corporatist subsystem. Consensus-building here largely takes place on the level of the top elite, the leadership of central interest associations, and depends upon their having a considerable freedom of action. Liberal corporatism thus has strong affinities for "consociational democracy" as it has been described by Lijphart (1969) and by this author (Lehmbruch, 1967, 1974b). This is not astonishing, since in both cases the threshold of consensus-building by necessity is high. As with conflicts of segmented religious, ideological or ethnic communities, those conflicts of capital and labor that stand in the way of national economic policy cannot be settled by majority decisions. Rather, they have to be resolved by top-level bargaining processes and the rule of *amicabilis compositio* (which one might perhaps translate into "business-like agreement"). And one of the reasons why most "consociational democracies" have come to adopt strongly corporatist devices may be sought in the fact that in these countries political elites have been socialized into that style of conflict management (Lehmbruch, 1974a).

THE CONSENSUS OF "TECHNOCRATS"

What distinguishes elite consensus in liberal corporatism even more, however, is the degree to which it is based on beliefs derived from economic theory. The comparative analysis of the Austrian and West German cases (to which other examples could be added) has already pointed to the crucial role of economic experts. On the one hand, as in other highly developed capitalist countries, advisory boards (which often consist of economists of high academic standing who enjoy considerable political prestige) have become increasingly important. Since economic forecasting by means of macroeconomic projections is one of their foremost functions, this approach has come to influence elite conceptions of economic policy-making. This is reinforced by the rising influence which economic experts enjoy within the interest associations. German trade unions, for example, have recruited more and more trained economists into their staffs, and it has convincingly been argued that this evolution has strongly contributed to preparing the ground for cooperative income policies (Institut für Sozialforschung, 1969: 204ff.).

In Austria, interestingly, both types of expert influence are fused. The approximate Austrian counterpart to, say, the U.S. Council of Economic Advisors or the West German Sachverständigenrat, is the *Beirat für Wirtschafts- und Sozialfragen* (Advisory Council for Economic and Social Questions), established in 1963 as a third subcommision of the Paritätische Kommission. The Beirat is clearly an institution of Sozialpartnerschaft and consists exclusively of experts from the associations without the participation of government representatives. Nonetheless, its explicit function is to advice the government, not the interest groups. Its tasks, however, are set not by the government, but by the Joint Commission, and publication of the expert opinions presupposes the agreement of the presidents of the four organizations represented there. This means that the Beirat can only be active if the experts and the leadership of the Sozialpartner reach unanimity.

In contrast to this is the procedure of the West German Council of Economic Experts. It may publish majority and minority opinions and not infrequently has done so. Minority opinions, however, may not simply reflect academic disputes among the "four wise men" (as they are frequently called). Occasionally, the dissenter represents a viewpoint favorable to organized labor, for example. Indeed, nominations to the council (which are made by the Federal President) take into account not only academic standing, but also political and interest group cleavages, and thus one of the "wise men" is expected to sympathize with the unions, another one with organized business. In spite of this, the experts continue to enjoy a large independence, and this distinguishes the German from the Austrian case. It might even be difficult in Austria to recruit a sufficient number of qualified academic economists who never have had formal ties with the interest associations. Due to the small size of the country and to factors such as the "brain drain" toward West Germany — which limits the number of personnel available in Austria — but also due to the fact that Austrians (including intellectuals) are "joiners," qualified economists very often have held chamber or trade union jobs at least for some time during their careers. Anyway, from the limited evidence of these two cases, it is apparent that for liberal corporatism to function social cleavages have to be taken into account (at least in an informal manner) if expert advice is to be institutionalized.

The growing influence of experts is, of course, not a peculiarly "corporatist" phenomenon. Liberal corporatism is not simply a technocratic regime based on scientific expertise. Obviously, the system would not work in the case of fundamental disagreements among the experts. A supplementary condition is thus the existence of at least some common outlook among academic economists who are recruited into the corporate system. Our hypothesis is that there indeed exists such a fundamental consensus in economic analysis and that this contributes to the ideological basis of liberal corporatism. Its essential element seems to be a macroeconomic "systems approach," stressing the interdependence of macroeconomic aggregates and at least some minimum of interventionism. It thus seems essential that experts be recruited among mainstream economists (representing the "synthesis" of neoclassic and Keynesian approaches). The growing importance of trained economists in trade unions in particular has served to promote such an outlook at the expense of more traditional, conflict-oriented strategies. The revival of a Marxian political economy might in the long run threaten such a system if, increasingly, neo-Marxist economists would be hired by trade unions staffs. On the other hand, a growing importance of strict liberals and monetarists (of the Chicago school, for example) within the ranks of employer staffs might equally endanger the fundamental consensus. There are indeed "technocratic" elements in liberal corporatism, but only insofar as the "technocrats" agree on a sort of basic "harmonic" outlook, stressing interdependence of competing interests, the importance of information about this interdependence, and an active orientation of "autonomous groups" toward collective goals.

THE WANING ROLE OF GOVERNMENT:
THE AUSTRIAN CASE

I have already pointed out that corporatist policy-formation is essentially based on a strong cooperation of interest associations with the government. However, in order not to dilute the concept of corporatism we should not label all cases of voluntary cooperation of interest groups with governmental incomes policies as "corporatist." The "social contract" which the British government has recently concluded with the Trade Union Congress corresponds much more to a "bilateral" model, whereas liberal corporatism as we understand it presupposes a clearing between unions and employers with regard to the overall goals of public economic policy. That does not exclude the government from playing a more or less autonomous role in the process. Even in Austria the two-step model is not fully realized, though certainly this country does constitute an extreme case. Of course, the Austrian government cares about economic policy, and the Sozialpartner are perfectly informed about its position. There exist strong informal contacts. Due to the high degree of centralization and concentration of interest associations, on the one hand, and due to the fact that Austria is a small country, on the other, all relevant actors form part of a rather tightly knit information network. Of particular importance is the interpenetration of political parties and interest organizations (which shall be discussed later). The Minister of Commerce and Industry and the Minister of Finance have almost invariably come from the ranks of the Sozialpartner establishment (especially from the group of influential experts in the subcommissions of the Paritätische Kommission). The central bank also forms part of this information network, since its top management not infrequently has the same background, and, in addition, the interest groups are already represented on the General Council of the bank. However, if we consider the importance of "summit diplomacy" by the presidents of the organizations, it is obvious that in Austria the autonomy of the associational subsystem from the government and its power to anticipate public policy decisions are strongly developed. Since one might ask whether this waning of the government is characteristic of the "pure" type of liberal corporatism, I shall investigate this case in some detail — again by comparing it to West Germany.

TRENDS TOWARD A "SPILLOVER" OF CORPORATIST POLICY-FORMATION

In Austria, much more than in other countries, the subsystem of liberal corporatist policy-making extends far beyond the domain of incomes and business-cycle policy and incorporates, in particular, the domain of economic Ordnungspolitik. Here, any political measure is subject to the prior agreement of the large interest organizations, and government is largely excluded from the bargaining process. The legal basis for this is the claim of interest organizations to be consulted on all legislative projects (*Begutachtungsrecht*; cf. Fischer, 1972). In practice, moreover, it is not uncommon that the bills themselves are prepared by the Sozialpartner. A most striking example is the history of Austrian legislation on supervision of cartels. The cartel law of 1951 had been prepared by a committee of experts who formally had been nominated by the Conservative and Socialist parties, but in reality were recruited exclusively from the specialists of the chambers. Afterwards, the amendments to the law in 1958 and in 1962 (which had been demanded by the Chamber of Labour) were prepared in the same manner. The amendment of 1958 introduced a paritätische commission with representatives from the Chambers of Business and Labour as an advisory body to the *Kartellkommission* (which is a law court). This was a compromise, since the Chamber of Labour did not obtain the creation of a paritätische administrative board (*Kartellamt*) which it had demanded as early as 1928. In 1967 the conservative one-party governments of Chancellor Klaus tried to depart from tradition. At the demand of the chancellor, a draft was prepared by the legal section (*Verfassungsdienst*) of the Chancellor's Office in consultation with the Federal Chamber of Business. But this draft met such violent opposition from the trade union representatives in parliament that Klaus decided to abandon it and to return to the former practice. The next text was drawn up with the collaboration of one expert from the Chamber of Business and another from the Chamber of Labour, and — after approval by the organizations — it passed the formal legislative procedure in government and parliament without being changed. Quite naturally, when in 1972 a new cartel law was adopted in parliament by a unanimous vote, this bill, too, had been prepared by the Sozialpartner, one of its innovations being an increase in the powers of the *Paritätische Ausschuss.*

(Characteristically, it has been pointed out that opinions which this consultative body passes unanimously are regularly confirmed by the Cartel Court, which has the final decision.)[18]

This two-step pattern of legislation on cartels in Austria is of particular interest in our context, since we may contrast it with the legislative processes which in West Germany have led to the passage of the cartel law of 1957 and to important amendments in 1965 and 1973. From different case studies (Bethusy-Huc, 1962; Grottian, 1974; Robert, 1976), the dominant feature appears to have been "pressure politics" in which the bureaucracy of the Ministry of Economy, which prepared the drafts, played an autonomous role, but under strong pressure from organized interests it had only a very limited latitude of action to push through its own preference. Furthermore, the process of consultation with interest associations was characterized by a strong asymmetry in favor of business. Trade unions were not peculiarly active, nor very eager about the matter. Finally, the party system was of rather limited importance in the process of policy formation. Neither in the fifties nor in the seventies has their role corresponded to anything like the Downs model ("parties formulate policies in order to win elections," Downs, 1957: 28). In 1956-1957 the parties of the majority only became active at the committee stage in parliament, but were divided (the Christian Democrats in particular) into supporters of the rather liberal position of the administration, on the one hand (plus some outsiders taking a still more consistent liberal position), and, on the other hand, supporters of the position of business. The latter obtained considerable modifications in the bill. Thus, the process corresponded largely to the classic pluralistic model of pressure politics. In 1969-1972 things were not fundamentally different. The essential bargaining continued to take place during preparation of the bill between the administration and business representatives and largely outside the party system.

Another relevant example in the domain of Ordnungspolitik has been legislation on codetermination in industry. Again, in Austria we see the predominance of the two-step model. The *Arbeitsverfassungsgesetz* (Law on Labour Relations) of 1973, which introduced a system somewhat similar to the West German *Betriebsverfassungsgesetz* of 1952, was worked out in negotiations between the Chambers of Business and Labour. In West Germany, by contrast, we observe an interesting evolution. In the first years of the Federal Republic the two-step model played a certain role in matters of codetermination, but soon afterwards was abandoned. When the trade unions tried to revive it more than twenty years later, this failed from the outset. In 1950 the government, through the Minister of Labour, had invited trade unions and employer organizations to "show to parliament ways how to arrive at a new social order." Indeed, the conflict on codetermination in the iron and steel industry and in coal mining was settled in this manner after Adenauer had successfully invited the employers to come to an agreement with the Trade Union Federation. On the basis of this agreement a government bill was drafted and adopted in parliament without major modifications. This course of events, however, was due to rather special conditions. For the largest part of the iron and steel industries, the agreement merely confirmed the status quo which the trade unions had obtained in 1947 when they enjoyed a strong position due to the situation under British occupation. The only major change was the extension of this formula ("parity" of owners and labor directors coming from union ranks) to coal mining. Since Adenauer wanted to avoid serious conflicts which could have resulted from changing the status quo in favor of business, he pressed for a bilateral agreement. Things proceeded quite differently as far as codetermination in other branches of industry was concerned. This issue clearly was perceived as redistributive in character (in the sense of the Lowi typology), since the status quo was expected to change in favor of labor. Negotiations between labor and business had already broken down in 1950, and Adenauer — under strong pressure from the smaller parties on the right wing of his majority (in particular the Liberals) — lost his interest in appeasing the trade unions. Thus, the Betriebsverfassungsgesetz (law on codetermination) of 1952 resulted from a process in which, contrary to that of cartel legislation, the parties of the majority (represented by their parliamentary spokesmen) played a pivotal role. Due to the "redistributive" character of the issue, it was no longer the administration that served as the "turntable," but rather the party system.

The Betriebsverfassungsgesetz certainly constituted a defeat for the unions, and thus reflected the shift in power relations which had taken place to the disadvantage of organized labor since the elections of 1949. In Austria they have remained much more firmly entrenched for a number of historical and political reasons, not in the least due to the strong ties between the unions and the Socialist Party. From the genesis of the recent West German law on codetermination, which since 1976 has largely replaced the Betriebsverfassungsgesetz, it seems that in West Germany even the Social Democrats stick to the autonomy and to the political priority of the party system in matters of Ordnungspolitik. Adoption of the law marked the end of an extremely laborious dispute within the coalition of Social Democrats, who adopted a position largely sympathetic to trade union demands, and Liberals, who in spite of their shifting towards positions more to the left maintained a position rather critical toward organized labor. It was clear that the dispute had to be resolved by the party system, for a definitive failure would have threatened the survival of the majority. Because of this vital importance for the parties, the protected negotiations were largely conducted within the inner circle of coalition leadership. And in order to retain the latitude of action necessary for arriving at a compromise, party leaders had to keep their distance from interest organizations involved in the matter. On the part of Social Democratic leaders, this apparently was due not only to tactical considerations, but also to some skepticism about what was precisely regarded as the "corporatist" implications of the trade union program for codetermination. (In the long run their program would have included codetermination on the level of the national economy, while at present codetermination remains limited to the level of the business firm.) Of course, there was a lot of bargaining with organized interests, but the decisive stages of consensus-building took place within the majority parties. A consequence of this was that trade unions, as well as employers, felt more or less frustrated, and in October 1975 the President of the Trade Union Federation, Vetter, even suggested to the employers' association that they should enter into negotiations in order to arrive at a common proposal. Not surprisingly, employers turned down this invitation. But more significant was the fact that coalition spokesmen considered it rather unrealistic. The final compromise certainly has only reluctantly been swallowed by both interest organizations.

The preceding, admittedly sketchy, comparative description of some processes of policy formation in contemporary Western Europe does not, of course, answer the question of whether "politics really mattered" and whether policy outcomes differed in an appreciable manner. Such a judgment would presuppose a more detailed analysis which is beyond the scope of this article. But the peculiar patterns of the Austrian policy process lead us to the question of what are the conditions that may explain such an extension of liberal corporatist policy-making.

One extremely speculative hypothesis might be derived from the asymmetry which may eventually characterize corporatist income policies in the perception of organized labor. Union leaders may be tempted, therefore, to demand an extension of the domain of corporatist policy-making to other domains of economic and social policy. This may include the control of private investments and a participation of labor in profits that are to be reinvested. Projects of this sort have been discussed in Sweden and West Germany.

Yet such a hypothesis does not seem to hold for the Austrian case. Rather, the broad scope of corporatist policy-making in this country seems to result from specific historical circumstances. It dates from the decades of the black-red coalition which seems to have discharged itself of some of its responsibilities upon the Sozialpartner in order to reduce the problem loads placed upon coalition leadership. And such a strategy appears to have been facilitated by the existence of strong corporatist traditions which go back not only to the authoritarian semicorporatist Dollfuss regime (1934-1938), but further into the late nineteenth century. These traditions, however, have lost most of their former antiparliamentary elements. For, as we shall now point out, in Austria as well as in Germany (which here stand as examples for all liberal corporatist countries) the associational subsystem has a strong symbiotic relationship to the party system.

INTERPENETRATION OF LIBERAL CORPORATISM AND THE PARTY SYSTEM

It has already been mentioned that the Austrian Federation of Labour Unions has strong ties to the Socialist Party. To be sure, in theory the ÖGB is independent of political parties, contrary to the former *Richtungsgewerkschaft* (union with a distinctive ideological orientation), and hence includes members of different parties. But it is precisely the system of proportional political representation within the unions which constitutes the decisive link. In the elected bodies of the union movement there are socialist, conservative, and communist *Fraktionen*, and since the socialists form a majority within the federation and all industrial unions (except the union of civil servants), decisions are effectively made by the SPÖ Fraktion. On the other side, union leaders exert considerable influence within the Socialist Party, and ÖGB President Benya is at the same time Socialist deputy and president of the first chamber of Parliament. Moreover, in the socialist government, the vice-chancellor is an important union leader. As for the conservative Osterreichische Volkspartei, its interpenetration with the subsystem of interest representation is still more pronounced, for its very organizational structure is based on corporate representation. Essentially, the party consists of three *Bunde* (leagues); The Business League (*Wirtschaftsbund*, ÖWB), the Farmers' League (*Bauernbund*, ÖBB) and the League of Blue and White Collar Workers (*Arbeiter- und Angestelltenbund*, ÖAAB). The latter, largely an organization of civil servants and employees in the state-controlled industries, plays an important role within the conservative minority in the trade unions, while the Business and Farmers' Leagues are very close to the respective chambers, in which the ÖVP has a strong majority. Therefore, on the conservative side a cumulation of offices in party and interest organization also plays an important role. Raab, for example, who was president of the Federal Chamber of Business, in 1953 became the Federal Chancellor of the coalition government. After his demission in 1961, he returned to the presidency of the Federal Chamber. In the last years the president of the Federal Chamber of Business has regularly been an influential member of the ÖVP in parliament. Negotiations of the presidents of the Sozialpartner, thus, have the character of meetings of influential parliamentary leaders. Indeed, if my information is correct, they used to take place in the very rooms of parliament. During the period of coalition government, the famous extraconstitutional "coalition committee," the most important steering body of the coalition, was composed of the top party as well as interest group leaders.

In West Germany the political linkages of interest organizations with political parties are not much different from those existing in Austria, but the boundaries of the party system and the subsystem of interest representation are much more clearly drawn. For instance, formal cumulation of leadership positions is rather exceptional. It is true that three ministers of the Brandt and Schmid governments have been presidents of industrial unions (Leber, Arendt, Gscheidle), but all of them abandoned their trade union functions upon entry into the cabinet. Though most trade union leaders are members of the Social Democratic Party and in general support its policies, while on the other hand the SPD in principle is

sympathetic to trade union demands, both organizations are eager
to preserve their freedom of action. We have already shown this in
the case of the Codetermination Law of 1976. On the other hand,
one could point to the attitude of the Union of the Public Service
and Transports, whose president, SPD member Kluncker, in the
wage dispute of 1974 consciously defied Brandt's government and
almost induced the Chancellor to hand in his demission (Brandt,
1976). These are important, but not exceptional, illustrations of the
relative autonomy of interest organizations from the party system,
and vice versa.

THE PROBLEM OF "FUNCTIONAL PRIMACY"[19]

The "problem of party government" has repeatedly been discussed
in contradistinction to "administrative government" (Rose, 1968).
In a superficial perspective, the Austrian case seems to present a
third alternative — namely, corporatist interest group government.
But such a conclusion would simplify our problem because of the
symbiotic relation of the subsystem of interest representation with
the party system.

If one takes as given the pretentions of classical theories of party
government, one might well conclude that the West German party
system has remained the "functionally primary" subsystem and
thus has a higher "directive capacity" than the Austrian. But we
doubt such a generalization is warranted by existing empirical
evidence. At best we might risk some more limited speculative
hypotheses. On the one hand, if there exists a high level of conflict
(in particular on "redistributive" issues), it is probable that the
party system possesses a greater capacity for consensus-building
since its flexibility is greater and thresholds of consensus are lower.
To put it the other way around, consensus-building and problem-
solving in a corporatist subsystem of interest representation depend
on a rather low level of conflict intensity because of the high
threshold imposed by (de facto or de jure) unanimity rules which
are essential to its functioning. Otherwise, conflicts over rules of
representation would be extremely difficult to resolve. Therefore, it
is highly probable that the liberal corporatist subsystem will not
tend to "supplant" the party system. "Overloading" of its capacity for consensus-building will in general only be avoided by functional self-restraint.

On the other hand, as I have argued, electoral competition may result in the party system giving precedence to short-run over long-run policy options. But since in policy-formation the long-term element is growing in importance, as is apparent in the emphasis increasingly placed upon planning and forecasting, such a short-term orientation of political parties may lead to a preponderance of the administrative subsystem on the condition that it retain a large autonomy from the party system. From this, in turn, may develop that "gap" in consensus-building we have discussed above, and it seems plausible that liberal corporatism may thus correspond to a functional requisite of highly developed capitalist societies. However, since its capacity for consensus-building is limited, it would be unrealistic to consider corporatism as a realistic alternative to representative government and the party system.

NOTES

1. Moreover, in some cases, such as the Austrian one, formal compulsory membership in the "chambers" is a characteristic element of the system. But here, too, the trade unions, one of its important pillars, retain the character of formally voluntary associations. This, on the one hand, demands permanent efforts of organizational integration of members, while, on the other hand, it contributes to increasing the unions' latitude of action.

2. Characteristically, in West Germany the Council of Economic Experts that has been an influential protagonist of "liberal corporatist" concepts usually speaks of the "autonomous groups," a term borrowed from the German version of pluralist theory (Fraenkel, 1964: 188).

3. In discussing the problem of party government, my premise is of course the institutional framework of parliamentary government. Prominent German theorists (Luhmann, 1969; Habermas, 1973) who adopt the material hypotheses of Parsons (1959) have overlooked the fact that the party system of the United States works under quite different institutional conditions.

4. I agree, however, with Schmitter on the need to define "corporatism" as a distinctive system in which "associationally organized interests" play a pivotal role. The concept should not be diluted into something as vague as "corporate society" (Harris, 1972), which lumps together the corporation as a special type of associational interest representative with the "modern corporation" of Berle and Means or the "mature corporation" of Galbraith, that is, the large business firm characterized by allegedly changing organizational motivations.

5. Characteristically, a leading expert from the Austrian Sozialpartnerschaft has placed a strong emphasis on this pattern (confusing, however, the terms "bilateral" and "multilateral"). In the "multilateral" (or rather "bilateral") model the govern-

ment deals with associations separately, and it is said to perceive its role as that of a "turntable," implying that it has some influence on the direction of the negotiative process. In the model called "Bilateral" (which corresponds to our "two-step" model and obviously has the sympathies of the author), its role in economic policy would be diminished due to prior agreements between the associations (Kienzl, 1974: 287).

6. Of course, this hypothesis should not be understood in the sense of a crude "historical materialist" theory. Rather, we are dealing with problems of "social guidance" which result from the functional relationship of the economic and the political system.

7. Rall (1975: 207) has proposed to distinguish the "imperative," the "indicative," and the "cooperative" varieties of income policies, the latter being characterized by the participation of labor unions and business in the process of policy-making.

8. When Samuelson (1964: 350) argues that "we have not yet arrived at a stage where any nation is likely to create for itself a set of constitutional procedures that will displace the need for discretionary policy formation," the underlying evolutionary hypothesis probably should be inverted. It seems more plausible that the need for discretionary policies will increase. This, in turn, involves increasing requirements for consensus-building.

9. The hypotheses I am developing here are admittedly of a somewhat speculative character. However, in the electoral campaign of 1976 in West Germany the government seems to have been successful when it argued that, since inflation and unemployment were due to a "worldwide recession," it could not be held responsible for them.

10. The problem of time required for consensus-building under different structural conditions (and in relation to the rationality of decisions) has been discussed in the penetrating study of Luhmann (1971).

11. Rose (1976: 94) has argued that in the months preceding a general election the governing party will try to artificially induce an economic boom and afterwards may adopt deflationary policies in order to compensate for that.

12. On Austria see, in particular, Pütz (1966), Klose (1970), several articles in *Österreichische Zeitschrift für Politikwissenschaft 3* (1974), and Bichlbauer and Pelinka (1974).

13. This system of parity is also reminiscent of the Austro-Marxist concept of an "equilibrium of class forces" characterizing a certain period of Austrian history (Bauer, 1923).

14. On incomes policy in West Germany, see Schlecht (1968), Hoppmann (1971), Adam (1972), Hardes (1974) and Pfromm (1975); on trade unions and incomes policy, see Institut für Sozialforschung (1969) and Bergmann et al. (1975).

15. These bodies form part of another subsystem of policy formation which has strong affinities to, and complements, the liberal corporatist subsystem. It has aptly been characterized as *Politikverflechtung* ("interlocking of politics") by Scharpf (1976). See, besides, Kock (1975) and Lehmbruch (1976).

16. On other West European countries, see Busch-Lüty (1964), Edelman and Fleming (1965), Ulman and Flanagan (1971) and Rall (1975). On The Netherlands, see Estor (1965).

17. Huntford (1972), who in his rather one-sided account so strongly stresses the "corporatist" character of Swedish society, would certainly deny it the label of "liberal."

18. Szecsi and Wehsely (1975). Further information in this paragraph comes from März and Weissel, in Pütz (1966), and from interviews conducted in Vienna.

19. The concept of "functional primacy" has been developed by Parsons (1959) and Luhmann (1970).

7

Corporatism, Parliamentarism and Social Democracy

Bob Jessop
University of Essex, UK

This paper attempts to locate current discussions of corporatism in relation to Marxist political economy and to assess the political and economic significance of corporatist tendencies in the capitalist state.[1] The critique of recent work begins with a review of the most influential definitions of corporatism, then considers the approaches to the state that underpin these definitions, and ends with a reformulation of corporatism as a form of articulation of political representation and state intervention. This critique is followed by some prefatory remarks concerning Marxist theories of the capitalist state with special reference to the analysis of state forms. We then discuss parliamentarism, corporatism, and tripartism and consider their nature, preconditions, and effects. The analysis is followed by some brief reflections on the social bases of different state forms. This helps us to distinguish the role of corporatism in fascist and social democratic regimes in terms of its differential articulation to other forms of representation and intervention and its significance in consolidating the social bases adequate to each form of regime. We conclude with some general observations on the theoretical and empirical analysis of corporatism and its future in advanced capitalist states.

DEFINITIONS OF CORPORATISM

The definition of corporatism most often cited in recent work is that of Philippe Schmitter. This definition belongs to a fourfold typology of political representation and is juxtaposed to definitions of pluralism, monism, and syndicalism [Schmitter, 1974; 1977]. Schmitter recognizes the abstract nature of his ideal typical definition and himself suggests the need to distinguish various sub-types. Thus he contrasts "societal corporatism" and "state corporatism". The former is characterized by the autonomy of interest associations from the state and piecemeal evolution from below, the latter is marked by the subordination of interest associations to the state and a crisis-induced, repressive impositon by authoritarian political forces from above [1974: 94]. Schmitter then discusses the origins, nature, and effects of each sub-type in relation to capital accumulation and the balance of forces in class struggle [1974: 102-5]. Finally he considers their characteristic internal contradictions and predicts that the future lies with syndicalism rather than state or societal corporatism [1974: 126-7].

An alternative approach favoured by Pahl and Winkler is also influential (at least in Britain). Their definiton of corporatism belongs to a fourfold typology of political economies which is produced through a cross-classification of two variables relating to the means of production, viz., private vs. public ownership and private vs. public control. Corporatism is defined as a system of private ownership combined with public control; and is contrasted with capitalism, socialism, and syndicalism [Pahl and Winkler, 1974; Winkler, 1976; Pahl and Winkler, 1976]. Pahl and Winkler then further specify corporatism (but not the cognate forms of political economy) through the introduction of a goal-orientation variable. Thus corporatism is finally defined as "an economic system in which the state directs and controls predominantly privately-owned business towards four goals: unity, order, nationalism, and success" [1976: 7]. They also distinguish two sub-types of corporatism: egalitarian (e.g., Sweden) and inegalitarian (e.g., Italian fascism) [1976: 13]. In contrast to Schmitter, however, no interest is shown in developing a general theory of corporatism and its sub-types. Instead Pahl and Winkler focus on the development of corporatism in Britain and suggest that "fascism with a human face" is almost inevitable within a decade [1974].

Somewhat different criteria are relevant for criticising the two approaches since only the latter is directly concerned with political economy. But both approaches involve problematic or inadequate views of the state and its articulation with capitalism. Neither

Schmitter nor Pahl and Winkler consider the specific qualities of capitalism as a mode of production and their implications for the specific form and functions of the state in capitalist societies. This creates various problems in their analyses of the relations between the political and economic domains in corporatist systems and in their understanding of the role of class struggle in capital accumulation and political domination. Since the problems are different in the two cases, however, we shall consider each approach separately before proceeding to a reformulation of the nature of corporatism.

Schmitter's typology is an abstract schema concerned with modes of interest intermediation. Its author correctly opposes the formal, static qualities of the four modes of political representation as defined in ideal typical fashion and the substantive, dynamic character of real political institutions and forces on the terrain of the state in particular societies. But his original paper on corporatism still embodies a number of ambiguities and inadequacies.Thus the typology of modes of political representation simply takes the state as given and endows it with the power to license, control, or, indeed, create corporations. Insofar as the state is not just anthropomorphized or seen as a sovereign legal subject, it is variously interpreted as a decisional structure, public officials, and "organized monopolists of legitimate violence" [Schmitter, 1974: 86, 104, 104]. Nor does the more recent paper contained in this volume clarify the issue through its parade of the three internally heterogeneous models of "civil society-association-state" relations. However, whilst the abstract typological analysis tends to treat the state as outside (if not above) conflicts rooted in the economy and civil society, the development of societal and state corporatism is explained largely in terms of changes in the capitalist mode of production and the balance of class forces. Thus societal corporatism is related to the need to associate or incorporate dominated classes in the political process as the state expands its facilitative, allocative, and regulative functions as guarantor of capital accumulation [Schmitter, 1974: 107-8, 108-15]. In contrast, the forceful imposition of state corporatism is explained as an instrument for rescuing and consolidating capitalism through the repression of autonomous organizations of the subordinate classes in situations where the bourgeoisie is too weak, internally divided, externally dependent and/or short of resources to respond in an effective and legitimate manner to their demands within a liberal democratic context [Schmitter, 1974: 108, 115-25]. Both explanations seem to instrumentalize the state and to endow the bourgeoisie with the power to restructure the system of political representation at will. This is just as unsatisfactory as the suggestion that the state is an autonomous subject and itself determines the forms of representation. It is also inconsistent with Schmitter's own account of the various tensions involved in these strategies for the bourgeoisie — with societal corporatism producing demands for authentic participation outside its representational straitjacket and state corporatism involving increasing costs in repression and capitalist irrationality [Schmitter, 1974: 126-7]. In short, despite the seminal nature of Schmitter's analysis of political representation, it is based on an inadequate theorization of the state in capitalist societies. But it is an account on which one can build with effect.

Pahl and Winkler forcus on political economy rather than political representation and discuss corporatism as a *tertium genus* distinct from both capitalism and socialism. In this context the *differentia specifica* of corporatism is not the amount of state intervention but the manner in which it is articulated with the economic order. Thus, whereas the reproduction of capitalism may actually be secured through the growth of intervention to facilitate and support private enterprise, the development of direct state control over the internal decision-making of individual concerns will lead instead to corporatism [1976: 8]. This involves not only the loss of private economic initiative and the decline of market forces; it is also linked with a fundamental reorganization of the state apparatus and its modes of conduct. Thus antinomianism replaces the rule of law, inquisitorial justice replaces adversary justice, strategic discrimination replaces universal and impartial facilitation and regulation, enforcement of government policies is delegated to private concerns and interest associations and/or mediated through quasi-governmental and quasi-non-governmental organizations, and there is official orchestration of public opinion and/or extra-legal coercion in support of official action [Pahl and Winkler, 1976: 14-22; also Winkler, 1977: 43-58]. Corporatism thus involves both the concentration of economic power in the hands of the state *and* the autonomization of the state in relation to the nation or people it is meant to represent.

This approach is interesting and provocative but it also entails major theoretical problems. Thus the argument for the specificity of corporatism rests on a narrow conception of capitalism and a subjectivist view of the state. In focusing on *private control* over *technical factors* of production and on *free market* competition among *individual capitals,* Pahl and Winkler overlook the *social nature* of capitalist production as a *valorization process* mediated through the *class struggle* and ignore all other forms of capitalist competition as well as the constraints imposed by *capital in general.*[2] Such an approach cannot relate the origins, effects, and limits of "socialism" (public enterprise) or corporatism (public control) to the process of capital accumulation and leads instead to the simple opposition and/or juxtaposition of different forms of political economy. Thus their explanation for the development of corporatism in Britain refers to technological change, the growth of monopolies, the profitability crisis in the private sector, the deficit on the balance of payments, the power of trade unions, and the growth of inflation [Pahl and Winkler, 1976: 6; Winkler, 1976]. None of these phenomona are related to the basic developmental tendencies of capitalism; nor to the specific location of the British economy within the international circuit of capital.[3] Instead they remain unexamined at the level of immediate appearances and no attempt is made to link corporatist developments to the reorganization of British capitalism. This neglect is matched by the failure to examine the different mediations between such economic changes and/or crises and the specific forms of public control in Britain. Instead Pahl and Winkler reduce state intervention to a simple reflex of changed technical and market conditions and/or treat the state as an autonomous subject which is able to impose its own goals on the economnic order. Their reductionism leads to the prediction that corporatism is inevitable regardless of electoral and political changes and makes it difficult to explain the differential development and success of corporatism in other societies.[4] Their subjectivism autonomizes the state vis-à-vis economic relations and favours a definition of corporatism in terms of the goals of public control. This leads to neglect of the struggle to elaborate such goals in particular programmes and policies and of the constraints on corporatist intervention imposed through the form of capital accumulation. Moreover, although Pahl and Winkler offer a useful account of the reorganization of the state apparatus in Britain, they do not relate it to the reorganization of political representation nor provide an explanation in terms of other economic and political changes. Indeed, whilst the brief reference to corporatist representation treats it as a ruse to reinforce state control [Pahl and

Winkler, 1976: 19; Winkler, 1977: 54], the extended discussion of the state apparatus tends to conflate the growth of state support *for* private capital with state control *over* private capital and nullifies the specificity of the corporatist form of state. In short, although this approach contains much insight and organizes a considerable body of material, it cannot be employed without some serious reservations.

Thus, despite their considerable influence on the study of corporatism, neither approach provides a satisfactory account of the political economy of corporatism. There is no attempt to analyse capitalism as a mode of production at different levels of abstraction; nor to examine the complex articulation between its economic and political determinations in different phases of capital accumulation. Hence the development of corporatism is examined in terms of technological, economic, or class reductionism and/or in an arbitrary, eclectic, and ad hoc manner. This is reflected in an inadequate view of the state. The latter is seen as an autonomous instance and both theories switch between instrumentalist and subjectivist views of state intervention. In another sense these approaches are complementary because of their differential focus on the forms of representation and the forms of intervention associated with corporatism. Yet even this is unfortunate since it is precisely the form of articulation between representation and intervention which determines the adequacy of corporatism in securing conditions necessary to capital accumulation. The rest of our paper is concerned to justify and elaborate this argument in terms of recent developments in Marxist political economy and/or state theory.

ON MARXIST STATE THEORY

If we are to locate the analysis of corporatism in terms of the Marxist theory of the state, we must first define the state. Moreover, although the search for guarantees that the state is capitalist is particularly tempting to Marxists, all forms of essentialism must be avoided. At the same time we want to avoid treating the state as a simple instrument and/or as an autonomous subject. The appropriate solution is to adopt the following assumptions: (a) the state should be seen as a set of institutions that cannot, qua structural ensemble, exercise power; (b) political forces do not exist independently from the state but are shaped in part through its forms of representation and intervention; (c) state power is a complex social relation which reflects the changing balance of forces in a determinate conjuncture; and (d) state power is capitalist to the extent that it creates, maintains, or restores the conditions required for capital accumulation in given circumstances and is non-capitalist to the extent that these conditions are not realized. Let us now elaborate these assumptions.

In advocating an institutional definition of the state we reject those alternative approaches that endow it with an essential unity as an autonomous subject and/or as the support of an essential function. This means that one can legitimately define the state in various ways since it has no essential unity which establishes unambiguous institutional boundaries. Corporatism is particularly important here as it highlights these ambiguities through the delegation of state power to quasi-governmental organizations, quasi-non-governmental organizations, and private associations. Thus, whilst some definition is a *sine qua non* of theoretical analysis, the choice is inevitably rather arbitrary. The legal distinction between "public" and "private" will suffice for present purposes. But, whatever one's choice of definition, it is essential to consider the complex forms of articulation among state institutions and between state and non-state institutions in the overall reproduction of capital accumulation and political domination.

The second assumption excludes a crude instrumentalist approach. For, although the state should not be seen as a subject able to exercise power, its institutional form does have unequal and asymmetrical effects on the ability of different forces to pursue their interests. This excludes the possibility that the state can ever be neutral. Instead the nature of political forces and what they can accomplish is at least in part determined by the forms of representation and intervention that characterize a given state. Thus, since changes in these forms will have differential effects on political forces, their access to the state, and their susceptibility to state action, it is wrong to see political forces as outside and independent of the state and able to manipulate it as a simple, passive instrument. This will prove important when we consider the implications of corporatism for the reorganization of class relations and the nature of the state.

The third assumption implies the firm rejection of all attempts to distinguish between 'state power' and 'class power' (whether as descriptive concepts or principles of explanation) insofar as they establish this distinction by constituting the state itself as a subject and/or deny the continuing class struggle within state apparatuses as well as outside them. This is not to deny the influence of political categories such as the military or bureaucrats; nor to deny that the class aspects of the state may sometimes be secondary to its nature and effects as a system of domination over the 'people'. But, whatever the relation between political categories and classes and/or between the twin determinations of the state as class and as popular domination, state power is a mediated effect of the balance among *all* forces in a given situation. This implies that state power comprises our explicandum and not a principle of explanation.

The fourth assumption implies a radical displacement of analytic focus from the search for guarantees that the state apparatus and its functions are necessarily capitalist in all aspects to a concern with the many and varied contingent effects of state power on accumulation in determinate conjunctures. These effects depend on a wide range of factors and cannot be reduced to a simple realization of the needs of capital. In this context capital accumulation has a dual theoretical function in our analysis: it is both a point of reference and a principle of explanation. We should not confuse the two nor stress one to the exclusion of the other. To treat capital accumulation only as a point of reference would endow the state with absolute autonomy in relation to capital; for accumulation to be treated merely as a principle of explanation would reduce the state to a more or less complex effect of the self-realization of capital. We should examine how the particular institutional form of the state and the character of state intervention affect capital accumulation and how capital accumulation conditions the state apparatus and circumscribes the effects of state power. In both cases we must avoid the invocation of general laws or tendencies and specify the various conditions of existence that serve as our points of reference and the causal mechanisms that mediate our principles of explanation. And in both cases these must be specified at appropriate levels of theoretical abstraction and complexity. For only in this way can we adequately account for the mutual presupposition and interaction of the political and economic instances of capitalist social formations.

Because the state and state power are critical to the reproduction of capital, the reorganization of the state and its articulation with other elements of the social formation may play a vital role in securing the preconditions of capital accumulation in altered circumstances. It is here that the form of the state is significant and we must therefore ask to what extent the development of corporatism furthers or hinders accumulation. But how should we tackle state forms?

The state is an institutional complex of forms of representation and intervention. This implies that state forms can be distinguished in terms of the differential articulation of political representation and state intervention. Such an approach offers several advantages. It provides a means to examine the linkages between the state, civil society, and economy in terms of the mediation of demands and support as well as the maintenance of accumulation and domination. This will prove particularly important when we consider the social bases of the state. It enables us to examine the effects of the inadequate articulation of representation and intervention on accumulation and domination and thus provides concepts useful in the analysis of structural crises of the state apparatus. It emphasizes the *hybrid* character of the state and thus points to the need to consider the pattern of domination and subordination among different forms of representation and intervention. This is particularly important for the analysis of the role of corporatism (whether societal or state) in fascist and social democratic regimes. In this context we must also recall that neither the forms of political representation nor those of state intervention are neutral; instead both structure the formation of political forces and their ability to achieve specific effects through the state. So, in considering the state as an institutional complex of forms of political representation and state intervention, we are also considering it as a system of "structural selectivity" [Offe, 1972: 65-106; Poulantzas, 1978: 135-78] or political domination.

PARLIAMENTARISM AND CORPORATISM

An analysis of state forms thus presupposes definitions of specific modes of articulation and disarticulation between representation and intervention. We do not intend to offer an exhaustive account of such modes but will focus instead on parliamentarism and corporatism. These are first considered as modes of articulation in which the form of representation is *formally* complementary to the form of intervention. We then define "tripartism" as a hybrid mode formed through the combination of corporatism with parliamentary (or some other form of) government. This is followed by arguments concerning the adequacy of parliamentarism and corporatism as forms of class and/or popular domination and the effects of disruption in the circuits of representation and intervention organized through them. We then assess the view that tripartism involves the structural-functional differentiation of the political system producing a consequent upgrading of its adaptive capacity. To this claim we counterpose an alternative account of the possible contradictions between parliamentarism and corporatism. Our analysis then concludes with reflections on the differential function of corporatism in securing the social base and forms of intervention appropriate to fascist and social democratic regimes.

Parliamentarism involves the fusion of political representation mediated through the participation of "citizens" in the policy-making of an elected government through their exercise of voting and related political rights and state intervention in the form of legislation or general policies enforced by a permanent rational-legal administration in accordance with the rule of law. "Citizenship" involves the institution of an individual juridical subject endowed with specific political rights and obligations and the extension of this status to all members of society without reference to their class location or other attributes. Definite legal freedoms (such as freedom of association, freedom of speech, and free elections) are also necessary to ensure the formal exercise of the citizen's rights of participation; and, to translate formal into substantive popular control, specific social conditions would also be required. However, since the formal structure of parliamentarism does not guarantee real popular control, popular-democratic struggles might develop to establish, maintain, or restore the legal and/or social conditions in which such control is possible. It should also be noted that, regardless of the outcome of such struggles on the formation of the "people" as a unified political force, various other political forces can develop in this context and engage in the struggle for state power. In this sense pluralism is a typical feature of parliamentarism [Schmitter, 1974: 95-7].[5] This system is also characterized by state intervention through the parliamentary enactment and subsequent impartial, rational-legal bureaucratic enforcement of general legislative codes regulating private and public activities and/or through the provision of general external conditions facilitating or supporting such activities without direct control over them. The latter field of intervention could include Keynesian macro-level demand management in the field of accumulation or welfare programmes oriented to the satisfaction of individual social rights.

Corporatism involves the fusion of political representation mediated through a system of public "corporations" which are constituted on the basis of their members' function within the division of labour and state intervention through these same corporations and/or administrative agencies formally accountable to them. Thus, in contrast to the characteristic institutional separation of representation and intervention in parliamentary-bureaucratic systems, corporatism implies their institutional fusion since the formal organs through which political representation is mediated are also responsible for intervention. Thus, even where this is not directly undertaken by the various corporations, the administrative agencies involved are accountable to the collective corporatist will through executive organs on which the corporations are represented. A determinate (although pluralist and non-unitary) sovereign authority would also be required to coordinate the different programmes and policies in a fully-fledged corporatist system. This supreme executive body could comprise a chamber of corporations or a collegial body recruited from and responsible to the various corporations. Moreover, if corporatism is to form the dominant element in a state form, the corporations would need to be all-embracing and enjoy representational monopolies in relation to their members' various functions [Schmitter, 1974: 93-94, 104-5].[6] For, in the absence of such compulsory and non-competitive "corporatization" of politics, serious deficiencies in both representation and intervention could occur. Finally, it is important to note that, just as parliamentarism has no immediate, unconditional implications for the balance of political forces, nor does the existence or dominance of corporatism in itself guarantee the accumulation of capital or reproduction of bourgeois political domination.

Tripartism is a hybrid in which parliamentarism and corporatism are combined into a contradictory unity owing to the formal participation in corporatist decision-making of representatives of the parliamentary executive ("government") and/or the delegation of corporatist policy implementation to the parliamentary bureaucracy and/or the formal participation of corporations in the decision-making of the parliamentary executive and/or the delegation of parliamentary policy administration to the corporations. The relative weight of the corporations and the parliamentary executive will obviously vary with the extent to which the conditions of existence of corporatism and parliamentarism are present and with the balance of social forces mobilized behind each form. It should also be noted that corporatism and/or parliamentarism can also be articulated with other forms of political representation and state intervention. This is evident in the articulation of corporatism with "monism" [Schmitter, 1974: 97] in fascist regimes or of parliamentarism with clientilism in various dependent capitalist systems. This phenomenon also underlies Manoïlescu's account of "corporatisme subordonné" — where corporations are created by and kept as auxiliary and dependent organs of a state basing its legitimacy and effectiveness on other forms of representation and intervention [as cited in Schmitter, 1974: 102-3]. Studies of specific states must take account of such hybridity and incorporate it into the analysis of state power.

STATE FORMS AND CAPITAL ACCUMULATION

Capitalist societies are characterized by many different state forms. Accordingly this section of the paper examines the adequacy of different forms to the preconditions of accumulation in different phases and conjunctures of capitalism. But it should first be noted that the state is located on the terrain of the social formation and not on that of the pure mode of production or, indeed, of a specific combination of forms of labour. Thus a full analysis ought to refer to other determinations besides the dominant relations of production.

Capitalist exploitation is based on free exchange of commodities and does not require the direct use of coercion in the organization of the labour process and the appropriation of surplus labour. But capital accumulation still requires political action to help secure its reproduction. Not only is state intervention necessary to facilitate the transition from pre-capitalist modes of production, it is also necessary once capitalist relations are dominant. Thus even the period of liberal competition presupposes the realization of the general external conditions of accumulation — such as monetary and legal systems; and the development of monopoly capitalism requires increasing state intervention to mobilize counter-tendencies to the tendency of the rate of profit to fall and/or to promote the socialization of capitalist relations of production in the attempt to bring them into correspondence with the increasing socialization of the forces of production [Holloway and Picciotto, 1977: 76-101; Fine and Harris, 1979: 113-145]. In turn the changing imperatives of capital accumulation in the field of intervention entail changing requirements in the field of representation. Here it should be noted that capital accumulation depends on the continued ability of capital itself to secure through struggle the many different preconditions of the creation and appropriation of surplus-value on an expanding scale. Thus the laws of motion of capitalism are not natural and inevitable: they depend for their realization on the balance of forces in the incessant struggle between capital and labour. It follows that a reorganization of this balance may become a prerequisite to restoring the conditions favourable to accumulation. Changes in the articulation of different state apparatuses, in the organization of access to such apparatuses, in the forms of political mobilization, in the character of state intervention, and in political strategies and alliances could prove significant in this respect. It is in this context that we can locate the growth of corporatism in the advanced capitalist states.

Parliamentarism is adequate as the dominant political principle only in certain situations and in others will prove incompatible with capital accumulation. As a system of representation it can encourage the formation of a unified "power bloc" among dominant fractions and classes and it can also facilitate the maintenance of hegemony over subordinate classes. Its function in the first respect is especially clear during the early stages of parliamentary development when the franchise was restricted and parliament was a significant forum for representatives of different propertied interests to establish common needs, negotiate compromises, and formulate shared strategies. Moreover, as the franchise is progressively extended, the imperatives of electoral competition stimulate bourgeois parties to consider the interests of the dominated classes as well as those of the propertied. This provides one basis for the reformist politics necessary to maintain that "unstable equilibrium of compromise" essential to bourgeois hegemony. Similar constraints discourage proletarian parties promoting policies that are electorally unpopular and reinforce moderation. In this context the emphasis on individual citizenship and the public or national interest may also inhibit or undermine the development of class consciousness. To the extent that these electoral and ideological constraints are ineffective, the parliamentary-bureaucratic system may still be so structured that effective radical policies cannot be implemented because of the separation of powers or similar institutional restraints. Indeed the separation of political representation and state intervention characteristic of parliamentarism performs important functions in this respect. For it permits the smooth operation of the permanent administration while changes occur in the balance of forces in the representational field. Moreover the system of rational-legal administration separates the masses from control over the means of administration and transforms them into its individuated subjects. Within this context it nonetheless provides stable, calculable administration according to the rule of law in a "Rechtsstaat"; and, through its articulation with parliament, provides the means to change the law. This is particularly appropriate during the phase of liberal competitive capitalism, when the principal role of the state is to secure the general external conditions of production and to restrict its more harmful effects through general legal or bureaucratic interventions. It is also compatible with general macro-economic intervention through fiscal and monetary policies working indirectly through market forces (e.g., international tariffs, investment allowances, or contra-cyclical budgetary policies). Lastly, as such forms of intervention maintain the separation between the economic and political domains of capitalist societies, they reproduce the dependence of the state on capital accumulation and thus render it vulnerable to market forces and economic crises when state intervention is inimical to the expanded reproduction of capital.[7]

But it is evident that parliamentarism also has its limitations and contradictions as the dominant principle of the capitalist state. It is liable to various political crises which restrict its abilities to function on behalf of capital and, even in normal circumstances, a number of dysfunctional consequences can occur. Thus its role in representation can be disrupted or paralysed through a representational crisis marked by a split between the parties in parliament and their supporters in the country, a parliamentary crisis which makes cooperation among parties difficult or impossible, or a substantial penetration of parliament by political forces committed to radical transformation of the relations of production and/or patterns of political and ideological domination. Such crises may reflect and/or intensify difficulties in the electoral mediation of hegemony, the unification of the power bloc, and the bourgeois domination of parliament. These problems will be aggravated to the extent that parliament has effective control over significant means of economic intervention and/or is also confronting an economic crisis. Dysfunctions may also be introduced through the normal operation of political competition. For adversary politics may encourage the abuse of executive power to secure electoral advantage at the expense of accumulation and/or create conditions in which long-term corporate planning becomes difficult owing to unpredictable changes in government policies. Again this provokes most problems where the amount and scope of state intervention within parliamentary control is significant. For, as the state acquires increased autonomy as a precondition of effective intervention to establish, maintain, or restore conditions necessary to accumulation, it also gains the means to disrupt and undermine these same conditions. This contradiction is aggravated by the fact that the requirements of capital in general cannot be fully determined *a priori* but often only emerge *post hoc*, if at all, as successive crises suggest that certain conditions of existence have not been realized. Thus an expansion in the means of intervention need not be matched by an increase in knowledge about their effective employment. Indeed the technical nature, enormous scope, and discretionary character of new forms of state intervention can itself lead to the decline of parliamentary control over the administrative branch and thus contribute to the disarticulation of parliamentary representation from state intervention. Among other effects this could result in increasing independence of the administration and/or in crises of political authority [Jessop, 1978].

It is in this context that corporatism is significant. For this involves two major shifts in the field of representation that realign it with new forms of state intervention. Thus, whilst the increasing disarticulation engendered by the continuing separation of parliament from an interventionist administration is solved through the corporatist tendency to merge representation and intervention in the same organs, the growing disarticulation between the concrete targets of state intervention and parliamentary representation formally based on territorial aggregation of votes is overcome through the corporatist reorganization of representation along functional lines so that the specific targets of intervention are directly and permanently represented. Corporatism thus entitles the political organs of capital and labour to participate in the formulation and implementation of policies concerned with accumulation so that responsibility for such intervention is placed on those immediately affected rather than mediated through parliamentary represen- taiton and rational-legal administration. This is particularly crucial when intervention concerns issues that cannot readily be effected without the cooperation of capital and/or labour; and/or that can- not be readily accomplished through rational-legal administrative means. Such issues would include reorganization of the labour pro- cess, industrial regeneration, welfare programming, infrastructural provision, incomes policies, and economic planning.[8] One should note here that such activities are not just technical in character but also require the consolidation of political support. Corporatism can function in both respects. For it organizes classes into func- tinally heterogeneous, politically equivalent communities represented through corporations and requires their compromise and cooperation as a condition of effective intervention. In turn this implies that the corporations are committed to the overall legitimacy of the existing economic system and confine themselves to demands compatible with its expanded reproduction. It is impor- tant in this respect for the corporations to ensure effective control over their members' conduct. This is true for capital as well as labour. For, whilst trade unions must be (re)organized on func- tional, centralized lines to facilitate control over the use of short- term economic strike power, industrial and financial capital must be politically centralized to ensure that competition between in- dividual capitals does not undermine the interests of capital in general. In these conditions corporatism can promote accumula- tion and reinforce bourgeois political domination.

But, just as parliamentarism is prone to various crises and con- tradictions, so too is corporatism. It would encounter problems even when bourgeois ideologies hegemonize the labour movement and there is a hegemonic fraction in the power bloc able to produce some mutuality of sacrifice among different capitals. For at best corporatism would block the growth of a revolutionary labour movement through the fragmentation of trade unions along func- tional lines and the institutionalization of reformist politics; and, secondly, facilitate the internationalization of competition through the strengthening of national capitals. It could not eliminate class conflict over the labour process (since it remains a *valorization* pro- cess as well as a *technical* process involving the transformation of nature) nor could it eliminate every form of competition among capitals (since it is competition that mediates the laws and tendencies of capital accumulation). This means that corporatism will reproduce class conflict within the heart of the state apparatus itself and threatens to disrupt the continuing realization of the political preconditions of accumulation. Such reproduction is facilitated under corporatism since it explicitly bases political representation on economic divisions. Thus corporatism can be disarticulated through union leaders' failure to control rank-and-file militancy and/or their own resort to industrial action to influence corporatist negotiations, decision-making, and intervention. It is also liable to disarticulation through the attempts of particular capitals to win a competitive advantage through selective compliance with corporatist economic programmes and/or through economic activities outside the national context. Moreover, since corporatism merges organs of representation and administrative agencies, a crisis of representation will have repercussions in the administrative field. In this sense corporatism is more vulnerable than parliamentarism to the effects of representational crises and thus potentially less stable.

FUNCTIONAL COMPLEMENTARITY OR CONTRADICTORY UNITY?

We have argued that tripartism is not pure corporatism but stems from the articulation of parliamentary (or other forms) of representation and intervention with corporatist forms. But does this reflect a structural-functional differentiation of the political system leading to greater adaptive capacity or does it result from other factors and intensify the contradictions of the capitalist state? It is such questions that concern us in the present section.

Lehmbruch rejects the view that corporatist policy-making will displace parliamentary government mediated through political parties. Instead he speculates that "it seems more plausible to interpret the trends in the relationship of 'liberal corporatist' patterns and the party system as an instance of increasing *structural differentiation and functional specialization* of the political system brought about by certain requirements of consensus-building specific to economic policy-making" [Lehmbruch, 1977: 91-126]. He notes that political parties are either unable to build sufficient consensus within a short time-span or produce irrational decisions; and/or orient their decision-making to electoral competition rather than economic performance in office. And he suggests that parties will shift responsibility for such matters as incomes or business-cycle policies to a corporatist subsystem involving organized interests and the permanent administration and thereby free themselves for electoral and parliamentary politics. Thus Lehmbruch discusses party politics and corporatism in terms of their functional specialization in different policy domains. But he qualified this argument by noting that liberal corporatism is most significant in societies where organized labour is integrated into politics through the dominance of a social democratic *party* or through social democratic participation in a "consociational" government system [1977: 11]. He also predicts a "spillover" of corporatism from incomes and business-cycle policies to the field of *Ordnungspolitik*, i.e., policies affecting the organizational and institutional framework of the economy; and attributes this "spillover" largely to successful demands from union leaders for just such an extension [1977: 116-120]. Its effect would be to reduce the role of parliament and elected governments and to increase that of direct business-union negotiations as a source of official policies. But Lehmbruch still concludes that liberal corporatism is most unlikely fully to supplant the party system since it functions on a unanimity principle and its own capacity for consensus-building would be "overloaded" if it had to cope with many of the antagonistic issues that are manageable through the party system. This means that the parliamentary system will be "functionally primary" and corporatism will play a subordinate role in some areas [1977: 121-2].

This analysis contains much of value but is somewhat marred by its narrow focus on party-corporation relations and its analysis of the consensual nature of corporatist issues. Lehmbruch recognizes an effective corporatism requires a high level of consensus between the social partners but oscillates between the views that corporatist issues are inherently consensual and that consensus on such issues is inherently fragile [1977: 98, 100, 110, 111, 112, 122]. Since it is also clear that party systems cannot always handle conflictual issues, it remains unproven that corporatism and party government will be complementary and stabilizing. Moreover, once we shift attention from the advantages to parties that would follow from corporatism and consider its relations with parliamentarism, it is far from obvious that they are functionally complementary. For the two systems have different decisional rules (unanimity vs.

majority), different principles of legitimacy (functional vs. electoral), and different political bases (corporations vs. parties). This at least suggests that the preferred policy outcomes in one system might be incompatible with those favoured in the other system and that conflicts and even immobilism could result. The participation of the political executive in both systems (hence tripartism) does not guarantee harmonization of corporatist and parliamentary policies and may even intensify conflicts and contradictions and/or provide the political basis for the independence of the executive through its exploitation of differences between the two systems. This indicates that we should rework the relations between corporatism and parliamentarism.

It is incorrect to deduce the nature of a political system from the formal institutional structure without regard to the balance of forces engaged in struggle on that terrain. This applies to tripartism just as much as it does to other state forms. Elsewhere we have argued that Lenin's claim, that "the bourgeois democratic republic is the best possible political shell for capital", holds only where the bourgeoisie is hegemonic [Lenin, 1963: 296; Jessop, 1978]. Likewise, since corporatism cannot eliminate the social bases of class antagonism, it can only work effectively when the "social partners" accept the overall legitimacy of the capitalist order. Where this does not occur and organized interests reject the "unstable equilibrium of compromise" on which capital accumulation is based, corporatism cannot reduce the burden of policy-making in a parliamentary republic and may intensify the strains and contradictions to which it is always subject. Conversely, where the corporatist system succeeds in maintaining the subordinate position of the labour movement through the reduction of the class struggle to negotiations between formally equivalent, functionally interdependent groups, it could well contribute to the reproduction of capitalism.

It is also incorrect to focus on capital accumulation to the exclusion of relations of political and ideological domination. Thus, even if corporatism proved effective under bourgeois hegemony in reproducing certain preconditions of accumulation, it would not necessarily help to contain popular-democratic struggles concerned with the relations of domination. Indeed, just because corporatism is appropriate to economic intervention (since it is constituted on the basis of function in the division of labour), it tends to be inadequate for other areas. Thus it might not offer the best means to link popular-democratic demands and interests with the imperatives of accumulation and thereby reinforce bourgeois hegemony.[9] Nor would it be able to resolve at all easily such issues as the demands for regional decentralization, a halt to coloured immigration, or enactment of a Bill of Rights. This is where pluralist pressure groups, political parties, and elected parliaments could continue to perform a central political function and, in this sense, corporatism and parliamentarism could be complementary rather than contradictory systems. But this conclusion still leaves unresolved the question of how these forms of representation and intervention are coordinated and which system is dominant.

THE SOCIAL BASES OF STATE POWER

This question can be clarified through consideration of the social bases of different state forms. The effectiveness of state power depends on the balance of forces in a given situation and is thus reinforced through the mobilization of support for official policies as well as through the monopolization of the means of coercion. In this context bourgeois domination presupposes the maintenance of a favourable balance of forces through a mixture of repression, moral suasion and indoctrination, and "economic-corporative" and popular-democratic concessions.[10] Strategies for organizing an adequate social base and disorganizing opposition forces will vary with the state of capitalism, the location in the world economy, the form of state, and the existing balance of forces. The complexity of specific social formations makes blanket generalizations inappropriate and it would be wrong to suggest that any given state form best secures an adequate social base in all situations. But it is clear that, as monopoly capitalism is consolidated and state intervention becomes more significant, the need to build a strong social base in the working class instead of relying simply on the dull compulsion of market relations and political repression becomes more pressing.[11] Thus social democracy has become more significant as a social base for capital accumulation in both monopoly and state monopoly capitalism. Indeed the crisis of Keynesianism has given even more impetus to this tendency and encouraged its attempted realization through liberal corporatism.

Such recent economic and political developments have interesting implications for the relations between parliamentarism and corporatism. For, whilst the consolidation of state monopoly capitalism accelerates the decline of the traditional petit bourgeoisie and small and medium capital, it increases the significance of the wage-earning classes of the proletariat and new petit bourgeoisie. The growth of corporatism reproduces these tendencies at the political level since it institutionalizes the representation of organized capital and labour and reinforces the concentration and centralization of state power at the expense of parliamentarism. In contrast, parliamentarism is still important as a field on which the traditional petit bourgeoisie and small and medium capital are organized as supporting classes and also seek to represent their interests. It is also provides a political terrain more favourable to the mobilization of popular-democratic forces (in the form of pressure groups as well as in the framework of electoral competition). This suggests that the social bases of corporatism and parliamentarism are becoming differentiated and that this might constitute an important source of conflict between the two systems. In turn this puts a premium on the social democratic movement as a means of integrating them since it provides important links between corporations and the party system. Indeed, if consociationalism, which Lehmbruch and others have interpreted as a means of securing labour movement participation in government decision-making through the consociational 'cartel of elites' rather than straightforward social democratic majority rule, is a declining state form (although, *pace* Lijphart, its disintegration probably owes less to its past successes than to the development of class conflict and new forms of popular-democratic conflicts), social democracy will become still more important in this respect [Lijphart, 1976]. It is certainly worth examining the tendential unification of various union confederations and the trend towards increased socialist party support in erstwhile consociational democracies and assessing whether they are being transformed into social democracies. Let us consider these arguments concerning social democracy in more detail.

THE SOCIAL BASES OF LIBERAL AND FASCIST CORPORATISMS

If we focus on the social bases of state forms, it is clear that liberal corporatism and fascist corporatism are very different. For, not only is liberal corporatism associated with parliamentarism, it is also grounded in consociational and/or social democratic politics. In contrast fascism was premised on the destruction of parliamentarism and social democracy and found its social base in the traditional and new petit bourgeoisie. Moreover, whereas corporatism is an important "efficient" element in the emergent tripartite system of liberal corporatism in a "normal" capitalist state (if still subordinate to parliamentarism and continuously subject to various contradictions and instabilities), corporatism in the fascist regimes was essentially a "dignified" element (or facade) and/or was firmly subordinated to the "monist" mode of representation and intervention in an "exceptional" capitalist state (even though it still provided some opportunities for class struggle, particularly at plant level, and even though business was able to circumvent or influence much of the state intervention). In this sense it is misleading to talk about social democratic and fascist corporatisms as if they were equivalent forms with identical economic and political functions. Thus the distinction drawn by Schmitter between "societal" and "state" corporatism (cf. that of Manoïlescu between "corporatisme pur" and "corporatisme subordonné") better expresses the differences between social democratic and fascist corporatism than the distinction between "egalitarian" and "inegalitarian" corporatism proposed by Pahl and Winkler. Indeed Trotsky was insistent that fascism and social democracy were antagonistic forms of capitalist state since the alliances on which the bourgeoisie founded its domination were mutually exclusive. For, whilst social democracy would be powerless without the weight of the organized working class in the parliamentary state, fascism could not consolidate itself without annihilating the workers' organizations and parliamentarism [Trotsky, 1975: 124-5, 276-7]. Now, although Trotsky was writing in the 1930s and was referring to social democracy in Weimar Germany, Ramsay MacDonald's Britain, and New Deal America, his comments are also applicable to the development of corporatism in the postwar world. Indeed, since there has been a massive shrinkage in the social weight of the old middle classes and the new middle class is now being unionized, the social bases for the fascist state have been dissolved. This means that the chief alternative to the development of liberal corporatism based on social democracy is a "strong state" based on the creation and incorporation of a labour bureaucracy, the depoliticization of organized labour, and the judicial repression of class and popular-democratic struggles. The nature of this alternative and its connections with liberal corporatism need careful specification.

Social democracy is the most appropriate social base for liberal corporatism since it secures the support of the largest and most powerful of the dominated classes in state monopoly capitalism. In turn, social democratic parties (or their equivalents) are the natural governing parties in liberal corporatism because they fuse several major roles in one political organization. They have close links with the labour movement whose involvement in corporatist organs is essential to their success; they have substantial electoral support among the organized working class and new petit bourgeoisie; and they manage to articulate "economic-corporative" and popular-democratic demands into a programme that supports state intervention in the interests of capital accumulation. In short, social democracy offers an appropriate means to fuse the parliamentary and corporatist forms of representation and domination and to adapt them to changing conditions. In this context we should mention the growing social democratization of Euro-communism and its implications for the development of state forms in southern Europe.[12] Moreover, given their great economic, political, and ideological presence in the working classes, social democratic parties also prevent or weaken the development of autonomous forms of working class mobilization that threaten to unify economic and political struggles against the rule of capital. This is not to say that such struggles cannot develop but merely to insist that they will be difficult to organize and make effective. Thus, rather than liberal corporatism being "fascism with a human face" (to quote Pahl and Winkler), it is more appropriate to characterize it as "the highest stage of social democracy" (to paraphrase Lenin).[13]

In this context we could say that the preceding stage of social democracy involved the consolidation of labour movement support in a parliamentarist state through the development of the Keynesian mixed economy and the welfare state. This stage can be found in most postwar European democracies even where government itself has *not* been dominated by a social democratic party or a consociational cartel with social democratic participation. It represents a response to various economic and political imperatives in state monopoly capitalism, especially in relation to the control of the business cycle, the maintenance of full employment, and the containment of working class dissent [Warren, 1972; Jessop, 1979]. In some societies it has been succeeded by the "highest stage of social democracy". This involves the transformation of parliamentarist states through the development of corporatism and/or tripartism and the transformation of the Keynesian mixed economy through the development of political intervention in the organization of production and in the determination of wages, prices, and profits. This represents a response to the problems of "stagflation" engendered by Keynesian contracyclical intervention in the absence of measures to reproduce the "purgative" effect of economic crises thereby postponed and, in some cases, to the growth of shopfloor militancy among trade unions. Lastly, bilateral corporatism and/or tripartism also occur in response to demands for participation in policy-making from union leaders in exchange for their securing rank-and-file compliance with wage restraint policies and industrial reorganization [Lehmbruch, 1974: 116-20].

Now, whilst the preceding stage was widely diffused, the current stage is much less well-developed and widespread. This reflects more stringent conditions of existence which are less often present. For, whilst Keynesianism and the welfare state involve only the accommodation of organized labour and its direct or virtual representation in parliament, bilateral corporatism and/or tripartism involve its full integration into executive decision-making and administration so that the labour movement becomes a virtual arm of the state itself. This presupposes that the labour movement is adequately organized to play such a role. Thus, in addition to close ties with a socialist party or cartel of parties influential in government, the unions should be strong bodies able to control their members and be organized into a unified central federation or confederation; and collective bargaining should be focused at national or regional, general or industrial levels rather than being focused at plant or company level [Lehmbruch, 1974: 109-112; Clegg, 1976]. Where unions are decentralized and shopfloor bargaining is widespread, it is hard to sustain a corporatist system without substantial material concessions to organized labour to induce voluntary compliance or to compensate for statutory restraint. Alternatively, where no strong social democratic party exists, a dominant bourgeois party may prefer to ignore unions and consult only with business interests, continuing to pursue a welfare state programme and employing a mixture of *dirigiste* and *sozialmarktwirtschaftlich* policies in maintaining economic stability and securing industrial reorganization. However, although there are significant differences among the metropolitan states in the development of corporatism and its articulation with parliamentarism (and other forms of representation and intervention), much more striking is the extent to which at least some corporatist forms have developed in all such societies. This suggests that there are powerful forces encouraging the development of corporatism and that variation in its institutionalization depends on the extent to which certain preconditions are present. In particular these concern the labour movement — as one would expect since it is the involvement of organized labour that is distinctive about corporatism and not the political incorporation of business interests.

Finally we discuss what might happen when the forces encouraging the development of liberal corporatism cannot be satisfied and there is also a crisis in parliamentarism. It is here that pressures for a "strong state" are likely to increase in association with a "strengthening" of corporatism and/or parliamentarism. For a "strong state" can emerge in small steps as well as in situations of catastrophic equilibrium or revolutionary crises. Thus a certain "creeping authoritarianism" is already evident in the metropolitan democracies with the development of legal and judicial restrictions on economic and/or political organization, the adoption of new technologies of political control, and the centralization and growth of security forces [Ackroyd et al., 1977; Center for Research on Criminal Justice, 1975]. Its effect is to increase the flexibility with which the state can react to internal dissent and to cloak political repression in legal garb. This is coupled with the autonomization of administration through the acquisition of new discriminatory powers and/or the creation of parastate apparatuses not accountable to parliament nor to corporations. However, as legalized repression and discretionary administration are insufficient to establish the conditions necessary to capital accumulation (witness the continued importance of the Labour Front's "economic-corporative" activities along with the constant attempts to win mass loyalty in Nazi Germany [Mason, 1966: 112-114; Mason, 1977: 124-208]), growth in these areas must be articulated with an attempt to build a social base among the people. But, since "strong states" are unnecessary when mass loyalty can be established through the process of hegemonization in liberal parliamentary and/or corporatist regimes, the social basis of the "strong state" is likely to be restricted. This suggests that the formation of privileged strata among the working class and the development of a labour bureaucracy in combination with measures to strengthen the power of labour organizations (unions and parties) over their members would be an appealing strategy for capital. In turn this implies the increasing marginalization of other strata and social categories and the resort to various measures to prevent the growth of alternative unions, parties, and extra-institutional forms of political representation [Hirsch, 1979]. This combination of repressive, administrative, and political tendencies might suggest that Pahl and Winkler were not wholly mistaken in predicting the development of "fascism with a human face". But it should be noted that these developments represent a response as much to crises in corporatism as in parliamentarism and thus that Pahl and Winkler tend to identify all recent changes in the state system with corporatism. Instead, we suggest that the strong state develops when parliamentarism has already lost, and corporatism has not yet acquired the faculty of securing capital accumulation and bourgeois political domination. And we would conclude with the observation that the "strong state" is strong in formal institutional structure but, since state power depends on the balance of political forces in a specific conjuncture, it may be weak and ineffective in its interventions.

CONCLUDING REMARKS

This paper has attempted to relate current discussions of corporatism to marxist political economy and to make an initial assessment of corporatism as an element in the capitalist state. We have argued that state forms should be studied in terms of the articulation between forms of political representation and state intervention and state power should be treated as an effect of the balance of political forces mediated through state forms in a determinate conjuncture. It is this orientation that has informed our analysis of parliamentarism and corporatism as elements of the capitalist state and of the social bases of different state forms. We have not managed to avoid certain instrumentalist and/or reductionist tendencies in this analysis and further work would have to develop the implications of our four assumptions about the state in capitalist societies to show more precisely how the interaction of different social forces is mediated through the state to produce certain conditions necessary for capital accumualtion. In particular we have neglected the contribution of crises in the sphere of representation to the development of corporatism (which would qualify the reductionist tendencies deriving from the more or less exclusive focus on intervention in the interests of accumulation) and the role of "spillover" from corporatist forms of representation to corporatist forms of intervention. But we have tried to bring out the changing conditions of existence of accumulation and their implications for the reorganization of the form and function of the state as a system of class and popular domination and to reveal the problems and contradictions involved in their realization. We have also tried to situate the analysis of the state in relation to its social bases in different forms of class alliance, etc. Finally, we concluded that the dominant tendency in the modern state is towards a social democratic tripartism based on the articulation of corporatism and parliamentarism and unified through the location of a social democratic party at the apex of both the corporatist and parliamentary systems. But we have also identified a secondary tendency towards the development of a "strong state" based on the attentuation of the corporations involved in political representation and intervention. This secondary tendency may become dominant if the international economic crisis intensifies and it is no longer possible to make the major concessions necessary to sustain the normal liberal corporatist and/or liberal parliamentarist state forms.

NOTES

1. This paper is a revised version of one presented at the sessions on 'Corporatism in Liberal Democracies' at the meeting of the European Consortium for Political Research, Grenoble, April 6-12, 1978. In revising that paper I have benefitted from discussions with Hans Kastendiek, Gerhard Lehmbruch, and Leo Panitch; but, since much advice from these and other colleagues has been ignored, it should be emphasised that I alone am responsible for the version given below.

2. For a short introduction to the nature of capitalism, see B. Fine, *Marx's 'Capital'* (London: Macmillan, 1977); a particularly good analysis of competition in a *dirigiste* economy is found in F. Neumann, 1942: 181-191, 237-240, and passim.

3. For an alternative account, see B. Jessop, 'The Transformation of the British State Since 1945', in *The State in Western Europe*, ed. M. Castells and R. Scase (London: Croom Helm, 1979).

4. Thus Sweden is cited as the exemplar of redistributive or egalitarian corporatism — but it is hardly characterized by state control of privately owned industry as opposed to facilitation and support; and it is never clear whether the British case will be egalitarian or inegalitarian.

5. Although parliamentarism is premised on citizenship, citizenship rights include the right to form associations on various bases; hence the combination of individualism with pluralism found in parliamentary democracies.

6. Unfortunately Schmitter does not justify the specific elements that enter into the construction and specification of his typology but the rationale for corporatism seems clear in this case.

7. The ideas in this paragraph are developed at greater length in B. Jessop (1978).

8. The emphasis on wage restraint in many discussions of corporatism may well be justified empirically but the need to control wages canot be a sufficient condition for its development; monetary and fiscal policies are technically adequate to securing such restraint in certain political conditions and thus incomes policies must be located in a political as well as economic conjuncture.

9. On the articulation of popular-democratic and economic corporate issues in the reproduction of bourgeois hegemony, see: E. Laclau, *Politics and Ideology in Marxist Theory* (London: New Left Books, 1978).

10. 'Economic-corporative' demands are based on consciousness of the solidarity of interests among all members of a class but they are restricted to demands for economic improvements, politico-juridical equality, rights to participate in legislation and administration, or even to reform them — but within the existing relations of production and domination. On this concept and its relevance for understanding the reproduction of hegemony, see: A. Gramsci, *Selections from the Prison Notebooks* (London: Lawrence and Wishart, 1971), pp. 181 and 161.

11. Cf. K. Marx, *Capital*, vol. 1 (Moscow: Progress, 1965) p. 737, on the 'dull compulsion'; and A. Sasso on, 'Hegemony and Political Intervention', in *Politics, Ideology, and the State*, ed. S. Hibbin (London: Lawrence and Wishart, 1978) pp. 9-39, on the need to supplement this compulsion with hegemonic mobilization.

12. On the social democratization of Eurocommunist parties, see: E. Mandel, *From Stalinism to Eurocommunism* (London: New Left Books, 1978).

13. This idea was first proposed in Jessop, (1978) and is best interpreted as a metaphor rather than genuine hypothesis.

8

Why No Corporatism in America?

Robert H. Salisbury
Washington University, USA

In the early 1970s, after President Nixon had created tripartite machinery to bring labor, business, and government together to try to halt inflation, several scholars proclaimed that the corporate state had arrived in America [Fusfeld, 1972: 1-20; Peterson, 1974: 483-506]. For the most part it was the strength of corporate business in the cricles of decision that most impressed these observers, but the new institutional arrangements were taken to be confirming evidence of corporatist tendencies stretching back through World War II, the National Recovery Administration, all the way to Theordore Roosevelt. But the evidence quickly disintegrated. Official labor-management collaboration in an incomes policy was ended and the machinery abandoned. Part of the reason could be found in the curious weakness of those peak associations that would be expected, in a corporatist system, to play crucial roles. Despite the temptations to seek unity major sectoral groups remained divided.

In January 1977, a small newspaper item announced that the national Association of Manufacturers and the US Chamber of Comerce had suspended talks about the possible merger of their two organizations. Later in the Spring, accompanying the accession of Douglas Fraser to the presidency of the United Auto Workers were speculations about whether the union would now reenter the AFL-CIO. These two stories were among the recent examples of a phenomenon that has long been known but not much examined;

peak interest group associations in the United States have great difficulty achieving enough comprehensiveness of membership to be
able effectively to represent their respective sectors in the political
process. The analysis of this condition provides the basis for this
paper.

To begin, let us say what we mean by the notion of peak associa-
toin. Comparativists may not think there is much difficulty here. In
Britain such groups as the National Farmers Union, the Confederation of British Industries or the Trades Union Congress include
some 80-90 percent of their respective potential members. In West
Germany the *Spitzenverbände* must be consulted in drafting
legislative proposals. And elsewhere in Western Europe the
phenomenon is not only familiar, it is a critical organizational ingredient in the emergence of what Schmitter calls societal corporatism. But in the United States it is not quite so clear which
organizations are the "peaks", and so we must seek definition for
our term.

It turns out that the interest group literature does not provide
much help. The term "peak association" is used, often in passing,
by such scholars as Key [1964] and Eldersveld [1958]. It is
employed as an important part of his analysis by Wooten [1970].
But none of these writers defines the words very clearly, and
Eldersveld seems to imply that he thinks the notion is unclear. My
own previous comments concerning "peak associations" are brief
but nearly all of what there is. I suggested that the term referred to
"sector-wide organizations which embrace a comprehensive array
of constituent sector organizations" [Salisbury, 1975: 187]. This is
a reasonable beginning but uncertainties remain. First, it is not
clear what is meant by saying that a peak association is composed
of other organizations. Indeed, the entire notion of group membership itself is far more ambiguous than is commonly realized. For instance, in the National League of Cities the unit of membership can
be either the individual city or the state leagues of municipalities.
The American Trucking Associations include both individual firms
and specialized associations. And the National Association of
Manufacturers has several different kinds of membership.
Moreover, there is a considerable difference between a group like
the American Farm Bureau Federation, a federation of state farm
bureaus, and the Consumer Federation of America, an amalgam of
over two hundred very diverse kinds of organizations. Yet both are
"organizations of organizations".

A second uncertainty arises over the definition of sector. The term is most commonly employed to refer to the major sections of economic self-interest in modern industrial society; labor, business and agriculture. What is unclear is how many such sectional or producer groups should be designated as sectors without destroying the meaning of the term. What of the professions? A good case can be made for including medicine, law and education as sectors. Each is reasonably well-bounded. Each has an "interest", a stake in society and in public policy. In recent years the "PIGs", the Public Interest Groups which include public official organizations of mayors, governnors, counties, and the like, have certainly emerged as a self-interested set with clear stakes in public policy [Stanfield, 1976]. The Nader groups and Common Cause are probably outside the definition. So perhaps are the environmentalists. Consumers are a borderline case. We need not come to a definitive position on the matter; only indicate the fuzziness of the boundary.

Let us attempt a definition. *A peak association is an organization which purports, and is taken, to speak for a particular sector of society.* The term leaves out those groups who defend the public interest for they deny a "selfish" sectoral concern. The term sector is intended to apply to larger rather than smaller slices of society. Neither the petroleum industry nor Texas constitutes a sector in this sense. The definition involves a reciprocal relationship. A group cannot simply declare itself to be the spokesman of a sector. It must be acknowledged to be so by those to whom it speaks; decision makers, elites more generally, or the broad public. Once the notion of audience response is taken into account, it makes the concept probabilistic rather than definitional. An organization may be acknowledged as the legitimate representative of a sector by some elites but not others. It may be supposed that there are threshold points beyond which a group achieves the status of peak association, and these points are located at the intersection of the organization's actual hegemony in its sector — density of membership, absence of intra-sector rivals, forceful assumption of sector leadership — and the recognition of that hegemony by the relevant "others". Presumably, the greater the hegemony, the fuller the recognition. But the opposite is also true. By conferring recognition on a group as the rightful spokesman of a sector, policy makers may greatly enhance its actual dominance. Indeed, it appears that many of the peak associations in Western Europe reached their hegemonic status with major contributions from the more or less official recognition by key government agencies, especially in the bureau.

In the United States, however, it has been unusual for official recognition to be granted any organized interest group, and it has been even more rare for such recognition to be given to groups purporting to speak for an entire sector. There are some examples, however, and let us note them. One of the best known is the support given through the Extension Service to the formation and continuing strength of the American Farm Bureau Federation [Block, 1960]. It took decades for this connection to be severed, and during at least part of the time from the Bureau's establishment in 1919 until the late 1940s there were many, inside of government and out, who asserted or acknowledged the Bureau's suzerainty [McConnell, 1953]. Yet all the while the Grange and the Farmer's Union existed as general farm organizations open to all kinds of farmers, and when there was a major consultation with USDA or Congress about farm policy they too were included [Campbell, 1962]. From the time of the Brannan Plan in 1949 until 1977 the dominant motif of American farm politics was partisan division with each party joined together in close working relationship with a general farm organization, Democrats with the Farmers Union and Republicans with the AFBF [Key, 1964: 159; Heinz, 1963: 952-78]. Even though the latter was much the largest, it could hardly be regarded as a peak organization when its access depended so heavily on having Republicans in power. And periodic efforts to transcend the partisan division by establishing ad hoc conditions of farm organizations have all quickly failed as the coalitions find themselves unable to contain the centrifugal forces generated by diverse and conflicting farm interests.

Another substantive area has witnessed several efforts of federal government officials to encourage the formation of interest groups [Zeigler, 1964: 94-109; Fainsod et al., 1959: 467]. First during World War I, again under Secretary of Commerce Hoover in the 20s, during the NRA period of 1933-35, and in World War II trade associations were organized with the active support of government, primarily in order to assist in the administration of federal regulatory programs. At other times federal policy has sought to restrict trade association activities, too, of course, but even during the periods of encouragement there was no sustained move to support or consult with groups that purported to speak for all of industry. Organizational recognition was confined to the level of the specific industry. When Washington officials wanted to acknowledge the importance of business (or labor) as a whole, to confer symbolic recognition, and to consult with private interests about public policy they worked with individuals, like William Knudsen and Sidney Hillman, whom they, the officials, not the sector organizations, chose [Blum, 1976].

A case for full peak status might be made for the AFL-CIO. Certainly since the 1955 merger there has been no rival organization in a position to speak on behalf of all of organized labor. Nevertheless, when compared, say, to the TUC, several points of difference appear. For one, the AFL-CIO includes only about seventy-five percent of unionized workers who consist, in turn, of less than one-fourth of the total work force. Moreover, any labor group that does not include the auto workers, the teamsters, or the mine workers must stand in stark contrast to the TUC in which the three equivalent unions are among the most significant. AFL-CIO hegemony is further reduced by its declining rate of success in winning representation elections. This is not meant to dismiss them as unimportant. Mr George Meany has certainly had a significant voice in national policy discussions, and Andrew Biemiller leads what is widely regarded as among the most skilled lobbying crews in Washington [Singer, 1976]. But neither lobbying strength nor electioneering clout has been sufficient to assure the AFL-CIO of a decisive, officially acknowledged, voice on labor questions. It is the President who selects the Secretary of Labor and other labor representratives on official bodies, not the AFL-CIO, even when a Democrat is in the White House.

A final example of the difficulties of sustaining peak association status in the United States can be drawn from medicine. When Oliver Garceau's splendid study was published in 1941 there was little doubt of the AMA's dominance over the "medical profession in politics" [Garceau, 1941]. This remained largely true through the 1950s. But it is not true any longer. Rival organizations of doctors have been formed, and other groups with different interests, such as the hospital administrators, have emerged to contest with the AMA for position and power in health policy making.

Thus peak associations in the United States are either weak and incomplete or ineffectual. None can claim quasi-monopolistic hegemony over a significant sector of socio-economic self-interest. Consequently, the United States lacks an essential ingredient of a corporatist polity, "a limited number of singular, compulsory,

noncompetitive, hierarchically ordered and functionally differentiated categories..." [Schmitter, 1974: 93-4]. Now there is a long
tradition among American intellectuals that asks, "Why no
Socialism in America?" [Laslett and Lipset (eds.), 1974]. To that
query, or perhaps instead of it, we now would ask, "Why no corporatism in America?" I propose to approach this question from
three quite different perspectives: one, macro-social; two, in terms
of the patterns of public policy; and three, as a problem in
organizational analysis.

SOCIAL DIVERSITY
AND INSTITUTIONAL FRAGMENTATION

Perhaps the most immediate and common response to the question
of "Why no corporatism?" would be the one that harks back to the
Federalist Papers and identifies two interrelated factors, social
diversity and institutional fragmentation as primarily responsible.
The relative extent of social diversity and its effects in American
life can be argued. Beeer and Sapolsky, for instance, both point out
that British agriculture is also diverse in commodity interest, yet
successfully brought under a single organizational tent [Beer, 1958:
130-140; Sapolsky, 1968: 355-76]. How much diversity is too much
to contain? To the element of heterogeneity one may add that of
sheer size. Compared to the nations of Western Europe the physical
scope and diversity of the United States is immense. This is undoubtedly true, yet corporate concentrations of power have emerged, despite the anti-trust laws, in sufficient proportion to suggest
that American heterogeneity can be overcome by skillful entrepreneurs.

A variant on the diversity factor, and one of considerable interest, is presented by those who contend that the pace and timing
of socio-economic growth significantly affects the prospects for
corporatist organization. At one end of the spectrum we find
Sweden with its rapid and nationwide advance into mature in-
dustrialism. The United States is surely close to the other end
[Sharkansky, 1975]. Industrialization sturck New England a century and a half before it reached many parts of the South or West;
today, while Utah, Wyoming and Montana emerge as fuel-rich industrial sites, the Northeast attempts to shore up its sagging
employment prospects. The unevenness of growth is not confined

to a single period of history. The late-starting sections do not eventually catch up and smooth out the differences. The Old South may become part of the Sun Belt, but Phoenix remains different from Savannah in the value and interests of those who live there.

Within any given sector, therefore, the tensions among competing groups will be greater and more difficult to reconcile to the extent that historical socio-economic growth and development has been distributed geographically in uneven pattern. If the historical pattern has been uneven, it will continue to be. Moreover, this tendency will be greatly accentuated if political institutions are designed to accommodate this spatially distributed diversity. And this is what American institutions are preeminently designed to do. The structural elements are familiar; federalism, separation of powers, legislators nominated and elected from single-member districts. The elements interact to perpetuate the pattern where groups have multiple access points and governmental officials find it extremely difficult to assemble enough authority to act on a comprehensive scale, whether it involves enacting policy or negotiating with a socio-economic sector. At the same time, the continued existence of dispersed centers of authority provides opportunities for influence to interest groups which are similarly organized in a fragmented, geographically dispersed manner [Truman, 1951; McConnell, 1966]. Simply to illustrate the familiar point: if lawyers are able to affect the selection of judges and the development of procedural rules at the state level for state courts, the need to act on a national basis is much reduced and the ability of the ABA to mobilize the legal profession is likewise reduced.

If federalism makes it difficult, or unnecessary, for a sector to be mobilized on a nationwide basis, so all the devices for fragmenting governmental authority make it difficult, or impossible, to assemble the capacity to act in a focused and forceful fashion. The other side of the corporatism equation is "the state", an entity capable of recognizing, licensing or creating a peak association and then bargaining with it in a substantively meaningful way. But in the United States no such monistic state exists in any real behavioral sense. The Department of Agriculture cannot meaningfully engage in an annual price review, even if there were an agreed spokesman for agriculture [Self and Storing, 1962], because neither that bureaucracy nor the administration of which it is a part can commit "the state" to a specific course of action except within a very narrow range. Congress has now allowed it even in its most extreme moments of delegation of authority. HEW cannot exercise even its delegated authority over universities or the medical profession without multiple end runs immediately going to Congress to mitigate the effects of the order. Corporatism is a form of collective bargaining. In the United States there is no party, on any side, with enough authority to bargain effectively and commit a sector-wide following to accept the result.

It is instructive to note that the partial exceptions to this statement have mainly occurred during emergencies. The extensive (and, as the Supreme Court ruled in the Schecter case, excessive) corporatist delegation contained in the NIRA was a response to the Depression. Trade association formation and cooperative bargaining flourished also during the wars, especially in conjunction with administering wage and price control. But even national emergencies have not suppressed for long the centrifugal tendencies built into America's governing institutions. And yet, governmental arrangements are, after all, subject to change. Public policy might have overcome the tendency toward fission. The mere existence of fragmented institutional structures does not guarantee their persistence, though it helps. Corporatist institutional possibilities might have been established by law, as they were in a good many countries after World War II. In the United States the functional need for a "stable, bourgeois-dominant regime" was surely as compelling as in other industrialized democracies [Schmitter, 1974]. But policy has not moved that direction. Why not?

INTEREST GROUP LEGITIMACY

The factors adduced already surely help to account for the predominant thrust of public policy. The central point to be added here is this. An important reason the American public policy has not enhanced corporatist tendencies is that monopolistic interest groups are regarded with deep suspicion in the American political culture.[1] It may seem absurd, at first blush, to suggest that in the United States, where interest group analysis was, in a sense, invented and given its most enthusiatic hearing, where associational membership has been the very hallmark of national character, the legitimacy of interest group activity is less than it is in other democratic systems. Nevertheless, it is the case.

First, we offer as evidence the point made earlier; namely, there is virtually no official incorporation of formal associations as participants in policy discussions. They are not invited to designate sector representatives on governmental advisory bodies, or to name key policy makers who are to deal with their sector. There have, of course, been occasional advisory relationships, such as the ABA's role in "clearing" judicial appointments [Grossman, 1965]. And we are in no way suggesting that groups have less *informal* influence in the United States than elsewhere. We shall comment on this aspect later. Here our point is only that their formal position is negligible.

A corollary to this is that bureaucrats in America deal directly with constituent units, not with associations. HEW negotiations with individual hospitals or universities, not with the organizations of hospitals or universities. The Defense Department does not contract with the Aerospace Industries Association but with individual firms. It is specific unions which must conform to pension fund regulations, and the AFL-CIO does not formally intervene.

A second piece of evidence bearing on the legitimacy issue is the amount of official regulation of group activity. We do not have a comprehensive survey on the matter, but it seems clear that no democratic nation even remotely approximates the seriousness of the American effort to regulate the details of group-government interactions. For a long time scholars seemed to believe that this was because there was so little group activity in other systems, but once interest groups were discovered abroad some two decades ago that illusion was swept away.

Lobbying regulation in American plainly rests on a deep suspicion of organized groups and of the probable consequences for the polity of their activities. This same suspicion permeates significant fragments of the academic community. In political science the heirs to the progressive tradition characteristically regarded interest groups as the enemy of the public interest.[2] Schattschneider, Lowi, and a rather disparate array of latter-day anti-pluralists have kept this perspective very much alive [Schattschneider, 1960; Lowi, 1969]. The point is that an anti-group orientation is widely diffused through the American polity, and it permeates both textbook literature and newspaper editorials. The organizational success of Common Cause, itself an interest group to be sure, cannot be understood apart from this profound conviction that organized interest groups are not fully legitimate participants in the processes of government.

Why, then, is this so? The matter can be approached from at least two directions. One is that fount of so much interpretation of American politics; John Locke, Louis Hartz and the Liberal Tradition [Hartz, 1955]. The argument is that American political culture is so rooted in individualist assumptions that groups have no integral place. Our theorists and publicists have sustained a mythic structure that was created in order to undermine an older corporatism of post-feudal Europe.

> [I] is clear enough why the democratic image these men gave us should be hostile to half of the machinery that was later invented to make democracy work...Seeking to emancipate men from the rigid pluralism of church, guild, and province, those thinkers were bound to be "individualistis." How could they say, even if they understood the fact, that democracy itself would function through a new pluralism of association, parties, and groups [Hartz, 1960: 13-14].

Presthus is one of the very few who has recognized how hostile American political culture is toward organized groups as policy-making participants [1974]. He regards Canada as possessing substantially more of a corporatist value orientation, though the empirical data he develops are not entirely compatible with this interpretation.[3] But we need not rest the argument entirely on the elusive variable of political culture.[4]

Tentatively, I would suggest that group legitimacy and group hegemony are mutually interdependent. What makes an organization the legitimate spokesman for a socio-economic sector? Confidence that the organization is representative of the values, opinions and interests (which terms may all mean the same thing) of the members of that sector. How can we be confident of this? From evidence that the organization encompasses a substantial portion of the sector in either actual or virtual membership; from evidence that the organization's leaders are not embroiled in internal conflicts over policy [Truman, 1951: 84; Masters et al., 1964]; from the existence of procedures, such as elections or referenda that give some reason to suppose the leadership to be reasonably representative of the membership. There are examples of this kind of unity/legitimacy which, in turn, results in a very impressive accumulation of group influence, albeit informal, over policy [Masters et al., 1964; Bailey et al., 1963]. But in the US these cases are rare and generally rather fragile. The overwhelming tendency is for membership to be fractional, cohesion to be threatened, and representativeness to be very doubtful. Hence, no legitimacy. Hence, no corporatist role.

The importance of the legitimacy dimension is that it makes it highly unlikely that American public policy will move in a corporatist direction, granting privileged access to particular organizations so that they gain enough organizing advantages to achieve quasi-monopolistic status vis-à-vis their respective sectors.[5] This being so, the only way for a corporatist system to develop would be for would-be peak associations to achieve hegemonic status through their own organizational processes.

PEAK ASSOCIATION AND ORGANIZATIONAL EXCHANGE

If it is up to organized groups to make themselves into legitimate peak associations, what would they need to do? To consider this question we employ the analytical framework that Mancur Olson and others have used to think about interest groups generally [Olson, 1965; Salisbury, 1969]. The would-be peak must offer prospective members selective benefits, unavailable outside the peak organizations, which are sufficiently appealing to induce a large proportion of the sector involved to join. (We pass over Olson's other possibilities, coercion or one member bearing the whole cost.) What kinds of benefits could hold such appeal?

Since we are dealing with peak associations we can assume that, despite the ambiguities we noted earlier regarding the nature of membership units, the prospective members of the peak are themselves organizations, such as labor unions, business firms or universities. It would be rare that material benefits in their usual forms — cheap insurance, charter flights, or strike funds — could be utilized to build a peak organization. The main reason for this is that the constituent units themselves are organized around the exchange of material benefits. Moreover, each of the constituent units typically has a substantial staff. This staff is unlikely cheerfully to surrender this autonomy nor the membership to subordinate a prospering benefit exchange to a peak association, and, conversely, the peak group cannot prevail merely by offering staff support or selective material benefits. American constituent groups tend to be far stronger in staff and material resources than their counterparts elsewhere, and hence less susceptible to this kind of appeal from peak organizations.

Let us consider four types of benefits that are sometimes utilized, or at least proposed, as having the potential, to attract and hold the requisite membership. These are information, the regulation of jurisdictional disputes, recognition of the sector organization as legitimate and/or expert, and increased sector weight in policy making. All are of material concern, but their value is not as direct as such things as insurance, and indeed their worth to prospective members is highly problematic.

Sapolsky suggests that a major benefit accruing to peak association members in Britain is access to information about ministry intentions regarding sector policy [1968: 368]. There is no doubt that information is a very valuable commodity. But in the United States two factors conspire to make it extremely difficult for peak associations to monopolize such information so as to make it a selective benefit available only to its members. One is that given the institutional fragmentation of American government there are multiple sources of information about what is happening in Washington. It is very difficult to imagine who could sign an exclusive dealing agreement on behalf of the government, effectively limiting the flow of information to a single peak group, and make it stick. The second reason is that there is a highly developed and enormously competitive information business already developed, and any organization already has many options available to find out what they need to know.[6]

Differential access to information gives advantages to specific organizations vis-à-vis competitors in their own sector. At some point, of course, such access may become too costly to maintain and a common information pool, as would be provided by a peak association, would then be attractive. Essentially, this is the calculus followed by a newspaper that uses a wire service rather than maintaining its own Washington correspondent. But it has not yet become operative in labor, business or the other major interest sections. Aspiring peak associations in most sectors seem not to have been as efficient in providing information to members as more specialized groups, and the prospects for peak group hegemony over this function are not at all encouraging.

The regulation of jurisdictional disputes is a different kind of matter. The possibilities can best be seen in the case of labor unions. One of the chief advantages of union participation in the

AFL-CIO is protection against raiding by rival unions and support from rival unions in organizing activities. A good recent example can be seen in the AFL-CIO support for the United Farm Workers against the Teamsters in their efforts to organize in California. Surely this kind of help can be of significant benefit to all but the very strongest organizational units in a sector. The Teamsters, of course, are very strongly situated and hence quite content to remain outside the AFL-CIO fold.

For other unions and in other sectors, however, there is an additional factor that limits the ability of organizations in the United States to establish sector hegemony by regulating jurisidictional disputes. There is an extensive array of extant public policy that already deals precisely with this problem in both positive and negative ways. On the negative side the antitrust laws preclude business organizations from allocating markets among competitors, and there is a considerable number of cases in which trade associations have been convicted on exactly those grounds. The NRA period was an exception, of course, and enforcement of competition has always been uneven, to say the least. But in large sectors of the economy peak associations would be legally forbidden to provide the "benefit" of settling jurisdictional arguments for the members.[7]

Consider also such policies as commodity marketing orders, which do indeed have the effect of regulating conflicts among potential competitors and which have been written into positive law as a result of the specialized pressures of particular commodity groups. In this situation there is no regulatory function left for a peak organization to perform. When an organization is put together, as the National Conference of Commodity Organization was in the late 1950s, it is left with the much weaker function of coordinating a log-rolling alliance based on the mutual support of each commodity group for every other group's needs. Hence the peak group does not long survive. There is a broad array of legislation regulating group operations, including representation elections and pension fund disclosures in the labor field, securities issues in business, and degree program certification in higher education, to maintain only a few which might have been subject to private control of strong peak associations. Conversely, it seems generally to be the case that in the more fully corporatist systems of Western Europe, with vigorous associations of comprehensive sector-wide scope, there is considerably less legislation regulating the internal affairs of that sector.

We have already discussed the question of peak association legitimacy at some length. In the present context the point is that legitimacy requires substantial sector unity and this can perhaps best be achieved by means of an effective peak organization. Let us consider further, however, what else is associated with sector unity, what kinds of groups especially need it, and what trade-offs there are against it. Professional groups provide good illustrations of the arguments. When doctors or lawyers or educators are cohesive and speak with one organizational voice, their associations are often regarded as legitimate spokesmen for their sectors. More broadly, the whole profession is conceded a degree of expertise that entitles its members to deference on sector-related public policy, and to substantial self-regulation. One aspect of this is the right to charge a fee for services which, if they are incompetent, will not be discovered until it is too late to do much about it, except, of course, to sue for malpractice. Such a reputation for expertise is thus highly valued and placed at risk whenever significant policy conflicts develop within the sector organization.

Once there is substantial internal disagreement about what is best for the sector, there is no choice but to have non-experts make the decision, in coalition with some portion of the sector and against some other part, and to do so according to standard political considerations. From the perspective of the sector, the thing to do is first to suppress the conflict or mask its expression. If the decisive forces cannot be contained, however, the indicated strategy is to cultivate political clout. Mobilized electoral strength can affect political decisions when deference is no longer afforded to expertise. In both education and medicine the decline in professional unity has been met by a rise in political militance.[8] The point is that wintin virtually every professional sector policy conflicts have erupted with increasing frequency and severity, reducing thereby the chances of sector hegemony.

The fourth possible basis for peak association formation is to increase the weight or influence of the sector in bargaining over policy. Surely there is appeal to potential members in enhanced influence, but this really is a problem in organizing for collective benefits, and Olson's arguments apply. He does provide for the possibility of small groups organizing for collective purposes and some sectors might already be organized into oligopolistic form with a sufficiently modest number of discrete units to qualify as a small group with the accompanying face-to-face pressures that help overcome free rider tendencies. Elsewhere I have argued that within some limits, that might be fairly broad, it would be in the interest of each potential member of large groups to join so long as it is uncertain whether that membership increment may be decisive to the establishment of requisite sector influence [Salisbury]. But above those limits free riderism must reappear in the absence of selective benefits, and, as we have seen, these are difficult to manage effectively in peak organizations. We cannot say, on these grounds, that strong peak associations are impossible in the United States but at a comprehensive sectoral level the odds are against them.

There is another factor in the American context that makes sector influence itself of problematic value. The assumption that influence is desirable for a sector is tied to another assumption; namely, that policy decisions will affect the entire sector in substantially the same way. For that to be so the policies themselves must be framed in comprehensive terms, and the members of the sector must be in sufficiently similar circumstances as to have a common interest in the outcome. In fact, however, heterogeneity of interest or situation characteristizes most sectors of American life. Pension fund regulation will not affect the Teamsters the same way it does the Steelworkers, for example. Nor are Harvard and Slippery Rock similarly situated regarding NSF policy. More than that, much American public policy tends to be highly disaggregated so that the differential effects within a sector are further heightened. The general point is that whenever a given policy has differential impacts, it adds to the centrifugal tendencies of the system, and in the United States the continued reinforcement of those tendencies constitutes a formidable obstacle for would-be peak associations to overcome. Again, medicine serves as an example of a sector where the expansion of explicit public policy has resulted in the steady proliferation of interests, each somewhat differently affected by existing programs and taking a distinct and separate posture toward new proposals.[9]

ANOTHER POSSIBILITY

In one sense the point of this essay is a small one, and perhaps some might consider it even trivial. We are not suggesting that organized interests are without influence over American public policy. That influence is informal and often suspect, but it is not necessarily less consequential because it is unofficial. Some observers indeed have interpreted American politics as very largely a public, legitimate, process that masks the exercise of private and unaccountable power of the business elite.[10] From this perspective the absence of corporatist mechanism might be regarded as irrelevant or even a matter of deliberate choice to hide the realities of economic power over political decision and to exclude potential rivals from the bargaining table.

If there were genuine corporatism in the United States, labor would have to be a full participant in the negotiations over economic policy. They would have a full voice in determining which social sectors were to get what share of the rational product. Government, in turn, would hold not only the swing vote between business and labor but an important potential for affecting the demands and interactions of both sides. Moreover, corporatist mechanisms presumably operate regardless of election outcomes, whereas informal access may be much affected by them.

Thus corporatist arrangements might well make a difference and a perceptive business elite might therefore wish to prevent a political evolution in that direction. Such an hypothesis cannot be refuted, of course, and the possibility, even as only a part of the total explanation, should not be dismissed. My own judgement is that insofar as a self-conscious business elite exists in the United States it has not devoted much attention to what economic planning mechanisms would or would not best suit its needs. Most of its energies have gone into the more general defense of the free market, on one hand, and the quest for specific subsidies and other direct benefits for particular industries, on the other. Still, the political strength of business in America and the concomitant weakness of labor may well help us understand why it has only been in times of severe crisis that both sides have been willing to sit together.

CONCLUSION

It is possible that there is a somewhat simpler answer, or partial answer, to our original query. The argument put forward by

Schmitter is that corporatism is a response, perhaps the model response, to the need for stability in an advanced capitalist system. Shonfield [1965: 231] stresses the need for stability but sees corporatism as one of three possible styles of national economic planning by which such stability may be sought. In addition to corporatist planning there is state intervention, utilizing the levers of public power, and indicative planning whereby the planners persuade rational economic men to accept dispassionate analyses and act accordingly. In the United States there is some of each of these kinds of planning but not much use of corporatist devices. On that policy area most representative perhaps of corporatist tendencies, wage-price or incomes policy, the American approach has been mainly to utilize jawboning, occasionally to exercise the levers of federal power, and to play off one sector against the other. But there has been almost no serious effort to cultivate consensus or to facilitate the development of labor-management agreements which would hold down inflation [Goodwin (ed.), 1975: 368-9]. Panitch has argued that in Europe corporatism has not really worked as well as Schmitter and others believe, that the stability it brings is brief and the problems soon return [Panitch, 1976c, also Wilensky, 1976 and Wheeler, 1975]. In the United States there has generally been enough slack within each sector that a relatively free market process could operate at least some of the time, to bring downward pressure on prices. But even in the face of stubborn stagflation there is not much corporatism in America.[11] Corporatism, in turn, is an aspect of comprehensive national economic planning and we may conclude this review by observing that there is not much planning in America either.[12]

NOTES

An earlier version of this paper was presented at the annual meeting of the American Political Science Association, Washington, DC, September, 1977.

1. For a parallel argument; *viz.*, that it is values that differentiate American from European practice, see Anthony King, "Ideas, Institutions and the Policies of Governments: Part III," *British Journal of Political Science*, Vol. 3 (Oct., 1973), pp. 409-423.

2. In a wonderfully revealing statement Professor Jewel Cass Phillips once distinguished between "good" pressure groups and "bad" pressure groups. He then asked, "Are good pressure groups desirable?" After careful deliberation he concluded that they were not! *State and Local Government in America*, New York: American Book Co., 1954, p. 122.

3. Another example is provided by Joseph La Palombara's characterization of the British style of operation: "When in doubt, clear it some more before taking action'." *Politics Within Nations*, Englewood Cliffs: Prentice-Hall, 1974, p. 354.

4. Roy C. Macridis is the author of another well-known argument embedding patterns of interest group behavior in the context of political culture. "Interest Groups in Comparative Analysis", *Journal of Politics*, Vol. 23 (Feb., 1961), pp. 24-45.

5. One might add that insofar as there is increasing insulation of elected officials from electoral insecurity, there will be still less reason to negotiate with organized associations. Rather, officials may feel more and more able to dominate the discussion. It would seem that such a development characterizes the contemporary politics of medical care more than would have been thought possible in the 1950's. On the increasing safety of electoral margins, see Morris P. Fiorina, *Congress, Keystone of the Washington Establishment*, New Haven: Yale University Press, 1977.

6. As a single example of a large and mostly uncharted area, see the large volume published by Congressional Quarterly entitled *Washington Information Directory*, 1977-78.

7. A notable exception to the general ban on peak organizations resolving disputes among their members is provided in the exemption from antitrust prosecution granted to organized baseball.

8. On the rising militance in the National Education Association, see "NEA's Growing Political Power," *National Journal*, August 30, 1975. An instructive recent evaluation of the politics of medicine is John K. Iglehart's "No More Doctor Nice Guy," *National Journal*, March 6, 1976.

9. A part of this proliferation process is treated by John K. Iglehart, "Health Report/Economy Takings Steam from National Insurance Drive", *National Journal*, January 18, 1975.

10. I am grateful to Professors G. William Domhof and Robert Alford for their perceptive and probing comments on an earlier version of this paper. Both of them, in somewhat different ways, made suggestions that persuaded me I could not ignore the relevance of *de facto* corporate influence in a discussion of corporatism in America.

11. N. H. Keehn has written a rather interesting essay, in part predicting and in part urging the coming of corporatism to the United States. I think he is wrong, but the analysis deserves attention. See "A World of Becoming: From Pluralism to Corporatism," *Polity*. Vol. 9 (Fall, 1976), pp. 19-39.

12. I have tried to address this side of the problem in another paper, "On Centrifugal Tendencies in Interest Systems: The Case of the United States," prepared for the World Congress of Sociology, Uppsala, Sweden, August, 1978.

9

Corporatism Without Labor?
The Japanese Anomaly

T. J. Pempel and
Keiichi Tsunekawa
Department of Government, Cornell University, USA

PROBLEMS IN CORPORATIST THEORY

Hitherto orthodox interpretations of politics and economics within advanced capitalist regimes are falling further from favor. It has been a truism for decades, if not for its entire life span, that the predominant position given to the notion of a free market has been based on assumptions divorced from the realities of individual and group motivation and behavior. More recently, the contemporary applicability and the explanatory power of traditional economic interpretations have been further undermined by a growing awareness of the centrality of the state in determining national economic priorities; the rise in the activities and significance of monopolies, oligopolies, and multinational corporations; increased sensitivity to the power of domestic and international finance; the persistence of class and the absence of significant redistributions of wealth; the growth in, and the recognized market impact of deficit financing for government; and the multitude of failures associated with Keynsian policies, to cite only some of the most obvious inadequacies (e.g., Galbraith, 1967; Shonfield, 1965; Hirsch and Goldthorpe, 1978; Lindberg, et al., 1975; Giddens, 1973).

Similarly, political assumptions undergirding liberalism and pluralism have also proven theoretically inadequate in dealing with the challenges posed by various contemporary phenomena. Many of these challenges grow directly out of the economic realities just noted (O'Connor, 1973; Galbraith, 1967). Others have been the result of dissatisfactions with the input-output models of politics so popular as an intellectual paradigm among pluralists. Such cybernetic models have, on the one hand, implied too much automaticity to the ways in which demands are "processed" by the state without sufficient attention to the capacity of state organs to generate, filter, shunt aside, suppress or ignore demands, according to preferences not accounted for by the model. Meanwhile, most of the presumed pluralist linkages among citizen opinion, party platforms, elections, legislative behavior, and public policies have been convincingly challenged (e.g., Bachrach and Baratz, 1962; Brody and Page, 1972; Connelly, 1969; Ellul, 1964; Campbell, et al., 1964; Hibbs, 1977; Key, 1966; Leeds, 1978; Loewenberg, 1971; Pempel, 1974; Tufte, 1978; McConnell, 1966). Relatedly, advocates of input-output models or pluralism more generally have tended to focus their empirical research almost exclusively on the "input" side, stressing citizen attitudes, political socialization, elections, interest group pressures, political party activities, policy-making process and the like without giving comparable attention to the output side of government. Many would surely agree that what governments do is at least as important as why or how they allegedly do it.

Such criticism of the dominant orthodoxies in both economics and politics has not as yet led to their replacement by any widely accepted alternative(s). Yet as a potentially viable alternative, corporatism has begun to attract the attention of a significant body of scholars. For many, one of its chief attractions lies in its alleged potential to overcome weaknesses in *both* the economic notions centered around the free market and in the political notions centering around pluralism. (Schmitter, 1974). Not all would agree that such a potential has as yet been shown, but certainly there is growing agreement that the motif of corporatism holds forth a good deal of intellectual promise in its efforts to deal with the state as a political actor, rather than as the simple black box processor of socially-generated demands; in its ability to examine the class and economic bases for the formation of interest associations and the development of public policies; in its concern for the fusion, rather than the separation, of politics and economics; in its potential ability to link social structure to state action; and, most significantly, in its potential to deal with these matters in a theoretically meaningful fashion. As a result, in the past few years, corporatism has become in Panitch's words a "growth industry". (1978).

In intellectual "industries" no less than in teenagers, however, growth is most frequently accompanied by blemishes, awkwardness and uncertainty. One of the most fundamental uncertainties within the area of corporatism concerns its ultimate explanandum: is corporatism truly a macro-level concept capable of replacing pluralism and the free market and capturing fully the supposed tidal shift toward the generalized corporatization of relations between the state and most, if not all, interest associations within a country? (Schmitter, 1974). Or, should the concept be more narrowly applied, focusing primarily on a shift in such relations within the area of economic policy (Lehmbruch, 1977, 1978; Panitch, 1977, 1978b; Jessup, 1978; Bonnett, 1978; Pahl and Winkler, 1976; Winkler, 1976)? Is the phenomena general within most capitalist countries, or is it largely a peculiarity of a few generally small states in Northern and Western Europe?[1] Is corporatism a generalizable description of either a country's economy or polity; is it a peculiar noncapitalist, non-socialist form of political economy; or is it more narrowly a distinct form of policymaking (Lehmbruch, 1978) or of "interest intermediation" (Schmitter, 1978)? Even more narrowly, is corporatism not even terribly widespread at all, either as a form of political economy, a form of policymaking or a form of interest intermediation; rather does it represent primarily the specific establishment of formalized tripartite bodies of government, labor and business to deal with problems of economic management and/or to coopt labor and legitimate wages and incomes policies (Panitch, 1978a; Jessop, 1978; Winkler, 1976; Pahl and Winkler, 1976)?

In the absence of basic intellectual closure concerning the level of analysis or the explananda for which the term "corporatism" might be most suitable, competing sides vie for the exclusive right to the appealing new label. If "corporatism" is a growth industry, it is one in which excessive efforts at product differentiation have led to what the Japanese call "excessive competition". In the absence of accepted authority, the sub-field has been characterized by "ungovernability". Not surprisingly, numerous component problems have arisen from such fundamental disagreements. Four seem particularly worthy of attention. The first two concern problems with corporatism as a *dependent variable*; the third and fourth concern important *independent variables* presumed to contribute to corporatism.

First, there is a need for greater disaggregation in all thinking about corporatism as a concept. Nedelmann and Meier (1977) have already pointed out that much of the conceptualizing on corporatism has been unduly undifferentiated and undoubtedly a natural outgrowth of the fact that early writing on the subject proceeded at the ideal-typical level (see especially, Schmitter, 1974). Particularly acute is the problem of generalizing about whole political systems. This may be helpful in isolating generically different patterns of socio-political relations from country to country but it too often degenerates into empty nominalism and definitionalism: is country A corporatist or not? As they state, "...corporatism as a structural configuration is rarely an adequate characterization of total societies." (Nedelmann and Meier, 1977: 49). Surely there is a greater need to specify conditions and degrees of corporatism so as to allow for more discrimination among countries presumed to manifest one or another trait associated with corporatism. This criticism can be further refined by noting specific areas where disaggregation has to date been most critically absent. Empirical and researchable investigation of different patterns of interest intermediation in specific historical contexts necessitates that one be more sensitive to at least three important differences: sector to sector; policy area to policy area; and institutional arena to institutional arena. Boldly stated, it seems intuitively probable that state-societal interaction will be more "corporatist" in regard to the activities of one economic sector or one interest (such as labor) than in regard to another (such as small and medium-sized industry). Similarly, one can anticipate greater or lesser corporatism in certain policy areas (such as incomes policy) than in others (such as monetary policy). Finally, one could expect comparatively high levels of corporatism within one institutional setting (such as the national executive branch or particular advisory committees) but fragmentation and pluralism in others (such as national or state assemblies).

Second, with such disaggregation in mind, it is also essential to be more sensitive to changes over time. Within individual economic sectors, policy areas and institutional arenas, as well as at the level of state-societal interactions generally, there is no inherent reason to expect that patterns of increased or decreased corporatism, for example, will be linear or will even vary in the same direction. History leaves a heavy residue on any present. The virtual absence of corporatist patterns of interest intermediation in the US or

Canada can be traced, for example, not to the absence of the economic pressures prevalent in more corporatist societies, or to the fact that they represent some peculiar mutation within the genus of advanced capitalism. Rather it relates to the specific historically rooted configuration of their political institutions, the role of the state, and the actions of the social sectors and political hegemony which have controlled the state apparatus over time. (Salisbury, 1977; Panitch, 1977a). To cite a different form of the same problem, Sweden, Holland and Denmark are far more corporatized in their present labor-management relations than Italy, Japan and, probably Germany, though the reverse was surely true in the 1940s. Finally, while it is generally suggested that Sweden or Austria manifest corporatist tendencies in most key policy areas, to the extent that anyone argues seriously that Britain is becoming corporatized, they do so almost exclusively in the context of economic policies, or even more restrictedly, in terms of incomes policy (and not, for example, in education, health, science or administrative reform) (though cf. Pahl and Winkler, 1976). And even within this narrowest of areas, the "neddies" have come, gone and come again in a new incarnation all within the short space of a decade. Hence, a disaggregated and dynamic approach is essential if corporatism is to become a workable concept.

Third, there is a much greater need for sensitivity to differing political ends, both of the state and of the socio-economic coalition that dominates its apparatus. At the broadest level of generality, of course, all capitalist states seek to reproduce capital and to retain their own legitimacy. Yet such a level of generality says very little about the different policy actions of separate capitalist states — why Britain followed an economic policy aimed at preserving the pound until the end of the 1960s, while Germany consistently sought to preserve the lowest possible levels of inflation among the capitalist economies and while France followed its own economic policy of developing "national champions". (Strange, 1971; Blank, 1977, 1978; Zysman, 1977; Katzenstein, 1976, 1977). Individual socio-economic sectors seek particularistic goals. Within the broad framework of a capitalist economy, which of these sectors, individually or in coalition, comes to dominate the state apparatus has a major impact on the specific aims particular states seek to achieve. In the course of seeking to achieve such differentiated goals, individual governments simultaneously engage in a number of actions influencing the development of patterns of public policymaking, interest intermediation, and political economy. Suffrage and electoral regulations; parliamentary procedures and powers; rights of association; criminal and civil codes; access to government controlled media; direct and institutionalized access to government ministries; permanent and guaranteed representation on executive or legislative advisory boards are but a few of the more important institutional ways in which particular social sectors and modes of behavior can be stimulated or discriminated against. The ultimate success of many social "outs", despite the most extreme combination of such barriers is testimony to the fact that obstacles can indeed be overcome; but historically they have been used successfully to reward those in power and hinder those who are not. The contemporary consequences of such past actions deserve far more attention than they have received by students of corporatism.

Finally, work in the areas of corporatism and interest intermediation has focused almost exclusively on domestic political activities, as though these took place in a hermetically sealed environment (though cf. Winkler, 1976: 108, 128-32). Historically, commerce and war have gone a long way toward shaping the "domestic" politics of most countries (Gourevitch, 1977, 1978b; Wallerstein, 1974) and the relative distribution of political, economic and military resources in the world has always had profound implications for the ways in which particular interactions among state and society have been shaped within individual countries. In the present world, it is difficult to talk meaningfully of key policies in advanced capitalist countries without some reference to the IMF, GATT, EEC, OECD, multinational corporations, OPEC, alliances, international capital and commercial flows, grain or arms sales, technology transfers and the like. There has been no agreement on the particular instances in which international stimuli influence domestic political structures more than the reverse (Keohane and Nye, 1972, 1977; Katzenstein, 1976, 1977; Gourevitch, 1977, 1978a, 1978b; Moore, 1966; Skocpol, 1973; Morse, 1973; Gilpin, 1975; Krasner, 1978; inter alia). But surely the arrows of causality run in both directions for most states. That there are instances where significant reshapings of domestic political institutions have resulted from international political and economic conditions seems beyond argument. The influence of international economic forces on the "dependent" countries of the Third World is widely acknowledged, but among advanced industrials the impact of the US Occupation on German and Japanese political institutions and social organization is undeniable (Montgomery, 1957; Dahrendorf, 1969; Kawai, 1960). So is the IMF's influence in restricting recent political possibilities in Italy or the influence of EEC policies in shaping both German and French interest intermediation in the areas of agriculture and small industry.

One thus confronts two somewhat different sets of problems. At the level of dependent variables, there is the broad problem of deciding precisely what the term "corporatism" means, how and where it can legitimately be employed, its degree of compatibility with contemporary capitalism and liberal pluralism and the like. What ultimately are the phenomena to be explained by the term "corporatism"? At the level of independent variables, there is a need for increased sensitivity to changes in state and sectoral objectives over time and a heightened consciousness of the ways in which domestic political patterns can be shaped by international conditions. In both instances, one confronts the need for greater differentiation. Obviously a good deal more work remains to be done on such problems. But no matter how high the quality of the theoretical work, it is unlikely to be sufficiently convincing to sweep into one harmonious camp all the many practitioners of the variant usages of the term while at the same time remaining sufficiently operationable to be of use in empirical research. Starting premises remain too widely differentiated while intellectual and psychic investments are too great. What can be hoped for, however, is a clearer realization of the ways in which different empirical phenomena are differentially identified as manifestations of one or another perceptions of corporatism. Once practical referents become clear, so should theoretical conceptualization.

Two things would appear necessary for this clarification to take place. First, there is a need for a framework capable of capturing in the broadest vein possible, the various phenomena now labelled "corporatism", yet sufficiently differentiated to take account of existing weaknesses in many of the usages. Second, there is a need for greater empirical research on specific situations potentially labelled corporatist. In this way parallels can be highlighted and differences in empirical referents can be isolated. The end result should not only be greater clarity in the practical application of the label, but also in its theoretical underpinnings.

TOWARD A FRAMEWORK
FOR CORPORATIST EXPERIENCES

A variety of definitions have been offered of corporatism and its many mutants, and the ultimate explanandum of corporatism continues to be widely debated. Along with others we would recognize that particular configurations of economic policies, or particular patterns of political economy are typically associated with corporatism. Yet distinctive as these may be, they do not to us constitute the ultimate tests for the presence or absence of corporatism. Although we will attempt to show the utility of a more differentiated sector-to-sector approach to the problem and we will stress somewhat different independent variables contributing to corporatism, in this paper we treat corporatism as a pattern of state-society interaction, or interest intermediation, roughly comparable to Schmitter's famous definition (1974:93-94). Despite the fact that we will eventually put them to use in a more particular way, we would contend that most of the questions with which the various approaches to corporatism are ultimately concerned — the character of the prevalent political economy, the nature of political outcomes, the pattern(s) of interest group organization and interest intermediation, the mechanism(s) of policymaking, including the specific presence or absence of tripartism, the active or passive nature of state institutions — devolve from three related elements. Most important is the nature of the social coalition which controls the state apparatus and ultimately the political economy of the country. Second, is the nature of the political institutions and channels of influence available, on the one hand, to the state and, on the other hand, open to the different social sectors within the country. Although this second feature is usually derived from earlier historical experiences of the first, it is worthy of attention in its own right because of its immediate salience at any specific point in time. Third, and also closely connected to the first, is the relative degree of dependence or independence an individual social sector and/or the state as a whole enjoys within the international political and economic system.

The basic argument presented in later sections is that the variations in the strength of corporatist linkages between components of the state and components of society will vary directly with changes in the character of the dominant domestic coalition and the relative place of a country within the international system. It will also be affected, although less directly, by variations in the channels of political expression. But to repeat, we believe that regardless of the relative weight given to them, and despite differences in presumptions about the directions of causality, these three elements themselves provide a useful basis for understanding "corporatism" in most of its diverse guises.

For some who are concerned with the elements of the corporatist phenomena, dominant coalitions and political institutions will be little more than the secondary political reflections of different modes and relations of production (e.g. Panitch: 1977; Jessup, 1978; Bonnett, 1978). For others concerned with distinguishing "corporatism" as a unique macro-level mode of interest mediation (Schmitter, 1974) or as a form of political economy (Pahl and Winkler, 1975) only the barest outlines of such elements are necessary. But if one wishes to distinguish types of corporatism, variations in the degree of corporatism, or changes in corporatist practices over time, it is essential that more fine grained sensitivity be shown to the broadly shifting alliances among social sectors, the timing of such alliances, and their institutional consequences, as well as the relative weight and autonomy each sector exercises individually and in coalition, and the power of such social sectors vis-à-vis state agencies.

The broad group of states called "advanced capitalist" enjoy the common characteristics of political democracy and economies in which, at some ultimate level, the state can be said to serve the interests of a capitalist class. Yet within such broad commonality there is a wide range in the relative powers of individual state bureaucracies, executive officials, representative assemblies, local governments, advisory committees, the individual ballot, court systems, police powers and a host of other institutional factors. (Tilly, 1975; Armstrong, 1973; Rae, 1967; Kornberg, 1973, inter alia). In addition, different social coalitions hold sway; dominance by "capitalists" involves coalitions composed of, and compromised by, differently balanced social sectors; the nature of opposition is different and the relative balance of all these factors shifts with time. (Bendix, 1969; Dahl, 1966, 1973; Lipset and Rokkan, 1967; Moore, 1966; Gerschenkron, 1962, 1968; Katzenstein, 1976, 1977, inter alia). Finally different states and different sectors encounter different international conditions.

In Canada and the United States, organized labor has at best enjoyed episodic control over government; in Britain and West Germany inclusion and direct influence has been more regular with recurring victories by the Labour or Social Democratic Parties; in the Nordic countries labor's inclusion has been institutionalized for at least a quarter century. Ethnic and/or religious factors are relevant to governance and opposition in Italy, Holland, or Belgium but not in Japan or England; an integrated and powerful banking community can be more readily identified in Germany than in France; organized agriculture plays a much more powerful role in the dominant coalitions in Japan and France or in the opposition in Norway and Denmark than it does in England or West Germany. The supremacy of parliament is more than a slogan in British political practice and the US Congress also is highly influential compared to most national legislatures. In Germany, France and Japan, by way of contrast, bureaucratic rule has been more prevalent than legislative rule.

In a related vein while the pulling and hauling among various groups and between these groups and the state will often take place in a more or less isolated domestic context, more often than not the relative strengths or weaknesses of particular social sectors and state actors will be helped or hindered by exogenous forces. These may be foreign armies, technical assistance, manpower movements, ideologies, moral suasion, nuclear blackmail, economic boycotts, tariffs, commercial penetration, trade embargoes, political asylum or whatever. The relevance of such external forces will of course differ from state to state and sector to sector as international politics persistently demonstrates the inequalities of power. But while the supposedly weaker states of the "South" have long been examined in terms of such vulnerabilities, it is well to recall the wide discrepencies in power among the capitalist states of the "North". Belgium is not France; Austria is not West Germany; Sweden is not Britain; and Holland is not the United States. Moreover, labor intensive industries are more vulnerable than capital intensive industries to international shifts in manpower availability; export dependent industries are more vulnerable than industries with primarily domestic markets; friendly or hostile neighbors can strengthen or weaken competing social sectors. Vulnerabilities and opportunities will clearly differ greatly, but it is important to realize that few states, social sectors or dominant coalitions will be totally immune to such external forces. "Domestic" political and economic arrangements will reflect such "international" differences.

Such examples could be multiplied almost indefinitely; the fundamental point is that such coalitional, institutional and international conditions make a difference in political outcomes, a point that has been amply demonstrated (Katzenstein, 1976, 1977, 1978; Shefter, 1977; Gourevitch, 1977, 1978; Zysman, 1977; Ashford, 1978; Heidenheimer et al., 1975; Pempel, 1977, 1979; Heclo, 1974; Katznelson, 1973, inter alia). Different coalitions in conjunction with different configurations of political institutions facing differing international conditions do make for different politics and different political outcomes. Although this point has been most amply demonstrated in the non-corporatist literature, the general point is not at all unrelated to corporatism. It has been widely argued that the impulse toward corporatism, or toward any of the prefix corporatisms, be they neo-, liberal-, pseudo-, or quasi-, is a consequence or general feature of advanced capitalist economies (e.g., Shonfield, 1965: 161; Beer, 1965; Galbraith, 1967; Panitch, 1977; Heisler, 1974: 42ff.). The economic systems in the advanced capitalist states are characterized by increased complexity and interconnectedness. Long-term planning, concern with market shares, guarantees of stable sources of raw materials and talented manpower, vulnerability to monetary and trade instabilities, the desire for employment security, a smoothing out of the extremes of the business cycle and a host of other pressures have pushed the state bureaucracy and the peak associations of labor and business into closer cooperation. But if the state has become increasingly powerful in the shaping of many capitalist economies, few have yet reached Pahl and Winkler's "fascism with a human face" in which ownership remains private, while economic control is governmental. And if closer cooperation characterizes relations between the state and interest associations, the nature of such cooperation, the degree of formal inclusion, the institutional nexus within which such cooperation occurs, the groups to which such participation is granted and the like differs drastically from context to context. The "iron triangles" linking interest group-congressional committee-bureaucratic agency within the US are haphazard compared to Holland's Social-Economic Council during the 1950s or to the present Austrian Joint Commission on Prices and Wages. Institutionalized cooperation is far more widespread in the Nordic countries and the smaller states of Western Europe than it is in, say, West Germany, where it is limited primarily to "concerted action" on incomes policy.

Such state-to-state variations have been dealt with in certain works on corporatism. Maier (1975) has identified a conservative corporatism between state and interest associations in France, Germany and Italy following World War I that exhibited both a general pattern and unique country differences, in part as an outgrowth of changes in international politics and the world political economy. In many other instances, variations in the degrees of corporatism and the areas where corporatism is most visible have been traced back largely to the nature of the political coalition(s) which have been in control within these countries over time and/or to the political institutions that have evolved. (Lehmbruch, 1977, 1978; Rustow, 1970; Schmitter, 1971, 1974; Olson n.d.; Hibbs, 1976; Cameron, 1976, 1978; Johansen and Kristensen, 1978 inter alia). Notions of "creeping corporatism" (Wassenberg, 1978) "societal corporatism" (Schmitter, 1974), "liberal corporatism" (Lehmbruch, 1977) or even "interest group liberalism" (Lowi, 1969) (which perhaps strictly speaking should not be included as a version of corporatism) all rely heavily on concepts of a state apparatus institutionally incapable or politically unwilling to fend off encroachments on its authority by organized societal interests. "State corporatism", in contrast, presumes a state (usually dominated by a politically reactionary coalition) with institutions and an international position strong enough so that it can force its will on recalcitrant domestic social sectors.

A final word on the general relationship among domestic coalitions, political institutions and international conditions is in order. Although much of the writing on corporatism has concentrated on corporatist behavior involving labor, business and the state and/or the political economy of a country, a total picture of political dominance and subordination, interest intermediation, policymaking and the like would perforce include an examination of the state in relation to a host of professional associations such as physicians, morticians, architects, engineers and the like; the assorted special interest groups pressuring for consideration of the interests of veterans, widows, sportsmen, athletes, teetotallers, conservationists and the like; plus emerging groups dedicated to more collective interests such as improvement in air quality or improvements in consumer benefits and the like. Significant as these may be on particular issues, however, certain limitations to their significance must be recognized. First, economically, their scope and influence are generally limited within the context of the total national economy: they account for a miniscule portion of the GNP; their economic activities are rarely at critical potential bottlenecks in the total economy; and their economic demands, even when met in toto rarely amount to little more than petty pilfering of the national treasury. Second, politically, they are usually similarly limited. Influential as many of these groups may be on the election of individual officials, or on single issues such as health, gun control, abortion, professional licensing, or pollution, they are rarely if ever in a position to force a drastic reorientation of the political regime, either through electoral power, lobbying efforts, or their collective withdrawal of support for existing governing arrangements. This is in sharp contrast to such sectors as big business, organized labor, agriculture and the like, whose economic might, while differing from country to country and from sector to sector is clearly substantial for all, and whose potential capacity to influence the shape of the political regime is generally unquestioned. From such a perspective, the existing bias in corporatist studies toward examining the few key economic sectors of a society in relation to the state and economic policy would appear to be a justified emphasis.

THE JAPANESE CASE

For the most part, recent work on problems of corporatism, particularly on the variants of neo-corporatism or liberal-corporatism associated with advanced capitalism, has proceeded primarily within the context of Western Europe, and to a lesser extent, North America (although cf. Schmitter, 1977a). But if the problems and approaches taken are truly related to political and economic phenomena integral to advanced levels of capitalism and industrialization, rather than to some specifically Western impetus such as the Judeo-Christian culture, the heritage of Rerum Novarum, or a reaction to the Protestant Ethnic, then the Japanese case should simultaneously bear out propositions deemed generally valid, and should possibly also provide an experience from which to enlarge and enrich the existing theoretical corpus.

The entire growth and development of the Japanese economy from the Meiji Restoration to the present is a success story of capitalism. Using 1913 as a basic year, Japan's total volume of output and total output per capita grew faster than that of any other industrialized nation for either the prewar or the postwar years (Maddison, 1969: 154-59). From the 1950s until the early 1970s, growth and industrial transformation were particularly impressive. Toy trains and terra cotta vases gave way to transistors and super-tankers; GNP grew at a rate of about 11% per year moving the country from a position as the smallest of the major powers to the third largest GNP in the world; the country's share of world exports tripled and its foreign reserves improved to the point of generating a near international economic crisis. Moreover, Japan's was one of the first economies to pull out of the depression that began to bedevil capitalist economies around 1974. By 1978 its inflation rate was 4.6%, while its official unemployment rate was 2.3%, both figures among the lowest of the OECD countries. Truly the country has been a highly successful example of the self-defined merits of capitalism.

For the student of corporatism as a mode of political economy, such as case poses obvious interests. Both in its earliest and its more recent transformations, Japan manifested the key attributes of a corporatist economy as defined by Pahl and Winkler (1974) — state direction and private ownership of the means of production aimed at insuring order, unity, nationalism, and success.

For those interested in "state corporatism", Japan from 1938 until 1945 provides an almost perfectly congruent example. With the formation of the Central Alliance for the Mobilization of the National Spirit, and the creation of the Imperial Rule Assistance Association in 1940 all autonomous interest associations were replaced by a monolithic organ of totalistic state control.

For the student of corporatism as a mechanism of interest mediation or policymaking, and particularly those interested in liberal corporatism, Japan should be of particular intrigue. At present, the country possesses the standard array of parliamentary, electoral and civil libertarian features associated with pluralist, liberal democracy. Indeed Neubauer's (1967: 1007) scaling of twenty-three countries on an index of democratic performance ranked Japan seventh, well ahead of such presumed stalwarts as Switzerland, Austria, Denmark, Canada and the United States. Yet at the same time, there is a high degree of corporatism in relations between the state and interest associations. Virtually all major industries are organized into powerful, hierarchical trade associations. The top 100 or so of these, along with about 700-800 of the largest individual firms are further aggregated into the influential Federation of Economic Organizations (Keidanren) (Yanaga, 1968: 42; Akimoto, 1968: 16). Over 99% of the 6 million farm families are locally organized into 7,000 branches of the efficacious National Association of Agricultural Cooperatives. Through these associations, both big business and organized agriculture participate directly in the making and implementation of numerous government policies. Various other groups ranging from doctors, housewives, veterans, private university presidents and local political officials, through cabaret hostesses and bathhouse owners, are organized in similarly influential and generally monolithic interest associations all receiving varying degrees of official state recognition and policymaking roles (Nihon Seiji Gakkai, 1960; Steslicke, 1973: 5-11).

Yet a most striking exception to the general pattern occurs in the area of labor. Only about 32-34% of the Japanese work force is unionized and of this one-third, only about 37% is affiliated with the largest labor federation (Sohyo); an additional 18% is affiliated with Domei, the second largest (Yano, 1977: 109-10). Neither enjoys an official state sponsorship, legal monopoly or even a de facto claim to being the "official" voice of labor. Hence the Japanese case presents a curious anomoly: a high degree of corporatized interest mediation in many sectors, but virtually none in the important area of labor.

Yet, as noted, overall economic performance is exceedingly good and official unemployment figures are exceptionally low. Furthermore, postwar strike volume, though clearly not as low as that in countries with highly corporatized systems of industrial relations such as Austria, Denmark, Switzerland, Sweden, Norway and The Netherlands, has been on a rather consistent and significant downturn ever since 1948 and strike volume has been in the middle ranks of the OECD countries, below that in Germany and not markedly above that in Sweden. (Shalev, 1978: 15). Crime rates are also exceptionally low (Bayley, 1976: 5-7). Furthermore, the relative quietude in Japan has not been the result of massive levels of government spending to insure social peace. Japanese goverment spending as a percent of GNP is the lowest of the major OECD countries. Such an anomolous situation — socio-economic success with a low level of corporatism in the area of labor — should surely command the interest of students of corporatism.

One obvious method of dealing with such a curious situation is to define it away: Japan has no meaningful corporatism if there is no single, monolithic peak association for labor, legally recognized or licensed by the state to engage in some form of economic planning or bargaining with a comparable unit representing business. But such an approach begs more important questions than it settles. Call the anomolous situation whatever one will, it is still one that should be perplexing to those who assume that some form of officially recognized and institutionalized bargaining betwen the peak associations of labor and capital is a logical and/or inevitable outgrowth of the developments of advanced capitalism, or even that corporatist patterns of interest organization and intermediation in one key sector will likely be parallel in other key sectors.

The remainder of this paper will be devoted to an examination of the domestic and international factors that led Japan to develop such an unbalanced corporatist structure, that is "corporatism without labor". Primary attention will be focused on how the corporatist mode of interest intermediation has varied according to sectors and over time. The basic argument presented is that the three key variables noted in the previous section, namely the dominant social coalition, the international political and economic context, and the alternative institutional channels of interest intermediation provide the keys to understanding variations in the corporatist pattern. Even for those who do not treat corporatism as we do, namely as a mode of state-societal intermediation, the explanation should provide some greater sensitivity to the problems of alternative explananda and levels of analysis, as well as showing the virtues of as more disaggregated, dynamic, state-goal and internationally sensitive approach to the entire problematique of corporatism.

LATE INDUSTRIALIZATION AND EARLY CORPORATISM

The essential starting point for an examination of Japanese corporatism must be the combined fact of Japan's late industrialization and its comparatively weak international position. The earliest nation-states to industrialize were characterized economically by the doctrine of laissez faire and politically by liberalism and pluralism. The relative political and economic power wielded internationally by the advanced economic sectors in these countries combined with the relative weakness of potential class-based opposition at home hardly suggested that a strong state would be essential to the advancement of their interests. Indeed, precisely the opposite seemed to be the case: the stronger the state, the more likely it would be to constrain the domestic and international advantages enjoyed by such groups. Strong legislatures and comparatively weak executive and bureaucratic agencies appeared in their best interests. Ultimately, however, when such legislatures proved to be open to capture, or at least influence, by mass-based political parties representing new social forces, these legislative institutions provided meaningful channels of influence over national policy for different interest groups and social sectors (Bendix, 1969; Gerschenkron, 1962; Moore, 1966).

A very different pattern can be found in the case of later industrializers who faced a set of international circumstances that seemed to force a choice between a rapid push to "catch up" or permanent international inferiority. With a major challenge to sovereignty posed from outside before industrialization began, it was essential for such regimes to insure unity within. A state resembling a strong marshall, rather than a night watchman, was needed. Nationalism provided the ideological glue used in minimizing internal economic competition and political dissent and in mobilizing key economic sectors. Close cooperation prevailed between the state bureaucracy and the more advanced sectors of the economy in the provision of capital, in the protection and nurturing of domestic industry, as well as in the suppression of opposition.

Meanwhile, the state, in effect learning from the experiences of earlier industrializers that some degree of mobilization of those left behind in the rush for rapid industrialization was inevitable, was able to follow a combination of repression on the one hand with paternalism and mobilization "from above" on the other. Legislative institutions remained weak, thus limiting their utility for the autonomous articulation of the specific interests of "out" groups. Instead the latter were more readily suppressed and/or absorbed into close cooperation with state bureaucratic agencies.

Throughout the entire period since the Western powers stormed into Japan obliterating its "closed country" policy in 1853, virtually all Japanese governments have seen the nation's sovereignty and independence as under serious threat from the international arena. In the early Meiji period, the state, under a modernizing oligarchy, committed itself to a policy of rapid defensive industrialization. State management of modern industries was attempted in military-related industries such as arms production, shipbuilding, coal mining, railroads, communications, and wool textiles, as well as in the cotton spinning industry for import substitution.

Such efforts at direct management, however, did not achieve their initial purposes. The increase in the import of machinery and raw materials far exceeded the rate of import substitution; government losses soared.

Around 1880, the government changed its strategy from direct management and import substitution to indirect inducement and export promotion. A new Ministry of Agriculture and Commerce was established in 1881 to promote exports (especially raw silk and tea) and to give technological and managerial aid to private industries (Oe, 1973: 73-76, 100-05).

Government factories were transferred to the private sector on highly favorable terms becoming a vigorous stimulant to the consolidation of the economic bases from which Mitsubishi, Mitsui and some other big merchant houses later developed into the large business conglomerates known as *zaibatsu* (Oe, 1973: 167-74). These conglomerates or holding companies were typically organized around one key bank, one key trading company, at least one representative of each of several key industries, and multiple subsidiary firms.

The early financing for Japan's industrialization came primarily at the expense of agriculture and small business. In the second half of the 19th Century, the major part of the government tax income was comprised of the land tax and the excise tax on *sake*, soybean sauce, tobacco and certain other basic consumer goods. (Ranis, 1959: 446).

Opposition by these sectors to the pro-big business policies of the government initially took the form of violent uprisings led by large or medium-sized landowners or by discontented ex-*samurai*. As it became clear that such resistance was futile before the well-equipped govenment army and police, the opponents of the dominant oligarchic coalition came to devote their major efforts to founding political parties and to securing the establishment of a publicly-elected Diet. When the Diet was finally opened in 1890, approximately half of its members were landowners while many of the rest were also from provincial towns, most of them small businessmen. Weak though it initially was, the Diet became a focal point of opposition, frequently vetoing government requests for tax increases (Irokawa, 1966: 478-87). Meanwhile, the two sectors had also begun to organize their own autonomous interest associations which were for the most part free of government control. *Nodan-kai* (Associations for Agricultural Consultation) or *Nojikai* (Agricultural Business Associations) sprang up in many local towns; in 1895, a National Agricultural Business Association was established to promote the interests of the agricultural sector through political activities (Kajinishi, 1973: 105). Chambers of Commerce also appeared as the spontaneous interest associations of merchants and small industrialists.

Government policy toward these sectors was initially a mixture of confusion and hostility. Not until the end of the century did the state begin to take steps to organize and control them. But the generation of foreign reserves required the successful export of the products of small and medium sized industry, such as pottery, tea, lacquerware, matches and brushes and continued political stability necessitated minimizing the extent to which political parties and the parliament could serve as anti-government vehicles by the exploited sectors. To separate these associations from political parties and to impede autonomous interest aggregation from below and to insure an ordered political economy, the state bureaucracy tried to reorganize the agricultural and the small-business sectors under its own initiative.

The Chamber of Commerce Ordinance (1890) obliged each chamber of commerce to be elected by all those in the district who paid business taxes (Imai, 1966: 85). This requirement impeded the smallest businessmen from organizing themselves according to functional lines, thus making specific interest aggregation difficult. The Agrarian Association Law (1899) ordered that *Nokai* (Agrarian Associations) be organized in each administrative district (city, town or village); *Nokai* participation by agricultural producers became compulsory in 1905. In 1910, the Imperial Agrarian Association (Teikoku Nokai) was established by a law replacing the National Agricultural Business Association. The state also distributed a limited amount of subsidies for technological innovations in agriculture through the *Nokai*, thus strengthening its authority over this organization (Kajinishi, 1973: 390-91).

In addition to the changes in organization, the government by the same year had significantly altered the tax structure of the country. Whereas the land tax had provided the bulk of government income until that time, following the revision only 34.5% of the total tax revenue was provided for by land taxes and much of the burden was shifted to business taxes, and less direct forms such as liquor taxes and customs duties. This meant an end to the period in which the agricultural sector and the small business sector had to bear the major sacrifices for industrialization.

Because of the increasing need for imported raw materials and machinery, Japan's trade deficit became especially serious during and after the Sino-Japanese War. In order to overcome this international weakness, the state bureaucracy adopted policies to promote production in the agricultural sector and small industries through the formation of cooperatives.

The Agricultural Cooperative Law and the Important Goods Producers Cooperative Law, both enacted in 1900, fostered the formation of cooperatives for credit distribution, for the purchase of production materials and for the sale of products from the agricultural and small industries sectors. Furthermore, in 1896 the government had set up the Hypothec Bank of Japan and the Agriculture and Industrial Bank, both of which were to provide special financing to agriculture. The number of agricultural cooperatives increased from 255 in 1898 to 11,160 in 1914 (Kajinishi, 1973: 392, 699). In the small industrial sector, the number of cooperatives reached 770 in 1909 (Kajinishi, 1962: 18). These cooperatives became the virtually exclusive channels for the distribution of government subsidies and public loans from the special banks.

Gaining such formal recognition and inclusion in formal policy making and implementation came at the expense of autonomous political development and articulation. Moreover, as Japan's economy soared following World War I, the critical economic role of small business and, to a lesser extent, agriculture began to wane. The drastic drop in exports in the latter half of 1920 and in 1921 hit the medium and small-size industries rather severely. Bankruptcies jumped from 93 in 1918 to 194 in 1920 and to 571 in 1921 (Ando, 1975: 109). The agricultural sector was also damaged not only by the deflation in the industrial sector but also by the increasing import of rice from colonies such as Korea and Taiwan (Kajinishi, 1973: 701-02).

The government moved quickly in the area of agriculture which still accounted for nearly one-third of the net domestic product and well over half the working population. The Rice Crop Law of 1921 authorized the government to partially intervene in the rice market to maintain the stability of rice prices (Kajinishi, 1974: 198-99).

Meanwhile, subsidies to the agricultural sector through the *Nokai* and the agricultural cooperatives increased sharply through the 1920s from 0.6% of total government subsidies in 1920 to 10.8% in 1929. (Ranis, 1959: 443).

The response of the state toward the difficulties in the small business sector was much slower. The only major policy for this sector in the 1920s was the encouragement of cartel formation among export-goods producers in 1925. However, since there were no membership restrictions, these cartels tended to become dominated by the large *zaibatsu* corporations, rather than the small businesses (Yamamoto and Kato, 1962: 8u4-93).

The decline in the autonomous power of these two sectors came to greatest fruition during the period of Japan's greatest international isolation, following the breakdown of the Washington Conference system, the autonomy of the military abroad, Japan's walkout from the League of Nations, and the outbreak of the war with China. Domestically, a decline in the influence of political parties and a surge in the power of the state bureaucracy accompanied these changes. After 1937, state corporatism became particularly conspicuous in the agricultural and the small-business sectors.

In 1931, the National Confederation of Rice Sales and Purchasing Cooperatives was established by a law which also gave the rice-producers' cooperatives exclusive authority to monopolize the purchase of the rice crop from individual peasants and the sales of rice to the government or retailers. Furthermore, the Rice Crop Control Law (1933) authorized the government to buy and sell as much rice as was necessary to maintain the government-determined rice price (Kajinishi, 1974: 571, 816). Since rice was (and is) the most widely cultivated crop in Japan, these laws greatly strengthened the power of the state bureaucrcy vis-à-vis the agricultural sector through the large-scale corporatist structure. Between 1939 and 1942 the system of mandatory purchase and rationing of rice by the government agency was consolidated, further strengthening state corporatism in the agricultural sector. In the same period, production materials such as fertilizer and agricultural machinery were also rationed through the cooperatives (Kajinishi, 1974: 1098-104). Needless to say, these measures were precipitated by the international economic and political crisis. In the meanwhile, the 1940 law authorized the *Nokai* to control all facets of agricultural production and, the Agricultural Group Law of 1943 merged the agricultural cooperatives and the *Nokai* into the *Nogyokai*, thus completing the unification of agriculture (Kajinishi, 1974: 1112-13).

In the small-business sector, the Industrial Cooperative Law of 1931 and the Commercial Cooperative Law of 1932 created control cooperatives which aimed primarily at cartelization. The laws also authorized the government to force non-participants to obey the control measures established by the cooperatives. The laws concerned with the control cooperatives were revised several times throughout the 1930s to strengthen the power of the state vis-à-vis small businessmen: in 1933, the punishments against those who did not obey the control measures of the cooperatives became heavier. Meanwhile, in 1937, the control cooperatives and their municipal and prefectural confederations were obliged to obtain government permission with regard to the election and dismissal of their directors. Finally, in 1943, the industrial and commercial cooperatives were placed under the direction of the *Toseikai* (control associations) which were the cartels of the *zaibatsu* (Yamamoto and Kato, 1962: 202-04).

While agriculture and small industry slipped rather consistently under state control in a corporatist pattern from 1900 until the end of the war, the pattern was rather different with regard to big business. It was the horizontally organized, and increasingly autonomous, *zaibatsu* which dominated interest mediation for big business, and although industrial associations were organized for specific industrial sectors, that for the cotton spinning industry was probably the only one which was highly developed. In 1890, eight years after the Spinning Industry Association was formed, it carried out the first coordinated curtailment of production (sotan) in order to overcome a recession. The SIA was also active in petitioning the Diet and the government to abolish the import tax on cotton and the export tax on cotton yarn, taxes which were abolished in 1894 and 1896 (Oe, 1973: 233, 238-43).

The SIA though was the exception. Instead of industrial associations, it was the *zaibatsu* which dominated Japanese economic politics through the first quarter of the century. In March 1917, the Japan Industrial Club was formed as a loose peak association of several of these *zaibatsu* (Imai, 1966: 84-85). And while the club and the individual *zaibatsu* maintained close ties with the state bureaucracy (especially the Ministry of Finance and the Ministry of Agriculture and Commerce) big business was hardly encorporatized by such actions. Moreover, as the political parties and the Diet came to gain bargaining power, the *zaibatsu* moved effectively to exercise influence over them as well, thereby broadening their channels of influence.

Big industry and the *zaibatsu* were initially quite in accord with most government perceptions of how Japanese economic policy should be conducted. Both sides were, in effect, partners in weakness vis-à-vis the much stronger and seemingly hostile countries of the West. And while there were disagreements among all sides on particular issues, big and small business, the state bureaucracy, and organized agriculture were united on one point: the basic threat posed domestically by organized labor.

The industrial development during and after the Sino-Japanese War (1894-95) brought about the first wave of unionization in Japan. Unionization further developed after the Russo-Japanese War (1904-05), and the period was characterized by the spread of frequently violent labor unrest and suppression by army troops (Sumiya, 1966: 329-38). Throughout the next three decades, the labor movement continued to achieve varying degrees of success. The number of labor unions increased from 107 in 1918 to 488 in 1926, reaching a peak of 973 in 1936. However, even at labor's prewar highpoint in 1936, the 420,000 workers organized represented only 6.9% of the total workforce (Ando, 1975: 129). Not until 1941 did labor organizations gain formal organizational status and recognition by the state, and this status came at the expense of institutional and sectoral autonomy, marking simply labor's cooptation into Japan's war effort. It was a classic example of state initiated encorporatization (Schmitter, 1974: 103-05). Despite certain levels of success, therefore, labor unions in pre-World War II Japan never became powerful enough to command autonomous legitimacy and recognition by the state. Nor were they sufficiently powerful to command any significant role in the economic policies of the state.

In addition to the fact that a large reservoir of surplus labor existed in Japan's agricultural areas, three essentially political conditions worked against labor. First, the labor movement and leftist parties encountered the frequent use of coercive measures by the state. In the face of the first wave of the labor movement toward the end of the last century, the government passed a Public Peace Police Law in 1900. Among other things, Article 17 of this law prohibited the following: (1) Forcing anyone to participate in groups aimed at collective actions with regard to labor conditions and wages; (2) Forcing strikes upon workers; (3) Forcing employers to concede demands concerning labor conditions and wages (Ando, 1975: 83). This law made the development of the labor movement extremely difficult. Although it did not prohibit voluntary unionization or strikes and negotiations with employers, the judgment of any strike's voluntariness was entirely entrusted to the police. Furthermore, the major move to enact a labor union law in the second half of the twenties was prevented by the strong opposition of certain business and state elements. In prewar Japan, therefore, labor unions had no status as legitimate entities.

Nor were the unions and the leftist political parties they supported successful in utilizing the electoral-parliamentary route to political influence, providing a direct contrast to the situation with agriculture and small business. Many reasons can be advanced to explain this weakness, but in addition to the general numerical weakness of the unions and to state opposition, one must note that universal male suffrage did not begin in Japan until 1925, and this was accompanied by a Peace Preservation Law, and the creation of the Special Police Force, aimed at weakening any "radical" organizations. The maximum penalty under the revised law of 1928 was death. Thus, even at their highpoint in 1937, the parties of the left failed to gain over 10% of the total vote, making their electoral and parliamentary voice extremely weak, and providing little real threat to the dominant coalition at the time.

A third reason for the early weakness of labor was the preemptive actions of the employers and the state in regard to the organization of labor along enterprise, rather than industrial, lines, and in the initiation of moderate factory laws. As Kaneko Kentaro, then Vice Minister of Agriculture and Commerce noted in 1896: "The advantage of being one of those who follow is that it gives one the opportunity to take note of the history of those who have gone before, and to avoid taking the same path" (as quoted in Marshall, 1967: 55).

Enterprise unionism was seen as important to the task of weakening the potentially disruptive capacity of labor on the existing political economy. In the rhetoric of management, the employer and his workers were supposed to be like a father and his sons. Workers would give total loyalty to their employer in exchange for which the employer would grant them paternalistic benefits such as family sickness allowances. The state cooperated actively in this policy. A conscious policy for the enterprise-level incorporation of workers started with the National Railways in 1906 and spread to the private sector, especially among the largest enterprises (Sumiya, 1966: 349-51).

Soeda Juichi, an official of the Ministry of Agriculture and Commerce, spoke strongly at the First Plenary Conference on Agriculture, Commerce and Industry of the need for state intervention in industrial relations

> Unless the State intervenes in some degree in the relations between employer and employee, there is no means of protecting the interests of the employees and hence there will arise social evils, disturbances, and social disorder (Marshall, 1967: 54).

At the same conference, government bureaucrats indicated their sensitivity to the likelihood of future problems if laws were not created on factory conditions. There was, it was claimed, an immediate need "to create the laws necessary to maintain in the future the balance between capital and labor, and harmonious relations between employers and employees, thereby protecting in advance against any disorders" (Marshall, 1967: 54).

Stressed by government and business throughout this period was the harmonization of the intersts of labor and management for the good of the country. One of the more noteworthy organizational results was the formation of the Kyochokai (The Association for Harmony and Conciliation) at the combined initiative of private business leaders such as Shibusawa Eiichi and the Ministry of Home Affairs.

Labor leaders, well aware of the dangers which family-type enterprises presented to the development of a cohesive labor movement, fought vigorously against it, and when the Great Japan Labor Confederation was organized as a peak association of labor unions in August 1919, one of its policies was to reorganize the member unions into industrial unions (Imai, 1966: 305). Most individual unions also sought to ignore the Kyochokai. But enterprise unionism and managerial and state paternalism dominated industrial relations throughout the prewar period. By 1938 military and right-wing labor leaders had created the Industrial Patriotic Movement to help the war effort in China. And in July 1940, existing labor unions and labor peak associations were dissolved and reorganized into the Industrial Patriotic Association. By 1942, the number of workers organized into the Industrial Patriotic Association through individual enterprises reached more than five million (Hayashi, 1966: 179-83). Thus, during the prewar period, organized labor was weak in virtually any autonomous articulation of its own interests and it never achieved a significant role in the national political economy.

While state-directed encorporatization was the trend in all of Japan's key economic sectors, the one significant exception was big business. Although big business and the Japanese government were usually in close agreement on the basic goals and mechanisms for achieving rapid economic growth, as Japan's international economic position improved, particularly following World War I, the partnership lost some of its closeness. The economic interests of the *zaibatsu* seemed no longer to coincide exactly with those of government, while correspondingly the protection of the government no longer appeared to be as critical to their continued economic success.

From the late 1920s on, right-wing bureaucrats, encouraged by young military officers, tried to reduce some of the power that had been lost to the *zaibatsu*. In the process of enacting the Important Industries Control Law, which aimed at "rationalizing" the economy and at overcoming the depression, some bureaucrats attempted to curtail *zaibatsu* influence and to generate state corporatist institutions similar to those in agriculture and small business. Industries were reorganized into industrial associations over which state control could theoretically be directly exerted. In practice, though, the *zaibatsu*'s insistence on "self-control" prevailed and most associations ended up as cartels dominated by the *zaibatsu* members themselves (Ouchi, 1967: 240-44).

Japan's economy suffered drastically as a result of the international depression, and received a second wave of shocks as a consequence of international opposition to the country's foreign and military policies in the late 1920s and 1930s. In the face of the collective national weakness internationally, a variety of corporatist, fascist and national socialist solutions gained increased credibility among a variety of military and civilian groups. Central to these ideas was the principle of the controlled national economy, and until the end of the war, efforts to create a state-controlled economy posed a key problem for the big business sector.

Ironically, it was the Diet which after the mid-1930s became a center for *zaibatsu* resistence to the state's attempt to control the national economy. In the late 19th century, landowners had used the Diet against the pro-business state. Now the *zaibatsu* came to rely on the Diet to resist the military-dominated state.

The *zaibatsu* continued to retain a good deal of autonomy throughout the war, but with the creation of the Planning Board in 1937 and the National Mobilization Law in 1938, all resources, materials, prices, wages, trade and other economic matters came formally under government control. The Important Industries Association Ordinance (August 1941) ordered the formation of control associations in each industrial sector. These were in theory to be placed under tight state control. But in practice, these control associations became little more than *zaibatsu* cartels under different names (Johnson, 1978: 71-72). Thus, there were important corporatist trends and elements in big business throughout the first half of the twentieth century, but the state was never in a position completely to dominate the leading industrial sectors in the way that it came to dominate labor, agriculture and small business. There was throughout the prewar period, however, and especially in moments of international weakness, strong pressure towards the corporatist version of a political economy written of by Pahl and Winkler — state direction and private ownership, plus pressures on all sectors toward order, unity, nationalism and success (1975). There was also ultimately a clear trend toward state corporatism, largely as an outgrowth of a weakened international position. but the trends were different from sector to sector, and at least in the area of big business, the state was never fully successful in exerting its dominance.

ECONOMIC NATIONALISM AND CORPORATISM WITHOUT LABOR: A ONE-SIDED JAPAN, INC.

With the end of World War II, and with Japan's occupation by the United States, significant changes occurred in the dominant political coalition, in the political institutions available to interest associations and in Japan's international position. Land reform eliminated the economic base of the Japanese landlord class as effectively as the parcellization of Germany had transferred the base of the Junkers to East Germany. Blunted though the policy came to be, the US dissolved several major *zaibatsu* and to the extent that one sees them as a member of the dominant prewar coalition, the Japanese military was also eviscerated. Although there was no direct attack on the power of the state bureaucracy (Pempel, 1978), the sovereignty of the emperor which had justified bureaucratic controls gave way to popular sovereignty and the relative powers of the Diet were considerably strengthened. The devastating effect of the war on Japan's economy coupled with the country's reputation as a wartime pariah, left it in an international position somewhat analogous to its isolation at the time of Meiji. One big difference internationally, however, was that with the outbreak of the Cold War and the success of the Communist Revolution in China, Japan became an integral regional link in the US system of military and economic alliances, a strong bilateral relationship unlike anything the country had enjoyed since the end of the Anglo-Japanese alliance in 1922. The United States provided certain generous security and economic benefits as a result of this link, as well as support for the creation and maintenance of the conservative coalition which has controlled the national government since the end of the US Occupation.

The overall consequences of such shifts in regard to corporatism are extremely interesting. In broad brush perspective, strong international pressures for a corporatized political economy existed and big business, in a much weaker position internationally and domestically than it had been in the 1930s, was more amenable to encorporatization from above. Weaknesses in agriculture and small business meanwhile, plus the dominance of the prewar heritage, left these sectors similarly ripe for such "top down" control by the state bureaucracy. At the same time, the increased significance of political parties and the Diet expanded the channels of influence open to these sectors and tended to counterbalance corporatist tendencies. Meanwhile, organized labor remained as hostile to the regime as the regime was to it, with the result that it neither succeeded in acquiring, nor faced the need to resist, any significant pressure for national level corporatist connections.

Economic reconstruction during the US Occupation became the task of the state bureaucracy since individual industries, for the most part, lacked the funds, raw materials and energy sources to recover alone. They needed the combination of US aid and public loans distributed through the state to survive and begin reconstruction. Simultaneously, they were undergoing critical struggles with the burgeoning radical labor movement, against which they also needed American and Japanese government assistance. Both combined to push business into the hands of the state.

Following the occupation, the government advanced policies of economic nationalism based on rapid growth through the selective development of certain key sectors of the economy. Importation of technology and raw materials and the export of high quality manufactured goods were central intermediate ends (Pempel, 1977). With the pro-business Liberal Democratic Party firmly in electoral control, the government was able to rely almost exclusively on the state bureaucracy to effect these policies.

The Ministry of International Trade and Industry (MITI), was entrusted with the task of sectoral development and export promotion. While encouraging the exporters of nondurable consumer goods, MITI allocated a major part of the available foreign exchange, raw materials and overseas technologies to heavy and chemical industries (the most promising sectors) and to basic industries (electric power, steel, coal). The Japan Development Bank concentrated its loans in these basic industries and the shipping industry. The Ministry of Finance (MOF) and the Bank of Japan led city banks to advance loans to these priority industries. Generous tax reductions were also granted (Tamagaki, 1977: 59-70; Johnson, 1977; Pempel, 1977).

Interest intermediation between the state and modern industries was carried out primarily through MITI's functionally organized bureaus and the peak trade associations; various industrial sectors were thus dealt with by directly corresponding bureaus (Honda, 1974: 11-12). This system was much more institutionalized and corporatized than anything big business had encountered during the prewar period.

Meanwhile, the "democratization" policies after WWII did little to change the basic structure of the interest associations in the agricultural and the small-business sectors nor their relationships with the state bureaucracy. The new agricultural cooperatives established in 1947 inherited the properties, tasks and employees of the old *Nogyokai* (Kajinishi, 1974: 1381). Although land reform weakened the influence of large landowners, paternalistic control over the peasantry by the state bureaucracy, through the cooperatives, continued.

The situation was similar in the small business sector. Most central to the government bureaucracy's ability to retain these tight links was the weakness of Japan's economic position in the world, and the ability of the state bureaucracy to serve as the effective gate keeper of all that came into and left Japan. With a minimum of natural resources, Japan had always been highly dependent on foreign sources for its needed raw materials. Under the US Occupation severe restrictions had been established over the ability of individuals and private firms to engage in international commerce, and thus the government bureaucracy obtained vast powers over the licensing of imports and exports, which it utilized to insure broad sectoral compliance with its fundamental economic policies.

Thus, although the new agricultural cooperatives were supposed to be non-compulsory associations, it was almost impossible for individual farmers to obtain production materials or credits and to sell their products without relying on the cooperatives which were assigned the role of intermediaries under the tight state control system for industrial and agricultural goods (Kajinishi, 1974: 1381). The agricultural cooperatives, in turn, relied on government subsidies and loans for their activities. Various fees paid by the government for the storage and delivery of agricultural products, for example, became important sources of cooperative revenue (Kajinishi, 1974: 1386).

The same pattern occurred with the industrial and commercial cooperatives in the small-business sector. The power of the state bureaucracy vis-a-vis this sector was also based on the system of rationing raw materials and intermediate products (Suzuki and Kajinishi, 1962: 84-93). Although the rationing system was abandoned in 1950, the dependence of the small-business sector continued as a result of the economic recession in the second half of 1951. The stagnation of exports following the initial boom caused by the Korean War further weakened the medium and small-sized industries. The Provisional Law on the Stabilization of Specified Medium and Small-Size Industries of 1952 aimed at relieving small businesses from this predicament by permitting the formation of cartels ("coordination cooperatives") which would coordinate production, marketing and investment in specified industries under specified conditions. MITI was granted vast authority by this law: when coordination cooperatives could not reach an autonomous agreement on the necessary coordination plan, the Ministry would be able to order the participants to obey whatever coordination plan it eventually wrote; although participation in the coordination cooperatives itself was not compulsory, MITI could issue a "coordination order" by which non-participants would be forced to obey the coordination plan written either by the cooperative or MITI. This provisional law became a "permanent" law in August 1953 (Yamamoto and Kato, 1962: 194-95, 215-16).

Simultaneously, the large corporations started to subordinate the medium and small-size enterprises as their subcontractors. This vertical integration by industry was regarded as necessary for the big businesses, not only to eliminate competition from medium and small-size enterprises but also to ensure the modernization of selected subcontractors. Thus this sector underwent a double encapsulization "from above", both by the state bureaucracy and larger firms, all in the interest of national economic success.

The stronger postwar role of parliament and the political party system did serve to mitigate certain of the seemingly total control from above. Business and organized agriculture formed the key social sectoral components of the Liberal Democratic Party which, along with its predecessors, has held power continuously from the end of the Occupation. In agriculture, farmers were able to utilize their electoral strength to insure relatively high rice prices through the price control system inherited from the prewar and early Occupation period (Donnelly, 1977: 143-200) and to gain protection from imports. Individual businesses and businessmen developed close links with individual politicians and LDP factions which provided them various advantages vis-à-vis competitors. On the other hand, the weakness of the horizontal organizations of smaller businessmen and the divisions within the sector tended to impede their autonomous political mobilization. As a result, the major part of the government subsidies for small and medium sized industries went to the medium sized firms (Sato, 1967: 104).

The major exception to the broad trend of encorporatization in the national economic interest was labor which although it became extremely powerful in the postwar period was consistently allied with political parties on the "outs". The power and role of the prewar Japanese state in suppressing labor can best be seen by recognizing the phenomenal organizational growth of labor immediately after the war under the American Occupation — the "new state". Under initial pro-labor policies the number of labor unions which was zero at the end of the war increased to 509 by the end of 1945, and ballooned to 17,266 in 1946 and to 34,688 by 1949. By 1949 55.5% of the total workforce was organized (Ando, 1975: 156). At about the same time, Japan enjoyed its only socialist led government (May 1947-February 1948). Yet such strength was not turned into a formalized role for labor in the making of state policy or in the political economy. The immediate causes were quite specific. The "socialist" government was based on a precarious coalition which included two conservative parties; labor was divided into two peak associations, one of which was completely hostile to any "conciliation" with business; US policy, reflecting its own changing domestic and international situation, was undergoing a shift away from support for labor and the socialists and toward the conservatives, business, and economic stability (Takemae, 1977; Sakamoto, 1978). Thus, labor was incapable of institutionalizing its short-term power and penetration of official policymaking mechanisms at the time of greatest potential.

Under the highly bipolarized politics of the 1950s and 1960s the conservative coalition enjoyed comfortable majorities and was in no mood voluntarily to provide a formal role for organized labor. Nor was labor able to force its way into such a role either through electoral or economic power, the two traditional routes to labor's national level influence in other capitalist countries.

Absolute size of the unionized workforce is, of course, a factor in utilizing each of these, and although there was over 55% unionization in 1949, the number of unions and union members did not increase between 1950 and 1956; by the mid-1950s, the organization rate had dropped into the low 30% range where it has remained ever since.[2] But other countries, such as West Germany, the Netherlands or even the United States demonstrate higher levels of labor inclusion in economic policymaking despite similar or lower levels of unionization.

Part of the problem for Japanese labor lies in the inability of the pro-labor parties to attract significant numbers of non-union voters. Still despite the fact that the Japanese electoral system is blatantly gerrymandered against those areas where labor has traditionally been strongest, parties of the "progressive camp" have managed to garner between 33-40% of the seats in the House of Representatives in all but one election since 1953. Yet they have not managed to translate this into a single cabinet seat since the late 1940s, and with only limited exceptions, the nearly 300 government advisory committees are devoid of labor representation.[3]

Strict party lines are enforced in committee assignments, parliamentary voting, and in the selection of a cabinet, so that little short of a majority provides significant influence. Moreover, bureaucratic control over the generation and implementation of policy proposals remains high so that the opposition's one-third translates into only a minor toehold for parliamentary influence and policymaking penetration (Pempel, 1974, 1975).

Labor has also been ineffectual in manifesting sufficient national economic power to force its way into the country's formal policymaking mechanisms. As noted, only one-third of Japan's workforce is unionized and Sohyo, the largest peak association accounts for no more than 37% of that unionized work force. More significantly, the bulk of Sohyo's membership is drawn not from manufacturing sectors, with clear importance for the national economy, but from government employees where such economic power is more veiled and where the right to strike is legally curtailed. These factors are obviously important in explaining labor's inability to demonstrate economic might. But undergirding labor's national economic weakness is the fact of persistent enterprise unionism. In the mid 1970s, enterprise unions comprised nearly 95% of Japan's unions and enrolled 83% of the nation's union members.

The heritage of prewar structure and ideology was important, but enterprise unionism was stimulated as well by several factors prevalent immediately after the war. First, there were conditions of extreme poverty. Stopping production through strikes was, therefore, not a good strategy for the emerging unions. It would only deprive workers themselves of a source of living. Many labor unions therefore tried to manage their enterprises by themselves in what were called "production control struggles". These, however, needed the cooperation of all workers in the enterprise and therefore contributed to unionization along enterprise lines without sharp distinctions in rank or status (Daito, 1977: 210). Furthermore, with the economic conditions of workers so dismal, differences in interest among workers were small. Both white-collar workers and blue-collar workers could unite around the single demand of securing some basic minimum level of well-being. In addition, there was a strong demand for democratization in enterprises as a reaction to the suppressive nature of the prewar regime. Hence, in many unions, differences between white-collar and blue-collar workers were consciously rejected for ideological reasons. Organizing all workers regardless of status, into one enterprise union rather than organizing along job, and hence unequal status lines, was seen as an expression of democratization (Kuriki, 1977: 228-29).

In the meantime, prewar business paternalist ideology combined with anti-union pragmatism. When the Federation of Employers' Associations was formed in April 1948, it guided employers in concluding collective contracts *inside individual enterprises*, in encouraging enterprise unionism, and where necessary in creating "second unions" loyal to management.[4]

Although some efforts were made by peak labor federations to reorganize their membership along industrial lines in the late 1940s and early 1950s (Hyodo, 1977: 102), and although certain "industrial unions" (Tekko Roren, Shitetsu Soren, etc.) do exist, these are essentially only conglomerates of enterprise unions within individual industrial sectors. The component enterprise unions retain a large measure of autonomy. Labor contracts are concluded between each enterprise and its union. In the now famous Spring Struggle, the closest approximation to national level wage negotiations, each union can decide, by a membership vote, whether or not it will participate in any industry-wide strikes.

This pattern of enterprise unionism has thus blunted the potential for peak labor federations to command representation in key economic decisions made at the national level, and the enterprise unions in conjunction with individual enterprises represent a more critical link between labor and capital. Cooptation has been the predominant feature of labor unions at the enterprise level although some unions have begun to exercise a slight impact on economic policy through collective bargaining actions at the level of the individual enterprise; however, as of 1978 there has been no formal inclusion of union representatives in the managerial structures of any firms, and Japanese enterprise unions have not gained the plant level powers of even German or British unions. Certainly, they have not achieved what Crouch correctly identifies as a most essential power, namely direct influence over investment policy (Crouch, 1978b). Thus, Japanese labor has been dealt with piecemeal at the level of the individual enterprise while economic growth in the "national interest" has been able to proceed without central regard to the specific demands of collective labor.

FLUX IN THE CORPORATIST PATTERN:
THE DEMISE OF JAPAN, INC.

Such a static picture of postwar Japanese "corporatism" does not do justice to the earlier call for increased dynamism and differentiation; nor does it take account of the fact that the dominant coalition in Japan is not as firmly entrenched in 1979 as it was ten or fifteen years earlier and that the international conditions that now face Japan and its component segments are also quite different.

The national level electoral margin exercised by the ruling Liberal Democratic Party became increasingly narrow through the last decade with the result that every vote becomes more important. Meanwhile, Japan's economic success has had the twofold effect of opening the country's economic policies to pressures from other major capitalist countries, including its primary ally the United States, while at the same time making it possible for certain sectors of Japan's big business community to depend much less on close cooperation with the state bureaucracy.

The increasing international success of Japan's economy brought pressures for, and a realization of, the liberalization of capital, trade and technology, and a reduction in the protective restrictions that heretofore had benefitted not only the most advanced sectors of the economy, but also agriculture and small business.

Meanwhile, there was growing internationalization of the Japanese economy and many of its industries and firms have become highly competitive internationally. Joint ventures, overseas investments, multinationalization, upstream and downstream integration, access to overseas capital, and the like have all soared, reducing the dependence of the individual corporation on government agencies and their own peak associations (Yoshino, 1976). No longer can the latter control capital, raw materials, technology, and export licenses with the same impunity as was true in the 1950s and early 1960s. What were once seen as necessary constrictions in exchange for broad economic development and close links to the government bureaucracy have increasingly come to be viewed as national albatrosses around the necks of international, rather than Japanese, firms. Thus, the close linkages between the state and the advanced areas of industry which so characterized Japanese interest intermediation for about twenty years after World War II have been weakening in the face of a growing capacity by Japan's most advanced firms to function effectively in the international economy without the direct, domineering and constricting partnership of the Japanese bureaucracy.

If the consequences of economic internationalization have worked against corporatist institutions and policies in the area of advanced industry they have had much the opposite effect on agriculture and small business. These latter sectors, most likely to be disadvantaged by such economic internationalization, have, wherever possible, sought bureaucratic and political allies and have pressed for ever more corporatist links between themselves and the state. The declining LDP margins have made officials and politicians more responsive to pressures from farmers and the chambers of commerce which have increasingly been used for electoral mobilization. At the same time they have sought to foil efforts by groups such as the Communist-led Democratic Commercial and Industrial Associations which have gained influence among small industrialists.

In the area of agriculture, for example, the oil shocks of the early 1970s had a significant impact. Destroyed was any presumption that may have existed in Japan to the effect that the internationalization of its economy could be both economically effective and free of political constraints. Japan's blatant vulnerability on energy imports only served to reopen questions about its potentially similar vulnerability on food imports. If the Japanese government sought to take advantage of cheaper food stuffs abroad, it was argued, Japan would ultimately lose whatever autonomy it might have once enjoyed in foodstuffs and would be open to political blackmail on rice, meat or citrus fruit in precisely the same way as it saw itself to have been blackmailed on oil (Sanderson, 1978).

Thus starting in 1973 the government began to plan to consolidate the smaller firms in the country so as to increase efficiency and to allow for a greater use of technology in agriculture. And since 1975 the Ministry of Agriculture and Forestry has been attempting to implement a program of "integrated food policies" aimed at the stabilization and development of imports, increased stockpiling, protection of fishing resources and an increase in self-sufficiency in food of 75% by 1985 (Donnelly, 1977). Much of the program will rely on incentive promotion and acreage payments, government loans and extension services, promotion of consumption of products which are domestically produced and the like, all in conjunction with the agricultural cooperatives.

Corporatist protectionism has come to dominate agriculture, fishing and small industry wherever immediate threats seem to appear, and/or wherever political pressure can be mobilized by the affected sector such as in livestock, whaling, citrus fruits and plywood (Yokota, 1977; Focus Japan, April 1977). The government has sponsored monopoly corporations, protective cartels, integration of related growers or producers associations, international negotiating teams composed of government and agricultural or industrial officials and the like. Farmers, fishermen and small businessmen for the most part have been only too happy to relinquish the burdens of independence for the assurances of close cooperation and aid from the government.

Thus domestic political shifts and international economic success have combined to produce some fundamental changes in patterns of Japanese corporatism. One of the more interesting manifestations of these changes came in early 1977 when agriculture and small business won a domestic political battle aimed at preventing larger firms from moving into areas traditionally dominted by smaller industry. The Small Business Sector Adjustment Law, passed on 27 May 1977, provides for close coordination between peak associations and the relevant government ministry (MITI in the case of industrial goods, MAFF in the case of agricultural products) to deal with any threats posed by the entry of larger firms. Preliminary authority to decide whether such entry is legitimate or not is given to the association, and if the association in conjunction with the government ministry cannot convince the big firms to desist, the government has wide powers to order revision in the plans of the larger firms (Focus Japan, August 1977).

CONCLUSION

In the early Meiji period, the dominant coalition composed of the state bureaucracy and big industrialists pursued a forceful industrialization policy sacrificing the agricultural sector, small business and, later, workers, The international threat to national security was always used as an excuse for such sacrifices.

However, once the agricultural and small-business sectors were able to rely on an alternative channel (the Diet) to defend their interests, the state preemptively moved to incorporate these sectors into semiofficial "associations" and "cooperatives". Agricultural and small-business accepted this encapsulation from above not only because of their domestic weaknesses but also because of their international weaknesses.

The agricultural sector needed state protection for production and price-maintenance for its crops, especially when domestic economic recession was serious or when there was serious competition posed by food imported from the colonies.

The small-business sector also needed state protection to defend itself from competition by big business and from the fluctuations in the export markets.

Thus, by early in this century, the dominant coalition of the state and big business was expanded to include, as minor partners, the agricultural and small-business sectors. One of the major political strategies chosen by this coalition was to systematically exclude labor from the national-level organizations and to incorporate them at the individual plant level, thus neutralizing their potentially disturbing influence.

In the meanwhile, international economic success and control over the Diet made it possible for the *zaibatsu* to maintain relative autonomy vis-à-vis the state bureaucracy, especially after World War I.

By the end of the 1930s, the autonomy of the *zaibatsu*, too, was largely curtailed because of the increasing influence of the military in the dominant coalition. However, the final blow came with the American Occupation which dissolved both the *zaibatsu* and the military.

The international weakness just after the war sharply curtailed the bases for autonomy of both agricultural and industrial sectors, thus strengthening the power of the state bureaucracy in all economic sectors. Corporatist structures were maintained in the agricultural and small-business sectors and even big business was incorporated under the auspicies of the powerful MITI.

Thus, the dominant coalition in the post-war period was composed of the state bureaucracy, big business and agriculture. Small and medium-sized industries joined as minor partners. Yet the political strategy of this coalition with regard to labor remained exactly as it had been in the prewar period: exclusion from the national level and incorporation at the plant level.

This state-dominated corporatist structure, however, is now in the process of change, primarily because of changes in international conditions.

The liberalization of trade, foreign investment and technology transfer has largely curtailed the legal authority of the state bureaucracy. Meanwhile, international economic success has led big business to demand more autonomy vis-à-vis the state bureaucracy. The Diet is now one of the arenas in which big business can resist the attempt of reincorporation by the state, which was fully shown, for example, in the process of the enactment of the Law on Structurally Stagnant Industries (Kozo Fukyo Ho) and the Law for Energy Saving (Sho Enerugi Ho).

In contrast, the internationally more vulnerable agricultural and small-business sectors have used the Diet and their ability to influence electoral results to capture portions of the state bureaucracy from below, thus strengthening the traditionally strong corporatist structures in these two sectors. This corporatist drive from below perfectly matches the desire of the state bureaucracy to maintain its declining power vis-à-vis society as a whole.

Thus, perceptions of international weakness have rather consistently pushed for corporatist solutions in Japan, both at the level of the national political economy and in the more specific patterns of mediation between economic sectors and the state. The specific forms and the relative inclination towards or against such solutions have, of course, differed over time and from sector to sector. Most generally, the strongest pushes towards corporatism have come from the state in moments of greatest weakness internationally and they have been mirrored by compatible drives on the part of economic sectors which see themselves as feeble in the face of extensive international competition. Conversely, strength presses in the opposite direction: the protections corporatism promises are not worth the sacrifices it demands of the strong. Political institutions become salient insofar as they do or do not provide alternative channels for an individual sector to either exacerbate a tendency toward societal corporatism or prevent unwanted capture by the pressures of state corporatism. But alternative domestic channels and international strength or weakness per se mean very little if a sector can be expediently ignored by the dominant domestic coalition in a country. This is clear from the isolated position occupied by Japanese labor under the varied corporatist situations during Japan's modern history. The perplexing question this poses is whether an anti-labor coalition can effectively design a political economy and political institutions so as to keep labor permanently on the outside, or whether some variant of corporatism, including the encorporatization of labor is inevitable either in advanced capitalist economies or in this supposed Century of Corporatism.

NOTES

An earlier version of this paper was presented at the International Sociology Association Convention, Uppsala, Sweden, August 1978. We would like to thank participants in the convention, as well as Gary Allinson, Peter Katzenstein, Patricia Giles Leeds and Sidney Tarrow for helpful suggestions.

1.   This is a point that is suggested as well by the seemingly high correlation between size and consociationalism; size and democracy and, in some cases, size and defensive foreign economic policy.

2.   Japans's labor force is characterized by the fact that most women in the labor force lack permanent employee status and union protection. The large shift from agriculture to industry, and the return to Japan of military and civilian personnel previously abroad also made for a rather generous and flexible labor supply, particularly during the early postwar years.

3.   For an examination of some exceptions see E. Harari (1974).

4.   "Second unions" are those created within the firm to counter the first, or existing, unions if and when the latter become unduly hostile to managerial policy.

10

Political Design and the Representation of Interests

Charles W. Anderson
University of Wisconsin, USA

The power of large organizations and interest groups and their role in the policy-making process are once more prominent political issues in all Western nations. The governability of societies in which competing groups vie for increasing shares of stable or declining economic resources has become a prominent concern of political leaders, commentators, and the public (Brittan, 1976). Populist suspicion of large aggregations of private power has become a touchstone for political appeals of a variety of kinds. To be sure, these are perennial issues of Western politics, but their salience ebbs and flows with the changing times. Today, they are once again a major topic of public controversy. The power of corporations, unions, and trade associations is very much on the public mind.

It is not only *that* large organizations are powerful, but *how* their power should be constituted and structured that is currently being debated. The place of interest associations in national economic planning or in the development of incomes policies is increasingly a concern of planners and the public. The issues of worker's control and industrial democracy have returned to the agenda of public action in a number of countries. The question of the legitimate institutional forms of corporate enterprise, of conglomerates and cartels, vertically integrated and multi-national industries, is being taken up seriously by policy makers throughout the West. The issues are not only those of the relationship of complex organizations to the state, but of the internal governance of these organizations as well.

Taken in their largest sense, these are questions of the total constitutional order of advanced industrial society. The issue of the appropriate relationship of the corporation, the trade union, and the interest association to the state, their role in the formulation and execution of public policy, like the issues of the responsibility and accountability of such organizations, are in essence questions of the architecture of legitimate political order. Unfortunately, these are seldom recognized as constitutional questions by political scientists, who tend to construe the problem of constitutionalism narrowly, as having to do only with the internal political order of the state. Nonetheless, the classic issue of constitutionalism was of course that of defining the appropriate relationship between the state and other organizations and associations.

It is not immediately apparent that interest group theory, as it is conventionally understood in political science, has much to do with such questions. The program of the Bentley-Truman approach, which has defined the dominant orthodoxy since the 1950s, was explicitly empirical and concerned with process far more than structure. The object was to explain public policy as the product of a configuration of pressures by contending interests. Bentley's motto, "Once the groups are stated everything is stated," captures the commitment of a generation of researchers in this field (Bentley, 1908:21). Nonetheless, like any useful paradigm, the Bentley-Truman model of interest group pluralism established a model case of expected behavior that posed puzzles and quandries, defined a project for theoretical inquiry and criticism, which had implications far beyond its own limited formulation of political dynamics.

The orthodox group process model gave rise to important intellectual controversies, the implications of which have not yet been fully digested by the discipline. The debate between pluralist and elite theorists evenutally bogged down in questions that had a distinctly medieval ring about them — such as the "essence" and "substance" of power — but it did pose the question of whether the group process model satisfactorily accounted for what it presumed to explain. The larger significance of this dispute, however, lies in its implicit relationship to a second realm of controversy provoked by the Bentley-Truman paradigm. This concerned the compatibility of group process with the norms of democratic legitimacy. The riddle of the relationship of "faction" to democratic majoritarianism posed by Madison and Mill was taken up again. The conservative "bias" in interest group pluralism was disclosed. The tone of interest group research shifted from empiricism to criticism. It is true that the relationship between the normative and the empirical questions raised in the analyses of Dahl (1956), Polsby (1963), McConnell (1966), Bachrach and Baratz (1962), and others was never made fully explicit, but that the controversy arose is significant, for to evoke standards of political order is to raise the constitutional question of legitimate institutional structure and procedure. By the time that Lowi's *The End of Liberalism* (1969) arrives on the scene, the transformation that has occurred is fully evident. The question is no longer whether interest group pluralism is an adequate empirical representation of the political process, but whether it is an appropriate procedural and institutional mechanism for public policy-making.

From a related line of interest group research a similar implication arises. The first generation of comparative interest group studies sought to universalize the Bentley-Truman model — to fit highly disparate institutional phenomena into the pluralist mold. Subsequent research has focused on distinguishing the process characteristic of interest group pluralism from other forms of interest group representation and activity. Particularly significant is the rediscovery by Schmitter (1974) and others of the logic of European corporatism. The ostensible purpose of this research was empirical, to define the limits of applicability of the paradigm case and to propose alternative models. However, the students of neocorporatism have become aware that their work suggests a fundamental revision in interest group theory. In the pluralist model, group pressures are generated autonomously within society. The role of the policy maker is hypothesized as that of "broker" between contending interests. In fully state corporatist systems, the policy makers define and channel the relationships of groups to the policy-making process. They delimit group formation and competition, "license" legitimate representative bodies, and may even create interest organizations. Elements of corporatist practice could be found even in ostensibly pluralist systems. (The orthodox group theorists were not oblivious to this fact. Truman, for example, gave considerable attention to the stimulus given such groups as the National Farm Bureau and the National Chamber of Commerce by public authorities in the United States.)

What these developments in interest group theory have in common is the idea of political design. The intervention of organized interests is not simply a "given" in the policy-making process. It is to some extent intentionally created, structured and institutionalized through state action. The political system is not merely a derivative from the configuration of group interests. It is also, at least in part, a conscious contrivance of public policy. This is a radical change in emphasis. As Stephan (forthcoming) observes, the state is no longer the passive recipient of group pressures, but an autonomous force in the political equation. This renewed sense for the autonomy of state action is of course shared by such neo-Marxists as Miliband (1969) and O'Connor (1973). All of this suggests a new program for interest group research. It is necessary to give a more satisfactory account of the role of the state as architect of political order. It is also essential to examine the implications of alternative designs for the representation of interests. These are problems we have hardly begun to consider.

INTEREST REPRESENTATION
AS POLITICAL ARCHITECTURE

The question of how interests are to be presented in policy-making is obviously not only a topic for empirical research, it is also a question for normative analysis, a problem in applied or positive political theory. At issue is the international and self-conscious definition of the appropriate relationship between interest organizations and the state. This is an aspect of the problem of planning in modern government. Normally we think of planning as having to do only with the design of measures, as the technical consideration of the *substance* of policy. However, planning is also a problem in the design of institutions, of the *procedures* through which decisions will be taken.

While the substance of policy is increasingly regarded as a technical activity, one that requires expert knowledge, to date there has been little systematic analysis of the structural aspects of planning. The few leading articles and books on participatory or adversary planning are on the whole hortatory, abstract, and vague (Davidoff, 1965). Decisions on the organization of participation in planning are generally taken on an ad hoc basis, guided by little in the way of theory or analysis. To admonish planners and public officials to have regard for political processes and the pluralist competition of interests does not tell them very much. These are not merely "political" questions, having to do with building consent for a specific policy design. They are technical and normative questions which require reasoned analysis. What principles or standards are to be applied to the composition of economic councils, to the structure of participation in national economic planning, to the design of regulatory agencies and wage-price boards? What criteria might be used to justify the inclusion of a specific group on such tribunals? How can one legitimate a specific pattern of interest representation?

To sharpen the focus somewhat, we can think specifically of the concrete problem of the design of public bodies — councils, commissions, boards, and the like — in liberal democratic societies where the principle of representation is to be in some sense functional, where representation is not based on partisan or popular democracy, or hierarchic position, or bureaucratic role.

As Ranney (1976) has recently reminded us, political science once was understood as an engineering discipline. For the founders of the American republic — as well, it might be added, for the reformers and progressives of the early twentieth century who had a substantial impact on the establishment of American political science as an independent discipline (Crick, 1959) — the preeminent problem of political science was the development of principles of political design and their application to concrete cases.

Is it still plausible to talk about criteria of good design in the creation of political forms? It is, of course, logically impossible to assimilate such as an exploration to the method of positivist political science. Empirically verifiable propositions are not to be expected. As Weldon (1955: 160-180) observed, political evaluation has more in common with art or literary criticism than with scientific inquiry. Hence, to extend the basic metaphor, what we are looking for are principles of political structure that have essentially the same standing as principles of design in architecture, canons of good practice that are not beyond criticism, that necessarily will reflect diverse schools of thought, but that nonetheless stand as a basis for appraising the workmanship of any political construction. From the standpoint of political theory, the object is to open up, and to make explicit, an arena of reasoned argument. Naturally, any such appraisal must be derivative from some normative system of political evaluation. We will here be looking for principles of interest representation that are compatible with the basic norms of liberal democracy. The basic question is whether *any* forms of functional representation can be reconciled with basic democratic criteria of political design.

INTEREST REPRESENTATION
AND DEMOCRATIC THEORY

Corporations, trade unions, and interest organization of all kinds are a prominent feature of the political landscape in all modern societies. They are part of the political order. They share in the distinctive functions of governance. As private governments they make rules and regulations that are enforced with sanctions. They create rights and duties (through such processes as collective bargaining) which may be enforced by the courts. They are a source of law, one that often regulates human conduct more intimately than does the legal authority of the state. In their relationship with public policy makers they take part in the "authoritative allocation of values" for society as a whole. They share in the task of giving definition and substance to some notion of the public interest. They play a role in planning and coordinating the product of society and its distribution.

That such private bodies are part of the political order is beyond dispute. Nonetheless, their position in that order is unclear and ambiguous. The legitimacy of their political role is tenuous at best. We talk of the power of organized interests. We do not speak of their authority. Classic democratic theory insisted on a clear-cut distinction between the private and the public realms. It eschewed any organic conception of state and society. The sovereign prerogative rests entirely with the people. Unlike medieval constitutionalism, there is no place for corporate entities in the modern theory of representative government. The canons of liberal democracy, then, provide a ground for criticism of any structured relationship between interest organizations and the state in the process of policymaking. The case against private power is readily available. To point out that interest groups operate in ways that are frequently incompatible with popular democracy is little more than a banality. What is more difficult is to propose criteria for the incorporation of complex organizations and interest associations into the framework of political order to provide standards that would enable us to judge how organized interests should be represented in the formal structures of policy-making. To discover that corporatist practices exist in all modern societies is one thing. To justify them is quite another.

The ambiguous legitimacy of interest organizations, the fact that we do not quite know where they fit in the political order of modern society and that consequently we have few credible principles for designing political institutions that incorporate them into the policy-making process, is a matter that most commentators on the subject recognize. Of the American experience, McConnell (1966: 51-52) writes:

> A curious feature of American politics in the twentieth century is the absence of any articulate body of doctrine that may be taken as orthodoxy on the central problem of private power. This lack is all the more striking in light of the vigor with which the wielders of power have been attacked by critics and reformers from the time of the Progressives onward...Nevertheless, the persistence and growth of private power have posed an embarrassing problem for all who are involved in exercising it. The problem is authority. What justifies the existence of power; by what principle is it rightful? For if it is not justifiable, power is properly open to attack and, if possible destruction.

Zeigler and Peak (1972: 35-36), in their work on American interest groups, are also conscious of the enigma: "From the beginnings of the American republic, the assumption has been made that pressure groups, irrespective of their goals, are evil because they conflict with the fundamental attributes of democracy." They go on to add: "This type of criticism is not based merely on the disapproval of the more harsh tactics sometimes employed by organizations, but specifies a rejection of the legitimacy of the very existence of such groups in our society."

This is not exclusively an American dilemma. Dion (1971: 292) notes: "Dans la plupart des sociétés libérales, la légitimité des groupes de intérêt est précaire." Lavau (1958: 60), in his treatment of French interest groups, writes:

> Although the concrete historical effort of multiple categories of Frenchmen has consisted for centuries in demanding from the State the liberty to form groups and to constitute in actual fact "partial societies", this has remained for French democratic tradition within the category of the *Sein*; it has not reached the level of political theory, the *Sollen*...Hence, there is widespread consensus to condemn interest groups morally, or more exactly, to condemn their unwarranted interference in politics.

And for Finland, Krusius-Ahrenberg (1958:34) comments explicitly on the problem of political design:

> The important economic interests which these organizations represent could easily be harmed if decisions concerning them were left to the mere decisions of the political and administrative organs. On the other hand, the question as to what form the political collaboration of the interest organization ought to take and to what point it should be allowed to develop, seems to give rise to difficulties everywhere. The answer obviously involves a theoretical and value commitment. The fact remains that so far, at least in Finland, no truly satisfactory forms for this collaboration between the interest groups and the corresponding political authorities have evolved.

There are two distinct questions about the compatibility of interest group politics with democratic government. The first concerns the legitimacy of interest group activity itself. The second is that of the propriety of any public action that structures representation for organized interests in the policy-making process. Most interest group theorists only address the former. Yet it is the second of these questions that is crucial for a theory of political design.

Nonetheless, it is helpful to see how the problem of democratic theory and group politics has been posed, for to do so makes explicit some fundamental criteria of institutional design in a democracy. If we examine the argument both of those who have tried to reconcile group politics with democracy and their critics, we begin to see wherein the dilemma lies. The problem may be stated thus: to be compatible with democratic theory, interest group process must be shown to be (1) capable of generating policies that are in the public interest rather than the interest of some "faction" of the community, (2) impartial as among the intersts present or potential in the community, (3) supplemental to the process of direct popular representation and not a substitute for it.

The first principle is Aristotelian, and from it the most familiar puzzle about group politics and democratic process derives. Any political system, whether of the one, the few, or the many, is appropriate if the rulers serve the public interest. Each is debased if the rulers govern in their own self-interest. How, then, in a system premised on the interested consent of individuals, to prevent government from becoming the instrument of some faction of the community, whether majority or minority? Mill (1929: 229-271) was less interested in the dilemma than the principle of political evaluation. Like Rousseau, his solution to the riddle was not intellectually elegant. Everything depended on "public enlighten-ment," on the willingness of citizens to make other-regarding as well as self-regarding choices. As is not uncommon in the writing of political theory, a higher state of civic consciousness is premised and the quandry dissolves. For Madison, more the realist, faction was a necessary dilemma of democratic theory, though its evils could be somewhat mitigated in a large and diverse polity and its impact cushioned through appropriate political engineering. Most modern American political theorists have tended to follow the Madisonian line. "Interest group pluralism" is regarded as com-patible with democratic theory where there is a broad array of overlapping and cross-cutting cleavages and interests. Of the modern theorists, only Polanyi (1951) and Lindblom (1965) have really ventured beyond either Mill or Madison's formulation of the problem. For them, the criterion of the public interest is really only satisfied through a politics of faction. A system of "partisan mutual adjustment" is more conducive to a workable realization of the general welfare than any process which has as its goal the com-prehensive, synthetic definition of the public good.

Impartiality is a second canon of democratic political design. Liberal democracy is rooted in a Humean skepticism, in a doctrine of human fallibility. Since no segment of the community can claim a license to rule on the basis of authentic knowledge of the destiny and purposes of humankind, all are equally entitled to render a judgment on the ends of public action, on the specific content of the public good. The normative imperatives of democratic struc-ture are purely procedural, and a prime characteristic of democratic institutions is that they be neutral with respect to alter-native ends. Hence, to reconcile group process with democratic theory it must be demonstrated that the system of group interven-tion in politics is impartial among the interests present or potential in the community.

This has been the normative point of reference for much of the debate on the legitimacy of interest group pluralism in the past generation. To validate group process, it must be demonstrated that interest group politics does not entail the dominance of any segment of the community. Pluralist theorists have invoked the ideas of multiple points of access and multiple and shifting group coalitions in support of their argument that group process is democratically tenable. Their critics have introduced the concept of the "unrecognized problem" in denying the neutrality of group process (Bachrach and Baratz, 1962).

As a criterion of political design, interest group pluralists seem to have appropriated the liberal model of competition in perfect markets and applied it to the realm of group process. Interest group politics are compatible with democratic politics so long as governmental institutions are impartial among interests, that none had privileged status in the structure of political institutions, and so long as equal rights of association, petition, and action are guaranteed to all potential groups. This was, implicitly or explicitly, the line of argument taken by the early Galbraith (1952), by Truman (1951), and by Dahl (1956), though all were less sanguine about the impartiality of interest group pluralism than they are sometimes made to appear. Again, critics have challenged the market metaphor as an appropriate defense of interest group pluralism. Inherent differences of organizability, power, and economic resources between groups make the system less than one of perfect competition. Neutrality of government toward groups is not sufficient to guarantee the impartiality of the group process itself. The argument has become deep and sophisticated. The canon of impartiality is even harder for the interest group pluralists to satisfy than that of the public interest.

The third principle is that group process must supplement direct popular representation. It must complement and enhance popular soveignty, but not displace it. Group process is not compatible with democracy if the basis of representation becomes in effect functional, if it substitutes for representative institutions based on individual equality, territorial constituency, and party competition. Formally then, group process must be shown to be an adjunct to representative process and not the essence of the process itself. Thus, defenders of the role of group in the political process may argue that group association is a social requisite of democratic stability and effectiveness. Intermediary associations act as buffers between the individual and the state and, thus, *enhance* popular representation; they give the individual supplemental and more differentiated access to decision makers and they protect against the development of mass movements destructive of democratic stability (Kornhauser, 1959). Conversely, critics allege that in the modern industrial state parliamentary institutions have been reduced to mere formalities and that group process describes the real dynamics of policy-making. (It is significant that the predominance of group process is never described as "progress" toward a higher form of legitimacy. The mode of analysis is either "realistic-empirical" or frankly critical — and the criteria on which criticism is based are the norms of democratic process.)

Interest group theory does make explicit certain fundamental principles of democratic political design. However, taken by itself, the issue of whether group process is compatible with democracy somewhat begs the question. Large organizations and associations are part of the political structure of all modern nations. Group theorists acknowledge that government creates institutional forms for the representation of interests in policy-making, that clientelistic relations are intentionally created between public agencies and affected interests, that government sometimes actually creates interest organizations. Corporatist practices exist in all modern polities, but we have no coherent theory of corporatist construction.

Classic democratic theory primarily serves as a ground for criticism of the interventions of organized interests in politics. The parsimonious model of popular sovereignty, the rigid separation of the private and public realms in liberal thought, provides no coherent doctrine of the place and role of intermediary associations in the political order. Liberalism arose out of rebellion against more organic conceptions of society. "Faction" is a *problem* for democratic theory, it is not a positive part of the theory of representative government. The result is that the legitimacy of the political order we have in fact created in the twentieth century is inevitably suspect in our own eyes.

The dubious legitimacy of interest group politics, the fact that all interventions of organized interests in the public realm seem vaguely suspect and illicit, is not very helpful. The giant organizations and associations that have been created, primarily in the past half-century, have a vital role to play in the governance of modern society. The problem is to specify how such organizations are appropriately represented in the political order, to define criteria for their incorporation into the planning and policy-making processes that are compatible with democratic practice. To this problem we now turn.

INTEREST GROUP PLURALISM

Interest group pluralism is generally taken to be the most

significant attempt to reconcile group politics with democratic theory. What I shall try to show is that it is not tenable as a basis for a theory of interest representation in public planning and policy-making. Interest group pluralism cannot legitimate the role of organized interests in the policy-making process. To be sure, it can be shown that group organization and advocacy are compatible with the democratic order. What cannot be demonstrated, however, is that any policy can be justified as the product of group interventions in politics. Interest group pluralism does not provide a sufficient basis for a *policy* of interest representation. It is not plausible as a model of institutional design in a democratic society.

The pluralist conception of political order follows from the rights of voluntary association and petition which are in fact the formal grounds of the legitimacy of interest organization in democratic theory (Finer, 1958: 108). The state endorses no overall design for political order. There is no conception of "right" order or of "natural associations" which the state is obligated to nurture, protect, and integrate into an organic whole as in medieval conceptions of the relationship of state and society. The organizational life of society as a whole is not a public problem. Rather, the larger political order derives from the notion of contract. Society takes its associational form from the voluntary contractual commitments of individuals. The role of government as political architect is restricted to that of assuring contractual probity. It may regulate the conditions of contract (as in labor relations) or establish and define standardized organizational forms (as in the corporate charter). It may establish rights both in and of associations and safeguard third-party interests. So long as such universalistic norms are applied and upheld, society takes its form and structure from the aggregate pattern of solidaristic and cooperative ventures freely entered into by individuals (Anderson, 1976).

The pluralist conception of the polity is compatible with the liberal doctrine of limited government. The more detailed elements of econmomic and social organization are in the hands of private bodies. Yet the authority of such institutions over the individual can never be arbitrary so long as there are multiple and competing groups. The individual is always free to renounce affiliation, to "exit" an undesired relationship, as Hirschman (1970) would put it.

Such organizations and association also perform a vital role in the political process. In expressing the differentiated claims and demands of groups they relate the structured order of society to the policy of the state. They not only provide a cushion between the individual and the state, but they provide a basis of representation that is more precise, more consistent with actual individual preferences than the raw conception of popular sovereignty. Intermediary associations provide a basis of representation that appropriately supplements majoritarian and constituency interests.

So far, so good. Interest group pluralism can make a strong case that associational freedom is both a necessary and a useful accompaniment to democratic process. However, the next step is more difficult. For what pluralism cannot do is to legitimate a policy as the outcome of a configuration of group demands.

Interest group pluralism as defined by the Bentley-Truman model was, of course, originally an empirical and not a normative construct. It was designed to decribe how the system worked in practice, not to justify it. The early group theorists, Bentley (1908), Odegard (1928), Schattschneider (1935), and the rest, sought to "reveal" the deeper forces at work in the system and to contrast a more realistic view of power relationships with democratic formalisms. Their purpose was precisely that of showing that the "system" was not consistent with democratic theory. How pluralism came to be regarded as both an empirical and normative theory is not entirely clear. The classic pluralists, Laski (1967) and Cole (1921) in particular, argued that a group basis of representation could be a legitimate foundation of popular sovereignty. But that approach to interest group pluralism is now virtually forgotten. The inference that must be drawn from modern group pluralism as a normative theory is that the policy product of the state is appropriate if it arises from a competitive configuration of group demands.

Interest group pluralism as a representation of the political process is one thing, but pluralism as a theory of representation is something else again. What in effect group pluralism proposes is a model of the political order in which functional representation is paramount over popular representation and this violates a cardinal principle of democratic political design.

The legislature referees the group struggle, ratifies the victories of successful coalitions and records the terms of surrenders, compromises and conquests in the form of statutes. . The legislative vote on any issue thus tends to represent the composition of strength, i.e., the balance or power, among the contending groups at the moment of voting. What may be called public policy is actually the equilibrium reached in the group struggle at any given moment, and it represents a balance which the contending factions of groups constantly strive to weigh in their favor.

Whatever else may be said for or against the empirical adequacy of this formulation of the dynamics of the political system, it does not state a procedural rule that is legitimate within democratic theory or in any other normative conception of political authority for that matter. "Majority vote" is a decision rule that is taken as definitive in any democratic polity. "The equilibrium of group pressures" is not a justification for policy by any standard of political legitimacy other than that of group pluralism itself. At this level, group process is not reconciled to democratic practice. It is completely at loggerheads with it.

The usual ground for criticism of interest group pluralism is that some interests are systematically neglected or disadvantaged in the competitive struggle. Schattschneider (1960: 47-61), for example, speaks of the "scope and bias" of the pressure group system, that it tends to favor relatively small but dominant elements in society. However, the problem is not only sociological, but also logical. Interest group pluralism is simply not a theory of representation. To be consistent with democratic theory, interest group pluralism would have to show that the configuration of interest that is "ratified" as public policy was in some sense appropriate to the definition of authoritative public purposes, and this it cannot do. The notions of "equilibrium" and "countervailing power" do of course attempt to cope with this. The system comes into balance over time. Past imperfections in representativeness are rectified by the "invisible hand" of group competition. Apart from all the doubts about the empirical worth of this principle, there is the larger question of its formal validity. How does the configuration of interest at a particular time authorize a public action? How does it obligate any citizen to comply with and submit to it?

By definition, interest group pluralism is not a theory of political design. It contains no principles for defining what interests are to be taken into account in the decision-making process. It provides no criteria for the inclusion or exclusion of any association, or for the weighting of influence as among interests. Any group that forms autonomously has a claim to be represented equivalent to any other group. For that reason, any policy attributed to group pluralist process can be irrefutably challenged by pointing to some interest that was not accounted for in the definition of policy. Democratic majoritarianism, for all its faults, at least has the virtue of being definitive as a procedural rule. Interest group pluralism does not have that attribute.

The theory of interest group pluralism, oddly, would be of no practical assistance if we were trying to develop a policy of pluralist representation of interests in planning and policy-making. To create councils or committees that are representative of "the important interests in the community" is a common enough aspiration of politics, but by this the decison makers usually mean the dominant interests, or the organized ones, or those it would be prudent to include in the particular public enterprise. Pluralism has no doctrine of "affected interests" that ought to be accounted for in any public action. It is, in essence, a theory of group power, and not of group authority. There is no representative theory, no way of saying that this particular configuration of interests was *entitled* to particpate in the formulation of this particular policy.

In fact, in interest group pluralism, almost any structured relationship between associations and government is suspect. To provide privileged access to any specific groups in the policy-making process violates the cardinal rule of the autonomy of group process. Clientelistic relationships between groups and government of course abound in all modern societies, but their status in political theory is, to say the least, anomalous. The basic function of journalistic and academic interest group analysis, at least in the United States, would seem to be that of "revealing" the privileged status of specific interests in their relationships with regulatory agencies, the legislature, administrative bodies, and so on.

This is not to say that pluralist theory cannot yield some, albeit rudimentary, canons of political architecture. For example, some would argue that it is necessary for government to offset the natural configuration of group pressures by creating specific mechanisms of access for disadvantaged or unorganized interests (as in the case of representation for the poor in American Community Action Programs) or to encourage the formation of associations to redress the balance of interest advocacy (as in the stimulus given to the U.S. Chamber of Commerce by President Taft). The logic here is similar to that of antitrust — that is in an appropriate function of government to sustain the competitiveness of the market, to break up monopolistic constraints on pluralist advocacy. However, such a policy has never been applied consistently or intentionally in any pluralist polity. Furthermore, representational "trust-busting" is paradoxical in pluralist theory, for to create "adversary" groups or to engage in a kind of representational "affirmative action" requires that goverment stipulate what interests are to be represented, how the configuration of interests is appropriately defined, and this is something, in pluralist theory, that is not a legitimate function of public policy.

CORPORATISM

By this point, it may seem that what I have in mind is some corporate theory of group representation and that my effort is to make this compatible with democratic theory and practice. Corporatism is the term that is properly applied to the structured representation of functional interests in the process of policy-making. Corporatism has come to be regarded as the dominant alternative to pluralism as a model of interest group intervention in politics. However, as we shall shortly see, it is difficult to provide principles of corporatist theory that could validate any given scheme of structured relationships between interest organizations and the state.

Schmitter (1974: 93-94) has aptly characterized the essential distinction between corporatist and pluralist schemes of interest representation. For Schmitter, corporatism is defined as "a system of interest representation in which the constituent units are organized into a limited number of singular, compulsory, noncompetitive, hierarchically ordered and functionally differentiated categories, recognized or licensed (if not created) by the state and granted a deliberate representational monopoly within their respective categories in exchange for observing certain controls on their selection of leaders and articulation of demands and supports."

In pluralist systems, conversely, interest organizations are multiple, voluntary, competitive, and not specifically licensed or regulated by public authority. They possess no representational monopoly, and their internal political processes are not explicitly regulated. It should be noted that Schmitter's definition is not merely an empirical model, nor does it pertain only to the structure of interest group process in a political system as a whole. Most of the characteristics Schmitter imputes to corporatist representation are logically entailed by any structure of functional representation. They are basic characteristics of corporatist political design, and particularly so, for reasons we shall note, in any corporatist representational scheme whose validity is to be judged according to democratic norms.

Corporate and quasi-corporate institutions abound in all modern industrial societies. One thinks immediately of the French and British systems of national economic planning, of the extensive and highly structured relations of interest organizations and administrative bodies in Scandinavia, of the more comprehensive corporatist designs for public order in modern Spain and Portugal, of regulatory and licensing bodies at all levels of American government, of the composition of commissions, boards, and committees in all nations. Despite the ubiquity of corporate practice in modern society, we have little in the way of doctrine about how it should be done, about the problems and desiderata inherent in any system of structured interest representation.

There is seldom much in the way of formal theoretical justification for most systems of corporate representation. European national economic planners offer little in the way of representative theory to support their often most elaborate institutions of interest consultation and participation. In most cases, it would seem, planners assume that the answer to the question of who should be represented is obvious. In fact, this is far from being the case.

In economic policy-making, the triune relationship of management, labor, and the public seems to constitute a natural and logical basis of representation. At least intuitively, there is a pleasing symmetry about the arrangement. But what in fact is the justificatory logic for this tripartite scheme? If the notion of the "public interest" is taken seriously, how to defend minority standing for what, in the classic conception, is the only justification for public policy? Or perhaps, as is often argued, "public interest" is to be taken as a euphemism for "consumer interest". This looks appealing. Enterprise has an interest in profit, labor in wages, the consumer in prices. Perhaps the representative scheme is designed to substitute for the equilibrium of the Manchesterian marketplace, or perhaps it is a modification of a class conflict or collective bargaining model. But though it seems in order, is it logically exhaustive? Does it account for "affected interests" in any significant sense — or third party rights? If public interest is taken to stand for consumer interest, then is not the state's interest recognizably separate? And what of environmental, natural resource, and amenity interests? Costs can be passed along in a number of ways. Should a logical scheme of corporate representation include a spokesman for generations yet unborn? If not, why not? If so, should the advocate for the future have equal voice and vote with those of labor, management, and the "public"? On what grounds to affirm or deny the proposition?

Any scheme of corporate representation has to have some kind of underlying rationale. Classic Catholic corporatism was grounded in an Aristotelian and Thomist conception of natural associations, those the state was obligated to nurture, defend, and orchestrate into an harmonious social order. However, Aristotelian logic is not particularly convincing in this day and age as a basis for political design, and few modern builders of corporate institutions have appealed to this in legitimation of their efforts with an entirely straight face.

More to the point, perhaps, most practitioners of corporatism have seen it as a way of engineering social peace and cooperation in place of class conflict. This was the putative motive behind the corporate schemes of European conservatives and American progressives in the late nineteenth and early twentieth centuries, and it is from the origin, no doubt, that we derive our sense that it is somehow natural to give pride of place to industrial and labor interests in a corporate scheme of representation. However, it is extremely hard in democratic theory to find grounds for investing the interests of capital and labor with the authority to make what are in effect public decisions. This is the flaw in any corporate theory of representation. How can one legitimate the legislative authority of powerful and contending interests over popular consent?

The effective rationale for most corporate systems however is probably pragmatic, a matter of administrative convenience or necessity. Those interests are represented whose collaboration is essential to give effect to a specific public purpose. This is often the logic of justification behind corporate arrangements in national economic planning and it is often defended explicitly and as a matter of principle. It operates as a working criterion of inclusion and exclusion in political design. The institution builders do not just represent anyone with social power and support. The structured intervention of an organized interest in policy-making must be justified as pertinent to the goals of policy. Of the representation of interests in the German program of industrial concerted action, Kuster (1974: 71) writes: "The privileged position of especially powerful interest groups was explained by the statement that the selection had been made according to whether the association 'caused one to expect optimum performance in the concerted action in consideration of their size and importance'." Such a criterion of representation probably also explains the biases in group influence in the French and Spanish planning institutions. The privileged position of powerful industrial and commercial interests is defended against charges that the planning system is undemocratic again on the grounds that the collaboration of specified groups is particularly important to the achievement of a legitimate public purpose.

While such structural influence for dominant economic groups is often offensive to democratic sensitivities, this does seem to be the one theory of corporate representation which is compatible with democratic design. Interest representation is seen as an administrative instrument, a means for the achievement of public purposes. The problem of political design is to create institutions for the effective coordination of organizations which have a vital role to play in the execution of public policy or it is to design forums in which putatively hostile or competitive interests will be caused to deliberate and arrive at a common policy. The interests that are appropriately represented are those that are essential to the achievement of a public purpose or those who overt conflict would be socially destructive. Such a conception of corporate representation is consistent with the fundamental canons of democratic political design. Interest group representation serves to give effect to some stipulated public interest, it is impartial among interests in that there is a rationally defensible rule for the recognition or nonrecognition of specific participants, and it is supplemental to popular consent insofar as public purposes are defined through parliamentary means. The quarrel of the critic is not so much with the principle of functional representation itself as with the statement of public purpose from which the logic of representation follows. (Thus, if the explicit goal of national planning is economic growth, it is appropriate that representation be biased toward the most efficient and productive enterprises. But if the goal is distributive justice, some other representational design is required.)

The difficulty in making such systems of corporate representation compatible with democratic theory then is not so much logical as sociological. Such structured relationships between important interests and the state take on a life of their own, become dominant over the formal institutions of representative democracy, and are extremely resistant to change. And in fact, this is the way the argument over the propriety of such systems of corporate interest representation is framed in all modern democracies: the defenders appeal to the formal grounds of legitimacy of such institutions and the critics base their objections on sociological reasoning.

Both in theory and practice, there are many problems in making any scheme of corporate representation compatible with democratic principles of political design. We have considered the question of the criterion of representation itself. However, when an interest organization comes to play a structured part in the policy-making process, there are also implications that follow from democratic theory for the internal form of government of the group.

In many corporate structures the conception of representation that is being endorsed is most unclear. Is it the "interest" itself that is being represented or are the interests of individuals aggregated through interest association? Is representation virtual or actual? This problem arises not only in connection with structures of group representation in public policy-making but also in efforts to redefine the constituency and accountability of corporations and other complex organizations. In what sense is a consumer or "public interest" member of a corporate board of directors representative? If the principle of political design is that of the adversary proceeding, with the consumer or public representative acting as trustee or advocate for specific interest, the scheme makes some sense. But if the metaphor is that of industrial democracy, if the representative is in some formal sense to be accountable to an enlarged conception of the constituency of the corporation, the problems of institutional design become overwhelming. One would have to create a consumers association for each industrial enterprise and insure effective and informed participation in each.

When an organization becomes the official representative of a particular interest it becomes, in effect, part of the political system. Furthermore, it becomes, in some significant sense, an involuntary organization. For both of these reasons, to be compatible with democratic theory, the internal government of the interest organization must itself be democratic. In classic liberal theory, democratic process was requisite only for involuntary associations, of which presumptively the only example was the state. The state could be indifferent to the internal political order of private bodies insofar as they rested on contractual voluntarism and the individual was always free to leave an oppressive political situation. Government by consent is a condition that can be satisfied in liberal theory either by individual choice in a competitive market or by democratic practice. However, when an interest organization becomes a licensed representational monopoly it takes the form of an involuntary organization, and a strong case can be made that democratic organization should be made mandatory for such groups as a matter of public policy.

When a corporate organization serves not only as the official representative of a particular interest but also takes on the function of administering public policy, the question of the appropriate constituency of the organization also arises. The authority to license and regulate certain occupations may be granted to professional associations, as is often the case, either formally or in practice, in law, medicine, architecture, and similar fields. The issue then is whether self-regulation by the profession is compatible with democratic practice, or whether the scheme of representation in such bodies should be itself corporate, whether consumers or the "public" should have voice and vote in the policy-making apparatus of the association.

Corporate systems of representation are not inherently incompatible with democratic practice. The position that only a pluralist conception of group process and interest representation is appropriate to democratic order is not tenable. However, to be consistent with democratic practice, corporate schemes of interest representation have to meet certain explicit criteria of institutional design. Some basic principles and problems have been suggested here but this is not a full-fledged theory of interest representation in a democracy. This is something that has yet to be developed.

ADVERSARY PROCEDURES

In pluralism, the basic model of political form is the competitive marketplace. In corporatism, it is the legislative body. The object of corporate political design is the creation of deliberative forums in which representation is based on functional rather than popular principles. These two approaches to the incorporation of interest organizations into the political order should be distinguished from a third possibility, which is that of the structured adversary procedure. Here we consider forms of interest representation in public policy-making that are logically distinct from either pluralism or corporatism though they are often assimilated to one or the other in interest group theory. We will deal specifically with political structures based on the models of collective bargaining and judicial process.

To sanction the collective bargaining relationship and to give it structure is an historical alternative to corporatist organization as a way of engineering mechanisms for the peaceful resolution of interest conflict. Institutionalized collective bargaining shares some characteristics of pluralist process and some of corporatist design. The basic model of interest group competition rather than organic solidarity is retained. However, institutionalized collective bargaining relationships also have some of the implications of corporatist forms. In "union shop" arrangements, a specific organization receives a representational license and a representational monopoly. In American practice, at least, the resulting involuntary nature of the organization is recognized, and democratic practice is imposed on the trade union organization as a matter of public policy.

As an approach to the problem of interest group representation, collective bargaining has particular appeal to labor parties. Collective bargaining is a privileged institutional form for democratic trade unions and it has a particular legitimacy for parties which are ideologically committed to advancing the interests of industrial labor through democratic processes.

Judicial procedure is another potential form for the representation of group interests in policy-making. This, of course, was the basic metaphor for the design of regulatory agencies in the United States. Affected interests appear in the role of litigants before an independent tribunal whose decisions are justified on the basis of explicit criteria of regulatory law. Once again, the combination of procedural and substantive principles in the model of political design is apparent.

The criteria for construction and evaluation of such a judicial procedures of interest group representation are quite distinct from those that apply to pluralist process or corporate structure. The impartiality of the tribunal, perhaps of the legal norms themselves, the actual adversary character of the proceeding, and the clarity and conclusiveness of the rules of judicial determination all become issues of public controversy, appropriate grounds for criticism and standards for reform.

Formally, of course, judicial forms of interest representation are compatible with democratic practice. The overriding conception of public interest is appropriately embedded in the norms of regulatory law. The adversary proceeding satisfies the conditions of impartiality among interests. And the adjudication of interest conflicts is supplementary to the legislative determination of the grounds that are appropriately invoked in reaching such determinations. It is because the criteria of judicial design are so widely acknowledged and understood in democratic polities that criticism of the actual performance of such quasi-judicial regulatory bodies is relatively coherent in political argument and discourse.

FORM FOLLOWS FUNCTION

It gradually becomes apparent that any coherent theory of political design must contain both procedural and substantive principles. This is why a political science of pure process, divorced from legal norms or any considerations of economic and social policy seems to be oddly truncated. In order to construct a prescriptive theory or a critical evaluation of political institutions we have to make some assumptions about what such institutions are expected to accomplish (Robertson, 1976: 1-22). All classic political theorist knew as much, though the point has been neglected of late.

The criteria of design for any system of interest representation compatible with democracy then follow from what those institutions are supposed to *do*. The sovereign decision on public purposes must rest with the people. There is no way of contriving a functional scheme for representation that is logically exhaustive of affected interests, that fully captures the bases of social or economic differentiation in a community. The most fundamental premises of liberal democracy stand against any effort to prefigure the interests that individuals ought to endorse. Thus, in a democratic order, interest representation is legitimate only insofar as it is instrumental to the achievement of stipulated public objectives.

From this it follows that two basic principles can be applied to the legitimation of any system of functional representation in a democratic polity. The first is that the criterion of interest representation itself be embedded in a substantive standard for policy-making. The second is that the decisions taken by bodies structured on functional lines are not rendered legitimate by virtue of the principle of representation on which they are based but by the conformity of their decisions to some substantive criterion of public action.

In designing systems of interest representation then, the first technical problem is to state the objectives of public purpose, the standards against which the propriety of policy decisions are to be measured, in such a way that the procedure for making decisions and the legitimate participants therein is logically entailed in the criterion of public policy itself. The system of representation is to be derived from the standards of justification for public action.

The classic example might be the institution of the jury in Anglo-American law. Whatever the historic conceptions of right that sanctify the principle of trial by jury, the central place of this representative institution in our system of justice is inherent in a specific norm of judicial decision, the concept of "reasonablenes." Reasonableness is a fundamental criterion of judgment in both criminal and civil law. "Reasonable care" is a ground of liability and of mitigation in the law of tort and contract, while "reasonable doubt" structures the presumption of innocence that is fundamental to criminal law. However, the idea of reasonableness is little more than an empty formalism until applied by a body representative of mature, responsible citizens. What "reasonable care" or "reasonable doubt" means cannot be derived from precedent or substantive rules. It is not a matter that judges can determine. What is meant by reasonableness in the law is that a representative individual would regard the actions of some person as reasonable in taking precautions to prevent harm to another. The nature and purposes of the jury as a procedural institution and the principle of representation to be applied therein are entailed in the substantive norm of decision itself.

The same rule can be applied to the design of corporatist bodies in the democratic polity. The question of who should be represented on a prices and incomes board cannot be determined in the abstract. The criterion of decision must be settled first. If the standard against which substantive policy is to be measured is that settlements be noninflationary without redistributing income in favor either of capital or labor, equal representation of capital, labor and public economic authorities is called for. If the criterion is that income be transferred either to investment or consumption, a different weighting of interests is required.

The second principle of design for such systems of representing interest organizations in public decision-making is that policies are not legitimate because they are made by a certain kind of representative body but because they conform to an explicit standard of public decision. That a corporatist wages and prices board representing labor and management decides that wage settlements reflect traditional occupational differentials does not legitimate policies made on that basis, for it begs the question of how such a group receives the entitlement to define the public interest. However, if traditional differentials are accepted as an appropriate basis for wage settlements by legislative prescription, then the decisions of a wages and price board that establishes a pattern of settlements on that formula are appropriate. The argument may be over the content of the substantive norm, but it cannot be with the institutional framework derived from the principle itself.

This is a problem with any scheme of industrial self-regulation, as McConnell repeatedly points out. In discussing the work of the Petroleum Council in relation to the US Department of Commerce, McConnell notes that the council took on the task of supervising voluntary agreements on various subjects of interest to the petroleum industry. The purpose was to make government control unnecessary. Of these agreements, McConnell (1966: 274) writes: "Perhaps in this and the exercise of other powers, the Council decided wisely. Once again, however, the problem of criteria arose: by what standards could *any* decision the Council made be justified?"

This way of looking at the problem of interest representation has implications for any structure of clientelistic relationships between government agencies and specific interest groups. By virtue of the first principle, it was not inappropriate for American policy makers in designing the Community Action programs of the War on Poverty to create representation for the poor as an aspect of institutional design. However, by virtue of the second principle, it was also essential to specify the criteria according to which the decisions that arose from such relationships were to be justified. This was also inherent in the Community Action program formula of institutional design. The local organizations created had explicit responsibility for choosing projects adapted to local needs from a long "shopping list" of potential activities appropriate for federal funding. And it is interesting to note that while the effectiveness of these programs has been severely criticized, the propriety of the scheme of representation itself has not.

In American regulatory policy, it is frequently argued that clientelistic relationships between government bodies and regulated interests corrupt a process that was structured to assure that such businesses operate according to the criterion of public interest (which is often taken to be equivalent to the consumer's interest). However, the Transportation Act of 1920, for example, explicitly provides that a crucial standard of decision-making is "the orderly development of the industry" (Noll, 1971: 37-38). The ICC is not *entitled*, formally, to give special privilege to consumer concern in making determinations on rates, routes and conditions of service. The quarrel, at one level at least, is with the formal substantive principle, and not with the close relationships that have grown up between the regulators and the regulated.

I think these principles can be applied to the evaluation — or the justification — of forms of corporate interest representation in any Western democratic system. For example, in Sweden, comprehensive nationwide agreements between peak labor and management associations have become a primary instrument of economic planning. However, when one examines the historical development and logic of this arrangement, it becomes apparent that its legitimacy does not rest particularly on a vesting of public powers in corporatist institutions. To be sure, collective bargaining is an institution which has particular significance for a labor party like the long dominant Swedish Social Democrats. However, the distinctiveness of the Swedish approach to economic planning rests in the combination of bargaining between peak interest associations with a specific conception of public macroeconomic management. The national wage bargain is justified not only on the ground that it arises from a process of deliberation among functional associations but on the basis that it meets certain explicit criteria of public purpose, including full employment, an active manpower policy, equal pay for equal work, and a capitalist system of industrial decision-making in which productive efficiency is measured in terms of international competitiveness (Martin, 1975). The Swedish theory of political design is highly sophisticated and its legitimacy rests on both procedural and substantive criteria of political engineering.

The idea we have explored herein is in some ways similar to

Lowi's conception of juridical democracy (Lowi, 1969). Interest representation in a democracy cannot be evaluated by reference to principles of pluralist politics of representative theory alone. The policies that arise as a consequence of group interventions in politics must be justified according to explicit criteria of public welfare and common good. The motto of the modernist movement in architecture applies to the long neglected art of political engineering. Form follows function in the design of political institutions in much the same way as it does in the design of buildings.

Concluding Remarks: Problems for Future Research on Corporatist Intermediation and Policy-Making

Gerhard Lehmbruch
University of Konstanz, Germany

It has repeatedly been pointed out that in the recent literature the concept of corporatism has not been employed in a uniform and consistent manner, but with quite different nuances and accentuations of meaning. To a certain degree, this has happened because normative elements from different ideological traditions have been brought into the discussion. But a more important reason seems to be that the observable reality to which those who employ the term are referring is a rather complex one, and that apparently divergent global conceptualizations are actually stressing different aspects of it. Moreover, this multiplicity of conceptualizations is largely due to different theoretical backgrounds. It is all the more remarkable that across these nuances, important convergences are emerging. In fact, the discussion on modern corporatism has become a meeting ground for different approaches and social science traditions. This could eventually result in mutual stimulation but, in the short run, it creates some obvious problems of communication.

AN ANALYTICAL FRAMEWORK FOR COMPARATIVE RESEARCH

Schmitter's well-known definition of "corporatism" as contrasted to "pluralism" and "syndicalism" (Schmitter, supra) has repeated-

ly been criticized for taking over the dimensions of the previously
"dominant" model of pluralism and "just changing or inverting
the empirical values of these dimensions or variables" (Nedelmann
and Meier, supra, p.   , as one example). It is true that the definition emphasizes formal organizational and inter-organizational
structures, in particular, the network of interest associations
(limited number, singular, noncompetitive, functionally differentiated), their internal organizational structure (compulsory, hierarchically ordered) and their structural relation to the state apparatus
(recognition by the state, representational monopoly). These certainly do not exhaust crucial dimensions of the phenomenon. The
definition leaves out the functional relationship of interest associations to the state, as well as to the economic system. In particular, it
does not tell us a priori whether corporatism is linked to capitalism
or, more precisely, to a certain stage of capitalist development. It
also leaves open the question whether corporatism is a universal
formula applicable to all sorts of interests (including, perhaps, the
Royal Society for the Preservation of Animals or the Free Masons)
or characteristic only of particular modes of class relations.

Yet these apparent ommissions are not necessarily shortcomings
of the model. On the contrary, the "formal" character of the
model, the stress laid upon organizational structures, which permits changing the values of some dimensions common to all three
models, are essential to the important and undeniable, advantage
of this approach. Until now, it is the only conceptualization that is
truly comparative in character, and it should allow operational
measurement in cross-national as well as longitudinal perspective.
One cannot measure "corporatism" without employing dimensions that are common to "corporatism" and "non-corporatism".
Thanks to this usefulness for comparative research, the definition
could well serve as the basis for a developmental model of interest
intermediation. The above mentioned problems, apparently omit-
ted in the model, in reality constitute empirical problems that probably might be fruitfully investigated with the aid of a descriptive
mapping based on Schmitter's dimensions and typology. Starting
with his analytical framework, we could ask whether "corporatist"
patterns of policy-formation are more regularly found at certain
stages of economic and political development than at others, and
whether these observable frequency distributions across space and
time are consistent with particular hypotheses about the functional
relationships between state, economy and interest intermediation.

CORPORATISM AND ADVANCED CAPITALISM

I have argued elsewhere (supra, p. 151ff.) that the emergence of corporatism as an important mode of policy formation is linked to problems of Keynesian economic policy. To this one might object that corporatist patterns of interest intermediation — as defined by Schmitter — have already been important in certain sectors of economic policy (in particular in agriculture) long before Keynes, or that traditions of compulsory interest intermediation by chambers (of commerce, handicrafts, etc.) are quite old in countries such as Germany and Austria. But that does not necessarily contradict the hypothesis which stresses the linkage of corporatism to certain crucial problems of policy formation in advanced capitalist economies. Rather, corporatist structures and practices — although they certainly have existed before — only acquire central importance in the relation between state and economy in a particular stage of capitalist development and under particular constraints of economic policy-making.

Thus, not all interest associations that conform to Schmitter's definition of "corporatism" have necessarily been integrated in the mechanism of making and implementing political decisions. For example, the German social historian, Heinrich August Winkler, has argued that the emergence of singular, compulsory, and non-competitive interest associations in Imperial Germany, such as the Chambers of Handicraft (*Handwerkskammern*) and of Agriculture (*Landwirtschaftskammern*), constituted "cases of organizational protectionalism. Two professional groups that were judged to be of particular importance for the state (staatspolitisch wertvoll) received preferential treatment in the protection of their interests against those of other groups. They received assistance from the state for an articulation of their demands which they were unable to accomplish by their own efforts" (H. A. Winkler, 1972, 18).

Compared to this "historical" use of corporatism for the protection of interests on the verge of marginalization, recent corporatist wage policies have a much more central role in economic policy, and corporatism now amounts to giving dominant interest associations a decisive share in policy formation. Longitudinally speaking, although we may have been living in the "century of corporatism" since 1900, the real "boom" in liberal corporatism apparently has taken place only in the second half of this century.

THE CORPORATIST STRATEGY AND THE
CONFLICT OF CAPITAL AND LABOUR

Generally speaking, corporatism as defined by Schmitter seems to be used mainly as a socio-political technique for the regulation of conflicts between important social groups by incorporating their interest intermediaries into the formal decision-making structures of the state (though not necessarily by formal institutionalization). Most important are those conflicts over the distribution of national income that may have repercussions for the process of capitalist accumulation and growth. In the earlier conflict between agrarian and industrial interests, the former were often "corporatized" in a "protectionist" manner, in order to make the preservation of agrarian social structures compatible with ongoing growth. Later, corporatism gained particular importance for regulating the distributive conflict of capital and labour in a manner compatible with the exigencies of continuous growth. Moreover, corporatist patterns may even be employed to regulate conflicts over secondary distribution, for example, in the public health system.[1]

THE ASYMMETRY OF INCOMES POLICIES

Given the strong impact of the capital-labour cleavage on the political structures of Western European countries and the growing importance of their distributive conflict for macro-economic policy, corporatist regulation of the relationship between capital and organized labour has become the most conspicuous aspect of the contemporary development of corporatism. This leads to intricate problems. Underlying corporatist regulation of this conflict is the assumption that it is a distributive struggle (and not a structural one over social domination, as in Marxist theory). But in the cultural tradition of the European labour movement, distributive conflicts have significant structural implications. Even reformist social democrats and established labour leaders have to consider that a given distribution of income has consequences for the distribution of wealth and, in particular, for the power to dispose of the means of production. Western European labour has, in general, experienced society as a dichotomous "class society". The demand for equality and, hence, the redistribution impetus have long been an important element in its tradition (however realistic or vague labour's concrete and immediate policy demands may have been). Now, normally, a cooperative incomes policy means that labour has to put aside redistributive objectives (see, in particular, Pfromm 1975; also Ulman and Flanagan 1971, 224ff.). This may result in stabilizing or even accentuating structural inequalities. Incomes policies may entail some "horizontal" redistribution among workers by leveling wage differentials (which, in a Swedish-style "solidary wage policy", may even be a deliberate policy of labour unions). But the "vertical" distribution of factor incomes between capital and labour normally cannot be challenged in favour of the latter (except in the case of restoring a long-term distribution ratio during certain phases of the business cycle). Under these constraints, wage restraint thus may easily be perceived by labour as asymmetrically favourable to capital.

As a consequence, union leaders ready to cooperate with the government in a "voluntary" incomes policy may come under heavy pressure from their rank and file. This has repeatedly been emphasized. Panitch, in particular, has taken issue with "the much-vaunted view of corporatism as representing a new avenue of democratic stability for advanced capitalism", stressing instead — as I have done myself — the instability of corporatism due to its inherent contradictions (supra, p.119ff.). The problem with this instability hypothesis is, in part, operational: Since "stability" and "instability" obviously have to be defined as the opposite poles of a single continuum, we must decide at which point to separate the relatively stable from the relatively unstable cases. Futhermore, we are often tempted to extrapolate from particular cases and, perhaps, from transitory situations. Panitch has convincingly analyzed the causes of the fundamental instability of corporatism in Britain (see, in particular, Panitch 1976). And some evidence for the same cyclical movements can be found in West Germany. However, we may have somewhat overestimated the importance of the outbreaks of militancy that occurred in 1969 and in the early seventies in countries such as West Germany and Sweden. The case of Austria, with the quite astonishing stability of its "social partnership", should warn us against premature generalizations. It will probably be necessary and certainly fruitful to invest some effort in more precise comparative measurement of the variable degrees of stability or instability of contemporary corporatism.

ORGANIZATIONAL AND CULTURAL CONDITIONS
OF CORPORATISM

The next step would then be to account for such variations. The most commonly-held hypothesis seeks to explain the relative stability and effectiveness of corporatism by organizational variables, in particular, by the degree of centralization of the labour movement (e.g. Headey 1972; Wilensky 1976). Indeed, organizational centralization seems to be not only a concomitant of but also an important condition for "corporatization".[2]

Centralization, however, or its equivalents seem to be a necessary but not a sufficient condition for the stability and effectiveness of corporatism. Another eventual explanatory variable may be "political culture", in particular that of the labour movement. To the degree that traditions of "solidarity" and "equality" prevent strong internal competition within the ranks of labour (in particular to defend wage differentials), union leaders may be more able to secure compliance with a voluntary incomes policy.

A NEO-CORPORATIST LOGIC OF EXCHANGE?

But this hypothesis leaves open the question: why union leaders themselves should be ready to cooperate at all. The leftist slogan, "traitors to the working class", has little empirical plausibility, even if it is supported by arguments concerning the oligarchic structure of union leadership and the apathy of members. We have to assume rational behaviour on the part of union leaders, and since, in the case of Western Eurpean unions, the corruption of individual leaders is, generally, not an issue, we have to search for the organizational quid pro quo that may explain the rationality of their cooperation.

To begin with, one quid pro quo may result from the very logic of post-Keynesian macro-economics which, as pointed out elsewhere (supra, p. 170ff.), has strongly affected the outlook of labour leaders and staff in a number of Western European countries. The notion of the interdependence of macro-economic aggregates leads to a number of interrelated reflections. On the one hand, different actors dispose of levers to restore the original ratio of income distribution (for example through an inflationary passing on of wage costs to prices). On the other hand, the level of employment depends on the propensity to invest and the latter in turn depends on the expectation of reasonable profits. Hence, if wage restraint should simultaneously guarantee monetary stability, full employment, and a long-term stable and fair income share for labour, "distributional neutrality" is supposed to be one of the conditions of success for this policy. The attempt to translate this logic into political action has been characteristic of the West German version of cooperative incomes policy (see supra, p.160ff.).

Although the *Konzertierte Aktion* had long since been quite controversial, it was not until 1977 that the German Trade Union Confederation (DGB), and the industrial unions affiliated with it, ceased to participate. Their motive was the employer organizations' action for unconstitutionality against the law on co-determination in large business firms, which the parliament had passed after laborious compromises. The employers' minimal intention was to obtain an opinion by which the Constitutional Court would set narrow limits to any eventual future extension of the law strengthening the influence of labour representatives on the "co-determined" boards. The latter, however, is a central long-term objective of German unions. Their walking out of the *Konzertierte Aktion* thus seems to indicate that co-determination was the payoff expected as a quid pro quo for their cooperation in incomes policy.[3]

Observations such as these lead us to speculate whether liberal corporatism in its most conspicuous form, the "incorporation" of organized labour into economic policy-making, is not subject to a particular logic of exchange. Since the core element of such an "incorporation" is a cooperative incomes policy, and since this requires from labour the reununciation of its traditional redistributive objectives, in the long run this will probably not take place without labour obtaining compensations in issue-areas outside wage policy.

AREAS FOR COMPENSATORY POLICIES

It seems plausible to assume that such compensations will be attempted in substantive areas both relevant to the conflict of labour and capital and "functionally" interdependent with wage policies. This suggests the following speculative hypothesis: the more durable and stable the form of liberal corporatism, the more it will be characterized by its simultaneous treatment of other interdependent problems arising from the conflict of labour and capital.

A particularly obvious example is taxation, whose relation to incomes policy is undeniable. Contrary to the doctrine of the "built-in stabilizer" function of progressive taxation, the progression may result in an intensification of the "struggle for income" as soon as, under inflationary conditions, it affects more and more wage-earners. In Austria, which has had a cooperative incomes policy since the fifties, it has not at all been uncommon for the Minister of Finance to discuss tax reforms with labour unions. On the other hand, taxation of business earnings is likewise relevant for a viable income policy.

A significant pattern which has recently appeared in several countries is the extension of incomes policy negotiations to include income taxes, social security taxes, prices, farmer's incomes and food subsidies. One important example has been the "Social Contract" in Britain, originally conceived as such a "package deal". Still more elaborate "combined packages" or "simultaneous solutions" of this type have been tried in several Scandinavian countries (e.g., Denmark in 1963, Finland since 1968, Norway in 1976). Yet such a broadening of incomes policy seems largely to be of an ad hoc nature and, thus, does not result in an institutional stabilization of corporatism since its continued success depends on a very precarious equilibration of public finance and economic conditions naturally subject to strong fluctuations (Schwerin 1979).

A higher probability of stabilizing corporatism exists in labour market policy since this has been marked by the development of quite strong institutional-bureaucratic structures. However, there are considerable cross-national differences in this institutional framework, in particular, with reference to the participation of labour and employers. To the degree that labour unions have an active stake in the making of employment policy this may yield certain compensations for wage restraint or compliance with a formal income policy. There may even be instances where an "active labour market policy" with strong union participation has been conceived as an alternative to incomes policy, as in Sweden (Ulman and Flanagan, p. 111ff.). Alongside labour market policy, regional and/or sectoral investment planning may eventually become characterized by corporative patterns of organizational participation.[4]

The West German developments discussed above point to

another relevant issue-area, namely, co-determination in industry. In spite of union rhetoric, one has to distinguish the quasi-syndicalist concepts of "industrial democracy" and "workers' control" from the corporatist concept of "co-determination" which, in its German version, is based on the principle of "parity between capital and labour" with the implication that labour is sharing the responsibilities of private enterprise. There seems to be a striking coincidence between the recent diffusion of co-determination schemes in other European countries and the growing importance of liberal corporatism which deserves further investigation. An aspect of particular importance would be the degree to which co-determination at the firm or plant level results in a sort of "firm egoism" on the part of labour representatives, or to which it is oriented towards taking into account larger economic consideration — be it by the co-optation of union representatives from outside the firm or by the establishment of regional or national "economic councils".

Finally, the possible impact of incomes policies on the distribution of income and wealth might be neutralized by a "policy of formation of wealth" (*Vermögensbildungspolitik*). The original problem is, of course, that an aggressive union strategy of wage increase cannot change the distribution of wealth in favour of labour because of worker's high propensity to consume. On the other hand, many schemes of workers' participation in reinvested profits simply tend to reinforce the financial assets of firms without challenging the control of original owners and management.[5] The corporatist strategy would be one of "collective capital formation" where workers' shares would be placed in funds under the organizational control of labour. Propositions of this sort have not yet been realized on a large scale. But at least in Sweden the discussion has led to concrete projects (Meidner plan), the future realization of which cannot be excluded.

SYNDICALIST AND NEO-LIBERAL ALTERNATIVES TO CORPORATISM

These speculations, however, provoke one to ask "who benefits?" from such exchange processes. It has been noted that liberal corporatism is accompanied by organizational centralization and increased influence of experts. These developments may evoke the theorem of organizational goal displacement, current since Robert Michels. The neo-corporatist logic of exchange sketched out here might then be attributed to tendencies toward organizational growth of labour unions. Indeed, it cannot be a priori ruled out that the advantages which labour may eventually obtain from corporatist policies will largely accrue to the organization and its élites in form of status and influence, rather than to the membership.

Critical awareness of these consequences might lead to the question of eventual alternatives to liberal corporatism. Two opposite strategies seem to be conceivable. One would involve the eventual transformation of corporatism into something like syndicalism by an increasing participation of the rank and file in the articulation of demands. This would probably tend to increase the intensity of conflict, and would jeopardize the corporatist objective of coordinating organized interests in a society characterized by antagonistic interests.

The other strategy would involve the restoration of a competitive market situation by reducing the power of economic actors, in particular, by regulating labour unions. This strategy would be of special importance for the success of the "monetarist" alternative to Keynesian policies. Its consistency and "symmetry" would, however, depend on effective curtailing of oligopolies and other concentrations of economic power. It is significant that in the last years concrete projects for regulating labour unions — such as the abortive British Industrial Relations Act — have been of a hybrid and inconsistent type, combining elements of an "incorporation" of unions with others aiming at reducing their control (Streeck 1978). Thus it may seem doubtful whether any clear alternatives to corporatism have a serious chance of being realized.

NOTES

1. In 1977, West Germany has established a "concerted action in public health", with the participation of medical associations, public health insurance schemes, the

drug industry and the government in order to check rising costs in the health sector, in particular, by restraining the rise in doctors' incomes and drug prices.

2. However, we should not exclude the eventuality of functionally equivalent mechanisms. In West Germany, in spite of the large autonomy of industrial unions, effects somewhat similar to centralized bargaining may be achieved by the "wage leader" function performed by the two large unions of metal workers and of public service employees.

3. In its decision of 1 March 1979, the Court has not only upheld the constitutionality of the law but has also refrained from limiting further legislative action. Upon this, the unions have immediately indicated their interest in a new trilateral forum for discussing economic policy.

4. It should be remembered that French and British (as well as Dutch) indicative planning had already been conceived with a strongly corporatist institutional framework.

5. The problem is somewhat similar with pension funds on the firm level as long as labour has no determinative share in their control.

References

ACKROYD, C. et al. (1977) The Technology of Political Control. Harmondsworth: Penguin.

ADAM, H. (1972) Die konzentierte Aktion in der Bundesrepublik. Köln: Bund-Verlag.

ADLER-KARLSSON, G. (1970) Reclaiming the Canadian Economy. A Swedish Approach through Functional Socialism. Toronto: Anasi.

AKIMOTO, H. (1968) Keidanren. Tokyo: Setsugesha.

ALMOND, G., S. C. FLANAGAN, and R. MUNDT (eds.) (1973) Crisis, Choice, and Change. Boston: Little, Brown.

ALFORD, R. (1975) "Paradigms of Relations between State and Society," pp. 145-160 in L. Lindberg et al., Stress and Contradiction in Modern Capitalism. Lexington, Mass.: Lexington.

ANDERMAN, S. D. (ed.) (1967) Trade Unions and Technological Change. London: George Allen & Unwin.

ANDERSON, C. W. (1976) "Public Policy and the Complex Organization," in L. N. Lindberg (ed.) Politics and the Future of Industrial Society. New York: David McKay.

ANDO (ed.) (1975) Kindai Nihon Keizaishi Yoran. Tokyo: Tokyo Daigaku Shuppankai.

ANTON, T. (1969) "Policy-making and Political Culture in Sweden." Scandinavian Pol. Studies 4: 88-102.

ARENDT, H. (1967) The Origins of Totalitarianism. London: George Allen & Unwin.

ARMSTRONG, J. (1973) The European Administrative Elite. Princeton: Princeton University Press.

ASHFORD, D. (1978) "The Structural Analysis of Policy or Institutions Really Do Matter," in D. Ashford (ed.) Comparing Public Policies. Beverly Hills: Sage.

BACHRACH, P. and M . S. BARATZ (1962) "The Two Faces of Power." Amer. Pol. Sci. Rev. 56 (December): 947-952.

BADE, K. J. (1975) "Organisierter Kapitalismus." Neue Politische Literatur 20: 293-307.

BAILEY, S. K. et al. (1963) Schoolman in Politics. Syracuse: Syracuse University Press.

BALBUS, I. (1971) "The Concept of Interest in Pluralist and Marxist Analysis." Politics & Society 1 (February): 151-178.

BAUDIN, L. (1942). Le Corporatisme. Italie, Porugal, Allemagne, Espagne. Paris.

BAUER, O. (1923) Die österreichische Revolution. Wien: Wiener Volks buchhandlung.

BAYLEY, D. (1976) Forces of Order. Berkeley: University of California Press.

BEER, S. (1969) Modern British Politics. London: Faber & Faber.

BEER, S. (1965) British Politics in the Collectivist Age. New York: Knopf.

BEER, S. (1958) "Group Representation in Britian and the United States". The Annals 319 (September): 130-140.

BELL, D. (1973) The Coming of Post-Industrial Society. New York: Basic Books.

BENDIX, R. (1969) Nation-Building and Citizenship. New York: Anchor.

BENN, A. W. (1973) "Heath's Spadework for Socialism". Sunday Times: 25 March: 61.

BENTLEY, A. F. (1908) The Process of Government. Chicago: University of Chicago Press.

BERGMANN, J. et al. (1975) Gewerkschaften in der Bundesrepublik. Frankfurt a.M.: Europäische Verlagsanstalt.

BETHUSY-HUC, V. G. (1962) Demokratie und Interessenpolitik. Wiesbaden: Franz Steiner.

BEVERIDGE, W. (1945) Full Employment in a Free Society. London: The New Statesman and Nation/Reynolds News.

BICHLBAUER, D. and A. PELINKA (1974) Wissenschaftliche Politikberatung am Beispiel der Paritätischen Kommission. Wien: Institut für Gesellschaftspolitik.

BLACKBURN, R. (1967) "The Unequal Society," pp. 15-55 in R. Blackburn and A. Cockburn, The Incompatibles. London: Penguin.

BLANK, S. (1978) "Britain's Economic Problems: Lies and Damned Lies". Paper presented to conference on Is Britain Dying? Cornell University.

BLOCK, W. J. (1960) The Separation of the Farm Bureau and the Extension Service. Urbana: University of Illinois Press.

BLUM, J. M. (1976) V was for Victory. New York: Harcourt, Brace, Jovanovich.

BOCKENFORDE, E. W. (1976) "Die politische Funktion wirtschaftlich-sozialer Verbände und Interessenträger in der sozialistaatlichen Demokratie: Ein Beitrag zum Problem der 'Regierbarkeit'." Der Staat 15: 457-483. (Berlin-West).

BONNETT, K. (1978) "Corporatist Developments in Advanced Capitalist Society: Competing Theoretical Perspectives." Paper prepared for the SSRC Conference on Institutionalization, Sussex (September).

BOWEN, R. H. (1947) German Theories of the Corporate State. New York: Whittlesey House.

BRANDT, W. (1976) Begegnungen und Einsichten: Die Jahre 1960-1975. Stuttgart: Deutsche Verlags-Anstalt.

BRENNER, M. J. (1969) "Functional Representation and Interest Group Theory". Comparative Politics 2 (October): 111-134.

BRITTAN, S. (1976) "The Economic Contradictions of Democracy," in A. King (ed.) Why is Britain Becoming Harder to Govern? London: British Broadcasting Corp.

BRODY, R. and B. PAGE (1972) "Policy Voting and the Electoral Process: The Vietnam War Issue," American Political Science Review 66: 979-995.

BRZEZINSKI, Z. (1970) Between Two Ages. America's Role in the Technotronic era. New York: Viking.

BUSCH-LÜTY, C. (1964) Gesamtwirtschaftliche Lohnpolitik. Tübingen: Mohr-Siebeck.

CALLEO, D. P. and B. M. ROWLAND (1973) America and the World Political Economy. Bloomington: Indiana University Press.

CAMERON, D. (1978) "Taxes, Deficits, and Inflation." Paper prepared for the Brookings Institution Project on Politics and Sociology of Global Inflation and Recession, December.

CAMERON, D. (1976) "The Expansion of the Public Economy: A Comparative Analysis." Paper prepared for the American Political Science Association Annual Convention, Chicago, September.

CAMPBELL, A., et al. (1964) The American Voter. New York: Wiley.

CAMPBELL, C. M. (1962) The Farm Bureau and the New Deal. Urbana: University of Illinois Press.

CANADIAN LABOUR CONGRESS (1976) Labour's Manifesto for Canada. Ottawa.

CARPENTER, L. P. (1976) "Corporatism in Britain, 1930-45." Journal of Contemporary History 11: 3-25.

CARR, W. (1972) Arms, Autarky and Aggression. London: Edward Arnold.

CENTER FOR RESEARCH ON CRIMINAL JUSTICE (1975) The Iron Fist and the Velvet Glove. Berkeley: Center.

CHATTOPADHYAY, R. (1975) "The Political Role of Labor Unions in India: an Interstate Study of Labor Unions in West Bengal, Karnataka and Rajasthan." Doctoral dissertation, University of Chicago.

CLEGG, H. A. (1976) Collective Bargaining Under Trade Unionism. London: Heinemann.

CLIFF, T. (1974) State and Capitalism in Russia. London: Pluto Press.

COHEN, S. (1969) Modern Capitalist Planning: The French Model. Cambridge, Mass.: Harvard University Press.

COLE, G. D. H. (1921) Guild Socialism. New York. F. A. Stones.

CONNOLLY, W. E. (1972) "On 'Interests' in Politics." Politics & Society 2. (Summer): 459-478.

CONNOLLY, W. (ed.) (1969) The Bias of Pluralism. New York: Atherton.

COORNAERT, E. (1941) Les Corporations en France avant 1789. Paris. 4th edition. Paris, Editions Ouvrières. New edition, 1968.

CORINA, J. (1975) "Planning and the British Labour Market," pp. 177-201 in J. Hayward and M. Watson (eds.) Planning, Politics and Public Policy. Cambridge, England: Cambridge University Press.

CRICK, B. (1965) The Reform of Parliament. New York: Anchor.

CRICK, B. (1959) The American Science of Politics. Berkeley: University of California Press.

CROUCH, C. J. (1978a) "The Changing Role of the State in Industrial Relations in Western Europe," in C. J. Crouch and A. Pizzorno (eds.) The Resurgence of Class Conflict in Western Europe since 1968. London: Macmillan.

CROUCH, C. J. (1978b) "Trade Unions Between Disruption and Stability." Paper prepared for the Brooking Institution project on the Politics and Sociology of Global Inflation. Washington, DC.

CROUCH, C. and A. PIZZORNO (1978) The Resurgence of Class Conflict in Western Europe since 1968. London: Macmillan.

DAHL, R. (ed.) (1973) Regimes and Oppositions. New Haven: Yale University Press.

DAHL, R. (ed.) (1966) Political Opposition in Western Democracies. New Haven: Yale University Press.

DAHL, R. A. (1957) A Preface to Democratic Theory. Chicago: University of Chicago Press.

DAHRENDORF, R. (1969) Society and Democracy in Germany. New York: Anchor.

DAITO, E. (1977) "Romu Kanri," in Nihonteki Keiei. Tokyo: Nihon Keizai Shimbunsha.

DAVIDOFF, P. (1965) "Advocacy and Pluralism in Planning." Journal of American Institute of Planners 31 (November): 331-338.

DELZELL, C. (1970) Mediterranean Fascism. London: Macmillan.

DION, L. (1971) Société et Politique: La Vie des Groupes I. Québec. Université Laval.

DONNELLY, M. (1977) "Setting the Price of Rice: A Study in Political Decision-making," T. J. Pempel (ed.) Policymaking in Contemporary Japan. Ithaca: Cornell University Press.

DORFMAN, G. A. (1973) Wage Politics in Britain 1945-1967. Ames: Iowa University Press.

DOWNS, A. (1957) An Economic Theory of Democracy. New York: Harper & Row.

DRAPER, H. (1961) "Neo-corporatism and Neo-reformers." New Politics 1 (June): 37-106.

DURBIN, E. F. M. (1940) The Politics of Democratic Socialism. London: G. Routledge.

DURKHEIM, E. (1964) The Divison of Labor in Society. New York: Free Press.

EDELMAN, M. and R. W. FLEMING (1965) The Politics of Wage-Price-Decisions. Urbana: University of Illinois Press.

EINZIG, P. (1933) The Economic Foundations of Fascism. London: Macmillan.

ELBOW, M. H. (1966) French Corporative Theory, 1789-1948. New York: Octagon.

ELDERSVELD, S. J. (1964) Political Parties: A Behavioral Analysis. Chicago: Rand-McNally.

ELDERSVELD, S. J. (1958) "American Interest Groups" in H. Ehrmann (ed.) Interest Groups on Four Continents. Pittsburgh: University of Pittsburgh Press.

ELLUL, J. (1964) The Technological Society. New York: Vintage.

ELVANDER, N. (1966) Intresseorganisationerna i dagens Sverige. Lund: CWK Gleerup Bokförlag.

ESTOR, M. (1965) Der Sozial-Okonomische Rat der niederländischen Wirtschaft. Berlin: Duncker & Humblot.

ETZIONI, A. (1968) The Active Society. New York: Free Pres.

FAINSOD, M., L. GORDON and J. PALAMOUNTAIN (1959) Government and the American Economy. 3rd ed. New York: Norton.

FINE, B. and L. HARRIS (1979) Re-Reading 'Capital'. London: Macmillan. 113-145.

FINER, S. E. (1958) Anonymous Empire. London: Pall Mall.

FISCHER, H. (1972) Zur Praxis des Begutachtungsverfahrens. Osterreichische Zeitschrift fur Politikwissenschaft 1: 34-54.

FRAENKEL, E. (1964) Deutschland und die westlichen Demokratien. Stuttgart: Kohlhammer.

FULCHER, J. (1973) "Class Conflict in Sweden." Sociology 7 (January): 49-69.

FUSFELD, D. R. (1972) "The Rise of the Corporate State in America". Journal of Economic Issues 6 (March): 1-20.

GALBRAITH, J. (1975) Economics and the Public Purpose. London.

GALBRAITH, J. (1967) The New Industrial State. New York: Houghton Mifflin.

GALBRAITH, J. K. (1952) American Capitalism. New York: Houghton Mifflin.

GARCEAU, O. (1941) The Political Life of the American Medical Association. Cambridge: Harvard University Press.

GATES, R. (1972) "German Socialism and the Crisis of 1929-1933". Paper presented at the American Historical Association meetings, New Orleans.

GELLNER, E. (1975) "The Social Contract in Search of an Idiom". Political Quarterly XLVI: 127-52.

GENDAISHI KENKYUKAI (ed.) (1960) Sengo Nihon no kokka kenryoku. Tokyo: Sanichi Shobo.

GERSCHENKRON, A. (1968) Continuity in History and Other Essays. Cambridge: Harvard University Press.

GERSCHENKRON, A. (1962) Economic Backwardness in Historical Perspective. Cambridge: Harvard University Press.

GIDDENS, A. (1973) The Class Structure of the Advanced Societies. New York: Harper.

GILPIN, R. (1975) US Power and the Multinational Corporation. New York: Basic.

GOODWIN, C. D. (1975) Exhortation and Controls. The Search for a Wage-Price Policy, 1945-1971. Washington, DC: Brookings.

GOUGH, I. (1975) "State Expenditure in Advanced Capitalism". New Left Rev. 92 (July-August): 53-92.

GOUREVITCH, P. (1978a) "The International System and Regime Formation: A Critical Review of Anderson and Wallerstein," Comparative Politics 10: 419-438.

GOUREVITCH, P. (1978b) "The Second Image Reversed: The International Sources of Domestic Politics," International Organization 32: 881-912.

GOUREVITCH, P. (1977) "International Trade, Domestic Coalitions and Liberty: Comparative Response to the Crisis of 1873-1896," Journal of Interdisciplinary History 8: 281-313.

GRAUBARD, S. (ed.) (1963) A New Europe? Boston: Beacon Pres.

GREENSTONE, J. D. (1975) "Group theories," in F. I. Greenstein and N. W. Plsby (eds.) Handbook of Political Science. Vol. 2. Reading, Mass.: Addison-Wesley.

GROSSMAN, J. B. (1965) Lawyers and Judges, The ABA and the Politics of Judicial Selection. New York: Wiley.

GROTTIAN, P. (1974) Strukturprobleme staatlicher Planung. Hamburg: Hoffmann & Campe.

HABERMAS, J. (1973) Legitimationsprobleme im Spätkapitalismus. Frankfurt a.M.: Suhrkamp.

HARARI, E. (1974) "Japanese Politics of Advice in Comparative Perspective: A Framework for Analysis and a Case Study," Public Policy 22: 537-577.

HARDES, H.-D. (1974) Einkommenspolitik in der BRD. Frankfurt a.M./New York: Herder & Herder.

HARRIS, N. (1972) Competition and the Corporate Society. London: Methuen.

HARTZ, L. (1960) "Democracy: Image and Reality" in W. N. Chambers and R. H. Salisbury (eds.) Democracy in the Mid-Twentieth Century. St. Louis: Washington University Press.

HARTZ, L. (1955) The Liberal Tradition in America. New York: Harcourt, Brace.

HAYASHI, S. (1966) Nihon no Rekishi 25. Tokyo. Chuo Koron.

HAYES, P. (1973) Fascism. London: Allen & Unwin.

HAYWARD, J. E. S. (1972) "State Intervention in France: the Changing Style of Government Industry Relations." Pol. Studies 20: 287-298.

HAYWARD, J. E. S. (1966) "Interest Groups and Incomes Policy in France." British Journal of industrial Relations 4 (July): 165-200.

HEADEY, B. (1972) "Trade Unions and National Wage Policies." Journal of Politics 32: 407-439.

HECKSCHER, G. (1958) "Interest Groups in Sweden: their political role," pp. 154-172 in H. W. Ehrmann (ed.) Interest Groups on Four Continents. Pittsburgh: Pittsburgh University Press.

HECLO, H. (1974) Modern Social Politics in Britain and Sweden. New Haven: Yale University Press.

HEIDENHEIMER, A. et al. (1975) Comparing Public Policies. New York: St. Martin's.

HEINZ, J. (1962) "The Political Impasse in Farm Support Legislation". Yale Law Journal 71 (April): 952-78.

HEISLER, M. (ed.) (1975) Politics in Europe. New York: David McKay.

HIBBS, D. (1978) "Mass Political Support and Macroeconomic Policy." Paper prepared for the Brookings Institution Project on the Politics and Sociology of Global Inflation, December.

HIBBS, D. (1977) "Political Parties and Macroeconomic Policy," American Political Science Review 71: 1467-1487.

HIBBS, D. (1976) "Industrial Conflict in Advanced Industrialized Societies," American Political Science Review 70: 1033-1058.

HIRSCH, F. and J. GOLDTHORPE (eds.) (1978) The Political Economy of Inflation. Cambridge: Harvard University Press.

HIRSCH, J. (1979) "The Transformation of the German State Since 1945" in M. Castells and R. Scase (eds.) The State in Western Europe. London: Croom Helm.

HIRSCH, J. (1974) Staatsapparat und Reproduktion des Kapitals. Frankfurt: Suhrkamp.

HIRSCHMAN, A. O. (1970) Exit, Voice and Loyalty. Cambridge, Mass.: Harvard University Press.

HOLLAND, S. (1975) The Socialist Challenge. London: Quartet.

HOLLOWAY, J. and S. PICCIOTTO (1977) "Capital, Crisis, and the State". Capital and Class 2: 76-101.

HONDA, Y. (1974) Nohon Neo Kanryo Ron. Tokyo: Kodansha.

HOPPMANN, E. (ed.) (1971) Konzertierte Aktion. Frankfurt a.M.: Athenäum.

HUNTFORD, R. (1972) The New Totalitarians. New York.

HUNTINGTON, S. P. (1974) "Postindustrial politics — how benign will it be?" Comparative Politics 6 (January): 163-191.

HYODO, T. (1977) "Rodo Kumiai Undo no Hatten," in Nihon Rekishi 23. Tokyo: Iwanami.

IMAI, S. (1966) Nihon no Rekishi 23. Tokyo: Chuo Koron.

INSTITUT FÜR SOZIALFORSCHUNG (1969) Die Funktion der Gewerkschaften im Prozeß der gesellschaftlichen Entwicklung Westdeutschlands. Frankfurt a.M. (mimeo).

IONESCU, G. (1975) Centripetal Politics. London: Hart-David.

IROKAWA, D. (1966) Nihon no Rekishi 21. Tokyo: Chuo Koron.

JESSOP, B. (1979) "The Transformation of the British State Since 1945," in M. Castells and R. Scase (eds.) The State in Western Europe. London: Croom Helm.

JESSOP, B. (1978) "Capitalism and Democracy: the Best Possible Shell?" in G. Littlejohn et al. Power and the State. London: Croom Helm: 10-51.

JESSOP B. (1978) "Corporatism, Fascism, and Social Democracy," Essex, England.

JESSOP, B. (1977) "Recent Theories of the Capitalist State," Cambridge Journal of Economics 1 (iv).

JOHANSEN, L. and O. Kristensen (1978) "Corporatist Traits in Denmark 1946-76." Paper prepared for the Internatonal Sociology Association Conference, Uppsala, Sweden, August.

JOHNSON, C. (1978) Japan's Public Policy Companies. Washington: American Enterprise Institute.

JOHNSON, C. (1977) "MITI and Japanese International Economic Policy," in R. Scalapino, The Foreign Policy of Modern Japan. Berkeley: University of California Press.

JOHNSON, H. (ed.) (1975) The New Mercantilism. London: Macmillan.

JONES, A. (1950) Industrial Order. London: Falcon.

KAJINISHI, M. et al. (1974) Nihon Shihonshugi no Botsuraku. Tokyo: Tokyo Daigaku Shuppankai.

KAJINISHI, M. et al. (eds.) (1973) Nihon Shihonshugi no Hatten. Tokyo: Tokyo Daigaku Shuppankai.

KAJINISHI, M. (1962) Gendai Nihon Shihonshugi Taikei. Tokyo: Kobundo.

KALECKI, M. (1971) Selected Essays on the Dynamics of the Capitalist Economy. Cambridge, England: Cambridge University Press.

KATZENSTEIN, P. (1978) "Economic Dependency and Political Autonomy: The Small European States in the International Economy," Cornell University Press mimeo.

KATZENSTEIN, P. (ed.) (1977) Between Power and Plenty. Special Issue International Organization 31. Also as hardbound book, 1978, Madison: University of Wisconsin Press.

KATZENSTEIN, P. (1976) "International Relations and Domestic Structures: Foreign Economic Policies of Advanced Industrial States," International Organization, 30: 1021-1034.

KATZNELSON, I. (1973) Black Men, White Cities. London: Oxford.

KAWAI, K. (1960) Japan's American Interlude. Chicago: University of Chicago Press.

KAYSEN, C. (1972) "The Corporation, How Much Power? What Scope" in M. Gilbert (ed.) The Modern Business Corporation. Harmondsworth: Penguin.

KEOHANE, R. and J. NYE (1977) Power and Interdependence. Boston: Little, Brown.

KEOHANE, R. and J. NYE (eds.) (1972) Transnational Relations and World Politics. Cambridge: Harvard University Press.

KEY, V. O. (1966) The Responsible Electorate. Cambridge: Harvard University Press.

KEY, V. O. Jr. (1964) Politics, Parties and Pressure Groups. 5th ed. New York: Crowell.

KEYNES, J. M. (1932). Essays in Persuasion. New York: Harcourt Brace & Co. This essay was initially published as a separate pamphlet in 1926.

KIENZL, H. (1974) Die Wirtschaftspartnerschaft. Osterreichische Zeitschrift für Politikwissenschaft (Vienna) 3: 287-293.

KING, M. "The UK Profits Crisis: Myth or Reality". Eco. Journal LXXXV: 33-54.

KING, W. L. M. (1973) Industry and Humanity (1918). Toronto: University of Toronto Press.

KLOSE, A. et al. (1974) Special Number, Osterreichische Zeitschrift für Politik-wissenschaft III, 3.

KLOSE, A. (1970) Ein Weg zür Sozialpartnerschaft: Das österreichische Modell. München: R. Oldenbourg.

KOCK, H. (1975) Stabilitätspolitik im föderalistischen System der Bundesrepublik Deutschland, Köln: Bund-Verlag.

KOCKA, J. (1974) "Organisierter Kapitalismus Oder Staatsmonopolistischer Kapitalismus? Begriffliche Vorbermerkung," pp. 19-35 in H. A. Winkler (ed.) Organisierter Kapitalismus. Göttingen: Vandenhoeck § Ruprecht.

KORNBERG, A. (ed.) (1973) Legislature in Comparative Perspective. New York: David McKay.

KORNHAUSER, W. (1959) The Politics of Mass Society. New York: Free Press.

KRAMER, P. E. (1966) The Societal State. Meppel: J. A. Boom en Zoon.

KRASNER, S. (1978) Defending the National Interest. Princeton: Princeton University Press.

KRUSIUS-AHRENBERG, L. (1958) "The political power of economic and labor-market organizations: a dilemma of Finnish democracy," pp. 33-51 in H. W. Ehrmann (ed.) Interest Groups on Four Continents. Pittsburgh: University of Pittsburgh Press.

KUSTER, G. H. (1974) "Germany," pp. 63-75 in R. Vernon (ed.) Big Business and State: Changing Relations in Western Europe. Cambridge, Mass.: Harvard University Press.

KURIKI, Y. (1977) "Keizai Kiki to Rodo Undo," in Nihon Rekishi 22. Tokyo: Iwanami.

LAPALOMBARA, J. (1964) Interest Groups in Italian Politics. Princeton, NJ: Princeton University Press.

LASKI, H. (1867) A Grammar of Politics. London: George Allen & Unwin.

LASLETT, J. M. and S. M. LIPSET (eds.) (1974) Failure of a Dream? Essays in the History of American Socialism. Garden City, New York: Anchor/ Doubleday.

LATHAM, E. (1952) "The group basis of politics." American Pol. Sci. Rev. 46 (June): 387-412.

LAVAU, G. E. (1958) "Political pressures by interest groups in France," pp. 58-70 in H. Ehrmann (ed.) Interest Groups on Four Continents. Pittsburgh: University of Pittsburgh Press.

LEEDS, P. (1978) "Issue Voting: A Reconsideration," mimeo, October.

LEHMBRUCH, G. (1978) "Corporatism, Labour, and Public Policy." Paper prepared for the International Sociology Association Conference, Uppsala, Sweden, August.

LEHMBRUCH, G. (1977) "Liberal Corporatism and Party Government," Comparative Political Studies 10: 91-126.

LEHMBRUCH, G. (1976) Parteienwettbewerb im Bundestaat. Stuttgart: Kolhammer.

LEHMBRUCH, G. (1974a) "Consociational democracy, class conflict, and the new corporatism." Paper presented to IPSA Round Table on "Political Integration," Jerusalem.

LEHMBRUCH, G. (1974b) "A Non-competitive Pattern of Conflict Management in Liberal Democracies," pp. 90-97 in K. D. McRae (ed.) Consociational Democracy. Toronto: McClelland & Stewart.

LEHMBRUCH, G. (1971) "The Ambiguous Coalition in West Germany" in R. Barker (ed.) Studies in Opposition. London: Macmillan: 168-192.

LEHMBRUCH, G. (1967) Proporzdemokratie: Politisches System und politische Kultur in der Schweiz und in Osterreich. Tübingen: J. C. B. Mohr.

LENIN, V. I. (1963) "State and Revolution". Selected Works, Vol. 3. Moscow: Progress Publ.

LEVITT, K. (1970) Silent Surrender. Toronto: Macmillan.

LINDBERG, L. (ed.) (1976) Politics and the Future of Industrial Society. New York: David McKay.

LINDBERG, L. et al. (1975) Stress and Contradiction in Modern Capitalism. Lexington, Mass.: Lexington.

LINDBLOM, C. E. (1965) The Intelligence of Democracy. New York: Free Press.

LINDROTH, B. (1975) Bingo! En kritisk granskning av folkrörelserna i Sverige 1850-1975. Stockholm: Bokförlaget Prisma/Föreningen Verdandi.

LIJPHART, A. (1976) The Politics of Consociational Democracies. Berkeley: University of California Press.

LIJPHART, A. (1975) The Politics of Accommodation. 2nd edition. Berkeley: University of California Press: 196-219.

LIJPHART, A. (1969) "Consociational democracy." World Politics 21: 207-225.

LIJPHART, A. (1968) The Politics of Accommodation. Berkeley: University of California Press.

LIPSET, S. and S. ROKKAN (eds.) (1967) Party Systems and Voter Alignments. New York: Free Press.

LOEWENBERG, G. (ed.) (1971) Modern Parliaments. Chicago: Aldine.

LOWI, T. (1974) "Interest Groups and the Consent to Govern: Getting the People Out, for What?" Annals (May): 86-100.

LOWI, T. (1969) The End of Liberalism. New York: Norton.

LUNDKVIST, S. (1973) "Folkrörelser och reformer 1900-1920," pp. 160-182 in S. Koblik (ed.) Fran fattigdom till överflöd. Stockholm: Wahlström och Widstrand.

LUHMANN, N. (1971) "Die Knappheit der Zeit und die Vordringlichkeit des Befristeten," pp. 143-164 in Politische Planung: Aufsätze zür Soziologie von Politik und Verwaltung. Opladen: Westdeutscher Verlag.

LUHMANN, N. (1970) "Wirtschaft als soziales system," pp. 204-231 in Soziologische Aufklärung: Aufsätze zur Theorie sozialer Systeme. Opladen: Westdeutscher Verlag.

LUHMANN, N. (1969) Legitimation durch Verfahren. Neuwied am Rhein und Berlin: Luchterhand Verlag.

MacPHERSON, C. B. (1973) Democratic Theory: Essays in Retrieval. Oxford: Oxford University Press.

MADDISON, A. (1969) Economic Growth in Japan and the USSR. New York: Norton.

MAIER, C. (1975) Recasting Bourgeois Europe. Princeton: Princeton University Press.

MALHERBE, J. (1940) Le Corporatisme d'association en Suisse. Lausanne: Imprimerie Henri Jordan Fils.

MANOïLESCO, M. (1936). Le Siècle du Corporatisme. Paris: Felix Alcan. Original edition 1934.

MARSHALL, B. (1967) Capitalism and Nationalism in Prewar Japan. Stanford: Stanford University Press.

MARTIN, A. (1975a) "Is democratic control of capitalist economies possible?" pp. 13-56 in L. Lindberg et al. (eds.) Stress and Contradiction in Modern Capitalism. Lexington, Mass.: Lexington Books.

MARTIN, A. (1975b) "Labour movement parties and inflation: contrasting responses in Britain and Sweden." Polity 7 (Summer): 427-521.

MARTIN, A. (1975) "Swedish experience with democratic control of unemployment and inflation." Paper presented to the Center for Comparative Policy Studies, University of Wisconsin.

MARX, E. and W. KENDALL (1971) Unions in Europe. Sussex: Centre for Contemporary European Studies.

MASON, T. W. (1977) Sozialpolitik im Dritten Reich. Opladen: Westdeutscher Verlag.

MASON, T. W. (1966) "Labour in the Third Reich." Past and Present 33 (April): 112-141.

MASTERS, N. A. et al. (1964) State Politics and the Public Schools. New York: Knopf.

MAYER-TASCH, P. C. (1971) Korporatismus und Autoritarismus. Eine Studie zu Theorie und Praxis der berufsständischen Rechts- und Staatsidee. Frankfurt a.M.: Athenäum Verlag.

McCONNELL, G. (1966) Private Power and American Democracy: New York: Alfred A. Knopf.

McCONNELL, G. (1953) The Decline of Agrarian Democracy. Berkeley: Univerity of California Press.

McRAE, K. D. (ed.) (1974) Consociational Democracy. Toronto: McClelland & Stewart.

MILIBAND, R. (1973) "Poulantzas and the Capitalist State." New Left Rev. 82 (November/December): 83-92.

MILIBAND, R. (1969) The State in Capitalist Society. New York: Basic Books.

MILL, J. S. (1929) On Liberty. London: Oxford University Press.

MILLER, A. S. (1972) "The Legal Foundations of the Corporate State." Journal of Economic Issues VI: 59-79.

MILLER, S. M. (1975) "Notes on Neo-Capitalism". Theory and Society II.

MISKIMIN, H. (1969) The Economy of Early Renaissance Europe. Englewood Cliffs: Prentice-Hall.

MONOPOLIES COMMISSION (1970) A Survey of Mergers. London: HMSO.

MONTGOMERY, J. (1957) Forced To Be Free. Chicago: University of Chicago Press.

MOORE, B. (1966) Social Origins of Dictatorship and Democracy. Boston: Beacon.

MORSE, E. (1973) Foreign Policy and Interdependence in Gaullist France. Princeton: Princeton University Press.

MOSSE, G. (1967) "The Genesis of Fascism". Journal of Contemporary History I, 1.

MURAT, A. (1944) Le Corporatisme. Paris. Les Publications Techniques.

NATIONAL ECONOMIC DEVELOPMENT OFFICE (1975) Financial Performance and Inflation. London.

NEDELMANN, B. (1975) "Handlungsraum politischer Organisationen." Jahrbuch für Politik 4: 9-118. München-Wien: Olzog Verlag.

NEDELMANN, B. and K. MEIER (1977) "Theories of Contemporary Corporatism: Static or Dymanic?" Comparative Political Studies 10: 39-60.

NEUBAUER, D. (1967) "Some Conditions of Democracy," American Political Science Review 61: 1002-1009.

NEUMANN, F. (1965) The Democratic and Authoritarian State. New York: Free Press.

NEUMANN, F. (1942) Behemoth, The Structure and Practice of National Socialism. London: V. Gollancz.

NEWBOULD, G. D. and A. S. JACKSON (1972) The Receding Ideal. Liverpool: Guthstead.

NICHOLSON, R. J. (1967) "The Distribution of Personal Incomes." Lloyd's Bank Review 83 (January): 11-21.

NIHON SEIJI GAKKAI (1960) Nihon no Atsurvoku Dantai. Tokyo: Iwanami Shoten.

NOLL, R. (1971) Reforming Regulation. Washington, DC: The Brookings Institution.

O'CONNOR, J. (1973) The Fiscal Crisis of the State. New York: St. Martin's.

ODEGARD, P. (1928) Pressure Politics. New York: Columbia University Press.

OE, S. (1973) Nihon Sangyo Kakumei. Tokyo: Iwanami.

OFFE, C. (1978) Industry and Inequality. New York: St. Martin's.

OFFE, C. (1975) "Introduction to Part II," pp. 245-246 L. Lindberg et al., Stress and Contradiction in Modern Capitalism. Lexington, Mass.: Lexington.

OFFE, C. (1975) "The Theory of the Capitalist State and the Problem of Policy," in L. Lindberg (ed.) (1975).

OFFE, C. (1972) Strukturprobleme des Kapitalistischen Staates. Frankfurt: Suhrkamp.

OUCHI, T. (1967) Nihon no Rekishi 24. Tokyo: Chuo Koron.

OLSON, J. (n.d.) "Organizational Participation in Government," mimeo, Bergen, Norway.

OLSON, M. (1965) The Logic of Collective Action. Cambridge, Mass.: Harvard University Press.

PAHL, R. E. and J. T. WINKLER (1976) "Corporatism in Britain," in The Corporate State — Reality or Myth? London: Centre for Studies in Social Policy.

PAHL, R. E. and J. T. WINKLER (1975) "The Coming Corporatism." Challenge (March/April): 28-35.

PHAL, R. E. and J. T. WINKLER (1974) "The Coming Corporatism," in New Society, 10 October.

PANITCH, L. (1978) "Recent Theorizations of Corporatism: Reflections on a Growth Industry." Paper prepared for the International Sociology Association Conference, Uppsala, Sweden, August.

PANITCH, L. (ed.) (1977a) The Canadian State: Political Economy and Political Power. Toronto: University of Toronto Press.

PANITCH, L. (1977b) "The Development of Corporatism in Liberal Democracies," Comparative Political Studies 10, 1: 61-90.

PANITCH, L. (1976a) Social Democracy and Industrial Militancy. The Labour Party, The Trade Unions and Incomes Policy 1945-1974. Cambridge, England: Cambridge University Press.

PANITCH, L. (1976b) "The Role and Nature of the Canadian State." Paper presented to the Canadian Political Science Association, Quebec.

PANITCH, L. (1976c) "The Development of Corporatism in Liberal Democracies." Paper presented to the American Political Science Association, September.

PANITCH, L. (1971) "Ideology and Integration: the Case of the British Labour Party." Pol. Studies 19 (June): 184-200.

PARSONS, T. (1959) " 'Voting' and the Equilibrium of the American Political System," pp. 80-120 in E. Burdick and A. J. Brodbeck (eds.) American Voting Behavior. Glencoe, Ill.: Free Press.

PEMPEL, T. J. (1979) Patterns of Japanese Policymaking. Boulder: Westview.

PEMPEL, T. J. (1978) "The Tar Baby Target: 'Reform' of the Japanese Bureaucracy Under the American Occupation." Paper prepared for the SSRC Conference on the US Occupation of Japan, Maui, Hawaii, July.

PEMPEL, T. J. (1977) "Japanese Foreign Economic Policy: The Domestic Bases for International Behavior," International Organization 31: 723-774.

PEMPEL, T. J. (1975) "The Dilemma of Parliamentary Opposition in Japan," Polity 8: 63-79.

PEMPEL, T. J. (1974) "The Bureaucratization of Policymaking in Contemporary Japan," American Journal of Political Science 18: 647-664.

PENTY, A. J. (1922) Post-Industrialism. New York: Macmillan.

PEPPER, B. (1975) "The Netherlands: From an Ordered Harmonic to a Bargaining Relationship," pp. 118-153 in S. Barkin (ed.) Worker Militancy and Its Consequences 1965-75. New York: Praeger.

PETERSON, W. C. (1974) "The Corporate State, Economic Performance and Social Policy." Journal of Economic Issues 8 (June): 483-506.

PETERSSON, O. (1974) "The 1973 General Election in Sweden." Scandinavian Pol. Studies 9: 219-228. Oslo: Universitetsforlaget.

PFROMM, H.-A. (1975) Einkommenspolitik und Verteilungskonflikt. Köln: Bund Verlag.

PIRENNE, H. (1914) "The Stages in the Social History of Capitalism." American Historical Rev. 19 (April): 494-515.

PIROU, G. (1938) Essais sur le corporatisme. Paris: Librairie du Recueil Sirey.

POLANYI, M. (1951) The Logic of Liberty. Chicago: University of Chicago Press.

POLSBY, N. (1963) Community Power and Political Theory. New Haven, Conn.: Yale University Press.

POULANTZAS, N. (1978) L'Etat, le Pouvoir, le Socialisme. Paris: PUF.

POULANTZAS, N. (1974) Fascism and Dictatorship. London: New Left Books.

POULANTZAS, N. (1974) Les classes sociales dans le capitalisme aujourd'hui. Paris: Maspero.

POULANTZAS, N. (1973) Political Power and Social Classes. London: New Left Books.

PRAIS, S. (1964) "A New Look at the Growth of Industrial Concentration." Oxford Eco. Papers XXVI: 273-88.

PRESTHUS, R. (1974) Elites in the Policy Process. London: Cambridge University Press.

PRESTHUS, R. (1973) Elite Accommodation in Canadian Politics. Toronto: Macmillan.

PUTZ, T. (ed.) (1966) Verbände und Wirtschaftspolitik in Österreich. Berlin: Duncker & Humblot.

RAE, D. (1967) The Political Consequences of Electoral Laws. New Haven: Yale University Press.

RALL, W. (1975) Zur Wirksamkeit der Einkommenspolitik. Tübingen: J. C. B. Mohr.

RANIS, G. (1959) "The Financing of Japanese Economic Development," The Economic History Review 11.

RANNEY, A. (1976) "The divine science: political engineering in American culture." Amer. Pol. Sci. Rev. 70 (March): 140-148.

ROBERT, R. (1976) Konzentrationspolitik in der Bundesrepublik — Das Beispiel der Entstehung des Gesetzes gegen Wettbewerbsbeschränkungen. Berlin: Duncker & Humblot.

ROBERTSON, D. (1976) A Theory of Party Competition. London: John Wiley.

ROBINSON, J. (1965) The New Mercantilism. London: Cambridge University Press.

ROKKAN, S. (1975) " 'Votes count, resources decide': refleksjoner over territorialitet vs. funksjonaliter i Norsk of Europeisk politikk," pp. 216-224 in Et Festskrift til Jens Arup Seip. Oslo: Gyldendal Norsk Forlag.

ROKKAN, S. (1970) Citizens, Elections, Parties. New York: David McKay.

ROKKAN, S. and STJERNQUIST,. N. (1966) "Norway: Numerical Democracy and Corporate Pluralism" in R. Dahl (ed.) Political Oppositions in Western Democracies. New Haven: Yale University Press.

ROSE, R. (1976) The Problem of Party Government. Harmondsworth: Penguin.

ROSE, R. (1968) "Party government vs. administrative government," pp. 209-233 in O. Stammer (ed.) Party Systems, Party Organizations, and the Politics of the New Masses. Berlin: Institut für Politische Wissenschaft an der Freien Universität.

RUIN, O. (1974) "Participatory Democracy and Corporatism: the Case of Sweden." Scandinavian Pol. Studies 9: 171-186.

RUIN, O. (1972) "Participation, Corporativization, and Politicization Trends in Present-day Sweden." Paper presented at Sixty-second Annual Meeting of the Society for the Advancement of Scandinavian Study, New York, 5-6 May.

RUSTOW, D. (1970) "Transitions to Democracy: Toward a Dynamic Model," Comparative Politics 2: 337-364.

SAKAMOTO, Y. (1978) "Nihon Senryo no Kokusai Kankyo." Paper prepared for the SSRC Conference on the US Occupation of Japan, Maui, Hawaii, July.

SALISBURY, R. H. (1977) "Peak Associations and the Tensions of Interest Intermediation or Why No Corporatism in America." Paper prepared for the American Political Science Association Annual Convention. September.

SALISBURY, R. H. (1975) "Interest Groups" in F. Greenstein and N. Polsby (eds.) Handbook of Political Science. Vol. 4. Reading, Mass.

SALISBURY, R. H. (1970) "An Exchange Theory of Interest Groups," in Interest Group Politics in America. New York: Harper & Row.

SALISBURY, R. H. (1969) "An Exchange Theory of Interest Groups," in Midwest Journal of Political Science, Vol. 13, February, 1-32.

SAMUELSON, P. A. (1964) Economics. New York: McGraw-Hill.

SANDERSON, F. (1978) Japan's Food Prospects and Policies. Washington: Brookings.

SAPOLSKY, H. (1968) "Organizational Competition and Monopoly." Public Policy 17: 55-76.

SARTI, R. (ed.) (1974) The Ax Within: Italian Fascism in Action. New York: New Viewpoints.

SATO, Y. (1967) "Chusho Kigyo 'Kindaika' Seisaku no Mondaiten," in The Annual of JEPA 15.

SCHARPF, F. (1976) Politikverflechtung. Kronberg/Ts.: Scriptor Verlag.

SCHATTSCHNEIDER, E. E. (1960) The Semi-Sovereign People. New York: Holt Rinehart & Winston.

SCHATTSCHNEIDER, E. E. (1935) Politics, Pressures and the Tariff. New York: Prentice-Hall.

SCHLECHT, O. (1968) Konzertierte Aktion als Instrument der Wirtschaftspolitik. Tübingen: J. C. B. Mohr.

SCHMITTER, P. (1977a) "Interest Intermediation and Regime Governability: A Japanese Epilogue." Paper delivered at the SSRC Conference on Japanese Interest Associations, May 13-14.

SCHMITTER, P. (1977b) "Interest Intermediation and Regime Governability in Contemporary Western Europe." Paper prepared for the American Political Science Association Annual Convention, Washington, DC, September 1-4.

SCHMITTER, P. (1971) Interest Conflict and Political Change in Brazil. Stanford: Stanford University Press.

SCHUMANN, M. et al. (1971) Am Beispiel der Septemberstreiks. Frankfurt a.M.: Europäische Verlagsanstalt.

SCHWERIN, Don S. (1979) "The Limits of Organization as a Response to Wage-Price-Problems". To appear in: Richard Rose (ed.) Contemporary Government under Stress. London and Beverly Hills: Sage.

SECHER, H. P. (1960) "Representative Democracy or 'Chamber State': The Ambiguous Role of Interest Groups in Austrian Politics," in Western Political Quarterly 23: 890-909.

SELF, P. and H. J. STORING (1962) The State and the Farmer. London: Allen & Unwin.

SHALEV, M. (1978) "Lies, Damned Lies and Strike Statistics: the Measurement of Trends in Industrial Conflict," in Crouch and Pizzorno (1978).

SHARKANSKY, I. (1975) The United States: A Study of a Developing Country. New York: David McKay.

SHEFTER, M. (1977) "New York's Fiscal Crisis: The Politics of Inflation and Retrenchment," The Public Interest 48: 98-127.

SHIRER, W. (1960) The Rise and Fall of the Third Reich. New York: Simon and Schuster.

SHONFIELD, A. (1968) "Note of Reservation by Mr. Andrew Shonfield," in UK, Royal Commission on Trade Unions and Employers Associations 1965-1968, Report. London: Her Majesty's Stationery Office.

SHONFIELD, A. (1965) Modern Capitalism, The Changing Balance of Public and Private Power. London: Oxford University Press.

SINGER, J. W. (1976) "Buttonholding and Buttering up for Labor — and 'the People'." National Journal (April 24).

SKOCPOL, T. (1973) "A Critical Review of Barrington Moore's Social Origins of Dictatorship and Democracy," Politics and Society 4: 1-34.

STANFIELD, R. (1976) "The PIGs: Out of the Sty into Lobbying with Style." National Journal (August 14).

STEPAN, A. (forthcoming) The State and Society: Peru in Comparative Context.

STESLICKE, W. (1973) Doctors in Politics. New York: Praeger.

STRANGE, S. (1971) Sterling and British Policy. London: Oxford University Press.

STREECK, Wolfgang (1978) "Staatliche Ordnungspolitik und industrielle Beziehungen: Zum Verhältnis von Integration und Institutionalisierung gewerkschaftlicher Interessenverbände am Beispiel des britischen Industrial Relations Act von 1971." In Udo Bermbach (ed.), Politische Wissenschaft und politische Praxis. Politische Vierteljahresschrift, Sonderheft 9.

SUMIYA M. (1966) Nihon no Rekishi 22. Tokyo: Chuo Koronsha.

SUNESSON, S. (1966) "Does Sweden Show the Way?" Int. Socialist Journal 3 (December): 588-600.

SUZUKI, T. and M. KAJINISHI (1962) "Sengo no Nihon Dokusen Shihon to Chusho Kigyo," in Kajinishi.

SZECSI, M. and H. WEHSELY (1975) Alte Kartelle neu geprüft, in Wirtschaft und Gesellschaft 1 (Vienna), pp. 33-51.

TAKAHASHI, H. (1977) "Shakaito Shuhan Naikaku no Seiritsu to Zasetsu," in Nihon Rekishi 22. Tokyo: Iwanami.

TAKEMAE, E. (1977) "Rodo no Minshuka," in E. Takemae and A. Amakwaw (eds.) Nihon Senryo Hisshi, I. Tokyo: Asahi Shimbunsha.

TAMAGAKI, A. (1977) "Nihon Shihonshugi no Saiken," in Nihon Rekishi 23. Tokyo: Iwanami Shoten.

THOMPSON, J. (1967) Organizations in Action. New York: MacGraw Hill.

TILLY, C. (ed.) (1975) The Formation of National States in Western Europe. Princeton: Princeton University Press.

TROTSKY, L. (1975) The Struggle against Fascism in Germany. Harmondsworth: Penguin.

TRUMAN, D. B. (1951) The Governmental Process. New York: Alfred A. Knopf.

TUFTE, E. (1978) Political Control of the Economy. Princeton: Princeton University Press.

TURNER, H. A. and D. A. S. JACKSON (1969) "On the Stability of Wage Differences and Productivity-based Wages Policies: an International Analysis." British Journal of Industrial Relations 7 (March): 1-18.

UK MINISTRY OF LABOUR (1965) Written Evidence of the Ministry of Labour to the Royal Commission on Trade Unions and Employers' Associations. London: Her Majesty's Stationery Office.

ULMAN, L. and R. J. FLANAGAN (1971) Wage Restraint: A Study of Income Policies in Western Europe. Berkeley: University of California Press.

VALIER, J. (1976) Le parti communiste francais et le capitalisme monopoliste d'Etat. Paris. Maspero.

VAN OTTER, C. (1975) "Sweden: Labor Reformism Reshapes the System," pp. 194-234 in S. Barkin (ed.) Worker Militancy and its Consequences 1965-1975. New York: Praeger.

VINCENT, J. M. et al (1975) L'Etat Contemporain et le marxisme. Critiques de l'économie politique. Paris: Maspero.

WALKER, J. L. (1975) "Structure of Company Financing." Economic Trends 263 (September).

WALLERSTEIN, I. (1974) The Modern World System. New York: Academic Press.

WARREN, B. (1972) "The State and Capitalist Planning." New Left Rev. 72 (March/April).

WASSENBERG, A. (1978) "Creeping Corporatism: A Cuckoo's Policy." Paper prepared for the ECPR Workshop on Corporatism in Liberal Democracies, Grenoble, April.

WATSON, M. (1975) "Planning in the Liberal Democratic State," pp. 445-483 in J. Hayward and M. Watson (eds.) Planning, Politics and Public Policy. Cambridge, England: Cambridge University Press.

WEINSTEIN, J. (1968) The Corporate Ideal in the Liberal State, 1900-1918. Boston: Beacon.

WELDON, T. D. (1955) The Vocabulary of Politics. Baltimore, Md.: Penguin.

WHEELER, C. (1975) White Collar Power. Urbana: University of Illinois Press.

WILENSKY, H. (1976) The New Corporatism, Centralization and the Welfare State. Beverly Hills, Calif.: Sage.

WINKLER, H. A. (ed.) (1974) Organiserter Kapitalismus. Göttingen: Vandenhoeck § Ruprecht.

WINKLER, Heinrich August (1972) Pluralismus oder Protektionismus? Verfassungspolitische Probleme des Verbandswesens im Deutschen Kaiserreich. Wiesbaden: Steiner.

WINKLER, J. (1977) "The Corporate Economy: Theory and Administration," in R. Scase (ed.) Industrial Society: Class, Cleavage and Control. London: Allen & Unwin.

WINKLER, J. (1976) "Corporatism," Archives Européenes de Sociologie, 17: 100-136.

WINKLER, J. (1975) "Law, State and Economy: the Industry Act 1975 in Context". British Journal of Law and Society II: 103-28.

WIRTH, M. (1972) Kapitalismustheorie in der DDR. Frankfurt: Suhrkamp.

WOOTEN, G. (1970) Interest Groups. Englewood Cliffs: Prentice-Hall.

YAMAMOTO, J. and S. KATO (1962) "Chusho Kigyo no Kozo," in Kajinishi.

YANAGA, C. (1968) Big Business in Japanese Politics. New Haven: Yale University Press.

YANO, I. (1977) Nihon Kokusei Zue. Tokyo: Kokuseisha.

YOKOTA, T. (1977) Gyuniku wa Naze Takaika? Tokyo: Simul.

YOSHINO, M. (1976) Japan's Multinational Enterprises. Cambridge: Harvard University Press.

ZEIGLER, L. H. and G. W. PEAK (1972) Interest Groups in American Society. Englewood Cliffs: Prentice-Hall.

ZEIGLER, H. (1964) Interest Groups in American Society. Englewood Cliffs: Prentice-Hall.

ZYSMAN, J. (1977) Political Strategies for Industrial Order. Berkeley: University of California Press.

Notes on Contributors

Charles Anderson is Professor of Political Science at the University of Wisconsin. He is currently writing books on 'Value Judgment and Political Decisions' and 'A Theory of Political Architecture', the latter related to the theme of the article in this volume. He is the author of *Politics and Economic Change in Latin America, The Political Economy of Mexico, The Political Economy of Modern Spain, Issues of Political Development and Statecraft.*

Bob Jessop is a Lecturer in Government at the University of Essex. He was formerly a Research Fellow, Downing College, Cambridge. He is the author of *Capitalism and Democracy* (forthcoming) and *Theories of the State* (forthcoming).

Gerhard Lehmbruch is Professor of Political Science, Konstanz University. He has published extensively on, among other topics, consociational democracy, in particular the book, *Proporz-demokratie*, 1967.

Kurt Meier is Assistant Professor at the Department of Sociology at the University of Mannheim. He has studied at the Universities of Mannheim and Freiburg and obtained his Ph.D. at the University of Pittsburgh, USA.

Birgitta Nedelmann is Privatdozent at the University of Mannheim. She has studied sociology and political science at the University of Munich and the Free University of Berlin, and obtained her Ph.D. in sociology at the University of Mannheim.

Leo Panitch is Associate Professor of Political Science at Carleton University. He is the author of *Social Democracy and Industrial Militancy*, 1976, and editor of *The Canadian State: Political Economy and Political Power*, 1977. He has also published several articles in *Political Studies, Politics and Society* and other journals. He is the joint general editor of the University of Toronto Press series, 'The State and Economic Life'.

T. J. Pempel is Associate Professor of Government at Cornell University. He is the author of *Patterns of Japanese Policymaking* and editor of *Policymaking in Contemporary Japan.* He is currently completing a book on Japanese public policy as part of a series he is coediting on comparative public policy.

Robert Salisbury is Professor of Political Science, Washington University. He is the author of 'Interest Groups' in Greenstein and Polsby (eds.), *Handbook of Political Science,* volume 4, 1975, and editor of *Interest Groups in American Politics,* 1970.

Philippe Schmitter is Professor of Political Science at the University of Chicago, with visiting appointments in Rio, Sao Paulo, Buenos Aires, Geneva, Paris, Mannheim and Zurich.

Keiichi Tsunekawa is a graduate student of government of Cornell University. He is currently writing a Ph.D. dissertation on the relationship between dependency and labor policy in Mexico.